The Successful Child

Sears Parenting Library

The Pregnancy Book
The Baby Book
The Birth Book
The Attachment Parenting Book
The Breastfeeding Book
The Fussy Baby Book
The Discipline Book
The Family Nutrition Book
The A.D.D. Book
The Successful Child

Parenting.com FAQ books

The First Three Months
How to Get Your Baby to Sleep
Keeping Your Baby Healthy
Feeding the Picky Eater

Sears Children's Library

Baby on the Way
What Baby Needs

The
Successful Child

What Parents Can Do
to Help Kids Turn Out Well

WILLIAM SEARS, M.D., AND MARTHA SEARS, R.N.
WITH ELIZABETH PANTLEY

LITTLE, BROWN AND COMPANY
Boston ◆ *New York* ◆ *London*

FIRST EDITION

LIBRARY OF CONGRESS CATALOGING-IN-PUBLICATION DATA

Sears, William, M.D.
    The successful child : what parents can do to help kids turn out well /
by William Sears and Martha Sears with Elizabeth Pantley. — 1st ed.
       p. cm. — (Sears parenting library)
    Includes bibliographical references and index.
    ISBN 0-316-77811-7 (hc)—ISBN 0-316-77749-8 (pb)
      1. Parenting. 2. Parent and child. 3. Emotional intelligence. 4. Emotions and
cognition. 5. Emotions — Social aspects. 6. Success in children. I. Sears,
Martha. II. Pantley, Elizabeth. III. Title.

HQ755.8 .S44 2002
649'.1 — dc21   2001038559

10 9 8 7 6 5 4 3 2

Q-FF

Designed by Jeanne Abboud

PRINTED IN THE UNITED STATES OF AMERICA

Contents

A Word from Dr. Bill

Children in America today enjoy many opportunities for learning and growing. They play sports, take music lessons, work hard at their homework, and acquire street smarts from television and the high-tech world of the Internet. But are they successful? Many children are less physically and emotionally healthy than they could be. The current epidemic of childhood obesity (which rivals smoking as a public health concern) suggests that children are overfed but probably undernourished. Even though immunizations have stamped out once common childhood diseases, asthma and diabetes are on the rise. Teens are feeling that if they can't handle a problem, then drink it or drug it. They turn to premature sex for thrills and assurance that they are loveable and popular. Many children — even of concerned and conscientious parents — seem lost, lacking the spiritual and emotional intelligence that would help them find their way in life.

Yet other children I have met are clearly empathetic, wise, and wonderful kids, destined to be a blessing to those around them and to pass their success along to their own children. These are connected kids, ones who will be reasonably happy and content as adults because they are successful at the things that matter most — relationships, values, human interdependence. It is our sincere desire to fill this gap by giving parents and other caregivers tools to raise connected kids.

Five years before writing this book, I underwent surgery for severe colon cancer. As when any major life crisis strikes, this event caused me to reflect on what was most important to me — and at the top of this list were my eight children. I spent quite a bit of time thinking about what it means to raise successful children and how parents help prepare them for a successful life. The evening before my surgery was, amazingly, one of the most peaceful times of my whole life. My mental peace came from the knowledge that my family was emotionally and spiritually healthy. I thought about the attitudes, education, and beliefs our children acquired during their growing-up years. I found great peace in feeling confident that Martha and I had done an admirable job in this area and that our children had the tools necessary to succeed in life as good human beings.

These reflections were a starting point for the material included in this book. Martha, Elizabeth, and I have combined our personal and clinical experience with information from scientific studies and, most important, from hundreds of parents to produce this book — which is essentially a collection of tools for success in life. We hope that this information will help you prepare your children to succeed in life.

Every child can be a star, shining in a unique and wonderful way. Some will light up the world with artistic, academic, or athletic achievements, some with service to others. My wish is that the tips throughout this book will help your little stars shine as brightly and happily as they can, with warmth and compassion for others and peaceful and contented hearts. Like stars, children are utterly, sublimely beautiful, and when watched, nurtured, and respected for who they are, they often guide us to a better understanding of what is truly important.

1

THE TOOLS OF SUCCESS

This book is about giving your children the tools to succeed in life. These tools are qualities that have been shown to lead to success in most children. You nurture the development of these qualities in your child's early, formative years and continue to foster them as your child enters school, high school, and beyond.

The first part of this book is about getting connected to your child and about how being able to form connected, trusting relationships is the main tool needed for success in life. Part II describes how to use this connection to help your child develop additional emotional and intellectual tools for success.

Parents begin to give their children the tools they will need to succeed as adults even before they are born. How you care for your child in the first years of his or her life is critical to developing trusting and sensitive ways of thinking. In later years, these good emotional habits influence the development of more specific skills for success: communication, compassion, health and fitness, self-esteem. This book takes you from the early years through adolescence, discussing new-borns, toddlers, preschoolers, school-age kids, and teens. We hope that along the way you will also learn what it means to be a successful parent. Instilling these qualities in your kids will help you be the kind of person you want your children to be.

1

What's Success?

THE FIRST OF OUR EIGHT CHILDREN was born thirty-four years ago, about the time I began pediatric training. As new parents, we wanted to do everything we could to help our child become a success in life, but we weren't sure what was most important. At the same time, as a new pediatrician, I found that parents often asked me what they could do to help their children turn out well.

To answer both these personal and professional questions, I began observing parents and children closely and recording my observations. I talked to parents about their relationship with their child, and I invited them to tell me what kinds of parenting challenges they faced and what kinds of parenting practices worked well for them. Meanwhile, at home, Martha and I had more children, learning more about parenting with each one. Many kids and many pediatric patients later, we believe we have found reliable answers to questions about how parents can help their children turn out well. We share what we've learned in this book.

How do we become who we are? This is the question I wondered about as I began my career as a parent and pediatrician. It is not an easy one to answer. Many factors influence how children turn out — heredity, nurturing, nutrition,

health, schools, peers, and, of course, a bit of luck. Parents can influence some but not all of these factors. Yet it seemed to me thirty-four years ago that there must be some common threads that run through the childhoods of children who are nice to be around. What factors in these children's environment contributed to their positive outcome? How do early experiences leave their impression on a child's inner being — for better or worse — and forever influence how the child thinks and acts?

To find answers to these questions, I decided to gather information on children who turned out well. I decided to find out what their parents did. Gather enough information, I thought, and some common themes were bound to emerge. So, for more than thirty years, I've used my office as a laboratory to study the development of babies and children, particularly the development of their personalities and relationships. After parenting our eight children, ages eight to thirty-four as of this writing, and participating in approximately 150,000 observation sessions (i.e., pediatric patient visits to my office), I feel I have a handle on what parents can do to raise a successful child.

In preparation for this book, Martha, Elizabeth, and I interviewed hundreds of parents, teachers, psychologists, and parent educators — anyone who works with children — to determine what correlations they notice between how kids turned out and what their parents did. We also turned to scientific studies on the relationship between how children are nurtured and the personal qualities they develop. Reading the research has helped us analyze our observations better and has confirmed our intuition about the importance of the connection between parent and child. Information from these research studies is sprinkled throughout this book in boxes labeled "Science Says." We even consulted the kids themselves, asking them to record what they believed about how their parents influenced their lives. Throughout the book we list these observations as "Kids Say."

Our observations tell us that parents should not take all the credit or all the blame for the person their child becomes. Certainly, the parents we talked to were not perfect parents who turned out perfect children, nor is this book written by perfect parents of perfect children. All of us must do the best we can with the information and resources we have. I wish we had had the knowledge and experience we have now when we were raising our first child, a time when our main concern was often just getting through the day. It wasn't until our sixth child that Martha and I felt truly confident about our parenting. However, we have learned not to beat ourselves up about the things we wish we had done differently, since we did the best we could and we can't change the past. Nevertheless, we'd like to help you scale the learning curve a little more quickly than we did. It is possible to be excellent parents even with your first child.

Our first two sons are now fathers themselves, and the way they saw us parent their younger siblings, along with the relationships we've established with them over the years, has been a positive influence on the way they and their wives parent our grandchildren. I am also beginning to see "grandchildren" in my pediatric practice — children of mothers and fathers whom I cared for as infants. I always ask them what their parents did that they will and will not carry over into how they parent their own children.

THE REAL MEANING OF SUCCESS

Every parent wants to raise a successful child. Yet many of us mean different things by "success." When our two elder sons, Dr. Jim and Dr. Bob, joined the Sears Family Pediatric Practice, I gave them a little doctorly and fatherly advice: "Your success in life, Jim and Bob, will not be measured by the money you make or the degrees you earn, but rather by the number of persons whose lives are better because of what you did."

The dictionary defines *success* as "attaining wealth, fame, or prosperity." Our definition goes beyond this conventional idea of success. Here's our wish list for successful children:

SUCCESS QUALITIES

These are the ten qualities we discuss throughout this book that will help your child be "success-full:"

1. To be a child who forms meaningful relationships with others
2. To be empathetic and compassionate

3. To be kind and polite
4. To be smart
5. To be healthy
6. To make wise choices; to think and act morally
7. To have confidence
8. To have a healthy attitude toward sexuality
9. To communicate well
10. To have a joyful attitude

We want these success tools to become part of the child's inner self — a way of thinking, a way of acting; something a child is, not only something the child does. Children take different roads to attain these goals. For some the way is smooth and straight; for others it's bumpy and winding. In fact, the children whose way lies along the more difficult roads are often the ones who best learn how to use these tools for success.

Does success mean rich and famous?

Rich and famous people make headlines, so it's easy for children to conclude that turning out well means being well-off. There are many success stories of people who gain wealth by using their talents and working hard, then live happily while giving to others to make this world a better place to live in. It is also true that among the rich and famous are some of the unhappiest people in the world. Tabloids are full of the "un-success" stories of celebrities: failed relationships, drug and alcohol addiction, suicide. Many financially rich persons are emotionally poor. As a psychologist friend once told us, "If you want to know how much wealth you have, count your friends."

We have worked hard to keep our children

from feeling that their value depends on how they perform. A child who makes A's is not "better" than a child who makes C's, provided they both are working to their full potential. While the A student is more likely to be voted "Most Likely to Succeed" at her high-school graduation, the C student might be more emotionally healthy. He may have talents in areas other than academics — sports, the arts, or the ability to get along with people. What we're trying to say is that you can't measure success in child rearing by children's accomplishments. In this case, "successful" refers to your personal qualities, not what you accomplish.

So, what does it mean to turn out well? We believe it's the depth of relationships we sustain, not the accomplishments we tick off, that makes our lives successful and happy: the relationships children have with themselves, as well as the other lives they touch. The goal of this book is to help you help your child become *relationship rich*.

Adding value to your child.

Children need to perceive themselves as valuable, based on what is within them; they also need external experiences that help them feel valuable. Our aim is to help parents raise children who not only regard themselves as valuable people but also, with their kindness, compassion, and ability to connect, grow up to add value to the lives of others.

One day an insensitive person was badgering Martha about having eight kids and contributing to the "world's overpopulation." Martha returned with: "The world needs my kids."

Lessons from "good" kids.

If you've spent any time at all reading books about raising children, you know that saying "bad boy" or "bad girl" is a no-no. Psychologists instruct parents to focus on good or bad *behavior,* not extend those value judgments to their child's personal self. But the fact is, there *are* good kids and kids who are not so good. Sometimes the "good" kids from "good" homes surprise us by making headlines for doing awful things. When we hear horrible stories of children and teenagers wielding guns, knives, and bombs against their teachers, classmates, and families, we search for explanations. Is it the video games these kids played? The movies they watched, the web sites they visited? Is it the all-black clothing they adopt, or some kind of exaggerated adolescent alienation? Psychiatrists, politicians, and religious leaders bemoan the state of our youth and the violence in our world. And everyone looks for ways to blame the kids' parents. But unless there's obvious abuse in the home, often no one ever seems to know how or why some children go wrong.

Good kids don't make bad headlines. In fact, good kids seldom make headlines at all. We are fortunate to work in professions that show us the inherent goodness of children every day. They are empathetic, kind, and friendly. They know who they are as people. They respect themselves and others, are responsible, and are fun to be around. They're not perfect. Some of their fine qualities are still in development, and sometimes anger or fear gets the best of them. Some may grow up to be rich and powerful, but, more important, they will be happy and content, have stable relationships, and make good parents for the next generation.

The parents of our world's "good kids" have much to share with us. These are parents who are willing to take responsibility for their children, parents who make an effort to learn about why children behave the way they do. They en-

NO GUARANTEE

There are no magic formulas for raising children. A child parented in a certain way may or may not turn out "well." Some great kids have risen above highly dysfunctional family situations, against all odds. Sometimes parents do their best to love a child and teach her what she needs to be a responsible adult, but she chooses a different path. There are no simple explanations for how we become who we are. Children receive all kinds of messages about who they should be from all kinds of sources throughout life. Their own temperaments and inborn abilities also influence who they become, as does the relationship they have with their parents. And, of course, there's some luck involved as well.

Consequently, we do not find it helpful to dwell on the age-old nature versus nurture debate. Parents cannot change their children's genetic heritage, and there are also circumstances in life over which they have no control. But parents do have choices about how they relate to their children, what to expect of them, and what to teach them. By focusing on the aspects of child rearing that you *can* control, you can give your child the skills to cope with who he or she is and whatever challenges may come along.

courage the good behavior while trying to change the bad. They learn from their own experience and that of other parents. As a result, parents of kids who turn out well have wonderful insights to share with less experienced parents. Throughout this book, we share with you what they have told us.

TURNING OUT WELL — BUT WITH A STRUGGLE

Martha and I are particularly sensitive to kids who have a tough start yet fight to become adults who turn out well. Humans are resilient, and what we become is not determined forever by what happens in childhood. We both had less than ideal childhoods — an understatement. Martha's dad drowned when she was four, and her mother never recovered psychologically, leaving her daughter to be reared by not especially nurturing grandparents. My father took off when I was a few weeks old, forcing my mother to work long hours to support us. Even though I was raised in a home with nurturing grandparents, they also worked long hours, making me a "latchkey kid" before there even was such a term. Yet, fifty years later, what I remember most about my childhood is how my mother did the best she could under less than ideal circumstances. She surrounded me with healthy role models. She carefully screened teachers, scoutmasters, caregivers, and other persons of significance in my life. She made sure I was connected to healthy attachment figures. Despite our poverty and the stigma of being a fatherless child (there was only one other child in my grade-school and high-school classes who came from a "divorced" family), I grew up in a loving home. Having to work for my luxuries taught me a work ethic and a sense of responsibility.

Although many kids do bounce back from less than ideal childhoods and turn out well, they carry emotional baggage into adulthood and spend many years trying to unload it. How much easier it would be for kids to grow up well and then be free to spend their adult years improving rather than repairing their emotional lives.

Yet problems can be turned into opportunities. As a child of divorced parents, I was determined to stay married. Working summers on assembly lines in steel mills motivated me to finish college. Still, this tough childhood left me unconnected in some important ways — which took me fifty years to recognize and correct. But I believe that the good things my mother and grandparents did for me in childhood helped me overcome the challenges I faced as an adult.

CREATING THE CAPACITY FOR RESILIENCE

How is it that some kids turn out well despite facing tough obstacles in childhood? Why are some kids more resilient than others? We suspect that early attachment parenting (which you will learn about in the next chapter) instills in a child a *blueprint* for future relationships. Children who learn early on what it is to be connected to others and to be able to trust them try to maintain or regain this connectedness as they grow into adulthood. They follow that early blueprint and bring the trust they learned in their first relationship into later relationships. That blueprint also shows them how to trust themselves, and this self-confidence sees a child through significant adversity. Children carry the connectedness they learned as infants through the rest of their lives. It becomes part of their overall well-being and makes them resilient.

Children who succeed despite multiple challenges usually have at least one important person in their lives to whom they feel connected.

SCIENCE SAYS:

Studies have shown that connected kids are better able to ride the waves of adversity than are children who are less connected. One study shows that the key to success in adulthood despite childhood adversity is the presence of at least one individual in the child's life who provided regular emotional support and who was a positive influence on the child's development. In this study, individuals who achieved success despite growing up around adversity had established a close bond with at least one caregiver in infancy. The researchers also found that other individuals in the child's life (e.g., grandparents, relatives, and other persons of significance) are able to provide compensatory support for children who are the victims of poor parenting. The presence of a positive male influence within the household seems to be an especially important factor contributing to the success of at-risk children.

TEN TOOLS FOR SUCCESS

1. Growing up connected
2. Having healthy eating habits
3. Becoming self-confident
4. Making wise choices
5. Making moral choices
6. Communicating well
7. Loving to learn
8. Understanding his or her own sexuality
9. Having a joyful attitude
10. Thinking and acting with empathy

Ideally, this person is a parent, but it may be a teacher, a coach, a scoutmaster, or another person of significance. Connecting with others is very important. The kids that high-school counselors worry about most are those who don't seem to belong anywhere. They also worry about those who, in their hunger to belong, connect with the wrong people. Kids with a blueprint for strong attachment in infancy and early childhood not only know how to connect with others but are also better able to sort out good and bad influences.

We have noticed two other characteristics of resilient kids. One is that trusted caregivers frame the child in a positive light: "You can do it," "You're smart and persistent," "You can get into that college." Children who hear statements such as "You're not good enough to make that team" or "You're too clumsy to be a quarterback" often live up to these negative expectations. Another characteristic of resilient kids is that some special person in the child's life discovered his "special something" — a talent, a unique ability — and helped him put that special something to work. Someone spots athletic ability in a marginal student and helps him become a star basketball player. A child may fail mathematics, yet excel in art, and someone helps him put that artistic ability to work in computer graphics — which also helps his math skills.

In an ideal world, every child would get everything needed for success in adulthood. In the real world, good parents try to do the best they can at each new stage that comes along. Children don't need perfect parents, just parents who are good enough. Get connected to your child and stay connected.

2

Raising Connected Kids

EIGHT-YEAR-OLD SUSAN, along with her mother and two-year-old brother, was in my exam room, waiting for her checkup. As soon as I entered the room, I felt comfortable. I liked being around these kids. Susan smiled and said, "Hi," as I sat down in front of her. Her eye contact was appropriate, an interested look that held my attention without being intrusive. Her little brother was, well, just being a toddler, busily exploring all the stuff in the room. He caught his finger in a drawer, and within a millisecond of his wail Susan reached out to comfort him. Her mother looked up with obvious pride and love. As the examination continued, I noticed a respectful independence about this young lady. She looked up and listened when her mother spoke, yet added her own insightful comments about her health. The family seemed to be so comfortable with one another that their warmth spilled over to include me. These were connected kids — connected to each other, to their mom, and to their world. I left the exam room thinking, "That's it — connected kids! That's the kind I like to be around." Raising connected kids is what parenting is all about.

GETTING CONNECTED

How we become who we are is rooted, to a large degree, in the parent-child relationship. The relationship you have with your child is the foundation on which all of his other relationships will be built. Even the way children understand themselves depends on their relationship with their parents. A loving, trusting, understanding attitude toward their offspring helps parents get to know them better, and parents can help children learn to know themselves and their values.

How do you get connected? And what is it about connecting that makes you a responsive, sensitive, successful parent? This chapter takes you on a journey from a child's birth to adolescence, describing connected kids and parents at each stage, in order to show how the relationship between parent and child develops and how it influences a child's opportunity for success. Consider this journey the heart of the book. The important parenting principles introduced here make the suggestions in the rest of the book work for you and your child. You'll learn more about many of these principles in later chapters — and you'll learn still more as you live them.

BIRTH TO ONE YEAR

What stage of development most influences how successful a child is likely to become?

   (a) birth to one year
   (b) preschool years
   (c) five to ten years
   (d) adolescent years
   (e) all of the above

You probably answered (e) — all of the above. Certainly the effects of the caregiving environment on a child's success is important at every stage of development. Yet, the question is: What stage *most* influences . . . ? The correct answer is (a) — birth to one year. Why? Because that's when caregivers can leave the most lasting impressions on a child's developing brain.

Believe it or not, parents' greatest influence over a child's personality and emotional development is during the first year. Babies do far more than just eat and sleep. They learn — a lot! Babies are also developing a sense of who they are and what the world is like. These beliefs will influence their behavior in the years to come.

Patterns of association.

As discussed in Chapter 4, the brain develops more during the first year than at any other stage in a person's life. Brain cells called neurons, which resemble miles of "wires," hook up and make pathways. These pathways receive messages and transmit thoughts to other parts of the brain. When babies are born, many of these neurons are unconnected. As babies grow and experience the world, the millions of connections made daily manage the way the brain organizes and stores information. Higher-quality experiences lead to better, more complex pathways. These paths and circuits determine a baby's early thought processes and how he learns to regard the caregiving world around him.

Another way to look at the infant brain is to picture it as a giant file cabinet storing cues and responses. When something happens in a baby's life — for example, "I cry, I'm comforted," or "I'm hungry, I'm fed" — the infant files away pictures of these scenarios. As the cry/comfort file begins to fill, baby forms a general impression of what the caregiving world is all about. This is the beginning of the infant's sense of self and others. These cue-response scenes, or *patterns of association,* become the baby's *norm* — what she learns to expect in a given situation. A baby's cerebral library of these patterns of association helps her anticipate the response that she expects or needs: "I cry, I expect to be comforted." These patterns set the stage for future reactions and relationships. One of the most important patterns of association, one that will forever influence future relationships, is *learning to trust.* In a nutshell, the right patterns of associa-

---

CREATING CAPACITIES

In the early years parents spend much of their time creating the capacity for healthy traits in their children. Returning to the file-cabinet analogy, think of how documents are organized on a computer. In the first couple of years you help the child create folders for, say, empathy and sensitivity. Then you spend the remaining years helping your child save experiences to the appropriate destination. The child who begins life without folders, or with the wrong ones, can't file subsequent experiences in useful places.

tion, planted in infancy and early childhood, will help your child turn out well.

First impressions, lasting impressions.

Early patterns of association in the infant brain are the precursors of such important adult qualities as trust, empathy, intimacy, and a sense of self. Like handprints in wet cement, the infant brain receives these early impressions, which become part of one's identity in childhood and adulthood. They form the infant's first impressions of what life is like. From responsive parents, babies learn

- to respond to someone in need
- to comfort someone who hurts
- to turn to other human beings for help
- to trust their own perceptions about themselves and the world
- to be happy

How might these first impressions play out in the later years? Imagine that a group of kids are planning to steal a bicycle. Some can imagine only how much fun they will have with that cool bike, and figure they are entitled to it. Yet the child who learned to care and was cared about in infancy and early childhood has an uncomfortable feeling about stealing the bike. He understands that the bike is important to someone else, and imagines how he would feel if someone stole his bicycle. He also remembers that his parents love and trust him and worries about disappointing them with his behavior. This child has empathy and sensitivity. He is able to stand in other people's shoes — to "get behind their eyes" — and imagine how they will feel. He realizes even before he acts that his behavior will affect another person's well-being, so he decides against stealing the bike.

Imagine a teen in another difficult situation: she's at a party, and kids are pairing off and "making out." She's being pressured into sexual situations she doesn't feel ready for, and feels confused and scared. But this teen was taught to trust her feelings by parents who have respected and responded to those feelings. This teen does not seek the gratification that comes from yielding to peer pressure. Because she has learned to trust her own feelings, she can respect herself, say no to peers, and call home for a ride.

Insensitivity and lack of empathy are the roots of destructive behavior in teens and adults. Kids who are not cared for sensitively grow up not caring about others. The infant who learns about empathy in the arms of a comforting parent is not likely to grow up to be a teen who shoots up a high school.

Baby training — an unwise investment.

Just what do we mean by responsive, sensitive parenting during infancy and early childhood? We'll explain in the next section, in which we outline the tools you need to build a good connection with your child. But first we want to warn you about a more distant style of parenting, an approach that we call "baby training." The goal of this kind of parenting is to make babies fit conveniently into parents' lives. Parents don't want their child to be "spoiled" or to "manipulate them." They want to be in control of their child. They may actually believe that baby training is the right approach, the way to teach their child about the "real" world.

Some parenting books and magazines tend to support this kind of parenting. Authors and advisers promise parents that they can and ought to train their baby to sleep through the night — even if it means that the baby is left alone to cry for hours. Parents are told to get their baby on a

BRAIN FILES

As you go through your day caring for your baby according to your natural parental intuition, you're making lasting impressions on your baby's brain without even realizing it.

What Parents Do	What Baby Stores in Brain	What Capacities Are Planted
• Respond sensitively and appropriately to baby's cries	• I speak, someone listens	• Trust in own ability to communicate
• Feed baby when hungry	• Caregivers will satisfy my needs	• Trust that people are caring and responsive
• Make frequent eye contact with baby	• Faces are fun and a good source of information	• The ability to read others' feelings
• Hold baby a lot	• Being held calms my fears and feels good	• Comfort with being intimate
• Comfort baby when upset	• Others understand my feelings and try to help	• Empathy
• Carry baby with them in a baby sling	• My world is an interesting place to be	• Curiosity, openness to new experiences
• Sleep close to baby	• Sleep is a pleasant state to enter and a fearless state to remain in	• Healthy sleep habits, the ability to relax
• Reflect love and happiness to baby	• Most of the time I'm happy, and I make others happy	• Happiness and contentment

feeding schedule — and not to respond when he indicates the need for food less than three or four hours after the last feeding. Parents try to train their baby to get used to playing alone in the playpen, which usually involves turning a deaf ear to his cry. Eventually, babies who are "trained" may become "good babies" (or more accurately, "convenient babies") in these authors' opinions, and the family congratulates itself on the results. But despite the short-term gains for this forced independence, the bottom line is a long-term loss. They have been trained to give up their attempt to have their needs for nurturing met.

A baby who is left to cry in her crib eventually ceases to believe in the value of her cries; if no one comes, she concludes that her attempts to communicate must be meaningless. Meanwhile, parents look to the clock or a book instead of learning about their individual baby. They lose trust in their ability to decode and respond to their infant's cries. The infant spends less uptime in parents' arms and more downtime out of touch with stimulating human contact. (In Chapter 9 we'll discuss how to help your child be a good communicator.)

It might seem that feeding on a schedule and enforcing a regular bedtime would make a baby's life more predictable. But in fact, the opposite is true. A baby subjected to baby training learns that life is unpredictable. Sometimes his cries are answered, sometimes they're not; sometimes he's fed when hungry, sometimes he's not. He is not able to anticipate how caregivers will respond, so he lays down fewer patterns of association. The patterns he does store tell him not to trust the world and not to be sensitive to his own needs. Parents get the same poor start. Letting a baby "cry it out" forces a mother to go against her natural inclination to protect, comfort, and nurse her baby. She learns not to trust herself and not to trust her ability to respond to her infant. Fathers who begin their parenting careers focused on getting their babies to fit into schedules miss out on the maturing experience of putting someone else's needs first. Parents who seek to establish some distance from their infant are at risk of spending the childhood and teen years feeling unconnected to their child and mystified by his behavior. They may try to play catch-up in the

THE NEUROCHEMISTRY OF ATTACHMENT

For several decades attachment researchers have speculated that early interactions with caregivers stamp lasting impressions on a child's developing brain, a process called imprinting. New insight into the neurochemical basis of attachment suggests that seeing her mother's face can actually stimulate a child's brain to produce neurohormones called endorphins. These are brain chemicals that bring feelings of well-being and pleasure. The infant begins to associate her mother's face and presence with feeling good.

Interaction with caregivers also induces beneficial structural changes in the brain. Stimulating encounters between caregivers and infants facilitate the growth of synapses, connections between areas of the brain. These patterns of association are known in brain development jargon as schema. Once these patterns are imprinted, a baby can frequently access this internalized image, or schema, of her mother's face as a source of comfort, even in her mother's absence.

years ahead, but it will take a great deal of effort to establish the close connection that should have formed during infancy.

Planting impressions of trust and sensitivity is best done in the early years, when children are forming their basic outlook on life. This is why many of our books, including this one, focus on sensitive parenting practices during the early years.

CONNECTING TOOLS: PRACTICE ATTACHMENT PARENTING

Now that you know the theory, you may be wondering about the practical applications. How do parents and kids get connected during babyhood and beyond? You've heard about the three R's of education: reading, 'riting, and 'rithmetic. You needn't worry too much about these until your child reaches school age, but getting connected depends on a fourth R, a very important one, which begins at birth — responsiveness.

Responsiveness is the guiding principle behind attachment parenting. Responding to your infant's needs builds trust between you, and trust is at the heart of a strong connection between parents and children. Responding doesn't mean you always say yes to your children. We believe that parents should be *appropriately* responsive, which means being caring and supportive when you say yes and knowing when it's better to say no.

How parents and baby get started with one another sets the tone for their future relationship. Certain parenting practices — we call them attachment parenting tools — build a strong connection between mother, father, and child during the first, formative years. The tools of attachment parenting help you get connected to your child. Use as many of them as you can, as much as you can. We realize that every family is different, so your lifestyle, your baby's personality, and your own temperament will influence how you put these attachment tools to work. If you find that medical circumstances or other issues get in the way of using some of these tools, keep in mind that the goal is to get connected to your infant. Attachment parenting is not about following rules; it's about strengthening relationships.

Below are the seven Baby's B's of attachment parenting — connecting tools that help you and your baby get started on the road to success.

SEVEN ATTACHMENT TOOLS: THE BABY B'S

1. Birth bonding.

The way baby and parents get started with one another can help the early attachment unfold. The days and weeks after birth are a sensitive period when mothers and babies are biologically primed to need to be close to each other. Staying physically close after birth allows the natural attachment-promoting behavior of the infant and the intuitive, caregiving qualities of the mother to come together. For example, newborns in the hour or so after birth enter a state in which they are quietly alert. They gaze steadily at human faces, and their vulnerability and openness capture the hearts of their mothers and fathers. When babies are kept close to their mothers during the first weeks of life, mothers can respond quickly to babies' cries, whimpers, and body movements. Mother and baby (and Dad, too) learn to communicate well right from the start. Bonding during the first few weeks, when the infant is most needy and the mother is most programmed to nurture, helps the whole family get off on the right foot.

Bonding is a process. Sometimes the concept of birth bonding is explained in such a way that people come to believe that there is a critical moment after birth when bonding occurs, as if it's now or never. As a result, a mother who is separated from her infant following birth because of medical complications may feel as if she's missed a critical moment in her relationship with her child. This isn't the case. Birth bonding is not like instant glue that cements the mother-child relationship forever. Bonding is a process that happens as you go through life with your child. "Bonding time" immediately after birth simply gives the parent-infant relationship a head start.

2. Breastfeeding.

Breastfeeding gives babies superior nutrition and protection against disease. Breast milk also contains unique brain-building nutrients that cannot be manufactured. In addition to all this magic in the milk, breastfeeding exercises a mother's baby-reading skills. Breastfeeding works best when mothers learn to read babies' hunger cues and respond to them promptly. Mother trusts baby to know when he is hungry or in need of sucking for comfort, and baby trusts mother to quickly offer nurturing at the breast. Breastfeeding gives both baby and mother a smart start in their life together. As an added bonus for bonding, breastfeeding mothers produce hormones, prolactin and oxytocin, that help them feel calm and relaxed and give their mothering a boost. Think of these lactation hormones as the chemicals of connection.

3. Babywearing.

A baby learns a lot when held in the arms of a busy caregiver. Carried babies fuss less and spend more time quietly alert, the behavior state in which babies learn most about their environment. The term *babywearing* refers to using a sling or some other kind of carrier to hold a baby on the parent's body while the parent does chores, takes a walk, or attends social gatherings, both inside and outside the home. Babies are very portable. When your baby is close to you, you get to know him better. Closeness promotes sensitivity and connection.

4. Bedding close to baby.

Responsive parenting doesn't end when the sun goes down and the family goes to bed. The night is a scary time for babies and little people, and being separated from the parents they trust increases their anxiety. Co-sleeping is a parenting option that allows parents and their little ones to stay within touching distance through the night. Babies learn that sleep is a pleasant state to enter and are not afraid to fall asleep. Bedding close to baby also makes it possible for mothers to breastfeed at night without having to wake up completely and leave a warm bed to tend a crying infant. Co-sleeping isn't for everyone, but many mothers find they get more rest when sleeping with their babies. Whatever sleeping arrangement helps all the members of your family get the best night's sleep is the right one for you. Parents who are busy during the daytime or are separated from their infant because of work often find that co-sleeping helps them reconnect with their baby at night.

5. Believing in the language value of your baby's cry.

A baby's cry is a signal. Tiny babies cry to communicate, not to manipulate. Crying is the only way that babies can communicate their needs, and communicating is necessary for their survival and for developing the parents' caregiving skills. Responding sensitively to your baby's cries builds trust. Babies trust that their caregivers will understand their language and take care of their needs. As parents respond to their baby's cries, they gradually learn to trust in their ability to meet their baby's needs. They get better at understanding baby's language, and baby also gets better at communicating with Mom and Dad. The whole parent-child communication network moves up a notch.

6. Being wary of baby trainers.

Parents who are sensitive to their baby's needs and signals become very discerning about baby-care advice. They avoid rigid and extreme parenting styles that teach you to watch a clock or a schedule instead of your baby. These more restrained styles of baby care create distance between you and your baby and keep you from becoming an expert on your individual child. Attachment parenting helps you get connected to your child; baby training focuses on controlling your child.

7. Establishing balance and boundaries.

Parents who zealously give to their babies often end up neglecting their own needs and those of their spouse. Their lives get out of balance. The key to family survival when children enter the picture is to stay balanced and to set appropriate boundaries. Here's where fathers play an important role. When Dad is involved in baby care and household chores, mothers have time to take better care of themselves and enjoy their husbands. Staying in balance also requires that you know when to say no to your baby. An infant's wants are the same as her needs, but a toddler doesn't need to have everything she wants and asks for.

An approach, not a set of rules. There may be medical or family circumstances that make you unable to practice all of these Baby B's. What's most important is that you open your mind and heart to the individual needs of your baby. As you do so, you will develop the wisdom to make on-the-spot decisions about what works best for both you and your baby. Do the best you can with the resources you have — that's all your child will ever expect of you.

This style of caring for babies is actually what many parents do instinctively. Our list of Baby B's just puts these instincts into words. Following these tips helps parents and baby get off to the right start, but parenting is too individual and babies too complex for there to be only one way. Think of the Baby B's as tools, not steps. When you follow steps, you dare not skip one. But you can pick and choose which tools make it easier to do a job well. Use our suggestions to work out your own parenting style — one that fits the needs of your child and your family. The goal is to get connected to your baby. As the connection between you and baby grows, stick with what is working and modify what is not. You and your baby will find many ways to fit together in a relationship that both of you enjoy.

TODDLER TIMES: GETTING MORE CONNECTED

Enter the toddler years from one to three. Baby now has "wheels" to run on and a "horn" to blow. Crawling, walking, climbing — toddlers are ready to explore, and parents may be hard-pressed to keep up. But children who have received sensitive, nurturing parenting during their first year enter toddler times with two qualities that make life easier for them and their parents: trust and sensitivity. Securely attached toddlers have the capacity to feel connected.

Toddler trust.

Trust makes living with toddlers easier. Between a child's first and third year, a parent's role as an authority figure becomes important. If your toddler trusts you to set limits for her, you will have little difficulty acting as an authority figure. When the two of you are a connected pair, your child is more likely to accept your limits and trust your guidance. Because a connected child trusts his parents to meet his needs, he also looks to them to help him behave. Trust makes a child obey because he wants to, not just because he's forced to.

During your child's toddler years, you continue to build her trust in you. You form reasonable expectations for her behavior. Toddlers can't sit still for long, can't wait, and can't resist grabbing things off shelves in the supermarket. Putting your child in a situation that overwhelms her and then losing your temper when she misbehaves bruises the connection between you. Set your child up for success at the grocery store by talking to her and having her help pick out oranges and apples. Your connection will grow stronger. When Grandma and Grandpa come to visit from far away, don't push your child to be friendly until she has a chance to get to know these interesting but unfamiliar people. A connected parent can imagine and respect what things look like from the toddler's point of view.

Parent sensitivity.

Connected parents have an easier time setting appropriate limits for their child. Their knowledge of their child gives them a head start on discipline as their child enters the rambunctious life of a toddler. Connected parents can see things through the eyes of a child and can predict what their children will and will not do; they can then intervene before kids get into serious trouble. This ability is especially important in toddler discipline because the drive that leads young children to explore and learn about their environment is the same one that sends them toddling into trouble. Parents who have learned to know their child well during the first year of life are better at knowing when to intervene and when to let a frustrated explorer work himself out of a jam.

Connected parents set wise limits while providing structure that makes it easy for children to obey. For example, they say no to the toddler who is heading for the steep stairs, but they also put a safety gate on the stairs, thus shaping their child's environment to make it possible for him to obey easily. Childproofing your home is actually a form of discipline, a way of setting firm limits and helping your child obey them. It's easier to maintain the connection to your child if you don't have to swoop down and remove precious objects from her exploring little fingers. Connected parents change their home environment to accommodate their children's needs so that they can find joy rather than terror in everything their intrepid two-year-old is learning to do.

Reading body language.

Because connected children are so in tune with the body language of their parents, it is easy to correct or redirect them.

All I have to do is give him "the look" and he stops misbehaving.

This child has learned to expect guidance and nurturing from his parents. When he sees that look, he immediately seeks to get back into his parents' good graces. Gentle correction is often the best approach with such connected kids. When parents respond angrily to a connected child's misbehavior, she may feel frightened or upset. Subtle ways of steering a child away from trouble build your relationship, since they show your child that you believe she can do the right thing.

It's harder to change behavior in an unconnected child. When parents develop a more distant, low-touch style with their child, restraining themselves from responding to infant needs and cries, the baby either cries harder (if he has a very determined temperament) or gives up and withdraws. In either case, the baby is at risk of becoming a toddler who is difficult to discipline. Since he can't depend on his parents to respond to his needs, he becomes angry, aggressive, or just plain stubborn. Parents complain that "this child just won't listen," turning to threats and punishment and whatever other techniques they can summon up to enforce their commands. With all this negative emotion swirling around him, the child can only defend himself. He never internalizes the behavior parents expect of him and does not learn to control his own behavior. Parents don't enjoy being around this kind of child, and the family drifts apart. For them, discipline becomes a struggle to muster up the right techniques to discipline the child, rather than a way of developing the right relationship.

The connected toddler wants to please. Because parents find such a child a joy to be around, they incorporate the child's needs and desires into their lifestyle. When you spend a lot of time with your toddler — sometimes at play, sometimes doing chores together — the parent-child connection grows stronger.

Becoming comfortable with closeness.

Many nights when we watched one of our two-year-olds inch over and snuggle next to us in bed, we have felt that even at this young age our toddler was acquiring a lifelong asset — *the capacity for feeling close.* Toddlers who enjoy lots of holding time, and perhaps also continue to nurse, are very comfortable with being held. They seek human contact when they are upset or out of sorts. Parents who want to raise a connected child welcome this closeness. They recognize that their toddler is still sometimes a

baby inside and needs to sit on Dad's lap or nurse at Mom's breast.

Toddler aggression.

Peer relationships between toddlers are often difficult. Even a connected child may find it difficult to tolerate another two-year-old. Squabbles follow, and the toddler loses control and hits the playmate. Aggression is easier to deal with in connected families. First, attached parents keep a close eye on play situations and are quick to step in and settle arguments in a way that respects the needs of both children. They don't insist that a child share a very special toy. Instead, they help small children to use simple words to negotiate a solution acceptable to both sides of the conflict. Second, instead of punishing the aggressive behavior, connected parents issue a reminder: "We don't hit, we hug." For the connected parent and child, the conflict becomes a teachable moment. The child learns two lessons: hitting is not acceptable to Mom and Dad, and there are other, better ways to solve problems between people.

Expressive kids.

Because connected toddlers spend so much "in your face" time with their caregivers, they are comfortable expressing themselves. When I walk into an examining room to meet a little patient, connected children make great first impressions. Their facial expressions radiate an "I'm interested in you" attitude even as they look to Mom for cues about how to behave.

You can spot connected children in a crowd. They are the ones looking at people instead of looking lost. They are the ones who seek eye contact, the ones who know that people and the natural world around them are far more interesting than anything on a television or computer screen. They are relaxed, yet full of energy. They are huggable and comfortable with closeness. They talk just enough to communicate their feelings and needs without being annoying. Even if they are a bit shy and prefer to remain close to Mom or Dad, they don't cling frantically, afraid that no one is paying attention to them.

One reason that connected toddlers are so expressive is that their parents listen to them patiently and respond to their attempts to communicate using clear, simple language. They stop what they are doing and focus on the child who is pulling on their leg and trying to say something. They watch their child closely for signs that he understands what is being said, rephrasing their communication if it has been too complex.

Parents often complain that they have trouble understanding what their toddler wants because the child doesn't use many words yet. We tell them to watch their child's eyes. You can get a clue about what small children need from their facial expressions. Your toddler knows exactly what he's telling you, and his eyes often speak more eloquently than his tone. Intently watching his eyes as your toddler "bares his soul" often helps the garbled words suddenly make sense. And by your body language, you're teaching him how to listen to other people.

Making mental connections.

What makes connected toddlers better behaved begins with a neurobiological principle called *person permanence.* During a child's first year of life, out of sight is out of mind. The infant does not yet have the intellectual versatility to realize that his favorite caregivers continue to exist when he can't see them. Sometime about their first birthday, babies begin to figure out that

objects and people are permanent. They can create mental images of caregivers even when they are out of sight. These mental images of favorite caregivers provide security. This is why peek-a-boo is such a favorite game with babies. The toddler can take his caregivers with him in his mind, even as he crawls farther away from them to explore and learn from his environment. Connected toddlers carry more trustworthy images of caregivers. When children learn that they can depend on predictable responses from their parents, they can explore more calmly and not fear independence. The parent inside their head encourages them and helps them feel safe and secure. Someday you'll see your child turn to a stuffed animal or doll and talk to it exactly as you talk to him. You'll see what kind of an image of you your child carries around in his head and heart.

THREE TO FIVE YEARS: THE CONNECTED PRESCHOOLER

The connected child enters this stage grounded. He has a three-year file of patterns of association that make up his sense of self. He now has a norm — a base of operations — that has formed his view of the world. By now he has the roots of trust and empathy, is comfortable holding and being held, and has the verbal and social skills to make known his needs and feelings.

Preschool-age children are able to *internalize* their parents' instructions and values. All the stuff that parents have been doing and saying since their child started to walk now begins to sink in. Internalizing makes discipline easier. You might have to tell a two-year-old a hundred times not to hit the dog. A three-year-old stores this bit of life wisdom in her memory and calls it to mind when the dog is pestering her for a piece of pizza. Connected children internalize parents' values and directions more easily, since they trust these important people so deeply.

Be sure that the values you reflect are the ones you want your child to internalize. Your example says far more than do your words. If you are constantly telling a preschooler to wait while you take care of the baby, she'll internalize the idea that the baby is more important to you than she is. If you make a point of spending special time with her every day and ask someone else to take care of the younger sibling during this time, she'll feel that you do care about her and enjoy being with her.

Sharing emotions.

Preschoolers notice when parents are happy or sad, and respond emotionally. Martha was having a bad day ("Too many kids," I jokingly told her) when three-year-old Matt put his caring hand on her shoulder and said, "You sad, Mommy. I sad, too."

Empathy and the ability to interpret others' feelings grow during the preschool years, but this means that the connected child is more easily bothered by upsetting emotions. A family illness, a move, divorce, or loss of a friend is more likely to upset the connected child. Although connected children are usually more fun and easier to live with, sometimes they can be more emotionally draining than less connected children. It's the difference between a child who is care-full and care-less.

During one of the emotional struggles that every large family has, three-and-a-half-year-old Matthew said to Martha, "Are you happy to me?" Connected children want to please, so naturally they worry when they sense that their parents are not pleased. Their sensitivity shows.

This mutual sensitivity between connected children and their trusted caregivers does not mean that you have to hide your emotions from them or put on a happy face whenever you are unhappy. (The connected child will often see through this facade.) You do have to acknowledge and explain your emotions in terms a child can understand. Having to do so is one way in which connecting to your child also forces parents to understand themselves better. If you have to explain why you're feeling mad or sad ("Grandma is very sick"), be sure to test your explanation by listening with your child's ears. Be honest but not melodramatic.

Outside influences.

During the first two years most of a child's worldview comes from her primary caregivers, usually her parents. For better or worse, between three and five years old, the child is exposed to a wider variety of personalities and influences. You may find that the most heavily quoted person at your dinner table is not your child's preschool teacher but the classmate who tells the most preposterous stories. Because of their deep sensitivity, connected children are easily bothered by another child's actions that go against their norm. You can strengthen the connection to your child by listening seriously when he puzzles over the things he doesn't understand about the outside world and the people in it. In some ways the connected child enters life as an idealist, which we believe is good. If you don't know what the ideal is, you don't really know what you're shooting for. It's your job as a parent to support your child's ideals while helping him find ways to live in a less-than-ideal world.

Connected children seem less aggressive. They still may hit and push, but they do so less often and less angrily. They don't have as strong a need to force others to do their will, since they are used to having their needs and wishes respected. During a toy squabble, the connected child is more likely to propose solutions; the unconnected child is more likely to hit. When you respect your child's feelings at home and help him use words to express them rather than acting out, you add to his ability to connect with playmates — even the troublesome ones.

FIVE TO TEN YEARS: SEARCHING FOR CONNECTIONS

During their elementary-school years, children search for meaning in life. What's important? Whom should I trust? Who are the models to copy? It's also a stage when peer influence increases and children are exposed to different values and different ways of responding to people. Hanging around with all kinds of children is a mixed blessing. On the one hand, it has great educational value and prepares a child for life. On the other hand, it can be confusing and can lead a child astray if she does not have strong roots in her relationship with her family.

The connected child enters this stage with the right tools:

- the capacity to trust
- the capacity to care
- a sensitivity to what's right and wrong

These virtues are not something the connected child has, they are what the connected child *is* — sensitive and trusting.

Early empathy.

A connected child enters this stage with a valuable tool: the ability to *get behind the eyes of another person* and imagine how her behavior will affect that other person. The capacity to care is the basis of the connected child's growing sense of morality. Because she can understand how another child feels, having been herself understood by her parents, she can imagine how her behavior will affect another person. Connected children are uncomfortable when kids are mean to other kids. Cruelty and teasing, even when they're not the object of the attack, really bother them. They may not know what to do when peers are ridiculing someone, but you can help them figure out what to do in difficult situations. This is a time when a connected parent spends far more time listening to what the child has to say than giving advice. Connected parents and kids work out a plan of action together. Parents don't dictate marching orders.

Healthy guilt.

Connected children enter middle childhood with an inner operating code of behavior, one that produces a healthy sense of guilt when violated. They feel right when they act right and feel wrong when they act wrong. A child who tells a lie is bothered by it until he sets the record straight. Connected children may rebel against family norms and try out other values, but they are likely to get back on track before any lasting damage is done. Parents who have been sensitive to kids' feelings have shown them how to listen to that inner voice that can tell right from wrong.

Not so the unconnected child, who grows up less trusting, less sensitive, and less caring. He has no inner guidance system, no internal norm on how to act or expect those around him to act. His values change according to his impulses, whims, and the friends he hangs out with. He becomes a moral marshmallow. A child who is seriously lacking in human connections may be unable to feel remorse or understand that her actions affect others. Unconnected children are less likely to get back on the right track if they deviate from their family's values, because they weren't on that track in the first place.

The saying "ingrained into the child" has a neurobiological basis. The patterns of association introduced in infancy leave their grooves in the brain. So does the emotional atmosphere of the home during childhood. Connected parents seek to guide their children by helping them understand the why behind family rules and moral values. Such an understanding helps kids feel more in control of their lives and destiny. Connected parents then trust their children to make wise decisions, and step in to help a child figure out a solution to a difficult challenge. More distant parents, who enforce the family rules primarily by punishing children for infractions, teach kids that they are powerless and that their own thoughts and opinions have no value. These children have trouble making moral decisions, both in childhood and when they grow up.

Fair rules.

"It's not fair" is the universal complaint of childhood. Whereas the connected child has a strong sense of fairness and understands the necessity of rules, the unconnected child may have less interest in them. "Not fair" to the unconnected child means "not fair to me!" This is symptomatic of living in a world in which everyone looks out for number one, and too bad for everyone else.

Morally literate.

The connected child follows his parents' example and chooses moral values that lead to the welfare of others as well as his own. Not so the unconnected child. Because he has no secure roots, he adopts values according to what's convenient or what will make him popular with his peers. He is prey to whatever influences come along.

HOW ATTACHMENT PARENTING HELPS KIDS AND FAMILIES SUCCEED

In this chapter we lay the foundation for a strong connection to your child. We have dubbed this parenting style "attachment parenting," or AP. Attachment parenting has a very positive influence on how kids turn out. Attachment parenting is a way of getting connected to your child, and this connection makes the whole parent-child relationship more natural and enjoyable. You'll see its benefits in every aspect of your child's life — health care, self-esteem, the ways you have fun together, and discipline. The better you know your child, the more your child trusts you, and the more effective you will be at guiding and correcting your child's behavior, from babyhood to late adolescence.

Just how does attachment parenting work for families? Here are some of the ways in which AP helps you get connected to your child in babyhood and beyond.

Attachment parenting is an exercise in getting to know your child.

Because AP infants spend so much time in close proximity to you, you develop a sixth sense about your baby. Mom, Dad, and other caregivers are able to read baby's body language and, by trial and error, learn how to respond appropriately and give baby what he needs to develop to his fullest potential. They also learn how to say no and, when appropriate, guide baby in a different direction. They really can tell what's he's thinking — an ability that becomes ever more important as baby grows more independent. This ability to understand what's going on in a child's mind is perhaps the most important part of attachment parenting. Everything else you do to help your child turn out right is based on your understanding of your child's uniqueness.

Attachment parenting makes discipline easier.

The connection that parents develop with their baby and toddler enables them to get behind the eyes of their child when she is older, so they know why she acts the way she does. They stay one step ahead of their child and are able to guide and shape good behavior, not just correct a child making a wrong move. Because AP parents have the right relationship with their child, they worry less about using the "right" techniques for discipline. Connected kids behave well — more often than not — because their parents let them know what behavior is expected and that they are secure, loved, and valued.

Attachment parenting is based on mutual trust.

When baby's cues are read and her needs sensitively taken care of, she learns to trust her parents. As parents respond over and over again to their baby's signals, they come to trust in their ability to read their infant's cues (at least most of the time) and to know how to respond. This trust between parent and child is very important. When children trust their caregiving environment, trust becomes an ingrained part of the child, and the world becomes a warm and trusting place in which to live. This may sound idealistic, but the ability to trust that one's needs will be taken care of is an important ingredient for contentment throughout life.

More distant, less responsive styles of parenting do not lead to a trusting relationship between parents and children. When parents are afraid of spoiling a child or are on their guard against the child manipulating them, they are not open to understanding the child's needs

from her point of view. Parents who want to be in complete control of their children see trust as a one-way street: their children should trust them to know best. These children, however, do not learn to trust themselves and their environment. Many parents honestly believe that a style of parenting that depends on set rules and schedules is better and more convenient for the whole family, but parenting methods that promise to get babies to sleep through the night and be less "demanding" depend on using some variation of the "let your baby cry it out" technique, which asks parents to ignore their baby's or child's needs and ultimately leads to insensitivity. Everyone is in trouble when infant cries no longer bother parents or when parents try to make an older child blindly obey their rules. Baby may become a "good baby" — or at least a more "convenient baby" — because he quits trying to communicate. The older child may comply with the rules without internalizing the wisdom behind them. Parents and children end up not trusting each other or themselves.

I once heard the story of the Chinese bamboo tree. After the seed is planted, you see only a tiny sprout for several years. During those years, the seed grows underground into a deep-branching root structure. Then in the fifth year, the bamboo tree can grow as high as a house. Why did it grow so well? Because it was nurtured with deep, secure roots.

We believe that the road to success begins with attachment parenting during the early years. Nevertheless, parents should not take all the credit or all the blame for the way their children turn out. You do your best to raise your children with the tools and resources you have at the time. The rest is up to the child. There is no perfect, 100 percent correlation between what parents do in children's early years and the kind of people their children become,

SCIENCE SAYS: CONNECTED CHILDREN ARE MORE LIKELY TO BECOME SUCCESSFUL

Attachment outcome studies — which look for associations between the quality of early parent-child relationships and later behaviors — are one of the hottest topics in psychology. Psychologists divide infants and children into two basic groups: securely attached and insecurely attached. Outcome studies are based on comparing these two groups of children over a long period of time. Here's a summary of what science says about the importance of getting connected early:

Connected kids play better with peers.

Researchers have studied the relationship between the degree of attachment that children experienced during infancy and how they played with other preschoolers. They found that preschoolers who were securely attached played better with similar securely attached children. They played less well with children who had poor attachment histories. Researchers noticed that children with insecure attachments were less socially competent and showed more aggressive behavior during play. They also found that preschoolers with secure attachment histories were more flexible and "held their own" against aggressive children. This study suggests that connected kids play better with other children because they are able to carry the sensitivity that was shown them during infancy into their play relationships as older children.

Connected kids become better lovers.

True lovemaking is, in psychological jargon, often called mutual empathy. In one study researchers found that securely attached children grew up to enjoy higher-quality romantic partnerships, an outcome the researchers attribute to the qualities of sensitivity and empathy associated with secure attachment. Being able to feel for and with another person, to listen sensitively to that other person, and to bring out the best in that person are qualities that make for a more connected romantic relationship. These researchers also found that adults who had a history of insecure infant attachment were able to overcome their insecure past when they became involved in a romantic relationship with a person who had a history of secure infant attachment.

Researchers feel that the capacity to love in adulthood goes back to the stable emotional bond formed between the primary caregiver (typically, the mother) and baby. Many studies have demonstrated a relationship between a cold and distant style of parenting and decreased emotional health in children. A study of one hundred adult women shows that insecurely attached women were not as happy in their romantic relationships. They were twice as likely to get divorced as securely attached women and had more difficulty remaining in committed relationships. The securely attached women showed qualities of interdependence — they learned to rely both on self and others. Another study of 154 women at the average age of nineteen shows that those who were securely attached grew up with a higher incidence of good self-esteem, interpersonal trust, and the capability of feeling at ease with intimate and interpersonal relationships, particularly romantic relationships.

Connected kids become better-adjusted students.

Studies show that children who have a secure attachment to their parents often tend to have closer relationships with their teachers. This seems like a logical consequence of attachment parenting, since children carry their capacity for being close to family members into relationships with friends, teachers, and other important persons in their life. One study of 408 first-year students entering a major university shows that students who had a positive attachment relationship with their parents (i.e., connected kids) adjusted more easily to university life. The students who fared the best had parents who were highly invested in their children and demanded a lot from them, yet were highly responsive to their children's cues and needs.

Connected kids become more resilient.

Studies have shown a fascinating relationship between early parenting and a child's ability to get through adversity. Specifically, the studies found that a key aspect in achieving adulthood success, even in the face of growing up in a difficult home environment, is the presence of at least one individual in the child's life who was an attachment figure throughout the child's development. If children had the opportunity to establish a close bond with at least one caregiver in infancy, they had a

greater chance of a good outcome, even with a poor start. Children who had the greatest capacity for recovery were the product of early sensitive parenting and came from homes in which parents were more highly invested in their children. Researchers also found that the presence of a positive male influence within the household contributes to the success of at-risk children. Researchers believe that a capacity for recovery from hard times is built into connected children. The psychologists also noted that children who succeeded in the face of adversity were extremely skilled in getting the resources they required from their environment. These children were particularly able to get connected to persons of significance, such as teachers.

Connected kids are better behaved.

Researchers studied four hundred students registered in kindergarten at age five years and interviewed most of these individuals thirty-six years later. The results of their longitudinal study relating the parenting practices at age five with social adjustments at age forty-one show that children who have warm and affectionate parents are more likely to be socially successful adults. Studies show that men with insecure attachments were more likely to call their mothers *controlling*. The parents' level of control seems to influence men more than women in terms of mental health. With men, the more controlling the parents, the less emotionally healthy these men became. The children who grew up with fearful attachment tended to have a negative view of themselves. This study also shows that adult women were better able to bounce back from insecure attachment relationships in early childhood and become emotionally healthy adults — as long as they developed secure attachment relationships during adulthood. Yet insecure adult men did not seem to benefit as much from their adult attachment relationships. In explaining these findings of gender differences, researchers suggest that women are more likely to choose mates for the type of emotional stability they will provide, while men (especially if they are insecure) often choose mates based on more superficial qualities, such as looks. Unconnected infants are more likely to show antisocial behavior and conduct problems in childhood and adolescence. The reason seems to be that connected kids are more respectful of authority, are more sensitive to others' feelings, and do not operate from the basis of anger that is characteristic of unconnected children.

Connected kids tend to grow up to be connecting parents.

More than eighteen studies show a clear relationship between the quality of attachment parents had when they were infants and the degree of attachment parenting they practice with their own babies. Getting connected early is your best long-term investment. A study of one hundred adult women showed that women who grew up in the most securely attached homes were more confident in social situations and less vulnerable to stress than those who were less securely attached. They were better able to form warm emotional bonds with others and to trust others. They also tended to be more independent and sympathetic than insecurely attached persons, who tended to be cold and

distant. Researchers have concluded that early attachment patterns become internal working relationship models that generally remain consistent over time. (However, they note that secure early attachments do not guarantee an emotionally healthy outcome.)

Connected kids have a greater chance of growing up to become connected adults.

A recent twenty-year study suggests that connected infants are more likely to grow up to be connected adults. As researchers wisely caution, however, attachment parenting in infancy is no guarantee that children will turn out well. These outcome studies suggest that getting connected in infancy and childhood gives the child the capacity for connectedness in other relationships. Yet whether or not the child uses this capacity and goes on to become a connected adult depends on the quality of attachments the child experiences at each stage of development. In essence, attachment parenting does not end in infancy but continues in other forms throughout the rest of the parent-child relationship.

Think of attachment parenting as an immunization that protects children in case of adversity. It helps them become resilient and bounce back, sometimes becoming even stronger. As with many immunizations, booster shots of attachment are usually necessary to maintain this connectedness.

In summary, these outcome studies all seem to come to the same conclusion: the child's early attachment relationships serve as a *blueprint* for all future relationships. Although there is not a perfect correlation, it's nevertheless true that the child who grows up connected tends to stay connected.

but in more than thirty years in pediatric practice, we have observed that AP kids generally turn out very well.

THE EARLY ROAD TO SUCCESS: HOW THE BABY B'S TRANSLATE INTO THE CHILDHOOD C'S

When we talk about kids who turn out well, we don't necessarily mean children who grow up to fulfill the typical American Dream. Real success in life can't be equated with a degree from an Ivy League college, a six-figure salary, or even the freedom to be your own boss. When we talk about success, we are focusing on emotional health and less tangible qualities: fulfilling and healthy relationships, self-respect, and happiness and contentment in whatever life may bring. It might seem a big jump from birth bonding and bed-sharing to an awareness of higher principles and the spiritual side of life. Yet we find that the Baby B's produce the Childhood C's, qualities that we think add up to real success.

1. Caring kids.

Attachment-parented kids show empathy. They are kids who care (e.g., care-full). From birth on, these children have been on the receiving end of nurturing. Someone cared for them. Caring, giving, listening, and responding to needs become the family norm, and these qualities become part of the child. Children who have received empathy learn how to give it. Because these children receive sensitive parenting, they learn to be sensitive to others' feelings. When friends are hurting, these children understand and rush to help.

Studies on kids who don't turn out well have shown that they do not care about other people. They feel no remorse for what they do, and they act with no thought whatsoever about the effects of their behavior on others. Empathy is completely missing. Often these individuals have a history of being abused or neglected as children. No one cared about them, so they don't know how to care about others.

Children who are the product of attachment parenting learn to consider the feelings of others before they act. They care about how their actions affect other people. They have a healthy sense of guilt, feeling wrong when they act wrongly and feeling good when they should. Connected kids care.

2. Compassionate kids.

Children from families who practice attachment parenting grow up with a deep inner sense of right. They are keenly aware of challenges to this sense of right and will strive to restore what they feel is just. I watch such children in play groups. Children who were "takers" during infancy become good givers. They actually share willingly — something that is difficult for many children. They are concerned about the needs and rights of their peers because that is the behavior their parents have modeled for them.

Attachment-parented children are supersensitive to the moods of family and friends. When you feel stressed, they'll feel stressed, too — and you'll see this reflected in their behavior. But especially as they get older, this sensitivity becomes an asset. When you feel bad, your children will do their best to help you feel better. I have witnessed our own children and children in other families console their upset parents: "Don't cry, Mommy, I'll help you," or "It's okay, Daddy, I love you." Having your sensitive three-year-old sympathize with and soothe you is one of the most beautiful payoffs of attachment parenting. No adult friend could ever offer words that have the same impact as those that flow naturally from the heart of a sensitive child.

In families that practice attachment parenting, kids aren't the only ones who become more compassionate. When you practice sensitive parenting, you find that your sensitivity to everyone and everything else goes up a notch. The ability to get behind the eyes of your child, to see things from his viewpoint, to think first of his needs, carries over to your relationship with your mate, your friends, your job, and your community. (You will learn more about teaching empathy and compassion in Chapter 7.)

3. Communicative kids.

From early on, AP children are rewarded for trying to communicate. Is it any wonder they become skilled communicators? Their communication skills extend beyond language. Because attachment-parented children are held a lot and get lots of face-to-face contact with their caregivers, they learn how to make appropriate eye contact and read body language. Because they are listened to, they don't hesitate to share their feelings and ideas. These communication skills are vital for later success in relationships and careers. (You will learn more about this in the chapter on teaching your child communication skills, p. 151.)

In watching how my daughter-in-law parents my grandson, I can see what I did wrong with my son, her husband. I let him cry too often for fear of spoiling him. He gradually just stopped trying to get my attention. As a result, he went through much pain trying to communicate as an adult.

4. Connected kids.

AP kids are comfortable with intimacy. Attachment-parented children enjoy being close to others, because these "Velcro babies"

spent the most formative months of their lives attached to mother's arms and breast. These kids have learned to bond with people rather than with things. They become high-touch persons even in a high-tech world.

Therapists whose offices are filled with adults who didn't get responsive parenting as children tell us that most of their energy is spent helping their clients learn how to get close to someone. They offer clients unconditional respect and support — in other words, reparent them. In contrast, children whose parents respond appropriately to their needs learn to thrive on interpersonal relationships. Being connected is their norm. The AP infant is more likely to become a child who forms deep friendships with peers and then grow into an adult who enjoys intimacy with a mate. The connected child learns to give and receive love.

5. Careful and considerate kids.

Connected kids are less accident-prone. They have a better understanding of their own capabilities and don't need to test their boundaries. In parent parlance, they are less likely to do "dumb things"! They carry within them images of caregivers telling them what they can and may do and what they should not do. Because the caregivers are important and respected, these images help curb childish impulses. Even children with very impulsive temperaments tend to get into less trouble if they are securely attached to a primary caregiver. One reason may be that connected kids are not angry. Anger adds danger to impulsivity. It overrides what little sense a child has, leaving her to plunge headfirst into trouble.

6. Confident kids.

The word *confidence* comes from two Latin words meaning "with trust." Children whose parents are responsive to their needs grow up as if *trust* is their middle name. From their relationship with their parents they learn that it is safe to trust others and that their needs will be consistently met. Trusting their caregivers translates into trusting themselves — in other words, self-confidence.

I felt he would never leave my arms, but when he became two, he often said, "Me do it." I know this is a phrase that many mothers dread (because it takes five times longer for the child to accomplish a simple task), but to the mother of a clingy baby, this phrase is a joy. Now that Jonathan is absorbed in trying things himself, he is rapidly leaving behind many of his old baby needs, such as demanding to be carried everywhere and never leaving my lap. I must admit that there are times when I miss being the exclusive interest in his life. But when one of those moments arises, all I have to do is give him a big hug and he stops whatever he is doing and returns to me. Mostly, I am proud to see him growing into a happy, loving, self-confident little person, especially when I realize he has done it on his own. I have simply given him the support he needed.

7. Cuddly kids.

AP babies enjoy a close physical relationship with their parents, thanks to babywearing, breastfeeding, and bedding close to baby. These kids are appropriately comfortable with touching and being touched. They'll come to their parents for a reassuring hug even as teenagers. They know how to seek appropriate human contact, making them less likely to seek out sexual relationships when what they really want is friendship and emotional closeness. The ability to offer a caring touch, such as a sympathetic hand on a shoulder, a warm handshake, or even an exuberant high five, enhances social relationships.

8. Confident parents.

Besides these seven C's for children, attachment parenting offers mothers and fathers an important C. Attached, responsive parents develop confidence in their parenting skills, along with the ability to adapt their parenting practices to their own lifestyle and their child's changing needs. During well-baby checkups I often ask parents, "Is your parenting style working?" I advise parents to periodically take inventory of what works and discard what is no longer effective. What worked at one stage of development may not work in another. For example, some babies initially sleep better with their parents but become restless later on, necessitating a change in sleeping arrangements. Other babies may sleep better alone at first but move into their parents' bed in later months. Confident parents use themselves and their baby as the barometer for evaluating their parenting style.

BENEFITS OF ATTACHMENT PARENTING — A SUMMARY

CHILD	PARENTS	RELATIONSHIP
• is more trusting • feels more competent • grows better • feels right, acts right • is better organized • learns language more easily • establishes healthy independence • learns intimacy • learns to give and receive love	• become more confident • are more sensitive • can read baby's cues • respond intuitively • flow with baby's temperament • find discipline easier • become keen observers • know baby's competencies and preferences • know which advice to take and which to disregard	Parents and baby: • share mutual sensitivity • enjoy mutual giving • mutually shape each other's behavior • show mutual trust • feel connected • are more flexible • show more lively interaction • bring out the best in each other

3

Ten Family Discipline Practices of Kids Who Turned Out Well

SUCCESSFUL KIDS COME FROM families of all races and religions, from families in all kinds of neighborhoods, and from families up and down the economic scale. They may have two parents at home, or just one parent actively involved in their upbringing. Some of these families live in rambling homes with a bedroom and computer for each child, shelves full of educational toys and books, and a family calendar filled to the brim with after-school activities and travel. Other families raising successful kids make do with the pots and pans from a tiny kitchen cabinet, and the children share a small bedroom. This family makes frequent trips to the local library and makes a learning experience out of a trip to the Laundromat. Wealth is clearly not a requirement for raising good kids. Many young children are not able to tell you from which economic level their family hails, knowing only that their lives are happy and fulfilled.

The home environments of families raising successful kids are also varied. Some of the families interviewed for this book have the neatest, cleanest home in the neighborhood; in others, the family pet can easily get lost in all the clutter. Some families have an orderly life with regular mealtimes, bedtimes, and chores, but others seem to thrive on the chaos of an ever changing array of activities. The families have different weekend rituals. Some spend every Sunday at church, while others spend it at the baseball field, on daylong bicycle journeys, or quietly at home.

Our success as a society depends not on what happens in the White House, but what happens inside your house.

— *Barbara Bush*

♦

It's comforting for me to know that I don't have to be rich or smart to be a good parent. I just have to be there and care.

No matter what the home environment, the families of kids who turn out well are remarkably alike when it comes to the way parents and children interact with and relate to one another. In this chapter we discuss ten parenting practices used by the families of children who turned out well. In the chapters that follow, we'll talk about the qualities that these practices nurture in children.

We have gleaned this list of top ten traits from interviews with parents of successful children. We have also drawn upon letters written to us by parents specifically for this book, letters in which parents describe their relationship with their children. We have further relied on the experience gained over thirty years of pediatric practice and more than thirty years of raising our own eight children.

Can you put all these practices into action all the time? Probably not. Lifestyle, economics, medical and social problems, and individual personality differences also play a role in the choices you make about raising your children. Yet this parenting style is more about *how* you do what you do than specific do's and don'ts. Most parents can adapt most of these practices to their families' circumstances. We hope that you learn from these families and employ as many of these practices as possible.

1. PRACTICE ATTACHMENT PARENTING

Top on our list of factors that influence how children turn out is the parents' overall style of childcare. Notice that we say *overall*. It's the predominance of good, responsive parenting over distant, unconnected parenting that makes the difference. All parents make mistakes, and certainly this book was not written by perfect parents. The overall message you send your kids is what matters most.

Parents who are trying hard to turn out good kids are emotionally invested in their children. They can be hard on themselves when they feel that they have fallen short of their parenting ideals. A dad once called me, feeling guilty about having lost his temper and slapping his child. I knew that he was basically a loving and nurturing father, but on that one occasion he just snapped. I reassured him that his overall gentle and nurturing ways with his children were far more important than this one incident.

His child might certainly remember the slap for a long time — because it was so different from the way his father usually treated him. I suggested that he talk with his child about what had happened, acknowledge that he was wrong, and apologize. He could turn the bad moment into a teachable moment — one in which both Dad and his youngster could learn something about anger and how to handle it.

Attachment parenting (AP) is an approach to raising children rather than a set of rules. It's a way of caring for your baby that gets the two of you connected. As children grow, attachment parenting focuses on guiding children in a way that respects their needs, feelings, and level of development.

The most concrete, easily described parts of attachment parenting apply to babies, because raising successful kids begins with the connection between parent and child — and that connection is most easily made during infancy. Babies are biologically programmed to learn to love caregivers, and caregivers are at their best when they respond to babies' needs. Becoming attached to your child is certainly an ongoing process, and you can work on becoming more attached at every stage of development. But we have found that parents who get off to the right start with their babies have an easier time making parenting decisions as the years go by.

The basic tools for getting attached to your infant are the Baby B's described in Chapter 1. If you'd like to read more about this approach to baby care, read our *The Attachment Parenting Book*.

In this chapter, we'll show how the Baby B's help you discipline your child when babyhood is over. The Baby B's, along with other ways of getting connected to your children as they grow, help you know your child well; as a connected parent once told us, "Knowing my children empowers me." The kid knowledge you get by practicing attachment parenting becomes like a sixth sense. Intuitively you get behind the eyes of your child to understand the world from her point of view. You can anticipate when your child might get into trouble or when she may need direction. With this knowledge, you can step in and reshape situations so that your child is able to behave better.

One day our daughter Lauren, then two, impulsively grabbed a carton of milk out of the refrigerator, and it went *splat* all over the floor. She had made a common, childish error of judgment, but it occurred during our family's morning rush hour. Cleaning up the mess was going to be downright inconvenient. Lauren was about to disintegrate completely. Then Martha stepped in. She got down to Lauren's eye level and connected with her. "Would you like me to help you clean it up?" she asked. Lauren nodded her head yes, and peace was restored as they worked together. Later I asked Martha how she had known that this was the way to handle the situation. Martha replied, "I asked myself, 'If I were Lauren, how would I want *my* mother to act?'"

Attachment parenting promotes mutual sensitivity.

Connected kids and their parents learn how to read one another. The messages flowing between them are often unspoken, yet very well understood. An attached parent can often correct a child's behavior simply by raising an eyebrow. An attached mom or dad can also send a look across a crowded soccer field to reassure a ten-year-old goalie whose confidence is fading as the opposition's score mounts. The mutual sensitivity between parent and child leads parents to look at the why behind their child's behavior. They address what's going on inside the child rather than focusing only on outward behavior. Connected parents naturally become experts on their child and know what behavior is appropriate for their child's level of development and personal temperament.

Connected children know what behavior their parents expect of them and try to live up to those expectations because they want to please their parents. Living up to their parents' standards makes them feel right inside. Displeasing parents leaves them feeling wrong. Because these kids are so accustomed to feeling right most of the time (something the Baby B's taught them about), they behave well most of the time. Of course, AP children misbehave, but their misbehavior is usually more easily corrected.

Mutual sensitivity also means mutual respect. Connected families tend to put their children at the center of the family rather than on the periphery. They go places together as a family. They share interests. They accommodate one another's needs and honor one another's opinions and feelings. But parents and children need occasional breaks from one another. (The senior Sears parents have been known to go on "adults only" vacations.) But on the whole, they value being together and truly enjoy one another.

The connected family's mutual respect may show up in something as subtle as the recording on the family answering machine. The other day I called one of our grown sons and heard, "Hi, you've reached the Sears family — Bob, Cheryl, Andrew, and Alex." Another subtle difference we've noticed is that attached parents tend to use the term *child*, more than the term *kid*. *Kids,* we'll admit, is a fun word, one that relays a certain exuberance associated with children, and we use *kids* a lot in this book. But sometimes we hear parents talk about "my kid" or "those kids" in a tone that clearly says there's

FAMILY NIGHTS

Many of the families that we talked to have frequent, scheduled times they spend together, events that many called family nights. It's a time to take the phone off the hook, turn off the television, and enjoy one another. Use the KISMIF principle: keep it simple, make it fun. Play games, sing songs, or play music together — whatever all of you enjoy doing together. As children get older, it can be challenging to come up with activities that everyone agrees are fun, especially when children are widely spaced apart in age, but it's well worth the effort involved.

Many families also hold family meetings, opportunities to discuss house rules, formulate ideas for happier living, and talk together about how to solve problems. We have found it helpful at times to use a chalkboard to make family meetings more businesslike. We have also used family meetings as a way to support a family member who is trying to solve a problem. When one of our children was having difficulty at school, we held a family meeting to discuss the situation and get input from the elder kids. Family meetings are another way to set kids up for success in life. No matter what occupation they choose, they're bound to spend some time in business meetings. Learning how to solve problems as part of a group will help them be more effective in meetings outside the home.

It's important that everyone gets a chance to talk in family meetings and that everyone's views are respected. This isn't always easy to do. Younger children may find family meetings boring, and older children may regard the younger children as pests. Establish rules about listening and speaking in a positive way. Model this behavior yourself. Don't let family meetings become a time when parents scold or lecture and children must sit still and listen. Hold family meetings regularly so that children learn that working together to solve problems is a normal and expected part of family living.

Kids say: I am now twenty, and the part of my childhood that stands out most are those special moments I spent together with my family, such as meals, traditions, game night, and family rituals. All outside influences, including television, phone calls, etc., were shut out while we intensely focused on just one another. This is an important legacy I hope to pass on to my family. With everything else that competed for their time, I know my parents had to be intentional about the family spending time together and made this a priority. I truly appreciate how my parents modeled this for us on a daily basis. As adults, we still look forward to special times when the family gets together.

something wrong with being a kid. Attached parents, especially when they're reflecting on their relationship with their children, tend to use the more loving, respectful word *child*. They also use the child's name a lot when speaking of them in conversation with other adults. These ways of speaking convey respect for the child's individuality and bring a certain dignity to people under the age of eighteen.

Attachment parenting promotes mutual trust.

You may be surprised to discover that being a trusted authority figure does not come automatically with the title of parent. Authority has to be earned, even when you're a full-grown adult and your child is an eight-pound newborn. Your infant's first impression of you is that you are someone she can trust to fulfill her needs. Trust is the beginning of respect for authority. As your child trusts you to meet her needs, so she will go on to trust you to set limits for her.

Being an authority figure to your child does not mean that you are engaged in a constant power struggle. Some parents confuse being in charge of their children with being in control. A child who is told he must "obey or else" may choose to behave, but he does it out of fear rather than out of genuine respect for his parents' wisdom and intentions. Parents may be able to control their children's behavior by making lots of rules and imposing punishments when rules are broken, but true authority is missing. *"Honor thy father and thy mother"* says the commandment in the Bible. Honor means respect. Obedience, of course, is likely to follow respect, but the parent-child relationship works best when respect and the trust it is based on come first. Attachment parenting teaches your children to respect you because you know their needs and respect them.

In my practice I often talk with expectant parents, and in these conversations I try to diffuse some of their worries. In one prenatal interview, a first-time mother confided that she was already worried about not knowing how to discipline her child. I asked her what her feelings were upon hearing a baby cry. She replied, "I just can't stand to hear a baby crying. I want to rush over and pick that baby up. It bothers me when mothers ignore their babies' cries." She didn't know it, but I had used this question as a sort of litmus test, to find out how sensitive she would be to her baby's signals. Having heard her answer, I could assure this mother

that she was likely to become a good disciplinarian because she was already someone who was sensitive to the needs of children and babies — and this sensitivity is what effective discipline is based on.

During another prenatal interview a mother-to-be stated quite firmly, "I'm not going to let this little person control me." Here, I thought, is a mother to worry about, and I set out to reframe her understanding of the mother-baby relationship. I advised her to begin life with her new baby by being more open to her baby's signals and her own intuitive responses rather than worrying about who was in charge of whom. I also helped her to think in terms of shaping her baby's behavior rather than always worrying about being in control. (See "Shaping versus Control," p. 47.)

When parents and children struggle over who's in control, they get into an adversarial relationship: in order for one person to win, the other has to lose. Families get along better, and kids turn out better, when everyone follows the "win-win" principle. Parents who believe that an infant comes into the world programmed to *control* the parents (and there are books and parenting advisers that promote this idea) respond by trying to control the baby first. Remember, *tiny infants cry to communicate, not manipulate.* When parents don't respond to infants' cries because they're trying to show the baby who's boss, they cut off the communication right from the start. Everybody loses. Similarly, by exerting their power over an older child, making decisions for him without taking into consideration his wishes, parents may actually lose authority in the child's eyes, and the child loses the ability to make wise choices for himself. If there is no discussion or explanation, the child sees parental decisions as arbitrary rather than wise and considered.

WHAT DISCIPLINE MEANS

In a nutshell, discipline means giving your children the tools to succeed in life. As parents of eight, we also regard discipline as doing whatever is necessary to like living with your kids. Eighty-five percent of discipline is encouraging good behavior; 15 percent (maybe less) is what you do about bad behavior. Encouraging good behavior depends mostly on building the right relationship. The techniques usually associated with the word *discipline* — time-outs, loss of privileges — are actually a very small part of what it takes to teach children appropriate behavior.

One day I was watching a family in my office waiting room. A busy toddler played happily a few feet away from his parents, but he checked in with them frequently. When he ventured a little farther away, he would glance back at his mother for her approval. She would nod and smile, giving him the reassurance he needed to explore new toys with confidence. When he started banging two toys together noisily, his mother gave him a cautioning look and Dad got up to take away the toys and redirect the toddler's attention to quieter activities. There was a natural authority in the parents' voices and actions, and the child was very receptive to their guidance. I could tell that they were connected.

I went over and complimented them: "You are good disciplinarians." Surprised, the father replied, "But we don't spank our child." Like so many parents, they equated the word *discipline* with punishment, not realizing that their day-in, day-out guidance of their child was helping him establish the inner control that would ultimately make him a self-disciplined individual. Their gentle, connected relationship with their child would help him feel right when he did the right thing and feel wrong when he transgressed. This guidance system would serve him well — at age four and at age forty.

Attachment parenting encourages obedience.

The word *obey* is derived from a Latin word meaning "to listen attentively." This is the kind of obedience you get with attachment parenting. Because of the mutual trust and sensitivity that connected families enjoy, a child wants to listen to parents, and parents have a way of talking so their child will listen. (See Chapter 9, Teaching Children Communication Skills.") Obedience follows naturally, and because they have been grounded in obedience to their parents, these children also find it easier to obey other trusted caregivers and authority figures: childcare providers, teachers, and coaches. (They may also choose to keep their distance from adults whom their gut feeling tells them not to trust.)

Parents often complain, "My child won't mind." As children become more independent and search for their own identity, they tend to mind their *own* mind and not always their parents'. Some children are naturally more compliant than others. How closely children follow your directions depends partly on their individual temperaments (which you can't control) and partly on the sensitivity of your parent-child connection (which you can influence). In a connected parent-child relationship, minds mesh rather than clash, so the child is more open to the parents' perspective. Even though you and your child will have some struggles and disagreements, if your relationship is a good one, he will be more likely to understand and accept your point of view. Connected children trust that their parents know best. Even when they're grown, connected children are more likely to respect their parents' opinions and judgment.

2. GIVE CHILDREN HIGH-INVESTMENT PARENTING

Children who turn out well come from families who are *highly invested* in parenting. Investing in your parenting is especially important in the early years, when great investments bring greater returns.

Most parents have a lot invested in their children: they invest a great deal of love in their children, and hope to be loved in return; children also carry their parents' hopes for the future. But this is not what we mean by high-investment parenting. Investing in your parenting means being willing to devote a significant amount of time and energy to raising your children. Especially in the early years, parents are the givers and babies are the takers. You're asked to give and give, even when you're tired or running out of patience. This is a realistic picture of what it takes to raise happy, healthy kids. Although it's important to take care of your own needs during these early, demanding years of parenthood, for the most part you're called on to invest yourself highly in your children. Doing so benefits not only babies and toddlers. You, the parents, grow and mature when you make this kind of investment in your family, and parenting becomes much easier as your investment begins to pay off.

Here's an example, pulled from the files of my practice. Nathan was one of those infants who fussed long and hard if he was put down, who protested mightily if he was asked to sleep in his own crib, and who nursed every hour or two. He asked a great deal of his parents, and they did their best to give him what he needed. During Nathan's four-year checkup his mother, Erin, made the following comment: "Initially, attachment parenting took a lot of energy and caused plenty of inconvenience. But now, caring for Nathan is easier because communication and discipline flow naturally between us. I'm finally beginning to cash in on my investment."

In his teen years Nathan was diagnosed with Asperger's syndrome, a type of high-functioning autism. With special help, he is turning out well. Because his mother intuitively knew early on that he was a different child who needed a high-investment style of attachment parenting, she brought out the best in her child. Nathan is now eighteen years old and is a "kid who turned out well," and he has a loving relationship with his parents.

High-need children.

High-investment/high-yield parenting is critical when you have a child with intense needs. Some children come into this world wired differently. (Some children come into this world wired, period!) We've affectionately termed these special kids "high-need children," because that's what they are. If babies could talk, they would come out of the womb, look up at their parents, and say, "Hi, Mom and Dad! I am not an average child, and I need better-than-average parenting. If you give it to me, we're going to get along fine. If you don't, we're going to have a bit of trouble down the road." Of course babies can't talk — even above-average babies. But they do have a way of letting you know pretty quickly that they need more of everything: more comforting, more holding, more nursing, more sensitive guidance through the years. In fact, we nicknamed our first high-need child, Hayden, More.

We coined the term *high-need* after figuring out how to survive and thrive with Hayden. It was a much more useful term than others we had heard through the years, terms such as "the fussy baby" or "the strong-willed child." High needs we could do something about, and we developed a parenting principle we call *the need-level concept*. We believe that every child comes wired with a certain level of needs; if those needs are filled, the child thrives and develops to his maximum potential — intellectually, physically, and emotionally. For example, some children *need* to be held a lot and *need* to spend hours a day in arms, at breast, and in a sling in order to thrive. The good thing about high-need children is that they also come wired with the persistence necessary to keep asking their parents for this level of care. They cry to be picked up, and cry harder if they're ignored.

Babies with high needs are half of the need-level equation; parents are the other half. When babies ask for a high level of care, parents need to learn to be more astute baby readers and more willing givers. They develop skills they might not otherwise have learned. Called upon to make a higher investment in their child, they find that the more they give, the more they get. They know their child well, the child trusts them, and they truly enjoy being this child's mother or father. The end result of this investment is the parent-child relationship operates at a higher level.

The best teachers in life are the ones that demand the most. I know how to be a parent because I was taught by a demanding teacher. If I had gotten the easy baby I dreamed of, I may not have the confidence and understanding I've gained in parenting my high-need child.

INVEST NOW FOR YOUR CHILD'S FUTURE

The best long-term investment you can make for your child has nothing to do with money or mutual funds. Parents, especially mothers, describe their commitment to attachment parenting as an investment, an emotional investment.

The good thing about making an emotional investment in your children is that you don't have to wait twenty years for it to pay off. Even in the short term, you get caring and empathetic children who are a joy to be around. Down the road you'll be rewarded with children who have the capacity to form healthy attachments as adults and who succeed on their own terms.

Make the emotional investment now and your children won't spend their whole lives trying to catch up on the nurturing they needed as infants and toddlers. They will be the kind of people who find comfort in feeling close to others. They will have the skills that make relationships last and will be good friends, good spouses, good parents, and good citizens. What better investment in the future could there be?

High-investment parenting helps disciplining challenging children.

Some children, to put it mildly, are less than compliant. Advice books for parents tag them with all kinds of labels: "the child with a persistent personality," "the spirited child," "the strong-willed child," "the difficult child," even the "high-risk child." Some children, regardless of how they are parented, are more challenging than others. While it's not exactly politically correct to say this, it's true — some children are nice to be with, and others can be downright annoying.

Parents who practice attachment parenting tend to be more accepting of their child's unique personality. Their knowledge of their child leads them to realize that they have a different and somewhat difficult child, and they have a realistic understanding of the challenges faced by both them and child. Yet they are also sensitive to their child's needs and realize that it's better to shape his personality gently than to squelch his exuberance and independence. Many of the characteristics of difficult children — persistence, intelligence, creativity, sensitivity — can work to the child's advantage. Invested parents of challenging children don't want clones of all the nice and easy kids in the neighborhood. They want their children to become the very best individuals they can be.

Of course, no matter how "different," "difficult," or "spirited," these kids must learn to live within the rules of their family, school, and peer group. Parents of high-need children have to adjust their expectations of "normal" childish behavior, yet they must also teach their children self-control. Disrespectful, annoying behavior from a child irritates the people around him and also harms the child. One day a group of children were playing together when one child became aggressive and pushed another child. One of the mothers watching said, "Oh, he's just being a boy." The child's mother replied, "I'm not going to excuse his behavior just because of his gender." She knew that her son needed to learn to respect others and to control himself. This connected mom took her son aside, talked to him about what he was doing, and helped him find another way to interact with his friends.

Children with special needs.

Some children's difficulties go beyond what we would call a high-need personality. They may eventually be diagnosed with A.D.H.D. (Attention Deficit Hyperactivity Disorder), autism, or other developmental or behavioral problems. Attachment parenting helps these at-risk children develop better, since the Baby B's give infants both appropriate stimulation and the help of a caregiver in organizing their responses. Attachment parenting in early infancy promotes quiet alertness — the calm, curious state that organizes baby's developing brain, leading to better-organized behavior. Simply put, attachment parenting helps the developing brain make the right connections, and better neurological organization means fewer behavioral problems later on — less distractibility, impulsivity, and hyperactivity. In addition, the mutual trust established between parent and child makes it easier for the child to learn self-control. This is a big plus as he enters school, a place where his behavioral problems can be a handicap to learning.

Our nine-year-old Ryan has Asperger's syndrome, which is a form of high-functioning autism. The diagnosis was a relief after years of struggling with a very high-need baby, toddler, and child and wondering what we had done wrong. I think I knew instinctively when he was small that allowing Ryan to nurse on cue, wean at his own pace, sleep in our bed, and ride in the sling was exactly what he needed. If I had allowed him to cry, he would not be the high-functioning, smart, and verbal child he is. He still has social and emotional issues, but think how much trouble he would now have if his obvious need for body contact had been rejected. I know without a doubt that if I had not done attachment parenting, we probably would not have a child with a promising future, despite our ongoing struggles. We would have lost him long ago. It's rewarding to me to realize that nine years later I have no regrets about having parented Ryan and his two sisters in an attached way. In fact, I celebrate it.

I try to spot children who are already at risk for problems of disorganization in early infancy. I advise their parents to study their child, her personality, her needs, her likes and dislikes, what she responds to, and what she is afraid of. You must become an expert on your child. You must, because no one else will. Through the years your child will change doctors, change teachers, change friends, but you will always be your child's mother and father — the people who know more about her than anybody.

One reason I'm so keen on getting parents and high-risk children connected is that these parents will have to advocate for their special child in the years to come. When a child has A.D.H.D. or other behavioral or learning problems, teachers, psychologists, and other specialists offer plenty of advice. But it's up to the parents to call the shots. If you know your child well, you can help professionals know him better, and they can then offer better solutions for teaching and working with your child. Your knowledge of your child will also help you tailor discipline techniques and behavior-modification programs to suit your child's needs.

My middle child, Eliza, has Down's syndrome. She's been in school, playschool, or at least speech therapy for most of her ten years. Many times I've stepped in and shared my knowledge of Eliza with the teachers who work with her. When she was about four, the school's new (and relatively inexperienced) speech pathologist thought that maybe Eliza didn't breathe properly to support her speech, since she talked very softly in speech-therapy sessions. I had a good laugh when I read this note from the speech teacher —

everyone in our home knew that Eliza could be plenty loud when she wanted to be. A week later, at parent-teacher conferences, I told the speech teacher that I thought she was on the wrong track. As I talked with her, I noticed that this young woman was very bright and animated as she spoke. (I think perkiness is almost a requirement for speech pathologists.) By comparison, I have always had a much more relaxed way of talking with my children. I realized that Eliza was probably content to sit back and be entertained during speech class, or maybe she was just overwhelmed. I found a tactful way to tell the teacher about my concerns. She toned down her approach, and soon Eliza had a lot more to say.

3. FRAME YOUR CHILD POSITIVELY

Children are sensitive to labels. Pin a negative label on a child and she begins to act accordingly. Call her "the whiny one" and you're likely to hear more whining, not less. You'll also desensitize yourself to the real needs behind the whine. Putting a more likable label on a child (even in her unlikable moments) can change how you see your child, how other people see her, and ultimately how she sees herself. It's easier to sympathize with a child when you stop and say, "She feels left out," rather than, "There she goes, whining again."

Connected parents are good at reframing a child's difficulties in order to understand them in a more positive way. Grandma remarks, "That baby sure is stubborn," when her grandson insists that he play with the toy cars rather than the stuffed dog. A connected father would respond, "He sure knows what he likes. He wants big-boy toys!" When the second-grade teacher comments, "She's always chattering away during class," an attached mom says, "My daughter really loves to connect with people."

These parents recognize that what are problematic traits in some settings may actually be positive qualities at other times and in different places. The "stubborn" child has the persistence he may later need to rise to the top of his profession or to find a cure for cancer. The chatterbox may have the social skills to be a friend to others in need. These positive observations are not only attitude changers, they also point to solutions to the immediate problem. The growing baby needs more interesting toys. Perhaps the second-grade girl needs chances to connect with friends outside of school (or maybe she needs less distracting neighbors in the classroom). One of our favorite examples of positive labeling comes from parents who instead of describing the infant as "clingy" thought of him as an infant who liked being with them.

Our term *high-need child* has helped many parents change their attitude about children with demanding temperaments. Parents actually discover that high-need children have many positive traits: "oversensitive" becomes "very sensitive." Instead of seeing their children as draining or demanding, parents think of them as intense or persistent. The "stubbornness" that keeps a toddler from minding his mother is actually the spunk that helps him get up and try again after a fall.

One day during a routine examination, an ultra-sensitive child, one who might be labeled "temperamentally difficult," was bouncing around my examining room. He started to climb on an expensive scale that is reserved for weighing infants and toddlers. Worrying more about my scale than his feelings, I admonished him to get down. Just those few words from me and he looked ready to disintegrate. His mother quickly added, "Because you are so strong." She put a new spin on the situation, and her son's self-esteem remained intact — as did my expen-

---

ADAPTABILITY

Studies on the long-term effects of early parenting show that attachment-style parenting produces kids that are highly adaptable. This is a very useful trait. Adaptable children are easily redirected from not-so-good behavior to better ways of doing things. They weather the trials of life better. They are more willing to accept correction from others and eventually learn to correct themselves. Even a child who, because of inborn temperament, is stubborn or strong-willed becomes more flexible when attached parents who know him well adapt their parenting to meet his needs. As one parent of a strong-willed child volunteered, "The stronger my child's will, the stronger must be our connection." Being connected gives confidence to parents and children alike and makes it possible for kids to change and adapt.

---

sive scale. (For more about the concept of framing, see p. 220.)

4. STUDY YOUR CHILD

The three most useful words in discipline are "know your child." To do so, you have to study your child's behavior and abilities at each stage. Read books or magazine articles to learn about child development. Talk to other parents — ones whose children are slightly older than yours. Most of all, try to see the world from your child's viewpoint.

Children don't think like adults. The world looks different to them, and they respond differently. Parents need to know what to ex-pect at each stage of development so that they can guide their children appropriately. Some kinds of childish behavior call for parental pa-tience, humor, and guidance. Eventually the child grows out of this stage, and the behavior disappears. Your parenting will go more smoothly if you learn to tolerate behavior that goes along with a child's age and stage. For ex-ample, most two-year-olds can't sit still for very long in a restaurant. You may have to focus all your attention on conversing with your toddler instead of with your spouse while you wait for your food to arrive. However, other behavior — what is disrespectful or dangerous — calls for a firm, immediate response: "You may not climb on the table."

Riding the waves.

Parents who study their children are able to "get in phase" with their children. Because they have a good sense of what's going on with their child, they are able to adjust their reactions to match the child's stage of dependence (or independence). As children step forward into uncharted territory, they find new friends and try new things. Parents who are in phase with their chil-dren expect some discipline problems as a result of the anxiety children encounter when experi-menting with more independent behavior. A preschooler may be in the "do it myself" phase and may need some coaching from the sidelines instead of hands-on help. Clued-in parents give their child some freedom as he tries to move away and grow up a bit. They understand if the child seems a little distant or a bit defiant. But these parents also stand by, ready to reconnect with a child when he needs more closeness.

Children move back and forth between de-pendence and independence, between phases when they change quickly and periods of rela-tive calm. Your six-year-old learns to ride a two-wheel bike and for a week spends every afternoon riding up and down the sidewalk, imagining she's a grown-up with a red sports car and a list of errands. Then one morning you wake up and notice this independent child next to you in bed. She has entered a reconnecting phase, a pit stop in the developmental journey that says to parents, "I need a bit of emotional refueling."

Parents who are in sync, or in phase, with their child learn to ride the waves of these de-velopmental phases. When parents and children are out of phase, discipline problems escalate. If you are trying to get closer to your child when she is trying to break away, you are likely to overreact when she asserts herself. If parents are too busy when the child is in a reconnecting phase, she may go to extremes to get her par-ents' attention. Meanwhile, parents miss an op-portunity to strengthen their position in the child's life as adviser, comforter, and authority figure. That same three-year-old who crawled into your bed every morning for a hug may be the teenager who comes into your room late some night and asks to talk. In both phases, wise parents take their cue from their child.

Get behind the eyes of your child.

Kids try crazy things and think crazy thoughts — stuff that seems perfectly logical to them. You will drive yourself crazy if you judge a child's behavior from an adult viewpoint. A two-year-old who runs into the street isn't in-tentionally defying his mother's authority, he just wants his ball back. Action follows impulse, with no thought in between. A five-year-old likes her friend's toy so much that she "bor-rows" it. She doesn't understand that, techni-cally, she's stealing. Her desire for the toy overrides consideration of the right and wrong

CALLS TO CONNECT

You wake up early one morning and discover your six-year-old nestled next to you in bed; your nine-year-old shadows you around the house all weekend; your usually distant teen invites you to go shopping. What's going on? These behaviors are calls to connect, signals that kids need some reassurance. In normal growth and development, children often take two steps forward and one step back as they move from dependence to independence and on to interdependence. One week your child is struggling to break away, and the next week she's trying to hold on. Be available and approachable when you notice your child calling out to reconnect with you. Reconnecting is as important to a child's emotional development as striving for independence.

of what's she doing, much less how her friend will feel. An adult may stop and weigh the necessity, safety, and morality of an act, but a child doesn't.

Parental decrees look different from a child's point of view, even if they seem reasonable to adults. At age two our son Matthew was a very focused child. He would become so engrossed in a play activity that it was difficult for him to stop what he was doing when it was time to leave. One day he was playing when we had to leave for an appointment. We were already running late, so Martha scooped up Matthew and carried him to the door. Matthew let loose with a typical two-year-old tantrum. Martha's first reaction was "Hey, I'm in charge here." She felt that she was justified in expecting Matthew to be willing to leave his toys and obey quickly. But as she was

carrying our flailing child out the door, she realized that her actions were a result of her need to leave, and maybe this wasn't the best way to handle the situation. She had forgotten Matthew's need for advance warning and a more gradual transition. He couldn't leave his play so quickly, even if we did have a deadline. He was not defying her, just being true to himself. He needed more time to let go of his activities. Martha calmly took Matthew back to the toys, sat down with him, and together they said, "Bye-bye toys, bye-bye trucks, bye-bye cars." Soon he was ready to leave his activities. It took only a couple of minutes, time that would otherwise have been wasted struggling with Matthew in the car. Martha's solution to Matthew's tantrum was not a parenting "technique" or "method." It was a strategy that evolved naturally from her knowledge of Matthew and her respect for him. Martha accomplished her goal — getting Matthew out of the house with the least amount of hassle. She also taught him a method of closing off an activity without resorting to a tantrum. That's what discipline is all about.

Realizing how much better our discipline worked when we considered our children's viewpoint was a major turning point for us. Initially we had to work through our fears about not being in control of our children. We had read, heard from others, and grown up with the idea that good parents automatically know best, with no arguments from their children. However, we found that considering our child's point of view actually helped us take charge. Knowing our children became the key to knowing how to discipline them. They knew we were in charge because we were able to help them obey. That left no doubt in their minds, or ours, that Mom and Dad knew best.

5. PROVIDE STRUCTURE, *THEN* SET LIMITS

Children need boundaries. They won't thrive (and you won't survive) without them. A child needs to learn and respect the family's rules. Home is the child's first society. How he learns to live in this mini–social world sets the pattern for other social interactions: in school, on a team, and later in marriage and in a career. Boundaries in the home help children channel their social and creative energies in a meaningful direction. Boundaries also make it possible for adults and children to cooperate and enjoy their life together.

It's up to parents to help children operate within the family's boundaries. Parents do this best by providing structure and setting limits — in that order. Providing structure means setting up conditions within the home that make it easier to respect the limits. Setting wise limits involves creating rules that are appropriate for the child's age and stage and communicating them so that children know what's expected.

Let's use the example of an exploring toddler to explain what we mean by limits with or without structure. A toddler is insatiably curious. His drive to explore helps him learn about the world, but it also gets him into trouble. Parents may find themselves constantly saying no to an exploring toddler. "No, don't poke your finger in the electrical outlet. No, don't pull on the lamp cord. No, don't jump on the table, don't knock over the chairs, and never, never run out into the street." These are all necessary limits, but it's very difficult for a toddler to remember them, much less call them to mind when his curiosity is about to get the better of him.

So how does a parent help the toddler obey all the nos and don'ts? Parents can structure their child's environment to make it easier to stay within the limits. Such structure makes life easier for the child and less stressful for the parents. Nobody likes to have to say or hear the word *no* on a regular basis. Obviously, the structure you provide for an exploring toddler is a childproof home. You put safety plugs in electrical outlets, hide lamp cords behind heavy furniture, and put away your breakables for a few years. You designate one cupboard in the kitchen as baby's cupboard and fill it with safe things to explore and bang on the floor. Then you steer baby to his own special things instead of forbidding him to get into yours. You take him to the playground so that he has a safe place to run and climb and blow off steam.

A parent's role as "structural designer" of a child's environment involves making the house safe *for* the toddler and *from* the toddler. Structure does not mean repressing the child, but rather setting conditions that discourage dangerous behavior and that allow safe and desirable behavior. Structure protects and redirects, freeing the child to be a child. It provides a generally positive "yes" environment, which lessens the number of nos you need to use.

"But my child won't sit still at the dinner table." Have you tried sitting for ten minutes or more with your feet dangling a foot and a half off the floor? You'd be restless, too. Structure your mealtimes so that children don't have to sit for long. Or get your child a tiny chair and table and let him eat there, with his feet planted on the floor. Allow him to have small toys at the table to play with while Mom and Dad talk and finish their meal.

Plan ahead.

Structure also means how you and your children use your time. "My two-year-old is absolutely impossible in a supermarket." "When I go to the store with my six-year-old, she wants every variety of junk food in sight." Whenever possible, connected parents structure their day around their child's moods. Preschool children tend to be better behaved in the morning, so go to the supermarket soon after breakfast if your trip includes a four-year-old. If you have an older child who can't resist colorful packages of sugary cereals, either shop without her or promise her a treat that you can both live with. This is not "losing control" or "letting the child run the show." It's simply respecting the needs of the child as a family member. As a bonus, it makes life as a parent easier.

Plan playtimes and playmates.

There are many subtle ways that parents can provide structure to encourage their child's good behavior. We have noticed that kids who play well with others have parents who guide them to select playmates with compatible temperaments. Even in the elementary-school years, you have a lot of control over whom your child hangs out with. It might mean changing after-school care providers or requesting a specific soccer coach, but such choices really do shape a child's behavior. You know if your six-year-old is ready to sleep over at a friend's house. If you don't think the evening will go well, find a way to avoid putting your child in that situation. If your child needs to run and play after a long day at school, don't insist that he do his homework the minute he walks in the door. Instead, set aside half an hour after supper for quiet study.

Structure remains important as your child grows. Set a curfew for a teen, but also make sure she knows where to reach you — and that you'll gladly come to pick her up — if she needs a ride home. Make a point of getting to know the parents of your child's friends so that you know their values and their house rules. Structure your home so that it's a friendly place for teens to

gather. All of these actions make it easier for teens to stay within the family boundaries.

Providing structure is a lot like being a coach. You instruct your children on how the game is played, you set up plays for them to run, and then you encourage them when they're out on the field. Dick Vermeil, coach of the 2000 Super Bowl champions, the St. Louis Rams, in discussing why some players show more discipline on the field than others, said, "Coaching begins at home."

As kids get older and move out into the wider worlds of school and community, connected parents use their intimate knowledge of their child to guide her *appropriately* — being neither too permissive or overly restrictive. They know how much their child can comfortably handle on her own and when to intervene. They continue to act as facilitators and guidance counselors.

Some connected parents may err on the side of being overprotective. That's okay, since it's an easy mistake to correct. You'll figure out when you need to back off a bit. Other parents whom you respect are often a good source of advice on when to clamp down and when to give your child more freedom.

Being underprotective is harder to fix. Children who are required to handle too many decisions and challenges without a parent facilitator can become angry with themselves, their caregivers, and life. In fact, a trait that often distinguishes the connected child from the unconnected one is anger. Less connected parents are more likely to give a child too many paths to choose from, too many tracks to follow. If he doesn't like playing violin after three months of lessons, they let him switch to drums. Naturally, because a child is open to new experiences, he wants to try everything. If parents adopt the philosophy that it's good for

REMIND + REWIND

(YOU REMIND CHILDREN) (CHILDREN REMIND THEMSELVES)

The combination of remind and rewind is a behavioral guiding principle we have used in learning to live with our children. Young children usually live in the present. They seldom reflect on lessons of the past, nor do they think about the future. Children are like that. They need adults in charge, usually parents, to frequently remind them about how they're supposed to act in the home or in a group — in other words, what is the normal way of acting. Yet children need frequent reminders to help them work through the many "but I forgot" excuses. As lame as this excuse sounds to adults, children do honestly forget and need reminders to keep their behavior on track. Reminders are cues that jog the hazy memory of a busy child. They may be subtle prompts such as a look that tells the about-to-be-mischievous child, "You know better," or a short verbal cue that turns on the child's memory: "Ahh, where does that toy belong?" Reminders are behavior motivators that work better than flat-out telling a child. By "reminds," you give a child

a clue, and the child fills in the blanks. You cast a disapproving look on a dirty plate left on the table, and the child gets the message that she's expected to carry her plate to the sink and clean up after herself. Sometimes a written message goes over better for the child who would otherwise perceive the reminder as nagging, such as a note we once placed on Erin's door: "Please remove the dishes from your room before they start growing things." Rewinds are an extension of the minding game. You've told the child ten times not to ride his tricycle out into the street or to stop at the curb and look both ways. If you catch the child about to forget your admonitions, simply say, "Rewind." You prompt the child to replay in his own mind the script you have gone through before. With that one word, you motivate the child to discipline himself, one step toward achieving inner control. Also, by remembering the remind and rewind principle, you avoid nagging or nattering. Children tire of and tune out your constantly reminding them what they have done wrong.

children to learn "a lot of different viewpoints" and "experience being around children with lots of different values," they may end up with a child who is headed in the wrong direction — or who has no direction at all. Children need guidance from their parents as they sort through all the possibilities that the world holds for them.

6. SHAPE RATHER THAN CONTROL YOUR CHILD

Parents of kids who turn out well know that it's their job to shape their children's behavior rather than to control it. Parenting is like gardening. Once you've planted a seed, you can't control the color of the flower you'll get or when it blooms, but you can pull the weeds and water and prune the plant to help that flower blossom more beautifully. That's what we mean by shaping a child's behavior. All children are born with some behavioral traits that need to be pruned, or even weeded out. Other traits you want to nourish so that they grow deep roots and produce beautiful blossoms in the person your child grows up to be. Connected parents tend to use gentle tools we call *shapers,* which weed out negative qualities without harming the positive ones. The tools change as your child's needs change at each stage of development. Eventually the child internalizes these shapers and develops his own control system.

Shaping versus control.

Shaping means providing your child with cues that direct and redirect behavior. You talk ahead of time about how she should behave on a visit to Great Aunt Caroline. You tell her what to expect and what she'll be doing while she's there. You help her choose a few books or quiet toys to bring along so she'll have something to do during the grown-ups' conversations. While you're there, you remind her of how she's supposed to behave; when she gets a little too rambunctious, you take her aside, calm her down, and play quietly with her for a few minutes. When trying to shape a child's behavior, you set her up to succeed by giving her the information and tools she needs to behave properly.

Controlling parents have a different attitude. They're more likely to take an authoritarian approach: "I'm the parent, he's the child, and that's that! I don't need all this modern psychology stuff. He should do what I say, and if he doesn't, he knows he'll get in trouble." Controlling parents are more likely to use punishment as a primary discipline technique. At Great Aunt Caroline's an unruly little girl would get her hand slapped, if not threatened with a spanking when she got home. Controlling par-

ents are more likely to see their children's behavior as a reflection of their own worth. They give their children few explanations beyond "This is the right thing to do" or "What will people think?"

It's not always easy to tell the difference between shaping and control, but the subtle differences are important. Parents who try to control their children tend to focus more on outward behavior than on the developmental process going on within the child. Attempts to control a child set up struggles between parents and offspring and invite rebellion, especially from intense or high-need children. Control squelches personality and prevents children from thriving and being all that they can be — physically, emotionally, and intellectually.

As you shape a child's behavior, you shape his growing personality. Connected parents tend to be more accepting of the child's unique self. They are patient and put up with their child's annoying quirks, even though they take their toll on parental energy. Connected parents celebrate their child's good qualities — even those that take some effort to recognize — and realize that their job is not so much to make their children behave a certain way as to produce responsible, caring adults who can care for themselves.

You can't change a child's temperament — his basic nature that is wired into his brain — but you can shape his personality. Personality is what a child does with his basic temperament. I once testified in a court case in Las Vegas on how parents can influence, for better or worse, a child's personality. Inspired by my surroundings, I came up with this analogy: "A child's temperament is like the cards he is dealt. The child's personality is how he plays the cards. Parents can teach their kids to play their hands wisely."

7. ALLOW APPROPRIATE FAILURES AND FRUSTRATION

Early on, parents of children who turn out well learn how to help their children manage difficulties rather than trying to prevent frustrations. Being able to deal with problems and bounce back from failure are valuable qualities needed to succeed in life. People who know how to turn a problem into an opportunity can make the best of whatever life brings their way.

Parents of children who turn out well allow their children to make mistakes and learn from them. What's equally important is that these children are allowed to see parents make mistakes, learn from them, and take responsibility for correcting them.

Don't ignore it!

Temper tantrums are a sure sign of frustration. Many advisers tell parents to ignore tantrums, but we have noticed that many parents of kids who turn out well do the opposite. They don't send a child to her room alone when she's having a meltdown. Instead, they get behind the eyes of the child and try to understand the reason behind the behavior. They don't step in and solve her problem for her, nor do they try to bribe her into settling down or distract her from her frustration. They listen, help the child understand what's going on inside her, and teach her how to manage those emotions.

These parents handle lower-level frustrations in a similar fashion. When a toddler is stubbornly trying to jam a round peg into a square hole, Mom neither ignores his difficulty nor rushes in with the right answer. Instead, she gently suggests that he try a different hole, or she helps him notice the roundness of the block and the straight sides of the square hole. When

an older child comes in from playing, slams the back door, and announces that her best friend is stupid, these parents don't jump in with "Watch your mouth!" Dad or Mom helps the child talk through the problem and find a solution.

Consequences.

Wise parents know that experience is the best teacher. When a child makes a foolish decision, they don't intervene to save the day. They allow children to make and learn from mistakes. They give their children lots of practice at making their own decisions during childhood, when the stakes are low. The natural consequences of these choices, good and bad, shape the child's decision-making abilities. A child who has to cope with the results of bad or impulsive choices learns that everyone makes mistakes, that mistakes are not the end of the world, and that one can take action to correct a mistake or at least learn from it.

8. JUST SAY NO!

One day when I was shopping with our seven-year-old, Lauren, we entered the checkout counter (universally dreaded by parents) and Lauren asked for one piece of junk after another. Each time she asked, I calmly said no. She probably knew what my response would be even before asking, but we had to go through the ritual. By the time we got to the cash register, the clerk half whispered to me, "I wish more parents would just say no."

Children want all the stuff they see, and they want it *now!* — "Collect them ALL!" screams the television commercial for itty-bitty play figures and all their accessories. "But everyone in my class has one," moans the preteen who wants the latest video-game equipment. One day I was giving a talk to a group of parents whose kids some might call privileged but who I honestly felt simply had too much stuff. I wanted to open my talk with three magic words — "Just say no" — but I realized the solution to kids' materialism isn't that easy. Many parents can't handle saying no to their children, because it is often much easier to give in and let the child have what he wants. This avoids a hassle and brings peace to the family, at least for a while. Yet it's another short-term gain that results in a long-term loss.

You are not doing your child a favor by always giving her what she wants. Reality says that when she's an adult, she will have to wait for many of the things she wants, she will have to choose which are most important to her, and she won't get everything she wants. Understanding the concept of delayed gratification is a valuable ability for success in life. So is learning not to make impulsive decisions.

Seven-year-old Andrew got some money for his birthday, and we went to the toy store. Naturally, he was overwhelmed by the variety of toys he could choose from, but I constantly reminded him that he had only a certain amount of money. If he chose the mechanical robot, he wouldn't have any money left over for some of the other toys he wanted. No, I told him, he could not have both the robot and the Lego set. He had to make a choice.

This wise mother acted as a facilitator, helping the child make choices that were in his best interest, helping him realize that he couldn't have everything he wanted, and showing him that he needed to set some priorities. "Which would you play with more?" "Which would last longer?" "What do you most want?"

If your child is clamoring for a certain new toy, it's usually wise to avoid rushing out and instantly gratifying his whim. Just tell him, "We'll wait another week" (or a couple of days — a week seems like an eternity to a preschooler). Give him some time to think carefully about his choices. He may want something completely different by the end of the week. Children who are the product — or the victim — of indulgent parents seldom value the possessions they have. They're never enough. On the other hand, children who grow up having to wait for a treat, or having to earn the money themselves, learn to place proper values on the things they own.

The stuff disease strikes families even before a baby is born. We are constantly amazed by all the equipment to be found in baby stores. We wonder how on earth we raised so many kids without all the high-tech stuff that promises, for a price, to make babies more convenient to care for while keeping them at a distance.

The baby market is a big one, and parents who want the very best for their child are all too ready to open the checkbook or hand over the credit card. Here's our advice on baby equipment, and on buying decisions that will come up all through childhood: say yes to items that help you stay connected, and no to all the stuff that gets in the way. The absolute best plaything for a baby is another human being. The face of a loving parent is infinitely more stimulating than any mobile. The arms of a parent are guaranteed to soothe and comfort in a way that no crib or bouncy seat can. Invest in a baby sling — or even two slings — and let your baby's enriched environment be the view from your arms, which is constantly changing. When you consider what to buy as your children get older, look for toys and games that you can play with together, as well as the usual popular toys.

It's easier for me to say no to my child because I'm so connected to her. I don't feel guilty not buying her a lot of things because I've given her so much of myself.

Giving children everything they want rather than what they need runs the risk of creating a stuff-oriented adult who looks for what he can get out of others rather than for what he can give. As you say no to a lot of stuff, naturally you want to say yes to time spent in personal relationships. The lesson you want your child to learn (and many adults never do) is that things don't make you happy, people do.

9. SCREEN PERSONS OF SIGNIFICANCE

Connected parents are not overprotective, they are *appropriately* protective. Besides providing healthy models for their children at home, they keep a close eye on what's going on in their children's lives outside the home. In today's mobile and diverse society, a child is exposed to a wide range of role models. Parents of successful kids keep an eye on the influence of these individuals. They choose substitute caregivers carefully. They get to know teachers and coaches, and the values these mentors are promoting. They also closely monitor their child's television watching, use of the Internet, reading material, and other mass-market influences.

We always got to know his friends' parents. We did not hesitate to call them if the need arose.

◆

My son has played youth baseball in our town since he was in third grade. He really enjoys it, and his baseball skills and confidence have come a long way, especially under the guidance of a coach he had two years ago, who was very positive about Kris being a good ballplayer. The next year, when he moved on to the junior-high level, he had a head coach whose heart, I believe, was in the right place but who tried to motivate his modestly skilled team of young adolescents by being tough on them, yelling a lot, and keeping the pressure on. His own son, of course, got the worst of this. During the season, Kris and I spent a lot of time talking about this coaching style and the effect it had on the kids. The coach's son was a nervous player — the more pressure, the more likely he was to mess up. By contrasting this man's coaching style with that of other teachers and coaches he had, Kris learned a lot about how to work with people, and he was able to keep some emotional distance from the pressures put on his fellow team members.

One way to lessen the risk of your child's getting involved with negative influences is to become more involved in your community's activities for children. If you worry about what kind of soccer coach your child might get, volunteer to be the coach yourself — or at least to assist with practices. If you're worried about the scout leader's influence, volunteer. Wonder what's going on in your child's classroom? Volunteer to help. At home, sit down with your kids when they're watching television. Keep the computer in the family room, not in the kids' bedroom, so that you can keep an eye on what they are doing online. Welcome your children's friends into your home. Be the driver when teens want to go to a movie.

Our house was the hangout for the neighborhood kids and my daughter's school friends. Her friends were always welcome in our home, and that way we felt we could stay involved. We felt that we were part of her life and that we had a handle on things.

10. EXPECT A LOT FROM YOUR CHILD

Parents who discipline well convey to their children the kind of behavior that is expected and help them meet these expectations. They expect desirable behavior, not as an option but simply as "how we act in our home." Also, by perceiving what behavior their parents expect of them, children have guidelines from which to operate. They become less confused. Your directives don't always have to make sense to your children. Sometimes the only message that's necessary is "Because this is what I want you to do." Your being the adult in charge frees them to be children.

Older children we interviewed told us that even when they did not understand why they were expected to act a certain way, down deep they believed their parents' directives would somehow help them turn out to be better persons.

When our children are acting obnoxious, I remind them often that I will not let them grow up to be jerks. My children know I mean it, and there was security there, and love.

As you will learn in Chapters 12 and 13, successful children had parents and other persons of significance who expected the children to always do their best. They not only believed the kids could do it but made sure the children believed in themselves. Self-belief is an important determinant of success.

"HANDS-ON" PARENTS CAN KEEP KIDS OFF DRUGS

This was the headline in *USA Today,* February 22, 2001. The article that followed reported on the Sixth Annual Teen Survey by the National Center on Addiction and Substance Abuse (NCASA) at Columbia University. This survey of a thousand teens ages twelve to seventeen found that "hands-off" parents double the risk that their teens will smoke, drink alcohol, and use illegal drugs. In the survey teens said that cigarettes are now more difficult to buy, but marijuana is relatively easy to get. The survey found that 61 percent of children ages twelve to sixteen are at moderate to high risk for substance abuse. More than 60 percent of high-school teens say that drugs are in their school; 30 percent said that drugs could ruin your life and cause harm; and 17 percent feel peer pressure to use drugs. For the survey, a "hands-on" household was defined as one in which parents took ten or more actions, ranging from monitoring what their teens watched on TV to knowing where their teens were after school and on weekends. "Hands-off" parents consistently failed to set rules and monitor their teens' behavior. They did not always know their teens' whereabouts. The recommendation was that parents be parents, not pals, to their children and that they should counter negative media influences. The "hands-on" parents took at least ten of the following twelve actions:

1. Monitor what your kids watch on TV
2. Monitor your children's use of the Internet
3. Put restrictions on CDs they buy
4. Know where your kids are after school and on weekends
5. Be told the truth about your teen's whereabouts
6. Be aware of your teen's academic performance
7. Impose a curfew
8. Make it clear that you will be extremely upset if your teen uses drugs
9. Eat dinner with your teen six or seven nights a week
10. Turn off the TV during dinner
11. Assign regular chores for your teen
12. Have an adult present when your teen comes home from school

4

Giving Your Child a Smart Start

NTELLIGENCE ITSELF DOES NOT guarantee success. It's what children do with the smarts they're born with that matters. Yet the fact remains that smart kids are more likely to succeed.

Once upon a time it was thought that intelligence was largely inherited. Either you had smart genes or you didn't. Now we know that the "smart genes" are only part of the story. Intelligence is shaped by experience as well as by heredity. You can influence how smart your children are by the way you nurture them. For more than twenty-five years infant-development researchers have speculated that infants go through certain critical, or sensitive, periods in development, during which their developing brains are most influenced by interaction with caregivers. New methods of studying how baby brains grow have confirmed these suspicions. There are indeed windows of opportunity when caregivers can most influence how baby brains grow. The biggest window of opportunity is during the first year.

HOW BRAINS GROW

New research in the field of neurobiology shows that parents can have a profound effect on how smart their children become. The brain grows more during infancy than at any other time. It triples in size during the first year and is virtually full-grown by the time a child enters kindergarten. Baby brains grow from about half a pound at birth to 1.5 pounds by the end of the first year, and then up to about three pounds, or full size, by five years of age. As the brain grows during a baby's first year, nerve cells within the brain (called neurons) grow, too. Neurons resemble miles of tangled electrical wire, with many of the ends unconnected. During the first year neurons grow larger and become encased in a coating of protective myelin. Myelin acts as insulation, helping electrical messages move more quickly and predictably through the neurons. The tip of each neuron resembles fingers, or feelers, that attempt to hook up with other nerves. The connections made by neurons and the circuits they form are what enable babies to store experiences in their brains, i.e., to learn. As the number of connections in the brain increases during the first year, the brain learns to work better, and babies learn to think, remember, and better control their bodies.

Scientists have found that one's environment stimulates neurons to grow and make better connections. For example, an infant sees his mother's or father's face. The nerves in the eyes transmit the image of the face to the area of the brain that processes visual information, and the infant stores the image of this face in a circuit of neurons. Seeing the face again and again stores more images and makes more connections between them. Eventually the brain not only recognizes the parent's face but makes a connection between the visual image and the muscles that control the baby's face. The result: baby smiles back at Mom or Dad. With continued neurological development, more connections are made, so eventually the baby can reach out and touch his parent's face with his hands. He can also figure out what kind of mood the parent is in and use that information to help monitor and control his own feelings. The moral of this neurological story is that the more the infant has organized interaction with his environment, the stronger the neurological connections he is able to develop. Brain researchers call all these nerve-connecting influences *environmental feedback*.

HOW BRAINS GROW SMARTER

Why are some brains smarter than others? Two aspects of brain growth are most influenced by parent-child interaction: how fast messages travel from one nerve to another, and how well connected these nerves are. Let's take a trip inside a baby's brain and marvel at not only how the brain develops but also how parents can influence its growth.

At the end of the billions of nerve cells are tiny fingerlike feelers that attempt to branch out and connect with other nerves. The connections between nerves are called *synapses*. Brains become smart by increasing and then pruning the number of synapses.

Suppose the developing brain were like billions of tiny telephones. Brains become smarter by interconnecting these telephone lines, or making synapses between telephones. First, you could call everyone in your neighborhood, then in your city, then throughout the country, and eventually all over the world. The growth of synapses, or connections, accounts for most of the brain growth. Researchers estimate that during the first two years, the growing infant makes some 2 million synapses per second. A lot of action takes place inside that little brain.

Faster lines of communication.

Besides the number of synapses, another factor that influences how smart the brain becomes is how efficiently and fast the messages travel across these "wires" — a process called *myelination*. A fatty coating, or myelin, insulates the nerves, making messages move faster and also preventing short circuits among neighboring nerves. As you will learn on page 57, nutrition can influence how well myelination occurs.

Better lines of communication.

While it would be nice to be able to call everyone in the world with one touch, it's not necessary — and you would need a huge phone. It would also be a cluttered and confused telephone system if these billions of lines were not correctly connected. So next comes the neural process of *pruning*. The more active synapses, or the calls that you make most often, become stronger and survive; those that are not used are pruned away — a sort of "use it or lose it" phenomenon. As we repeatedly stress, smart parenting, especially during the early years of rapid brain growth, helps the developing brain make the right connections. Pruning lets the brain circuits work more efficiently, sort of like being left with a user-friendly phone system with your most commonly called numbers accessible by a one-touch dial.

Use it or lose it.

With this "use it or lose it" principle, there are critical periods in brain development. This window of opportunity, or critical period, is narrow for sensory abilities, such as vision and hearing, in which synapse formation and myelination occur most efficiently during early infancy, but it is wider for social functions, such as language and emotions, whose pathways continue to prune their synapses and myelinate the nerves throughout childhood.

Neuroplasticity.

The child's developing brain is endowed with billions more synapses than it will ever need or use. Consequently, if a child is understimulated or undernourished during a critical period of brain development, some catch-up growth can occur. But researchers have concluded that once a critical period is over, though the window may not be completely closed, the opportunity to rewire the brain becomes very limited. Because of neuroplasticity, or excess pathways, some rewiring is always possible, but the brain will never be as malleable as it was in infancy

and childhood. That is why it is easier for a child to learn a second language (especially if exposed to it in infancy) than it is for an adult.

Dr. Lise Elliott says in her excellent book, *What's Going On in There — How the Brain and Mind Develop in the First Five Years of Life:* "Everything a child sees, touches, hears, feels, tastes, thinks, and so on translates into electrical activity . . . of the synapses. On the other hand, synapses that are rarely activated — whether because a language is never heard, music never made, sports never played, mountains never seen, love never felt — will wither and die. . . . Once those excess synapses are gone, the critical period is over, and the brain must make do with its existing circuitry; there's no trading up for a faster computer. For many abilities the critical period is mercifully long, extending throughout childhood and even early adolescence. For others, it closes in just a few months or years of life."

Nature versus nurture.

How much of what a child acts and thinks is due to the genes, and how much is influenced by the child's caregiving environment? This nature versus nurture debate has been battled for decades. With new insights into brain development, modern researchers have come to the conclusion that it's about a 50-50 split: half genes and half nurturing. So, if only half of a child's intelligence is due to genes, there's still plenty of room for parents to play a significant role. Brain researchers believe that the basic hardwiring of the brain is genetic, yet how this wiring is connected is determined by nurturing. It's like nurture finishes a job started by nature. The child-rearing environment enables the basic wiring of the brain to make better and more efficient connections. In a nutshell, bigger and better brains become that way by making more and better connections. The brains with the best connections are most successful. These connections form *patterns of association* (as discussed in Chapter 2), which become a child's blueprint for life.

Parents are often confused about what the terms *IQ, intelligence, talent,* and *temperament* really mean and about how they can influence these traits. The term we use throughout this book is a child's *abilities,* the sum total of intelligence, talents, skills, temperament, experiences, and self-belief. Abilities are the bottom line for each child's success; they are most influenced by parents and other persons of significance in a child's life.

Parenting makes a difference.

Infant development used to be viewed as a sort of elevator. As a baby grew and reached each new floor, the door would automatically open and a new skill would get on. Given a reasonable amount of nurturing, good health, and adequate nutrition, babies would graduate from one developmental stage to another at a pace determined largely by nature (inherited genes), with good parenting and a stimulating environment playing only a minor role. However, researchers have now come to believe that interaction with the caregiving environment has a significant effect on how babies develop. Using the elevator analogy, the baby reaches each developmental floor already equipped with certain competencies. For example, a baby is ready to reach for objects or is ready to make speech sounds. How these competencies flower into skills depends upon whether objects to reach for are readily available or whether the baby's first experimental syllables are greeted with smiles and responses from a caregiver. When caregivers respond to a baby's new skills, he practices them more and enjoys them more. He rides up to the next developmental floor with more skills to

build upon. The interaction on the next level of development is then even more rewarding. The responses the baby gets from the caregiving environment are what help him thrive, meaning to develop to his full potential and use his natural gifts to the fullest.

TWELVE WAYS TO BUILD A BRIGHTER CHILD

Some parents recently came into my office with their three-year-old for his annual checkup. Disappointedly, they reported, "He didn't get into the top preschool we wanted." The child appeared to be bright and happy, but the parents looked as if their child had just flunked out of college. I reassured these caring parents that there's absolutely no correlation between what kind of preschool a child attends (or whether he even goes to preschool) and his chances of getting into Harvard fifteen years from now. (I wanted to add that getting into Harvard was no guarantee of a happy life, either.) Yes, quality schools and academic success are important, yet what goes on at home is even more important, especially if the goals for your child include happiness and contentment as well as academic achievement. You want your child to be smart — at school and at life. Here are some suggestions:

1. A Smart Womb Start

The development of the fetal nervous system is affected — for better or worse — by what mothers do during pregnancy. Cigarette smoke, alcohol, and narcotics have all been shown to adversely affect fetal brain development and increase the risk of a child's having learning and behavioral problems later. Besides the don'ts of drugs, alcohol, and nicotine during pregnancy, there are some do's as well. A healthy diet is a must during pregnancy. In general, the better you nourish your body, the better you nourish your baby's growing brain.

Although it takes serious malnutrition to significantly harm a baby's development in the womb, the lack of certain nutrients may contribute to subtle developmental problems. For example, many nutritionists are concerned that pregnant women do not get enough of the right kind of fats in their diet. Best fats for growing brains are omega-3s, and the best source of these brain-building fats are cold-water fish. In our pediatric practice, we encourage expectant mothers to eat at least a four-ounce serving of fresh or frozen ocean salmon or tuna at least three times a week.

Another important nutrient for pregnant women is the B-vitamin folic acid. A deficiency of this vitamin can increase the chances of abnormal development of the spinal cord or cause brain defects. Folic acid is especially critical to fetal development in the first weeks of pregnancy, before a woman may even realize that she is pregnant. For this reason, pregnant women and those who are trying to become pregnant are advised to take 400 mcg of a folic acid supplement daily. It's also important to eat bread, flour, and cereals fortified with folic acid.

The mother's thoughts and emotions can also affect a baby's development. There is growing evidence that a baby's developing nervous system is influenced by the womb environment and events outside the womb. Mother and baby share hormones through the placenta, and an environment full of stress hormones can, fetal researchers theorize, produce a child with a more nervous or anxious temperament. Of course, stress is inevitable during times of change, such as pregnancy. It's how the mother handles it that determines what the baby's womb surroundings are like. Working through fears and anxieties during pregnancy, instead of letting them build up, helps a mother stay mentally calm as she nurtures the baby growing inside her.

Be happy, get moving.

Substances called *endorphins,* known as natural feel-good hormones, counteract stress hormones and relax Mommy and, therefore, baby. Laughter and exercise increase endorphin levels. Give yourself and your preborn baby the smart effects of these hormonal perks. (For a more in-depth discussion of maternal fetal health, see *The Pregnancy Book,* by William and Martha Sears and Dr. Linda Holt.)

2. Smart Carrying

Think about what's more educational for babies: lying in a crib, watching a developmentally appropriate mobile turn in the air, or being carried on Dad's shoulder as he pokes around the house, sorting junk mail or talking with Mom? What's more interesting? A playpen well stocked with the latest in educational toys, or the kitchen where Mom and Dad are unpacking a huge variety of groceries? If you had to take a ride through the stores at the mall, would you rather that your eyes were eighteen inches off the ground, or up near Mom's shoulder, where all the most interesting merchandise is displayed?

It's surprisingly easy to give your baby a stimulating environment. Most babies, from newborns to toddlers, find the adult world endlessly interesting. When you carry your baby as you go

---

SMART TIP

Babies learn a lot in the arms of busy caregivers.

about your daily tasks and errands, you give her the stimulation she needs to develop her sight, her hearing, and her understanding. Plus she gets added input from you as you talk to her and share your observations and feelings with her.

Infants who are carried more cry less, thereby giving them more time for productive interaction with their environment. They learn more. The closeness to Mom and the gentle motion of her walking keep babies calm. Newborns who are carried spend more time in the state of quiet alertness, which helps them adapt more quickly to the outside world. They also enjoy better-quality "conversations" with Mom and Dad. Left lying in a crib or baby seat, newborns flail their arms, arch their backs, and waste a lot of energy in unnecessary motion. When they are carried in a parent's enfolding arms or in a baby sling, these movements are contained and babies can focus better. A baby carried facing forward in a sling has a wide view of her environment — she is able to scan her world. This might be more than a tiny baby can cope with (that's why you tuck newborns *into* the sling), but for a baby of three or four months of age, there is no better vantage point from which to learn about the world. Baby chooses what she wishes to look at and shuts out what she doesn't.

As a speech-language pathologist and a mother of two, I'm a strong believer in the value of carrying babies — in a sling or in arms — for a substantial part of their early lives. When babies are carried, they are exposed to adult conversation. They have ample opportunity to watch people talking. They observe the turn taking and eye contact to communicate. They develop an understanding of language by hearing intonation patterns that express emotions — happiness, sadness, anger. By viewing the speaker's mouth up-close, they learn to imitate

correct speech movements for accurate articulation patterns. All these parts come together for a baby learning to talk.

Because we recognize the value of babywearing on a baby's intellectual development, every new parent that comes into our pediatric practice gets a demonstration on the art of babywearing. Babies love to be carried, and though some take longer than others to learn to enjoy being worn in a baby sling, it's well worth the effort. Babywearing parents often tell us, "As soon as I pick up the sling and put it on, my baby lights up and raises his arms, as if in anticipation that he will soon be in my arms and in my world."

From the beginning, I carried my daughter in a sling wherever we went, whatever we did. I talked to her — kind of as a running commentary — as I washed the dishes, walked the beach, visited a bookstore, went shopping; basically, everything I did, she did, too. She was right there, securely in my arms as she was seeing all the sights and sounds of the world. Sure, time and again people looked at me as though I were crazy, talking to a baby as I did. But I'd just smile and continue to comment on the lovely red apple or the loud airplane. Sure, we're biased, but even strangers comment that she is one of the happiest, most secure, confident, inquisitive, imaginative, humor-filled kids they've ever seen.

3. A Smart Nutritional Start

MOTHER'S MILK: FOOD FOR SMARTER KIDS boasted the headline in a 1992 issue of *USA Today*. Over the past decade researchers have accumulated increasing evidence that breastfeeding makes babies smarter. Studies have found that breastfed infants scored higher on IQ tests when they were older. Researchers have also noted better scores on developmental scales and better grades in elementary school among children who were breastfed.

Here are possible reasons why breastfed children enjoy an intellectual advantage:

Smarter fats. Human milk contains a significant amount of a brain-boosting fat called DHA (docosahexaenoic acid), an omega-3 fatty acid. DHA is a vital nutrient for developing and maintaining brain tissue. Until recently, infant formulas made in the United States did not contain DHA. Yet in May 2001 the overwhelming scientific evidence on the importance of DHA compelled the FDA to approve the addition of DHA to infant formulas made in America. In our medical practice, we advise all pregnant and lactating women to eat foods rich in DHA (fresh or frozen ocean salmon and tuna) or take a 200 mg DHA supplement daily, since the amount of DHA in mother's milk is influenced by the mother's diet. Cholesterol is another fat needed for optimal brain development. Breast milk contains a lot of cholesterol, but infant formulas currently contain none. While low cholesterol may be good news for adult diets, babies need cholesterol to build brain tissue.

Smarter sugars. Lactose, the main sugar in breast milk, may be another reason why breastfed babies are smarter. The body breaks down lactose into two simpler sugars — glucose and

---

SCIENCE SAYS:

Breastfeeding mothers who eat smarter fats have smarter babies.

Researchers compared two groups of breastfeeding mothers: one group ate extra omega-3s (in the form of DHA supplements) for eight weeks postpartum, and the control group received a placebo (a dummy supplement). At two and a half years of age the toddlers of the supplemented mothers scored higher on developmental tests.

---

galactose. Galactose in particular is a valuable nutrient for brain-tissue development.

Smarter connections. There's more to breastfeeding's developmental boost than just nutrients. Because breast milk is digested faster, breastfed babies feed more often and therefore probably interact more with their caregivers. Breastfeeding mothers also tend to be more sensitive to their infants' needs. Because a mother can't keep track of ounces of milk consumed, she must learn to watch her baby's hunger cues. This helps her tune in to other baby signals as well. The more tuned-in, responsive, and predictable the mother is, the easier it is for the baby to make sense of his environment. Predictable responses also encourage a baby to initiate more interactions. Breastfeeding itself — with its skin-to-skin contact, the variations in milk flow, and the interdependence of mother and baby — is likely to be more stimulating than bottle-feeding.

Smarter touch. Breastfed babies are guaranteed to be touched a lot, and many sleep in the same bed with mother for all or part of the night, a healthy parenting practice that further increases

---

SMART TIP

The milk, in addition to the mothering, gives babies a head start. At least eleven scientific studies have shown that breastfed babies are smarter. And the more frequently and longer infants are breastfed, the greater this intellectual advantage.

daily "touch time." Infant-development specialists believe that touch — or the lack of it — has a powerful influence on a child's physical and intellectual development.

4. "Smart Talk"

Babies don't have to be taught to use language, but the more of it they hear, the better they learn to speak. Note that language is more than using words. Language is communication, and babies communicate long before they begin to use words. Early on, a newborn learns that she can use sounds and gestures to get attention and have her needs satisfied. Your responding to these cues helps her understand how communication works. When her cue — say, a "pick-me-up gesture" — gets the expected response, she is motivated to give more cues. Because the cue-and-response system is the foundation for communication and language, it's important for parents to put their energy into responding rather than worrying about "spoiling" their baby. This is one of the many ways in which following the Baby B's (as listed on pages 14–16) contributes to children's development and success. (See Chapter 9 for communication tips.)

"Talking" with parents also helps babies pick up on the subtleties of communication. From attentive parents, babies learn that eye contact is part of communication. They also learn about *turn taking*, a fundamental language and social skill. Mothers especially tend to talk to babies in short bursts of slowly rising crescen-

dos and falling decrescendos, with pauses in between thoughts. Even though Mom is the only one talking, she acts as if baby is talking back. And in fact, video analysis of mother-baby interactions shows that baby moves in response to the rhythm of mother's "dialogue," holding up his end of the conversation with body language rather than words. These early responsive conversations shape the baby's ability to listen; as with other developmental skills, more opportunities for practice allow the baby to develop to her full potential. Parents of children who turn out well enjoy these early interactions and make the most of them.

Mothers and fathers use an enriched form of language with their babies that has been dubbed *parentese*. They raise the pitch of their voices and s-l-o-w the rate at which they speak. Parents brighten their faces and open their eyes wide when talking, so that it's easier for a baby to focus on the message. They exaggerate some words or facial expressions in order to relay meaning. A baby doesn't have to depend on words alone to know that something fun or exciting is about to happen. She can associate words such as "go for a walk" with a pleasant smile and her mother bustling about getting ready. How parents talk is more important to a baby than what they say. Most important of all is to spend lots of time in conversation with your children.

Probably because I'm such a talker, both of our girls have strong communication skills. I talked to both of them from the time they were born, all the time. I sang to them, too. I never thought twice about this and found they were so responsive early on. I think just talking a lot to your babies from the word "go" makes a hundred different kinds of differences over time. And not "baby talk." I talked to them as I would with anyone, maybe with different voices, but with normal words.

SMART TIP

Talking to your baby has a profound effect on his brain development. Here's where parents, especially mothers, really shine.

BABY TALK TIPS

Look at the listener.

If you engage your baby's eyes before beginning a conversation, you will be able to hold her attention longer and are more likely to get an appreciative response.

Mimic your baby's sounds.

Babies tend to watch a speaker's mouth and try to mimic the tongue and lip movements. Parents can encourage this by making fun sounds, exaggerating words, and encouraging their baby to repeat them. Mimicking the *baby's* sounds also encourages him to practice his sounds and try new ones.

When my babies started making noises, I repeated them back but turned the sounds into a word that it sounded like, rather than just repeat baby talk.

Address your baby by name.

While a baby may not associate the name with herself until she is several months old, hearing it frequently triggers pleasant associations. This special sound means that someone is paying attention to *her*.

Keep it simple.

Use short, two- or three-word sentences, and one- or two-syllable words with drawn-out, exaggerated vowels: "Sweeeet baaby."

Keep it lively.

Say, "Wave bye-bye to Grandma," as you wave. Babies are more likely to recall words that are associated with *animated gestures,* which is why babies love sign language. Give your speech some spark with inflection at the end of the sentence. Exaggerate cue words. Babies become bored with the same old sounds. Infants and toddlers are more attentive when you talk in a singsong way.

Ask questions.

"Suzy want to nurse?" Talking in questions will naturally raise the pitch at the end of a sentence as you anticipate your baby's response.

Narrate.

As you go through the baby's daily maintenance — dressing, bathing, and changing diapers — talk about what you are doing. (Note to dads: this is much like a sportscaster describing a game, "Now Daddy takes off the diaper. Now we put on a new one. And there goes baby, making a break for the other side of the bed. . . .") It's normal to feel a bit foolish initially (unless you already talk to yourself regularly), but you are not talking to a stone wall. There is a little person with big ears and a developing brain processing every word she hears. In my pediatric practice, I have noticed that infants of chatty mothers who are also good listeners tend to become more talkative toddlers — and attentive listeners.

Sing out!

Researchers believe that singing uses more language centers in a baby's brain than do words alone. You don't have to be an opera star to have an admiring audience of one. Babies at all ages love the songs they hear over and over again, whether they're made up by Mom and Dad or borrowed from familiar sources. File away your baby's top ten favorites and replay them frequently. Babies thrive on repetition.

Expand.

Expanding on a child-initiated word is a valuable language-learning tool. Suppose your toddler points up at the "buh" (bird). You add: "And birds fly in the sky. . . ." Words or ideas that a child initiates present a teachable moment.

According to an interesting bit of research, it's "real life" language — coming directly from a person's mouth — that is important to a baby's development. Words on television, tapes, or the radio just don't offer the same learning benefits. This may be because babies need to see the people who are speaking — perhaps even smell and touch them. Language means the most to babies and children when it is about their world and when it comes from people they care about. It stands to reason that well-connected kids will be good language learners.

I talked to my baby almost constantly. I always tried to talk "above" his level — that is, to give him colorful and interesting verbal messages. I'd often narrate my activities: "Mommy is making soup. Look at the orange soup. See the pieces of the carrot in the soup?" I spent lots of time describing items that he could see. He was an early and prolific talker, and I like to think all of this conversation helped.

As children grow, it's important to keep talking to and with them. You can talk about people you know, things you see while driving to baseball or soccer practice, events at school, other family members, your own and your child's feelings. You are helping enlarge your child's worldview by talking about the television show you watched together (or the commercials), commenting on a new car you see on the road,

or talking about how Aunt Sophie is having a hard time since her dog died. Children feel special when adults make time to have genuine conversations with them and listen to their

TABLE TALK!

In our surveys, we noticed that the dinner hour is important to many families raising successful children. Parents and children both look forward to this social time. The focus is on being together and sharing experiences, as well as on eating. Although family dinners may not be possible every night because of busy schedules, try to eat together as a family whenever possible — more often than not. Be sure that each child gets a turn to speak and feel important. Keep your expectations realistic, based on the ages of your children; three-year-olds can't sit as long as ten-year-olds. Don't limit the conversation to child-centered topics. This is a good opportunity for children to hear adult conversation and participate in it. You can discuss current events, family business, and what's important to Mom and Dad, as well as what happened at school that day. Children — even little ones — enjoy the buzz of conversation.

SMART TIP

Responding to your baby's cues builds brain connections.

---

observations. Just as in those long-ago infant dialogues, remember to watch for and respect your child's responses, verbal and nonverbal.

5. Smart Responses

Building a brainy baby depends not only on how you talk to your infant but also on how you *listen*. Many studies have shown that the quality of the attachment between parent and infant is the most powerful influence on brain development. A sensitive, responsive style of parenting reinforces a baby's learning at critical moments. When you are connected to your child and can intuit what she is thinking, you can often provide the crucial bit of information that helps her understand why she's crying or what she wants — and what to do about it. A responsive parent can help her fit the blocks together or understand why her sibling is upset right at the time that she is wrestling with these problems. When babies cry or cue, they expect a response. That's the fourth R of learning. By listening to all her language, the actions as well as the words, you can respond with the most effective kind of educational stimulation — the kind that comes with love and caring attached to it.

Despite the many classes, toys, and programs available for babies, toddlers, and preschoolers, parents remain the most important educators in their children's lives. Your child's intellectual development does not depend on what things you buy or what classes you sign up for. The toys are fun and classes are full of helpful ideas, but it depends on what you *do*. The parents' role as playful companions and sensitive nurturers is

---

SMART TIP

Relationships, not things, build brighter children.

---

far more influential than formal or even informal teaching. In the keynote address at the 1986 annual meeting of the American Academy of Pediatrics, infant-development specialist Dr. Michael Lewis reviewed studies of factors that build brighter babies. In summarizing the research, Dr. Lewis concluded that the single most important influence on a child's intellectual development is the responsiveness of the caregivers to the cues of the baby.

The responsive relationship that you establish with your child during infancy will carry over into later learning. Secure, confident children learn better, no matter their natural abilities. The knowledge of your child that begins with responding to cries and other cues in infancy will help you help with homework in years to come.

6. Smart Reading

A study conducted by the U.S. Department of Education titled *A Nation at Risk* found that children whose parents read to them performed better in school than those who were not read to at home. It's never too early — or too late — to read to your child. Babies love to hear nursery rhymes and poems with a singsong cadence. They also love to look at books with pictures of other babies. Older children, even those who read well on their own, enjoy sharing more grown-up books with Mom and Dad.

Reading aloud to children is the single most important activity for building knowledge and eventual success.
                        — *U.S. Department of Education*
                        Commission on Reading

BRAIN-BUILDING DADS

For most dads, a regularly scheduled time to do something means it's more likely to get done. And routines can develop relationships. So pick a regular time several nights a week for "Daddy and me" reading time. Your arms, your lap, and male vocal intonations go a long way toward enhancing future reading skills, as well as your child's interest in learning. In fact, studies show that children have a higher degree of academic and social competence when their fathers are involved in their learning.

Reading to your child involves more than just following the text. With a baby or toddler, you'll do more talking about the pictures than actually reading words on the page. Look for books for your baby with one large, simple picture on each page — or make them yourself. Then ask, "See the lion? What does the lion say?" Your toddler will love the ritual of roaring together. Then you can talk about the lion at the zoo or the stuffed lion on his bed. Lift-the-flap books and others that incorporate interaction are lots of fun for toddlers and preschoolers and get them hooked on reading at a young age.

I would involve the kids in the reading time process by saying "turn" at the end of each page so they knew they could then turn the page. You know, kids like turning pages!

♦

As a mother of three, I've learned a few things about reading to children along the way. Now I don't feel that I have to stick to the words that are on the page. I feel free to read those, and to also talk about the pictures, or even to ask what the child thinks is going on or what might happen next. I've escaped the box of simply reading along, and now make it a fun, interactive adventure.

Read to me!

Books can open doors to conversations about important events in your child's life. A book about a visit to the doctor's office can prepare him for his upcoming appointment. A book about his day can bring back memories about last week's outing to the local zoo. A book about an airplane trip can help prepare her for your vacation. A book about a new baby can help you explain the changes that are expected in your home. Picture books lend themselves to dialogue between reader and child: "Where is the kitty?" "Why do you think Pooh Bear is so happy?" "How many red apples can you count?"

Young children love books about themselves. You can create these for and with your child, using photos or simple drawings, scrapbooks, or even the computer (depending on how good at crafts or ambitious you are). Homemade books are a great way to prepare for an important family event, or remember one.

The home is the child's first school. Parents are the child's first teachers. Reading is the child's first subject.
— Barbara Bush,
the Barbara Bush Foundation for Family Literacy

Besides reading for pleasure, children enjoy looking forward to reading as a ritual. We always enjoyed our family bedtime routine, as we read lots of books to lots of kids. Occasionally we would try to take shortcuts and skip a paragraph or page, but more often than not we got caught, indicating that even half-asleep children really were paying attention.

We began reading to our child when he was a toddler. Our bedtime ritual was to cuddle up in a rocking chair and read a bedtime book. At first, the books were short, like Goodnight Moon, *but they increased in length with his growing attention span and procrastination at bedtime. Sometimes we would fall asleep while reading and he would wake us up to continue.*

There's more to reading with kids than just picture books for the seven-and-under crowd. Reading longer, more involved chapter books out loud is a wonderful family activity to share with grade-school-age kids. Reading a book together is like entering another world with your child. You'll have lots to talk about as you read — and at other times, too, as you discuss the characters and events. Some families listen to books on tape during long car trips. Other parents make a point of sharing articles in newspapers or magazines with preteens and teens. This can open important conversations about sports figures, political scandals, or high-school shootings. As with other interactions with your children, *what* you read with your children is not nearly as important as just making the time for it. Your example speaks volumes. Besides, reading together is pleasurable for both parents and children.

We are reading the Anne of Green Gables series together, and I feel as though I'm revisiting my childhood.

7. Smart Music

New research suggests that music can make infants and children calmer and possibly smarter. The interest in music as a cerebral stimulant stems from observation that premature infants in newborn nurseries seem to thrive better when exposed to classical music. Studies done in schools have shown that the attention and

---

SMART STORIES

Tell me a story! Telling stories is another great way to share imaginative experiences with your children and to expand their minds. When listening to a parent-created story, children must pay close attention. They are free to create their own pictures in their minds, and their requests can even influence how the story turns out. You can personalize your stories to include your children as characters, which allows them to picture themselves in the adventure. Children also love to hear stories about what their parents did as kids. Some stories might have a moral or social lesson. Others are just pure fun.

I tell my kids made-up fairy tales at bedtime. Princess Julia and Princess Amanda stories are their favorites, as the princesses share my daughters' names! With these stories I can spark imagination and creativity skills. In these stories my kids become the tiniest bugs or ride magic horses to castles in the clouds.

---

performance of students improves when they are listening to classical music in the background. Scientists theorize that music helps organize the brain, especially those areas associated with creative reasoning. They attribute music's calming effect to the release of endorphin hormones, the body's own mood-calmer.

It is never too early to begin playing good

SMART TIP

Music relaxes mind and body.

music! In fact, babies in utero can hear the music their parents are listening to. You may have heard the claims that classical music builds brighter brains, dubbed the *Mozart effect*. Controlled studies have shown mixed results, but parents don't necessarily need scientific backup to justify playing music for their children. Enjoy classical music; your baby is likely to enjoy it, too.

What about early music lessons, on piano or violin? Absolutely! Researchers at the University of California, Irvine, have shown that three- to five-year-olds who took piano lessons improved their spatial-temporal reasoning skills, which helped them do better in math. But when it comes to developing your child's musical talents, use your good judgment. Don't concentrate all your efforts on music and neglect other important areas. Everyone's talents and interests are different. Your child also needs physical activity and sports, imaginative activities, experiences with visual arts, and social opportunities.

8. Smart Play

Play is children's work. From a baby's first attempts to grab a rattle to a teen's mastery of the intricacies of a computer game, children learn reasoning, concentration, and motor, social, and language skills from play. Parents can learn about what their children are thinking and feeling by watching them play and by entering their play when it's appropriate. When you play with your child or just observe his play carefully, you discover all the decision-making and

problem-solving processes going on in your child's mind during play. You also get a glimpse of how the world looks to your child and which experiences stand out.

My eldest son went through a period as a three-year-old when he loved to play restaurant. He would be the waiter and I would be the customer. I'd sit down at his little table and he would come to take my order. But very often I would order something and he would tell me that the restaurant didn't have this particular food on this day. Where was he getting this from? I wondered. And then I remembered that we had been to a neighborhood eating place for lunch recently, had ordered milk for my son, and had been told they didn't have any that day. This concept of being "all out" was so fascinating to my son that he repeated it in play for several weeks. His restaurant at home was always out of milk — though you could get orange juice instead. And then he would be out of root beer, or salad dressing, or some other item. He could tell me this with a perfectly straight face, but I found myself almost choking on a laugh. This was serious business to him.

Play is spontaneous and open-ended, not something parents can make happen. Yet you can set the stage so that your children play better. More varied ways of playing enrich children's learning at every stage of development. Basically play is *doing*, rather than watching. It involves the senses — hearing, feeling, seeing. Play at its best offers choices, possibilities, different ways to explore a problem. Children can make things happen while playing that can't happen in the real world. This can be a source of power for them, a way to feel bigger or more competent even when they are overwhelmed by the grown-up world. Don't swoop in and crush their big imaginations with a load of reality — not unless your Superman is about to jump off the porch railing!

SMART TIP

To a child, play and learning are the same thing.

You can learn a lot about your child's attention span, preferences, temperament, strengths, and weaknesses by observing him play. Some children play well alone; others prefer to have companions, especially as they reach the elementary-school years. Some children love to manipulate objects and figures; others pretend that they are themselves part of the story. Some focus on one-to-one relationships, some concentrate on families, and others build entire towns and social systems. Sometimes stepping in with a needed prop, costume, or idea helps children expand on their play ideas. Sometimes parents are needed to settle squabbles and help children work out controversies as they play together. Sometimes it's best to stand back and let children's play unfold on its own.

Here are some ways that you can encourage smart play:

Play with your baby.

Baby takes a swipe at the ball placed on the floor and discovers that not only does it roll away, it makes music! Baby stretches, reaches, tries to crawl — whatever it takes to make that noise happen again. Blocks piled one on top of another make a tower that toddlers can be proud of. They also enjoy the fun of knocking it down and starting over again. The best activities for babies and young toddlers are those in which they get to make things happen. This teaches cause-and-effect relationships and also contributes to their developing sense of individuality.

Babies love it when parents play with them, and they respond more readily than older children to adults who wish to shape their play. But don't be too pushy. Take your cues from the baby. What does that two-month-old most like to look at? Play with that toy, not your preferred stuffed animal. Often the simplest games are the best. Mirror your baby's facial expressions. Let her take the lead in this game. And pay attention to your baby's "stop" signals. If she turns away or seems to lose interest, she may need a break from the stimulation. Respect her need for a pause in the action. This is how you teach her to pay attention to her own feelings and be in charge of them.

I believe that babies don't need a lot of extra stuff or planned activities. I gave my babies what I believe they needed most: me. I breastfed them, knowing that this enhances visual acuity, brain development, hand-eye coordination, and jaw development for future speech. I carried them, knowing that movement also enhances brain development. I took them with me everywhere so that they were fully immersed in my world, and I talked to them. My children have grown into bright and independent young people.

Join the game.

Smart parents make time to play with their children, from babyhood until adulthood. There will be times when you think, "I'm getting nothing done. I could be wading through all that work on my desk. Instead I'm just sitting here on the floor playing blocks with my three-year-old." Playing with children is not always intellectually stimulating for you. It may not always be your first choice of activity. But it's very important. You're building your connection with your child. You're learning how to be a better parent. You're letting your child know that you care about her and her world. All of these factors contribute to your child's developing sense of competence and confidence. On a philosophical/spiritual level, you're learning to live in and enjoy the moment, something that children are very good at and adults must relearn. You're also making special memories. Children and their play can remind us that life is at its best when we take time to relax, use our imagination, and just have fun. Children are likely to remember the time spent with you as much as the activity itself.

When you play with older children, just as when you play with babies, it's important to take your cues from the child. Whether you're learning from your child about the very latest in trendy fashion dolls or enjoying a building session with good old-fashioned wooden blocks, try to enter your child's world. Gain her trust there and she'll be more willing to try activities and games that interest you. Careful observation of your child's play will help you discover how your child learns best and what she is ready to do. Then you can tailor your suggestions for fun and recreation to suit her developmental skills and emerging preferences.

9. Smart Toys

You can learn a lot about your child through play: your child's attention span, preferences, temperament, strengths, and weaknesses. Toys not only teach children about the world, they teach parents about their children. Toys are the icing on the brain-building cake. Your relationship with your baby is the real cake. The developmental basis for baby toys is called *contingency play,* in which a baby discovers the cause-and-effect relationship: "I poke the mobile, it moves." Basically, a toy should stimulate as many senses as possible so that your baby can see, hear, feel, and do something with the toy.

Tips on choosing toys.

When selecting toys for a child, think carefully about the toy and the child. Choose toys that

---

BRAINY BABY GAMES

Games babies play can stimulate those billions of brain nerves to make smart connections. However, when playing these games, be careful to respect your baby's need to rest now and then. Your baby will let you know when to end the game, by turning away from you.

Face-to-face game. From two weeks to two months a baby's favorite games (and they don't cost you a dime) are facial games. When your baby is in the quietly alert state, hold her within the best focusing distance (about eight to ten inches) and slowly stick out your tongue as far as you can. When your baby begins to move her tongue, sometimes even protrude it, you know you've registered a hit. Try the same game by opening your mouth wide or changing the contour of your lips.

Facial expressions are contagious. You may catch your baby making you yawn.

Mirroring games. In playing face-imitation games, you mirror your newborn's expressions back to her. When a newborn frowns, opens her eyes or mouth wide, or grimaces, mimic her expressions and exaggerate them. A baby sees her face in her mother's. Mirroring is a powerful enforcer of a baby's self-awareness. Babies love to mimic your changing facial expressions. Like a dance, you lead and baby follows. Nothing can entertain a baby like a face.

Fun and Games with a Four-Month-Old

- **Grab-and-shake games.** Babies love games with rattles, rings, rag dolls, and small cuddly blankets.

- **Sit-and-hit games.** Dangle an interesting toy or mobile within your baby's reach. Watch him punch at it or try to gather it in his arms.
- **Kicking games.** Kick toys are a favorite at this age. Pom-poms, rattles, and pleasant noisemakers can be attached to your baby's ankles for her to activate with her kicking.
- **Finger games.** Give your baby six-inch strips of yarn to play with. See how she uses her fingers, hands, and arms and how intently she focuses on the string. Note: Supervise your baby closely when you play any game with strings in order to avoid a choking hazard.

Babies in this stage are very curious about the relationship between toys — how a big toy is related to a little toy and how a little object fits into a bigger one. This is the stage of container play, in which a baby can figure out play combinations of objects (like banging, stacking, and the ever favorite fill-and-dump).

- **Banging games.** Put cotton in your ears and bring out the pots and pans! Babies delight in the noise of banging and dropping.
- **Stacking games.** They also delight in putting little pots into bigger ones. Plastic bowls and measuring cups are great for these games, too.
- **Fill-and-dump games.** Give your baby hand-size blocks and a shoe box or a large plastic cup and watch how little hands and minds work together to figure out how to put the blocks into the container and, of course, dump it out. While you are doing laundry, place your baby in a large laundry basket half full of small clothes, preferably socks and baby clothes. After she takes the clothes out of the basket, put your little helper outside the basket and show her how to put them back in, picking up a sock and putting it back into the basket for her.
- **Water play.** Encourage bathtub and sink play, *always under supervision,* which gives the master dumper an exercise in filling and pouring. Scooping up a cup of water and pouring it out makes a big splash on a baby's list of favorite games.

Fun and Games with the Six-to-Nine-Month-Old

- **Play ball!** Balls and blocks are and always will be some of the best baby toys. Babies can do so much with these simple toys.
- **Mirror play.** Sit your baby within touching distance of a mirror (floor-to-ceiling mirrors are the best). Watch your baby try to match her hands and face with the image in the mirror. When you appear alongside, she becomes fascinated at your image next to her in the reflection.
- **Roll games.** Playing on foam bolsters, which you can begin at about four months old, becomes even more fun at this age because babies can crawl up and over these cushions and entertain themselves. Drape your baby over a bolster cushion and place a toy just beyond her reach. Notice how she digs her feet in, pushing and rolling herself forward on the foam cylinder in hot pursuit of the toy.

Nine-to-Twelve-Month Fun and Games

From nine to twelve months, the master mental skill that begins to mature is the concept of object permanence — the ability to remember where a toy is hidden. Previously, out of sight was out of mind. If you hid a toy under a blanket, baby showed little interest in finding it. Try this experiment: Let your baby see you place a favorite toy under one of two cloth diapers lying in front of her. Watch her momentarily study the diapers, as if figuring out which diaper is covering the toy. By the "I'm thinking" expression on her face, you get the feeling that she is trying to recall in her memory under which diaper the toy is hidden.

• **Hide-and-seek.** Baby's new ability to remember where a parent's bobbing head was last seen makes this game a favorite. Let your baby chase you around the couch. When she loses you, peer around the edge of the couch and call her by name. She will crawl to where she saw you peering. Eventually she will imitate you by hiding and peeking around the couch herself.

• **Hide-and-seek with sounds.** Next, add the game of "sounding." Instead of letting your baby see where you are hiding, stay hidden but call her name. Watch her crawl, and later toddle, around the house in search of the voice she mentally matches with the missing person. Keep sounding to hold the searching baby's interest.

TEN TOY-CHOOSING TIPS

In selecting the right toy for your child, ask yourselves:

1. What will it teach my child?
2. Will it hold my child's attention?
3. Is it safe?
4. Is it annoying for me to see or hear?
5. Does it promote creativity and social interaction?
6. Is it noncombative, nonaggressive?
7. Does it foster hand-eye coordination and problem-solving skills?
8. How many senses does it stimulate?
9. Will I enjoy playing with this toy?
10. Will the toy have a long play life?

SMART TIP

Interaction, not stuff, builds brighter brains.

---

are developmentally appropriate, build on skills the child already has, and provide a few challenges. What does your child enjoy playing right now? Give her the tools — the toys — that will help her do it better.

Choose toys that can be shared with friends as well as enjoyed alone. Choose some toys that you know you both will like playing with, then take time to play with your child. Remember, you are the best "toy" your child could ever have.

Play style and temperament.

A child's inborn temperament reveals itself in his play. One three-month-old baby may be described as laid-back, happy to kick his legs and make the wrist rattle jingle all by himself, while another three-month-old may need to be constantly entertained. Your child's play may be rambunctious and intensely physical, or more thoughtful and quiet.

By encouraging different kinds of play, you can help your child channel his energies and skills into new areas. A shy child might benefit from toys that require interaction with other people — games that use the thinking skills she excels in but also require structured interaction with a partner. A very active or aggressive child probably should not have an assortment of toy weapons at his disposal. Instead, think sports equipment or skates or balls — toys that channel energy away from violent play. If you feel that an aggressive child needs to learn more about caring for others, your first thought may be to give that child a baby doll or a teddy bear. But will he play with it? Instead, try toys that encourage caregiving activities on a heroic scale — equipment to play police officer (minus the gun) or firefighter. Don't forget to rotate toys frequently, as children easily get bored with the same toys.

Playmates.

Whom your child plays with influences how she plays. When you encounter a child who seems a good match for yours, help the friendship along. Invite the child for play dates or trips to the park. Get to know the parents and families of your children's friends. Note whether your child plays best in larger groups or with just a single friend. Preschool and kindergarten teachers can often help you choose suitable playmates for your child. Children learn and polish their social skills in their play activities, so giving your child lots of opportunities to play with others contributes to her social development.

Children's squabbles.

Conflicts occur when children play together. Kids who can play together and never fight or never have hurt feelings are rare. Wise parents know when to intervene and when to let children work things out for themselves. Younger ones especially may need assistance in putting their feelings and wishes into words that playmates can understand. Kids also may need help

working out compromises when controversies erupt. Smart parents try to be fair — they don't force their child to give in to the guest's wishes, nor do they let their own offspring manipulate playmates who are less assertive. There are many opportunities to teach your child valuable life skills in connection with play and playmates, mostly having something to do with conflict resolution.

Video games and other electronic babysitters.

Much has been written in the popular press warning parents about the dangers of too much TV and too much time spent with video and computer games. The trend toward increased obesity in American children has been linked to too much time in front of the screen. Yet PlayStation, Game Boy, and Nintendo are words well known to children around the world. Parents of kids who turn out well recognize that video games limit a child's play options. Even though players are pushing buttons and manipulating figures on the screen, they're still sitting and watching rather than actually experiencing the sports game, auto race, or pursuit of the bad guy. In small doses of the right kind of games, these activities are fun and pass the time on a rainy afternoon. Violent video games should not be part of anyone's childhood. (See Chapter 16, "How to Monitor Media and Technology Influences.")

10. Discover How Your Child Is Smart

My many years of parenting and practicing pediatric medicine have convinced me that there's more to intelligence than can be measured on a standardized IQ test. Different children are smart in different ways. One child may be more adept at mathematical calculations or spatial thinking, another more gifted in language and

TAMING HIGH-TECH TOYS

Dogs that bark, dolls that dance, and animals that carry on conversations at the push of a button or click of the mouse — high-tech toys are big business. Could "smart toys" be causing children to be dumber? Buyer beware! We have always been suspicious of toys that run on batteries rather than kid power, and we're equally suspicious of games and toys that depend on computer chips. Here are our concerns.

Kids bond to things rather than to people.

Toys with flashing lights and lots of noise and action are so exciting that kids are naturally drawn to them. Playing with mere human beings seems boring by comparison. And you can make a robot do whatever you want, whenever you want, with no need to negotiate or worry about the robot's feelings. Playmates are not like that. Children need to play with other children in order to learn to give and receive, cooperate, and empathize. No matter how sophisticated, a high-tech toy can't offer that kind of complex play experience.

Kids become less creative.

Technology often takes the imagination out of play. High-tech toys ask kids to sit back and watch rather than to participate. These kinds of toys are being marketed to younger and younger tots. As infants spend more time watching or pushing buttons, they spend less time stacking blocks, chasing balls, and exploring containers. They miss out on important opportunities to develop motor skills and understand spatial relationships.

Instead, toddlers learn to crave entertainment rather than use their minds and imaginations. The answer to these cravings then becomes more technology. Educators fear that tech toys may create a world of "crib potatoes," in which infants grow up preferring to just sit there and be passively entertained at the push of a button.

They shorten attention span.

In a world where more and more children are being diagnosed with Attention Deficit Disorder (A.D.D.), do we really need toys that shorten attention spans and require little concentration? In real play, and real life, things don't happen quickly. A child has to stack blocks patiently to build a finished tower. The pleasure of finger painting is in exploring all the possibilities, not in quickly finishing the picture. Lightning-fast high-tech toys bring instant gratification. Even with toys where children are supposed to solve problems and thoughtfully key in answers, many kids just keep pressing buttons to see what happens.

And don't forget the expense. Something is wrong when parents must work long hours to earn money to buy the stuff they believe their kids need for "an enriched environment." What kids need most is their parents. Children who learn to think and learn will never be "technologically behind," at least not for long.

So what's a parent to do? The answer is balance. Start your toddler off with blocks, balls, crayons, finger paints, and plain old junk around the house, to let his imagination run wild. No matter what the toy, play with it along with your child and encourage him to share it with others. Watch how the child plays with the toy. If the technology seems to be controlling the child rather than the child manipulating the technology, set some limits for how long and how often the child may use it. Apply the same guidelines to the purchase of high-tech toys as you do to other toys:

How many different ways can this be played with? Will this toy encourage open-ended play activity?

Finally, like so many aspects of parenting, study your child. If your previously imaginative and creative child is slowly becoming more connected to the video-game controls than to real life, it's time to pull the plug, get out the Legos, and call some friends.

using words and images clearly and colorfully. One child may be more "intelligent" in the visual arts; another expresses herself in music or always seems to be dancing. Some kids are natural athletes; others are gifted with the dogged persistence it takes to keep shooting baskets or kicking the soccer ball until they excel, regardless of their natural talent. Some children have superior social skills or have the emotional intelligence to help them cope well with adversity or adapt to different situations easily.

Multiple intelligences is currently a buzzword in developmental and educational circles. Teachers are encouraged to present lessons in different ways so that children can learn through visual, auditory, or experiential means. Parents who want their children to do well in the world can help them discover in what ways they are smart and how they learn best. Your knowledge of your child, gained from all your close interaction, makes this relatively easy. All kids are intelligent, but in different ways. As you discover your child's special gifts and learning style, you take on the role of facilitator. You look for opportunities for your child to develop her talent and then you motivate her to do so. You also use your knowledge of your child to find positive ways to help her when she is struggling to learn something that is hard for her. Parents who recognize a child's strengths and

help develop them boost their child's chances of success. Positive approaches work much better than harping on deficiencies.

Children who are successful academically usually have other interests outside the classroom, such as athletics, art, or music. They may learn a second language, or engage in fascinating hobbies, often excelling at these interests just as they do at academics. As a perk, children who are involved in after-school extracurricular activities have less time to waste watching TV. Children who are involved in productive pursuits replace passive television-viewing with more active and meaningful experiences. Yet it's important to have some balance in outside activities. More is not always better. Overbooking creates stress that can negatively affect both the child's studies and outside activities.

DR. BILL'S TOY TIPS:

The two Baby B's — blocks and balls — are the best baby toys, as babies can do so much with these simple joys. The famous architect Frank Lloyd Wright attributes much of his skill to his early fascination with blocks.

Downtime.

Children need time for fun, time for family, time for friends, time for work, and time to be alone. Children need downtime, when they are doing simply nothing, just sitting, daydreaming, or playing with toys. A bit of idle time is important as a counterbalance to school and other directed activities. This quiet time gives a child the chance to recharge his batteries and rest his mind and body.

Do your best!

These are the three golden words to smart teaching. You have heard motivational speakers say, "Success is ten percent inspiration and ninety percent perspiration." There is a lot of truth in this statement. In fact, one explanation often cited for why immigrant children do so well in American schools is that their parents pay less attention to their children's innate gifts and talents and, instead, place a high value on how hard the child works at developing academic skills. The most common thread that ran through families of successful children whom we interviewed was that the parents expected their children to "do their best" — no more, no less.

Parents of successful children stress that the effort a child makes is the most important issue in any task, not the actual grade the child receives. Parents of successful kids do not hold unrealistic expectations for their children. They do not expect all A's or perfection. They don't regard grades as the primary focus of education. Parents of academically successful kids concentrate their energy on the *learning process*. They help their children take pride in their work. They help them learn how to learn. Yet they do expect that their children will, at all times, do their best.

I've always told my children that what's most important is not the final grade but that they do their best work. If their best efforts result in a C, that's fine. But if that C is a result of sloppy, careless work, then they know I will not be pleased. I want them to learn to be proud of their efforts.

11. A Smart School Start

Make schoolwork a priority. A common trait in families of children who turn out well is that on school days, schoolwork takes priority over all other activities.

I have always maintained that children must attend to their jobs now — scholastic education. All schoolwork and homework must be completed before television or any other noneducational activity. In fact, my children rarely watch television during the week. We tape favorite programs and watch them when time permits on weekends.

THE CARRYOVER PRINCIPLE

Time and again, we've noticed what we call the carryover principle. When a child excels at one special thing, the boost to her self-esteem carries over into other endeavors. For example, if your child is doing poorly academically, discover his special something and run with it. Don't threaten to keep him off the soccer team until his grades improve. He needs to feel successful somewhere. Support his soccer playing, praise his achievements, and let him carry this self-confidence into his schoolwork. This really works!

HOMEWORK HELPERS

Homework is about more than academics. It teaches children how to manage time. It reinforces the priority of learning and ensures that home and school are working together toward this goal. It's also your chance to find out what your child is studying in school and observe how he works and learns. Since children think and learn differently, it helps to customize a homework plan for your child. To get you started, here are some tips from parents who are well acquainted with or who have overcome homework hassles.

- Consider giving your children an hour or so of relaxing playtime after school before they begin homework. Some children really need this time to unwind after hours of concentrating at school. Yet be sure that kids know homework must be completed in a timely fashion.
- Your children can sit at the kitchen table doing homework while you make dinner. That way, if they have any questions, you are right there to help them. Organize a homework hour after the evening meal. Children can sit around the kitchen table to do homework. Set aside a "family homework hour" when your child sits at the table and does her schoolwork while you also sit at the table and pay bills or catch up on your reading. You're available to help or answer questions.
- As children become teens, they need a quiet place to study, usually their own room.

Some preteens develop more efficient homework habits if given their own private place to study. Other children regard homework as less of a chore and more of a family activity if they're allowed to do homework with Mom or Dad close by to encourage and help.

- To complete homework tasks efficiently, store needed supplies in a convenient place, easily accessible to all. Doing math problems is frustrating when it takes fifteen minutes to find a pencil with an eraser. Stock up on poster board, report covers, markers, and crayons to avoid last-minute runs to the store when special projects are due.
- If your child is struggling with a certain subject, take a special field trip or turn it into an arts-and-crafts project to make what's in the book applicable to real life.
- Many children drudge through homework because they don't see its relevance. Help your child make connections between schoolwork and the world around him.

By regarding homework as a family activity rather than a chore that interferes with quality family time, you reinforce that learning is an expected priority and that it can be fun. It's up to parents to point this out. Although some parents complain that their children have too much homework, statistics show that most children spend more time watching noneducational TV than doing productive homework.

Be involved at school.

When teachers gather together to share tales from the front, they often complain about parents who just don't understand what's going on at school and who don't give their kids the support necesary to learn. Don't be shy about getting involved at school — it is one way of demonstrating to your children that their education is very important. Find out about what's being taught to your child. Volunteer as a classroom aide, or field-trip chaperone, even if it's only once every month or two. (This is an excellent way to discover how your child's peer group operates.) Develop your personal PTA — parent-teacher association. Work with your child's teacher. Wise teachers want to know any special learning tips that the parents have observed about their student at home, and wise parents pay attention to what the teacher has to say about their child at school.

When I go to a parent-teacher conference, listen to the teacher's report, and am able to respond, "Yeah, that sounds exactly like Lauren," I'm reassured. It means the teacher and I both share a similar understanding of my child's strengths and weaknesses, and we're working on the same challenges.

You owe it to your child to get involved in his school. Successful students most often have parents who take an active interest in their education. These parents are involved at school and know their child's teachers, attend parent-teacher conferences, supervise homework, and are informed about what's going on in the classroom. When parents are involved, they convey the message of encouragement and support.

We have always been involved in the children's schools. This tells our children that we believe school is important and valuable. Our children are quietly proud that we are in these roles.

How to react to poor grades.

A twenty-year study at Stanford University on parents' reactions to poor grades shows that a negative reaction is likely to have a negative impact on a child's academic success. Instead, this research reveals that poor grades got better in time if parents responded with positive support rather than faultfinding. Criticizing a student for poor performance will not make the child work harder, but it is likely to create more stress, which can result in even worse grades.

THE PTA (PARENT-TEACHER ASSOCIATION)

In gathering the material for this book, we interviewed a lot of teachers. Many complained about being expected to do for kids what parents should have done, or should be doing. Teachers believe they should be an extension of the home, not a replacement for it. They didn't use the term *connected kids,* but teachers noted that children from homes where nurturing and discipline were priorities were better behaved and more of a joy to teach.

The relationship between parent and child affects the teacher-child relationship. At home a child learns that a respectful way of talking, communicating with eye-to-eye contact, and a positive approach to kids means love. So, when his teacher pays the same kind of attention to him, he may think, "This is how Mommy and Daddy treat me, and they love me, so my teacher must love me, too."

HOMESCHOOLING

As classroom sizes increase, school campuses expand, and national literacy scores flounder, many parents choose to take direct responsibility for their children's education by homeschooling. An estimated 1.5 million children in the United States are schooled at home.

Parents cite a variety of reasons for choosing to homeschool: wanting to have more influence over their children's social interactions, wanting children to learn the family's values and morals, and wanting to provide children with high-quality learning experiences. Homeschoolers also enjoy the flexibility of being able to personalize the curriculum to meet a child's individual needs.

We homeschooled our children for a year or two because we felt that a little more time in the "green house" would give them added strength for facing the cold winds of reality. Academically, they certainly did better with a ratio of one adult to four children than they would have done in a classroom of thirty children.

Given that parental interaction is critically important to the success of children's education, it's not surprising that research shows that on standardized tests home-educated children repeatedly score as well as, or better than, those students in conventional schools.

We have the advantage of homeschooling our children, so every day presents many opportunities to learn new things — our whole life is school! We expand what we are learning into our everyday activities. We've always let them help cook; exploring new recipes and inventing their own is a wonderful learning experience. We also let them help with the laundry, work in the yard, and shop. Our children can delve into the topics of their interest with no bells ringing to stop their progress.

Schooling children at home can be a wonderful alternative to daily separations for parents with unusual work schedules. Often both parents are involved in teaching the children. Homeschooling requires commitment from the whole family.

Homeschooling keeps our family close. It's hard to be close when you are just not with your children. My husband doesn't always have the weekends off, so having our children home during the week makes it possible for him to see them.

Children who have special academic needs may thrive in a homeschooling situation. Since parents know their children better than anyone else, they can often meet atypical needs in a more meaningful way.

My son is very easily distracted, and I felt he was not learning well in school. I came to believe that I could provide him with an education far better and broader than he could get through institutional learning. My husband and I can offer the very best personalized education for all of our children.

Homeschooling can be a wonderful alternative for your children, but it's not for everyone. Some children need the social outlets that school offers. Some families like the structure that school brings to their lives. Employed parents simply can't be home with their kids. Not every parent enjoys schooling children at home.

I've tried homeschooling and have not found it to be rewarding for them or me, but I do have that homeschooling mentality that says school should be interesting, challenging, meaningful, and rewarding. I work with my kids' teachers to make sure the kids are getting a valuable education and to see that my kids are showing respect and responsibility for the teacher and their schoolwork. I think this helps them succeed.

Regardless of whether or not you do formal homeschooling, all parents can be sure that their home is an extension of the school, and vice versa.

Communicate grace. When a parent replaces judgment with mercy, however, the child begins to trust parents to help. Consider the guilt and embarrassment your child already feels about his poor grades. Parents must separate who their child is from the grades he receives. Be sure that your child does not feel he is valued less or loved less because of his poor academic performance.

Discuss your child's grades with him in a nonthreatening, friendly setting. Go out for ice cream and talk about his struggles over a cone or a sundae. Tell him that grades are a serious matter, but let him see love, not anger, in your face. Then ask your child how you can help him set a course for better grades next time. Be firm but affectionate.

Finally, energize your child's hope. As the old saying goes, "Nothing succeeds like success." Struggling students need to believe that they can succeed. Many educational specialists see hope as the most important ingredient in a student's success. If the child does not believe he can succeed in school, sooner or later he will give up, feeling, "I can't do it, so why try?" Be sure your child is in classes that are not too hard for him, and show and tell the teacher that you are working with your child to help him pull up his grades. Teach your child to learn to ask teachers for help when he needs it. Working with a child to improve poor grades can be an opportunity to strengthen the parent-child connection.

12. Smart Learning from Life

Everyday life is a masterful teacher, and to a curious child the whole world is a classroom. Instill a love of learning in your children and they will go far, not just in school but in life. In a study of high academic achievers, one trait stood out: a genuine love of learning. Opportunities to enjoy learning are yours to give. Such occasions are easy to see when you're the parent of a child who is gathering information at every turn.

Let babies explore the world, pick up things, get involved. When they start crawling, they are discovering many things for the first time. Let them touch, taste, and smell. With my children, I let them get into everything — of course, while watching them to be sure it was safe. Babies naturally like to explore, so we let them. We didn't put them in a walker or playpen.

Parents don't need to do formal, classroom-type teaching at home. You can make everything you do with a child a learning experience. For example, when you put groceries away, you and your preschooler can talk about the alphabet. Notice and comment on letters everywhere — the *C* on the Cheerios box, the *A* on the bag of apples, the big *Q* for Quaker Oats. When you're driving along the freeway, you're moving through a real-life classroom. Read the billboards. Talk about why traffic is so heavy at this time of day. Count all the green cars or the sixteen-wheeler semis. Notice license plates and street names, architecture, and landscapes.

Talk about nutrition, food, even ethnic eating, when you walk through the supermarket with your children. Since you're there anyway, you might as well take an extra few minutes to explore the aisles and talk about the items that catch your child's curiosity. Teachable moments happen all through the day. Children are most eager to learn when the opportunity is right in front of them.

I always tried to be sure he got what I call the "basic five" every day: reading, outside play, arts/crafts, music, and quiet play.

Take time to smell the roses. Suppose you're going for a family walk. You may have been hoping for vigorous exercise, but for a child it's an exploratory expedition. Make frequent stops to watch and comment on the birds. Inspect bugs and caterpillars. Look at all the different kinds of trees. To a child, nature is one of the most captivating classrooms.

Sometimes just before the kids go to bed, one of us steps into the hallway and calls out in a loud voice, "Pajama ride!" The kids know what that means. They race out of their room and hop into the car for a ride to view the sky in search of falling stars, or drive high up on the mountain and look down at city lights. The kids never know which night it will be or what they will see! We want to keep learning fun.

Answer questions.

The love of learning is rooted in curiosity, of which most children have an abundance. Those endless questions ("Why?" "How?") are opportunities. When your child is in the mood to learn, he naturally goes to his most trusted teacher. Although incessant questions can be annoying or inconvenient, answering them promptly is an investment in your child's future. As you provide answers or help your

---

THE SECRET OF SCHOOL SUCCESS

Why do some students succeed in school and others struggle? Part of the answer lies in the attitude toward learning in the home and the school. Learning begins at home, and parents are the child's first teachers. In one sense, all children are homeschooled, even those who also attend school. Here's a summary of what parents and other educators can do to help children become academic high achievers (AHAs):*

Implant a love of learning.

Not surprisingly, research shows little correlation between IQ, economic status, a privileged childhood, or even early preschool and later academic success. The most influential factor in children's academic success was parents who instilled a love of learning early on. Learning is rooted in curiosity. Kids are naturally curious, and from

* An excellent parental resource for influencing your child's school success is the book Top of the Class: Guiding Children Along the Smart Path to Happiness, *by Arline L. Bronzaft (Norwood, N.J.: Ablex Publishing Corporation, 1999).*

early infancy onward, parents, as teachers, act as facilitators, guiding those curious, exploring hands and eyes toward interesting objects. This doesn't necessarily mean lots of "educational toys." Babies learn a lot riding in a baby sling, where they can be in on adult conversations and see the world near adult eye level. Learning tools for toddlers can be as simple as a kitchen drawer or cupboard full of pots and pans, paper-towel rolls, and plastic dishes that the child is allowed to play with. Basic balls and blocks are also great toys for stimulating and satisfying curiosity.

Kids say: I'm a good student because my parents tell me to do my best or I won't do well in life. (Tony, age twenty)

Foster free play.

Let children play, for this is how they learn. While one-on-one time with parents and other sensitive and responsive caregivers is certainly important to facilitate early learning, be sure to give your toddler and child ample time alone to simply "mess around" with toys and safely explore the environment. Pre-school children do not need to have every minute of the day filled with one planned lesson or activity after another. Observation of the homes of AHAs showed that parents allowed these children to take reasonable risks. They childproofed the home and had a lot of "yes touches" around the house. These children were not constantly supervised by adults warning, "Be careful," or "Don't touch." Learning usually involves some risk taking.

It's all attitude.

Another feature that sets AHAs apart is their attitude toward learning. Rather than viewing learning as an obligation or chore, they love to learn because of the feeling of self-satisfaction it gives them. They view school as a privilege rather than a problem. In fact, interviews with AHAs reveal that children who achieve high academic success look forward to the opportunity to shine on tests. They make a connection between hard work and good grades, and see themselves succeeding.

Kids say: I'm a good student because my parents taught me from the time I was little that education was really important. (Susan, age nineteen)

It's all in the family.

AHAs' love of learning is most influenced by putting a high value on learning. Research shows that the homes of AHAs tend to be quieter, with no blasting TV or stereo. Noise gets in the way of learning. Children reared in noisy homes are slower to develop language and cognitive skills. Students tend to achieve better in school when family life is harmonious. You may not think of your marriage as a tool for your child's academic success, but studies show that children who perceive harmony and commitment between their parents feel less anxious and more grounded — freeing them up to do better at school. Academic outcome studies also have shown that students who eat meals with their families more often enjoy greater academic success.

Parental guidance advised.

A U.S. Department of Education survey of 26,000 students found that parental involvement ranked high on the list of factors influencing AHAs. Academic success also correlated to how frequently parents checked in with teachers on their child's progress. Parents of AHAs also ask for teachers who demand more of children. Studies confirm that a child's level of success in school tends to parallel both parents' and teachers' level of expectation. Studies further show that parental attitudes toward learning influence academic success. That immigrant Americans see academic achievement as a stepping-stone to success is the most likely explanation for their high achievement. These families also tend to be highly involved in their children's homework. To cultivate a love of learning, parents need to persuade, but not pressure, their children to work hard in school; parents and teachers need to stretch, but not stress, students.

AHAs are not nerds.

Contrary to popular belief, academic high achievers are not isolated and asocial bookworms. Because they enjoy the self-satisfaction that learning and academic success give them, these kids also want to be successful in other areas. Studies have shown that well-liked and emotionally healthy children tend to do better in school and that unpopular children and those with poor social skills are more likely to become school dropouts. Once children taste success in one area, it carries over into others; the combination of academic and social skills is the prime determinant of later career success. Because academic excellence carries over into a child's overall self-confidence, AHAs tend to be less influenced by peer pressure. As we repeatedly emphasize, character is more important than achievement. AHAs even tend to value their physical health more than academic underachievers. In summary, children who are smart enough to value learning are also smart enough to take care of other parts of their life.

Kids say: I'm a good student because my parents made sure I had a balanced education, not only study but participation in sports and clubs. (Allison, age twenty-four)

Value the teachers.

Parents of AHAs not only tend to be highly involved in their children's schools but also go out of their way to match their children with the right teachers. Dr. Arline Bronzaft, author of *Top of the Class: Guiding Children Along the Smart Path to Happiness,* relates that over the past ten years the average verbal SAT score for people going into the teaching profession has been about 400, which is less than average. Two lessons can be learned from this dismal statistic: teachers need to be more highly valued and better compensated so that more qualified people will enter the field of education, and parents need to take charge of their child's education rather than depending upon teachers who may not be qualified to guide gifted students or those who struggle with challenges. Perhaps teachers should be treated more like doctors (after all, the word *doctor* means *teacher*); they certainly have tremendous influence on how kids turn out.

child find answers, you also teach life skills —
seeking knowledge, analyzing problems, working together. If your preschooler or grade-
school-age child finds you approachable with
small questions, she'll be more likely to bring
the big ones to you in the teenage years.

*We have always listened to every thought and an-
swered every question, no matter how tough. No topic
was off-limits. Our daughter always gets the real explanation, as fully as we can offer. Now, as a high-
school freshman, she is very open to new ideas and can
defend her positions and opinions fully and logically.*

5

Planting Healthy Sibling Relationships

BROUGHT TOGETHER BY circumstances of birth, brothers and sisters share a common life, profoundly affected by one another's presence. They are bound together through good times and bad, through disagreements and anger, yet often with an undercurrent of strong attachment. During childhood and adolescence their connection may wax and wane, but it often reemerges strong and vibrant in adulthood.

There are many ways in which life as a child in a family is like boot camp for living in the adult world. Chief among these is the basic relationship training that children receive from their interactions with siblings. In sibling relationships, children build upon the blueprint about human connection they have learned from their relationship with their parents. They learn how to negotiate, compromise, forgive, be forgiven, and love someone even when they don't like him. Children take this knowledge into adult life, to their relationships with others outside the family. A healthy sibling relationship, even with the inevitable rivalry, provides learning experiences not easily found elsewhere.

Healthy sibling relationships don't just happen. There's no law of genetics that says children born of the same parents will have compatible temperaments and personalities. In fact, having to share the same parents is the basic challenge of being siblings. But parents can help their children get along better, ensuring that the lessons learned from siblings are good ones. Here are fourteen building blocks to help your children build successful sibling relationships.

1. PRACTICE ATTACHMENT PARENTING

Attachment parenting helps parents know their children well, making it easier to deal with differences between siblings. When you understand that each child has different needs, it's easier to help everyone get what they need to be happy. Children with a secure attachment to Mom and Dad find it easier to love their siblings. When each child in the family feels loved and respected, children get along better. They may argue and fight at times, but underneath they are not seriously threatened by or jealous of one another. With attachment-parented children, their love for one another and for their parents overshadows their rivalry.

Parents find that attachment parenting really pays off when a new sibling arrives. Because the

THE TRICKLE-DOWN EFFECT OF AP

Our first child, Jim, was our "trial baby." We were young parents searching for a parenting style that would work for us. We learned by trial and error, practicing on Jim, then Bob, and then Peter. When our high-need daughter, Hayden, arrived, we finally signed on for the full spectrum of attachment parenting. We had learned with our eldest three that bonding at birth is important, that breastfeeding is best, and that a baby's cries are signals that demand appropriate responses. Hayden was the first of our children to benefit from babywearing, bed sharing, and extended breastfeeding.

Does this mean that we somehow failed our three eldest sons? That there is something lacking in our relationship with them? Not really. We have learned not to waste energy worrying about what we should have, or could have, done with those first babies — we did the best we could with the resources and information we had at the time. Even without the constant closeness of AP, we followed our hearts and instincts when it came to meeting their needs. (All three were easy, laid-back babies. If they had been more demanding, we might have found the AP style a lot sooner.) And as we have parented their younger siblings, the responsiveness we have come to value so highly has certainly influenced our relationship with our elder boys.

It's never too late to try the AP approach with a child. It can be more difficult to figure out what an eight-year-old needs from you than to understand a baby who at eight days needs mainly food and comfort. But if you are someone who is wondering whether you have somehow shortchanged an elder child, ease up on yourself. Look for age-appropriate ways to become closer to that child. You can't haul a four-year-old around in a baby sling, but you can set aside time each day for focused, one-on-one time. Read stories and cuddle at bedtime. Enjoy your child for who he is.

As you practice the Baby B's of attachment parenting with your new baby, you are also teaching your elder children how to parent and how bigger, more powerful people care for little ones. Your sensitivity to your baby will deepen the other relationships in your family, including those with elder children, which to us is the ultimate testimony.

The big payoff is that your elder children will one day model their parenting on the way they saw you care for their sibling. Two of our three elder sons are now married and have children of their own. Dr. Jim and Dr. Bob, and the wives they brought into our family, are now practicing attachment parenting with their own children.

toddler has had her needs met as a baby and young child, she is less likely to feel jealous of all the attention paid to a new brother or sister and, in fact, is often a leader when it comes to lavishing love and attention on her sibling. Having been attachment parented helps elder children understand that bigger people — whether parents or siblings — treat little people with care and sensitivity. The way you parent your elder child plants the seeds for how he will relate to a younger sibling. Attachment parenting two or more children simultaneously is not easy, especially with small children who are close in age. Yet all the effort is a wise investment. Your sensitivity to everyone's needs sets an example that your children will follow in all the coming years of living together as a family. This is how you teach your children to be sensitive to the needs of others and how you establish the family values that you want your children to practice all their lives.

2. PREPARE THE EXPECTANT SIBLING

Even the most well adjusted, most attachment parented child is likely to have some doubts about adding a sibling to the family — if not before the birth, then sometime after. You can help your child handle the inevitable anxiety by taking away some of the mystery. She'll cope with changes better if she knows what to expect.

You may not want to tell your child that you're pregnant at the first sign of a missed period or a bout of nausea. Nine months is an eternity to a three-year-old. But remember, children pick up on their parents' feelings, and since they are normally so egocentric, they will worry that the change they smell in the air is going to affect them. As Mom changes — physically and emotionally — with the pregnancy, children need to know what's going on. It's wisest to share the news with your child early in your pregnancy.

Get acquainted before birth.

Show and tell your elder child about the new arrival before he or she comes. Let the elder children be involved in getting ready for their little brother or sister — buying clothing, finding baby toys, choosing a name. Encourage the big sib to talk to and pat the soon-to-be brother or sister, and feel baby kick.

My daughter attended prenatal checkups with me and got to hear the baby's heartbeat and watch the ultrasound pictures. She also attended our hospital's classes for expectant siblings and learned so much about what a new baby would be like. She liked to lie on my chest and go to sleep at nap and bedtime. When the baby would kick her, I would call him by the name we had chosen and say, "Your new brother is kicking you."

◆

Elizabeth says: When I was pregnant with their brother, my elder three children loved to shop for baby things and, once home, would gather around oohing and aahing all over our purchases. They spent hours setting up his bedroom and arranging his toys and books. I let them select his outfits for coming home from the hospital, right down to his little socks. They reveled in this privilege and took it very seriously. They would hold up his little clothing, marveling at the idea of such a tiny human being who was to be their brother.

Being involved in plans for the new baby helps siblings feel that the big event is happening to them, too. The new baby is theirs as well as Mom's, not only to play with but to care for.

Talk about what's going to happen.

Prepare the sibling for all the changes that will occur in family life when the baby is born. Get out the photos from your elder child's baby days and show and tell her about what she looked like when she was only minutes or hours old. Show her pictures of how she nursed and was carried or worn in a baby sling. Talk about the presents she got when she was a baby and the visitors who came to meet her. Talking about the sibling's baby days prepares her for what babies are like and reminds her that she, too, got lots of attention when she was tiny. Tell her, "Visitors will bring baby presents," "Tiny babies really need their mommies, so Mommy will carry baby a lot — just as I did with you," "Baby is going to nurse a lot — just like you did." Children need to be prepared for the reality of a new baby in the family. Change is easier to handle if you know ahead of time what these changes are likely to be.

Before I went to the hospital, I wrapped several little gifts for Jessica. I put these away for when people came to visit the new baby. Many people bring gifts for the new arrival but often don't bring anything for the sibling. So, once in a while I would surprise her with a "big sister" gift.

♦

We talked a lot about what babies are like to have around and the fun things that my daughter could do to help me. I explained that babies need a lot of holding and attention to thrive, and explained what thrive *meant. I said we would all help the baby to grow feeling happy, healthy, and well loved. She found this to be really fascinating. I told her all the things she could do to help me with the baby, wrote a list, and got her to circle the ways that* she *wanted to help, and told her that we could add to that list as time went on or change the things she liked to do. I wanted her to know she was welcome to help, but I wanted her to have some choices about how.*

♦

When we were expecting our adopted children, we wondered how the girls (then three and six) would adjust to adopting two preschool brothers. We talked regularly about how day-to-day life would change ("When the boys come, we'll put more chairs at the table") and tried to give honest answers to any questions the girls had: I carried pictures in my wallet of all four of them and spoke as if their brothers were already ours. We set up the boys' bedroom, and the girls added books and toys. By the time our adopted children came, they were already part of our day-to-day lives, and the girls adjusted with remarkable grace.

3. GET THEM CONNECTED — EARLY

Parents whose children get along well envision their children as lifelong friends from the beginning and do what they can to make this vision a reality. Parents can take advantage of their children's natural fascination with babies to get siblings connected during the early days of the baby's life. This is the time to help your elder child understand that the baby is a real person, with real needs and real feelings. Be a go-between. Do the talking for your baby and explain to your toddler or elder child what you imagine baby is thinking or wants to say.

When the baby grabs you and holds on tight, the baby is telling you how much he loves you.

♦

When the baby makes little mouth motions, we told the kids she is trying to figure out how to give them kisses. I'd often put words to the baby's reactions or expressions. It made my [elder] daughter laugh and helped her see her sister as a real person. I knew we were making progress when our child persuaded me to bring her three-week-old sister in for "show and tell."

Many parents of kids who have turned out well told us that tandem nursing (continuing to nurse an elder sibling as well as the new baby) did wonders for helping their children get connected. Mothers don't usually plan on tandem nursing, but when an elder child clearly needs to continue to nurse partway through a pregnancy and afterward, they find themselves nursing two. This is easier on the elder sib than pushing him to wean before he's ready. Tandem nursing makes it easier for baby and sibling to share mother, and mothers treasure the image of their elder child stroking the younger one's hand when both are at the breast. But it isn't always easy. Mothers who are tandem nursing may find that they have mixed feelings about the elder child who is still nursing, especially since he looks so big compared with the new baby. Elder sibs may want to nurse longer and more frequently in the first weeks after birth, a response to Mom's more plentiful milk and their own worries about being supplanted by the baby. Of course, the new baby should get first dibs on Mommy's milk, and mother may want to set some limits on the elder child's nursing. Certainly, tandem nursing won't appeal to every parent, yet don't imagine two children nursing all day long. Toddlers and preschoolers who still nurse may do so only at naptime and bedtime. One-on-one attention from Mom can substitute for nursing at other times.

Tandem nursing worked briefly for fostering sibling relationships between our fourth and fifth children, Hayden and Erin. Allowing Hayden to nurse one or two times a day for a few weeks helped one-year-old Hayden share Mommy with her baby sister, Erin, and helped get their connection off to a sharing start.

*Karen was still nursing during the early part of my pregnancy. She was delighted when her baby brother arrived with the gift of more milk, and asked to nurse again. I think that being able to relax her once or twice a day while her baby brother napped gave us special quiet time together and helped the two of them get off to a great start. Now at age five, with a sparkle in her eye and a huge smile on her face, she assures other children awaiting siblings that the baby will bring along a wonderful gift for them . . .
MORE MILK!*

4. YOU'RE SPECIAL, TOO!

A new baby naturally attracts lots of attention. Friends shower gifts on the new baby, and par-

ents are constantly holding, feeding, changing, or comforting the new arrival. Elder siblings can easily get lost in the whirlwind of activity a new baby brings into the house. It's understandable that elder children may feel that no one notices them. Do what you can to keep them from feeling left out. When an admirer says, "What a beautiful baby," add: "Now we have two beautiful children," or "And she has a beautiful big sister!" If Mom is busy feeding baby, Dad can step in and give the elder child some special attention. Or find special books or quiet activities that Mom and the elder child can share while baby nurses or naps.

My sons are twins and attract tons of attention. I made sure that when people asked about them, I would also introduce my daughter as the best big sister in the whole wide world. I would also try to tell people something about her so that she would get recognition apart from the twins.

Ever been given a job that made you feel important? One way to make a child feel important is to let him know that he is needed. This elevates the elder child's position in the family, thanks to the baby, which is likely to get their relationship off on the right foot. Tell big sister that you need her help and show her what to do. In our large family we refer to this as "give her a job in the family organization." Give her a fun job title: Mommy's helper, Mommy's assistant, or Mommy's go-fer. "Bring me a diaper, please." "Pick out some clothes for the baby." "Let's dress and bathe baby together." Feeling important helps many children relish the big-sister or big-brother role.

Soon after Benjamin was born, our four-year-old showed a turnabout in personality. She reverted to bedwetting, throwing temper tantrums, waking up at night, and becoming increasingly defiant. She made herself a general nuisance. I gave her a job as "mother's assistant." After a few weeks she not only became more pleasant to live with but enjoyed learning some mothering skills.

Keep in mind that you are bringing up someone's future husband, wife, mother, or father. How children eventually handle these roles depends on the role models they see at home. As your "mother's assistant" is helping you take care of the baby, the elder child will mimic many of your mothering skills. As we would wear Stephen around the house in a baby sling, Erin would wear her dolls around in her own little minisling.

I helped my elder children feel they were an important part of taking care of the baby. They would get me a diaper, hold a toy, open a baby gift, and make the baby laugh. I would always say, "Thank you for being such a good big sister." We emphasized the big-sister and big-brother aspect a lot.

Adjusting to the presence of a younger sibling is challenging for a young child. There will be times when your elder child is delighted to be a big brother, and other times when he will wish that you would take the baby back to where it came from. Be sensitive, and don't overdo the "big boy" routine. Your child will miss having you to himself; sometimes you will miss those days, too. Ignoring these feelings won't make them go away. Allow your child to express them, and acknowledge that it's not easy being older. When your elder child regresses into baby talk and thumbsucking, allow her the luxury of being babied a bit while at the same time focusing on the benefits of being the big kid in the family. Talk about all the fun things big boys can do, but not babies: "Big boys can eat ice cream, but babies can't." "Big girls can climb the monkey bars, but not babies." Your child will gradually realize she really doesn't want to be a baby again.

My son told us to call him "little brother," not "big brother." Being a big brother, he said, was too hard.

5. ENCOURAGE TOGETHER-ALONE TIME

Siblings need time together to create their own relationship. Whether or not they can verbalize it, they know that "sometimes what we're doing is just between us kids." This "alone time" allows them to explore each other's personalities. When the elder child is a toddler or preschooler, it's important that there always be an adult around to supervise. But do let the elder sibling set the pace for interaction while you go on standby to prevent any potential accidents. Your children will discover ways to delight and entertain each other that you as an adult would never dream of trying.

My son and daughter spent much of their time together when they were little. They were together like two peas in a pod. She followed him around and imitated his every move. He seemed to love being the leader and the attention that he got from her.

It's important to respect and protect the elder child's needs and possessions. Be sure he has places of his own where he can retreat to when he doesn't want his block towers knocked down.

My kids are real buddies. They play together almost all day, but sometimes my eldest one wants some space to play with his toys or just be alone. I do my best to help him get that space. Once he's had this time, I can count on him to search out his younger brother once again.

6. ROLE-PLAY

Setting up different roles for different children in different situations helps them become the best of friends. This comes back to the parents' role as facilitators, finding ways to foster healthy sibling relationships. Here are some of the possibilities.

Protector role.

Teach your elder child that he has a responsibility to protect the younger one, which includes modeling good behavior. "Be sure to pick up your toys so that the baby doesn't fall over them and hurt himself." "Would you make sure that the baby doesn't crawl out of this room while Mommy finishes cooking supper?" (Meanwhile, you are constantly checking on them.)

Helper role.

Helping each other can bring out the best in both the helper and the one being helped. Doing things for each other promotes a good relationship between siblings. The giver feels empowered and successful; the receiver feels cared for, valued, and loved; and both parties feel connected through the act of helping. Helpfulness builds loyalty. In the process, children learn how to accept assistance gracefully and thankfully — a social skill that's critical to relationships. You want your children to grow up knowing how to give and how to receive.

As mentioned above, the elder child can help take care of the baby and feel important. That's in the earliest stages of the growth of the sibling relationship. As children get older, it's the younger one who may "help" the big kids with a task like watering the flowers on the patio or putting away toys, and elder children can help younger ones build towers or create Lego masterpieces.

I encouraged our elder child to help our younger one by pretending to confide in the elder child: "Christie doesn't know how to put blocks on top of each other yet; how about you pile some up so she can knock

them down." I think making it a game that the elder child felt in control of helped her feel important. And the younger one always enjoyed this special attention from the elder sibling.

There's an old saying that if you want to deepen a friendship, let your friend help you. This concept works especially well between siblings. Children find it easy to run to parents all the time for help. Encourage them to look to each other as well.

With a big family we had what we called "special helpers." Each sibling had another sibling as his special helper. When shoes were missing for Sunday school, and a child would call on Mom and Dad for help, we would say, "Have you asked your special helper to help you find them?" What a surprise it was when our elder kids discovered that their younger special helper could actually help them in certain situations! Not only did this help us as parents, but it helped the bond between siblings.

Teacher role.

Elder siblings shine when they pass a skill on to a younger one. Encourage your child to take on the role of teacher: When Matthew took on the role of baseball coach to his younger brother, Stephen, they spent more time together and grew closer. Encourage elder school-age children to help the beginner with homework. Of course, you have to make sure that the young teacher's patience is not sorely tested and that the student has fun as well.

Adviser role.

Trying to get your younger child to care a little more about how he looks, to neaten up his room, or get involved in a new activity? Enlist the help of a big brother or sister. A big sibling, who knows how all the kids at school dress, can be a helpful fashion adviser, one whose taste is trusted more than Mom's. (Have a private conference with the sib first, if necessary, to set some guidelines.) When it comes time to hang posters on bedroom walls or store doll clothes in an orderly way, siblings can advise and help, resulting in a room that's really cool. If your youngster has doubts about playing soccer or moving on to second grade, let the elder sibling share wisdom gained from recent experience. The big kid feels important when called upon for advice, the younger one enjoys the attention, and Mom and Dad can often get the results they're looking for — a clean room, no more jeans with holes — without a battle.

Doctor role.

Encourage siblings to comfort one another. When one child gets hurt, ask another to help care for the injured one. Give your assistant a job title: "Dr. Lauren, would you hold Matthew's leg while I wrap his ankle?" "Mr. Paramedic, please put this Band-Aid on Susie's cut." The title *doctor* defines the sibling's role as a compassionate, helpful one, and the patient, who a moment ago may have yelled, "I hate you!" at the sib, is now on the receiving end of caring. It's hard to hate the hands that help and comfort you.

Minister role.

A ritual we have used in our family is one we call "laying-on of hands": the sib in need (whether because of an upcoming test, a big wish, or an emotional or physical hurt) sits in the middle while family members place a hand on his shoulder, arm, head, or wherever the hurt is. They pray and each one offers a kind thought or word of encouragement. The family is the child's first and most enduring support group. Years ago when we started doing this,

Martha and I would tell each other that we hoped our children would continue this ritual into adulthood — and they have.

Co-workers.

Set siblings up to cooperate. Give them assignments that require cooperation and motivate them to work together: "Bobby and Jimmy, please clean up the garage together. The sooner you two finish, the sooner we can get to the movies." Giving sibs a job to do — with a little incentive — is particularly helpful when they are squabbling or simply not getting along. The task forces them to focus their energies on working together — a valuable life skill. Part of your role as facilitator is to monitor the working relationship and be sure that it remains cooperative — that both are helping and that neither is acting bossy.

We would frequently encourage co-ventures, such as setting up and running a lemonade stand together. Naturally, the adult in charge keeps a bossy-submissive relationship from developing. Role-playing activities reflect an important parental role: to promote sibling sensitivity. Throughout this book we use the term *sensitivity*, which is the foundation of interpersonal relationships. During toy squabbles and apparent insensitivities, constantly keep in mind your goal: raising sensitive siblings.

7. CONVEY THE BEHAVIOR YOU EXPECT

Your expectations will greatly influence the relationship between siblings in your family. How much fighting and teasing will you allow? How much time should siblings spend together? In what ways will your children help one another? Your children's perception of how you expect them to treat one another sets the tone for their expectations of how to treat others outside the home. Let your children know that you expect them to respect one another. Remind the elder ones that they are to set a good example and that their younger brother or sister looks up to them. Create lots of opportunities for them to work together and have fun together so that they look to siblings for help and recreation even when you are not setting the stage for it. Sometimes you simply have to draw the line on what is acceptable and what is not. One day at the height of Jim and Bob's bickering, Martha said to them, "If you two want to fight like dogs, we'll build a doghouse in the backyard and you both can live out there." They got the point.

Your family is your child's first social group. It should have a positive effect on how he or she relates to others later in life.

From the time my second son was born, I made a commitment to help my children learn to be friends. I wanted to reduce sibling rivalry. I worked hard at being fair and didn't tolerate a lot of jealous behavior. They were expected to be nice and helpful to each other, so they were. I set limits on their behavior to each other and kept reminding them that they are related and need to be nice to each other.

8. KEEP SIBLINGS CONNECTED

Modern life has a way of keeping family members apart. Dad and Mom work away from home, at separate jobs. Children spend six or seven hours a day in school, separated by same-age classrooms from brothers and sisters. Siblings may also spend their after-school hours in separate Scout troops, in different sports leagues, or with their own friends. It's hard to stay connected when you're always going off in different directions. Parents, however, can structure their homes and their children's leisure time in ways that encourage sibling bonding.

Include friends in play groups.

When kids are at home with no friends around, they automatically search each other out for company. Close-in-age siblings don't feel they always have to go outside the home to find a friend when they want one. When children reach school age and begin making same-age friends, these new relationships often compete with sibling relationships. When a friend enters the picture, the sibling may be shut out — if parents let it happen. Step in and monitor the situation. You might suggest activities that they can all share, or offer space in the family room or basement to open up more inclusive play activities. Let your elder child know that you expect him to include the younger one, at least part of the time.

We've always had a rule in our home: No one who wants to play is to be left out. That means that Angela sometimes finds her little brother, David, joining in with her and her friends. We found that our children's friends readily accept our rule.

A technique for helping the elder child endure the company of a pesky younger sibling is to remind her that she, being more mature and experienced, can teach the younger child what and how to play. It never hurts to add something about how much that younger sibling looks up to the elder one and tries to be like her. This puts the elder child and her friend in the position of teacher or leader.

Enjoy family travel.

Family travel is like a retreat — away from all those influences that tend to pull family members outside the family circle. Family vacations are a way to bring everyone together and focus on one another. With no distractions from peers, daily lessons, sports practice, and ordinary chores, brothers and sisters rediscover the fun of being with one another. Family vacations also give you something to talk about together in the months to come.

Limit electronic influences.

You can't have fun with one another if everyone is wearing headphones. There may be a place for Walkmans or Game Boys on long car trips or boring plane rides, but these devices shut people off from one another. When going on family vacations, we've had to monitor the use of TV, Walkmans, handheld computer games, and other electronic influences that interfere with our children spending quality time together. Nobody wants to have a lot of rules on vacation, but you can't create family togetherness in a van full of kids with their ears plugged into their own music and their eyes focused on some electronic gadget. Set some limits, and then be prepared with alternative activities. Many families enjoy listening to a book on tape as they travel together, or they play games.

Share bedrooms.

Bonding in the bed is not really a new idea. It's done by families the world over. We have noticed that in our family, and many parents have shared this same observation, children who sleep together play more peacefully together. Sleeping side by side strengthens the sibling bond. It's a good feeling to check on your children before you go to bed and find the arm of the elder sibling draped over the shoulder of the younger one. When siblings share a bedroom, or a bed, they learn about living with another human being in a shared space. When children share a bedroom, they must learn how to resolve disagreements and make compromises. They must respect each other's space and deal with the consequences when one sib feels the other has violated an agreement. Remember, one of the tools that your child needs to succeed in life is to be able to live in harmony with others. Sharing a bedroom helps children acquire this tool.

Each pair of our children, boys and girls, shares a bedroom. We hope this will nurture a deeper relationship between them. I'm certain they feel safe at bedtime, as they have never had nightmares. They need to learn to cooperate, negotiate, and handle conflict as they share space. Both pairs sleep in the same bed by choice. It's lovely to see them curled up together, especially if they were squabbling during the day. Sleeping together helps them restore their relationship.

Many parents report that children who share a room also share a special connection. It's as if they belong to their own special "club," with their own private "clubhouse." The bedroom becomes a place for quiet conversation or uninhibited giggles. Many parents we interviewed felt that having their children sleep together in the "family bed" when they were young was the first step toward their wanting to share a bedroom.

It's very heartwarming to see how much the girls care for each other. In the mornings, it's one big cuddle fest! Sometimes my elder one will read to the younger for quite a while before we get up.

◆

I've always cherished the way our two children wake up in the morning in our family bed (which consists of two mattresses pushed together on the floor). Our elder one snuggles up to the younger one upon awakening. When they are both finally awake, they greet each other with the warmest smiles and snuggles.

Those dreamy moments upon awakening set a lovely tone for the day. For us, the family bed arrangement has been an incredible tool for sibling bonding.

◆

My ten-year-old son loves to read to his one-year-old sister. One night he asked if he could snuggle up to her in bed and read her a story. I said, "Fine," and he popped her in with him and I went off to finish the dishes. I came back half an hour later and they were both fast asleep holding hands. It melted my heart.

9. GET THEM BEHIND THE EYES OF THEIR SIBLINGS

Children seem to forget at times that brothers and sisters have feelings. The things they say and do to one another can make a parent cringe. When you step in to help settle a conflict, remind your children that they must respect one another's feelings — even when one is convinced that the other is completely wrong. It's hard to hate a person who understands and cares about how you feel.

Help your children understand one another's feelings. This requires them to look at a conflict or a difficult situation from another's viewpoint. Children often can't make this mental leap on their own, especially not in the heat of battle, when they feel it's more important to be right than to be compassionate. When it's time for you to blow the whistle and referee a fight, don't just make a simple call as to who's right or wrong, who's following the rules and who is not. Take time to talk about the feelings involved and the actions they produce. This is the first step toward a true negotiated settlement, not just a temporary, parent-imposed cease-fire.

When one of them hurts or upsets the other, I ask the offender to look at the other's face and tell me how he

thinks he feels. Then we turn it into a question and ask the child offended, "Is that true? Do you feel sad?" That gives the other child a chance to say yes and explain why he's feeling that way. The formula we use is "When you [do a certain behavior], I feel [a particular emotion], and I want you to . . ." Then we ask the offender how she can make it right. Usually it ends up in hugs and apologies; then things are more peaceful again.

We don't believe that siblings are born adversaries. In fact, there's no one who can know you and love you quite the way a brother or sister can. Once children get into the habit of trying to understand their siblings' feelings, they will be able to apply these empathy skills to other relationships, too.

10. AVOID COMPARISONS

Children grow up in a world in which they're constantly being evaluated relative to others — grades and test scores in school, the batting order on a baseball team, which part they get in the school play. Even informal peer groups have ways of letting kids know just where they stand in relation to others. Home should be a place where children can count on being valued for themselves and not being measured against others. Nevertheless, children do compare themselves with their siblings and suffer when they don't feel that they measure up.

Try to avoid comparing one sibling with another. One child may feel she can't possibly measure up to her big sister and deliberately try to be different in nonconstructive ways. Each child has unique qualities, with unique strengths and weaknesses. Help them see themselves as individuals without judging their accomplishments against those of their siblings. If

Suzie gets better grades than Sally, Sally will be well aware of it. Instead of saying, "Why can't you be more like your sister?" focus on Sally's strengths and how they can help her become a better learner. Try to help each child find special strengths and talents. Help children enjoy their own gifts, in addition to appreciating and enjoying their siblings'. It's a delicate balancing act. It would be unfair to prevent one child from achieving her full potential just to spare the feelings of another, but it's also unfair to let a child monopolize the family spotlight. Here are some suggestions.

Help each child shine — differently.

Not every child can shine all the time. Try something like the "Star of the Week" approach. Suppose one child has gotten the leading part in a play. She is the star that week. She gets praise and encouragement from everyone. This is her week to shine. Next week another child is the star — say she got an A on the spelling test that she studied hard for. This is her week to shine — in a different way. Though there will always be some competition for time in the spotlight — kids are like that — don't let your children draw you into this childish contest. When one child stands tall in the light of his accomplishments, be sure the others are not left in the shadows. A great way to do so is to let the kids nominate the star and give a reason. It helps them learn to enjoy and appreciate another's accomplishments.

When one child shines because of an accomplishment, be sure the other siblings share in the excitement. Learning how to rejoice with another person's success is a valuable tool for happiness in life. "Tonight we're all going to go out for pizza and congratulate Tony for working so hard to get a good grade on his test." Do some PR (parent reminding) behind the scenes:

"Madison, it would really make Tony feel happy if you would give him an encouraging 'Way to go, bro!' when we congratulate him for his good grades at dinner tonight." When one child plays on a championship baseball team, give everyone a treat after the final victory. Make the nonbirthday child a part of the preparations for the party. Include her in picking out presents, making the cake, putting up decorations, and organizing the party games. Be sure that the birthday boy knows that his sister played an important role in making his birthday fun.

Teach your children to respect and appreciate one another's differences and to value and support one another's talents. One week the whole family attends one child's recital, the next week another's ball game — and all cheer appropriately. If you have one child who has a special talent that attracts a lot of attention, it's important that the other children don't fade into the shadows because of your "gifted child." Remember, all children are gifted; they are just gifted differently. Celebrate the gifts of all!

Fair does not mean equal.

Children place immense importance on fairness, but to them fair often means exactly equal. The standard comment from our second son, Bobby, on almost everything his elder brother Jimmy did was "No fair!" One evening at dinner these two scorekeepers counted the number of peas on their plates to be sure they got an equal number. After that, we let them serve themselves. When they saw we wouldn't get involved in this game, they realized how ridiculous it was and stopped — though when Jim got married first, Bob's first comment recorded on the wedding video was "No fair!"

Parents soon learn all kinds of tricks for addressing the fairness issue. When our children share a cake, we let one cut it and the other choose his piece. Be fair, but you can drive yourself crazy trying to keep everything equal. It is impossible to treat all your children the same all the time, nor should this be your goal. Not all children's needs are the same. "Why did Susie get a new pair of shoes and I didn't?" quibbled Mary. "Because her shoes were too small, and you got a new pair last month," says Mom. Let children perceive that their individual needs will be met but that they are not necessarily the same as their siblings'.

One mother we know tells her three children regularly that even if things don't seem fair at the moment, she is sure everything will balance out in the end. Children need to be treated individually, but not necessarily equally. An eight-year-old's needs differ from those of a fourteen-year-old. One child may need a lot more attention during a particularly difficult stage. The time you spend attending one child's dance recital is less than the amount of time you spend watching the other's baseball games. Often your job as a parent is to explain to your children why different children receive different privileges: "Daddy, why do I have to go to bed at nine o'clock and Erin gets to stay up until ten?" "Because you're growing faster, and because Erin has more homework to do." A simple matter-of-fact explanation will often ward off sibling grumbling.

Don't expect to give each child "equal" opportunities every day or even every week. Aim for balance in the big picture, not equal amounts of peas on the plate. Fairness can become a trap, leading parents to count out M&M's, measure the size of pancakes, or buy every child in the family a gift when one has a birthday. This kind of fairness is doomed to failure. Life, after all, is not fair. It's more important for children to feel sure that they will get what they need, even if what they get is not the same as what their sibling has.

11. PLAY FAVORITES — EQUALLY

Even the admonition "never play favorites" is unrealistic. Any parent who thinks it possible probably has only one child. Some parents' and some children's personalities mesh; others clash. Some children are easier to be around and bring out the best in a parent; others push the wrong buttons. The best you can do is recognize where you and one of your children clash and where you get along. Then do your best to accentuate the positive and avoid the problematic situations.

Try not to let your children perceive you as playing favorites, and listen carefully if they complain that you do. At one time or another you'll get the question, "Who do you love more, me or Jason?" Be ready with an emotionally correct answer: "I love you both in special ways." We've often compared love to sunshine: "Sharing the sun doesn't mean you get less, and our love shines on you all like sunshine." Help your children realize that they are loved in special ways: "You are my first daughter, and no one else will ever be my first daughter." "You are my very own Jennifer, and no one else is quite like you."

12. TAUNTS AND TEASING NOT ALLOWED HERE

Siblings learn to take a certain amount of ribbing from one another. It's part of the fun of being in a family. Yet parents need to draw the line when good-natured teasing turns into put-downs that hurt individuals and relationships. (Making jokes at another's expense is a sorry way to boost one's own self-esteem.) Groups of people — whether families, friends, or business organizations — function best when everyone gets a chance to shine and no one has to be the victim of others' crude humor. Keep your ears open for signs that what seems to be good-natured fun is actually hurting someone's feelings. Teach your children to be aware of the difference between teasing that says "I love you just as you are" and put-downs that say "I'm so much better than you because you are so stupid." When one sibling is down, sometimes others jump in and criticize, pulling that brother or sister down further. Use one child having a problem as an opportunity to teach siblings how to pull someone up — without teasing or taunting. "Jessica really feels bad about not being picked for that part in the play. How can we help her feel better?" you ask the other children. Let them all contribute ideas on how to help Jessica feel better about herself. Remind them that teasing her would be cruel and that you will not allow it.

AGE-GAP PARENTING

In today's world of blended families and parents who have children later in life, there are more and more siblings who are many years apart in age. These sibling relationships are very different from those of children who are spaced two or three years apart. Sibling rivalry is less of a problem. The challenge is to find ways to help these children build a close and loving relationship. Since two-year-olds and twelve-year-olds have little in common as far as interests and abilities, parents must give some thought to how to bring these children together. Relying on an elder sibling to babysit regularly for a young one is not the way to create a healthy relationship between them. The elder child may resent the younger one's intrusion upon his free time and privacy, and he may not enjoy having to watch his "pesky little sister" when his own friends are visiting. It's okay to use a willing sibling as an occasional babysitter (consider paying him if that makes him more agreeable), but try not to overdo it. A better way to help build their relationship is to help them spend time together doing something fun. Making elder children the teacher, the baseball coach, or the fashion adviser helps them feel special and important as a big brother or big sister.

When my elder children use an old baby toy to entertain our one-year-old, it's fun to watch them find renewed joy in that forgotten object. It's been said that having a baby in your forties keeps you young. I think it has a similar effect on elder siblings. It allows them to step back into their childhood and be silly and playful, no matter what their age.

One night Martha and I were sitting in the family room when we heard six-month-old Erin crying from our bedroom, probably because she had just awoke from her nap. As we approached the door of our bedroom, we noticed a touching scene that is implanted forever in our memories. Our fifteen-year-old, James, was lying next to Erin cuddling and comforting her. We were happy to witness this teen sensitivity.

13. LET CHILDREN WORK OUT THEIR OWN SQUABBLES

In our interviews with parents about sibling issues, we heard repeatedly that it is important to let children work things out between themselves whenever possible. Doing so teaches children how to negotiate and compromise. Parents should be there to help but should not take over. Disagreeing (to a point) is healthy, and talking about disagreements can strengthen a sibling bond.

When to step in and when to remain a bystander is a round-by-round judgment call. Let your children know in no uncertain terms that you expect harmony to prevail in your home. Martha's favorite squabble-stopper is the phrase "You're disturbing my peace." Don't intervene at all in minor arguments. Try not to listen to them. When bigger eruptions obviously call for adult supervision, prepare to act diplomatically and help the kids talk to each other more effectively. Don't fall into the trap of figuring out who's at fault: it's usually difficult to tell, and most of the time both are at least partly in the wrong. Taking sides will often drive children apart rather than bring them together. Sometimes the most valuable thing a parent can do is step in and impose a "cooling off" period when one child is so angry with another that he or she cannot listen to reason.

We would always wait for the kids to cool down a bit before trying to heal a relationship. Stepping in and helping each one vent his own viewpoint as the other listened without interrupting was the first step to finding a solution to the squabble. We would echo their feelings: "Bob, you feel that Jim wronged you." "Jim, you feel that Bob was being unfair." Then we would encourage them to work out a solution between themselves: "You're big boys and you're brothers, and this sounds like something you guys can work out. You both go to your bedroom and talk it over. I expect you to come out as friends." Imposing a deadline for a solution can be helpful, or simply tell them that no one is going anywhere until they have solved the problem.

My own parents never let my sisters and me fight. The minute there was conflict of any sort, our parents would solve the problem their way and we were told to go to our own rooms. Now that we are adults, we are still separated. We never learned how to talk to each other. I'm determined not to let that happen to my boys. I'm always watching and helping when needed — but I let them have arguments. They always get solved, and then the boys end up playing together again.

No physical violence tolerated here.

For some children it's a natural reaction to hit, bite, or lash out when they are frustrated or angry. This is normal childhood immaturity. Learning to control these impulses is part of growing up. Children need to be taught that any physical violence against another human being is intolerable. There is no room for wavering on this point.

I have zero tolerance for one child putting another child's safety at risk. If one child hits the other, the two are separated, to keep them both safe until the offender is able to come up with, or agree to, a plan to make things right.

It's your problem, handle it.

Problem solving is critical to success in life. In fact, when companies are having difficulty, wise executives follow a Japanese motto of business management: "Show me the solutions, not the problem." Early on, teach your children to quickly take responsibility for their own problems and fix them. Let them know that you're not going to be drawn in to a squabble between siblings and that you will not expend energy on figuring out who is right and what went wrong (though sometimes these issues merit some consideration). The best message to give children is "It's your problem, now fix it." Take children's arguing or fighting as an opportunity to help them learn new skills and build a better relationship.

One of my best solutions was to have the two fighting children hold hands until they figured out a solution themselves. If they started to argue with me about the other child, I would answer, "No, I'm sorry, it's not my problem. It's yours. When you have a solution, let me know." I tried hard to stay cheerful and walk away. Believe me, holding hands with your six-year-old brother when you're nine is a killer! Things got worked out pretty quickly.

◆

Children need to know early on that the world may be their oyster, but they are participants and not just recipients. They need to learn to give and let others go first. So many children are growing up with a competitive "me first" attitude. How can families cope with a houseful of "me firsts"? Everyone in the house needs to recognize the value of giving.

14. FRIENDS COME AND GO, BUT FAMILY IS FOREVER

Here's some more PR (parental reminders) to use with your kids. Repeatedly impress upon your children the true meaning of "brother" and "sister." Remind them of the importance of family, especially of sibling relationships. Even school-age children sense that blood is thicker than water. Brothers and sisters are a live-in support system. Nobody knows you, warts and all, quite the way a sibling does, and few people in your life will love you as much. During family gatherings, on the phone, and during hard times and family crises, let your children see how much you care about and need your own brothers and sisters, their aunts and uncles. Let them know that friends — sometimes even spouses — come and go, but a brother or sister is a friend forever.

6

Raising Healthy Kids

AN IMPORTANT KEY TO SUCCESS — and one that parents can greatly influence — is health. Healthy children put their energy into growing and learning. They miss less school, have more opportunities for normal social and emotional growth, and enjoy life more. Kids who are sick a lot miss out on learning experiences and fun.

In my years of pediatric practice, I have noticed that connected parents and kids fare better healthwise. There are lots of reasons why one would expect children who receive attachment parenting to be healthier. Breastfeeding tops the list. Also, children with a strong connection to Mom and Dad are less stressed. As babies they don't have to cry hard to have their needs met. As older kids they're less likely to find themselves in conflict with their parents. Less stress means more health. These children also benefit from how well their parents know them. If an attached mother tells me that something is wrong with her child, I pay attention. In all likelihood, she's right, and her detailed observations will lead me to an accurate diagnosis.

Getting connected is your first step toward keeping your children healthy and helping them get well if they do get sick. Here are some of the ways in which connected parents can contribute to their children's good health.

NINE NUTRITIONAL TIPS FOR SUCCESS

"Let food be your medicine," advised Hippocrates. Over the years I have observed that children who have the healthiest eating habits are often the healthiest kids. They do better in school, have fewer behavioral problems, and are sick less often. I first noticed this in my early years of pediatric practice, when I met the first of what I call "pure moms." They are mothers who do not allow any junk food to pollute the minds and bodies of their children. Their children eat fruits and vegetables, whole grains, little refined sugar, more fish, and less meat than most Americans. These pure moms also limited their children's exposure to other "pollutants," such as scary television and violent toys. I noticed that I rarely saw these "pure children" in my office, other than for checkups, since they were rarely sick. When their children started school, these mothers were not the ones who made appointments with me to discuss teachers' judgments that their children had behavioral or learning problems. Over the years these "pure moms" and "pure kids" have made a believer out of me: there truly is a connection between how kids are fed and how they act and learn. Diet is not the answer to every physical, emotional, or learning problem a child might have, but when kids eat healthy foods, I believe that their problems are less severe and that both parents and children are better able to cope.

In recent years I, too, have become a bit of a health nut when it comes to nutrition, because I know that good nutrition is the key to good health and an overall sense of well-being. Here are the top nutritional tips for successful children and their parents.

1. Breastfeed Your Child as Long as Possible

The incidence of just about every illness you don't want your child to get is lower in children who are breastfed. This includes everything from ear infections, colds, and tummyaches to childhood cancer, asthma, allergies, diabetes, and heart disease. Breast milk is more than just calories. It's a living food that offers your baby protection against disease and provides nutrients needed for optimal development.

Breastfed infants are leaner and are less likely to be obese later in life. As discussed in the previous chapter, they're even smarter on average than formula-fed infants. The longer your child is breastfed, the more she benefits.

I hoped my children would learn the importance of breastfeeding because I breastfed them. One day in a restaurant, I pointed out to them a cute baby lying in his mom's arms enjoying his bottle. My children looked disappointed. "What's wrong?" I asked. They both quickly said, "The baby is holding his own bottle and the mom isn't even looking at him." I'm so pleased that my children, ages eleven and thirteen, realize what natural infant feeding is supposed to be like.

So how long should mothers breastfeed? Answer: How healthy do you want your child to be? The Committee on Nutrition of the American Academy of Pediatrics recommends that "breastfeeding continue for at least twelve months, and thereafter for as long as is mutually desired." A former Surgeon General of the United States, Dr. Antonia Novello, after reviewing the scientific research on the health benefits of extended breastfeeding, stated, "It's the lucky baby, I feel, who continues to nurse until he's two." Our advice: Think of breastfeeding as one of the best investments in your child's health. If you run into difficulties in the early weeks, get help to solve them. If you must return to employment outside the home, consider buying or renting a high-quality pump so that you can express milk for your baby while you're gone and continue to breastfeed when you're together. Putting some effort into breastfeeding pays off. You give your baby the best possible nutritional, emotional, and intellectual start in life. You also enjoy the wonderful closeness that can continue well into your child's toddler and even preschool years. (For the effects of breastfeeding on emotional development, see p. 15; for the intellectual benefits, see p. 57.)

I'm grateful to have been able to nurse my children long enough into their childhoods that they each remember the feelings of love and security shared there.

2. Shape Young Tastes

Your child forms lifelong eating habits in the first three years of life. A child who grows up nourished first by mother's milk, with wholesome, fresh foods added to his diet as he is ready for them, will learn to prefer healthy food. These flavors become his norm, rather than the oversalted, artificial flavors of high-fat, processed, packaged foods. This child is then more likely to prefer healthy foods because that's what his body is used to.

This strategy has worked with our own children — in fact, some of them were seriously "junk-food deprived" in their early years. As toddlers and preschoolers they wore T-shirts that proudly displayed IF YOU LOVE ME, DON'T FEED ME JUNK. When these "pure" children went out on their own into the sugarcoated, fat-filled world of birthday parties and trips to fast-food restaurants with friends, they ate french fries and licked icing from their fingers, but they did not overdose on junk food. They quickly made the connection between junk food and "yucky tummy." These junk-food-deprived children knew that when "I eat good, I feel good."

Besides shaping young tastes, you can also shape young cravings. Nutritional science has shown that food cravings have a biochemical basis and that food and mood are connected. When you give your child nutritious foods in her early years, her body becomes biochemically programmed to crave these good foods and shun the less nutritious ones. When you eat a steady and varied diet of healthy foods, your body secretes just the right balance of serotonin and endorphins, hormones that give you a feeling of well-being. Children who learn to know this good feeling at an early age instinctively crave the good foods that keep these hormones in balance. How you feed your infants and children also shapes their attitudes about feeding practices.

When you shape your children's tastes to prefer fresh foods, you also shape their eating behavior. If you are disciplined about what you feed them in these early formative years, your children will have better self-discipline about food choices in the years to come.

WISDOM OF THE BODY

The nutritional principle called "the wisdom of the body" says that the body intuitively craves the nutrients it needs; if a person is deficient in a particular nutrient, the desire to eat foods that contain that nutrient increases.

In the 1920s, pediatrician Clara Davis made a landmark study on the concept of the wisdom of the body. She offered exclusively breastfed but newly weaned toddlers all-natural foods that were unprocessed, unseasoned, and unsweetened (that "pure mom" diet again). She offered a dozen food choices. She noticed that the children instinctively chose foods that provided them with balanced nutrition. They had followed the wisdom of their body.

Unfortunately, most children and adults are exposed to so many non-nutritious food choices that they have lost this wisdom of the body. By eating a diet of junk food for a long enough time, the body decides that this is the norm. It craves more junk food rather than more nutritious choices. However, if junk food makes only a rare appearance in your diet, your inner body wisdom will remind you that you need to get back on the right track. "Pure children" have this gift of the wisdom of the body — thanks to the "pure parents" who are careful about what they eat from day to day.

3. Allow Grazing for Good Behavior

When you have lots of children, you don't have time to be a short-order cook who caters to each child's eating whim. Through the years we have come to realize that our job as parents is to buy nutritious foods, serve them creatively, and then sit back and let our children choose what to eat. We noticed that without parental pressure to clean their plates, our children ate throughout the day. Sure, they ate meals at regular mealtimes, but they also "grazed" their way through several minimeals in between. We did a bit of research and realized that little growing bodies (and grown-up bodies, too!) are biochemically better off with many minimeals throughout the day rather than gorge sessions at breakfast, lunch, and dinner.

Children have tiny tummies, about the size of their fist. Next time you place a heaping plateful of food in front of your three-year-old, compare the size of her fist to the amount food and you will see why she leaves so much on her plate.

Grazing actually improves children's behavior. When a child eats a lot of food at once, especially foods high in refined sugar, her blood sugar rises quickly. Sensors in the body send a message to the pancreas: "We've got too much sugar here in the blood, let's get it out." The pancreas then releases insulin, which drives this excess sugar out of the bloodstream into the cells but may also send blood-sugar levels plummeting. Low blood sugar causes stress hormones to kick in, which affect children's behavior and make them crave more sugar. Both blood sugar and behavior go on a roller-coaster ride enjoyed by no one. Children who graze throughout the day don't experience these ups and downs in blood sugar and the resulting behavior swings that occur when children go without food for several hours.

Teens and older children will graze naturally on their own (check their rooms if you seem to be running out of dishes). For toddlers and preschoolers, try the "nibble tray" — an ice-cube tray, muffin tin, or a plastic dish with several compartments. Place bite-size portions of colorful and nutritious foods in each section. Give them fun names, such as banana wheels, broccoli trees, cheese blocks, avocado boats, and pasta shells. Reserve a compartment or two for the child's favorite nutritious dip, such as yogurt or mashed avocado. Set the nibble tray on a low table near your child's play area or keep it on a low shelf in the refrigerator. Kids should have opportunities to graze at school (send along a nutritious mid-morning snack) and on family outings or shopping trips. Don't leave home without something to stave off the blood-sugar blues.

The best foods for grazing pack a lot of nutrition into a small volume. Kid favorites include:

- Avocados
- Broccoli
- Cheese
- Slices of hard-boiled egg
- Chunks of fish (salmon and tuna)
- Pasta
- Peanut butter
- Pieces of cooked chicken
- Sweet potato chunks
- Kidney beans
- Whole grain breads and crackers
- Yogurt

4. Keep Children LEAN

Lean people live longer and healthier lives. Children who lug around extra fat are at an emotional and physical disadvantage. Studies have shown that obese children are more likely to develop a poor self-image, are more prone to

---

Lean is the most important health word.

social isolation, and are less able to compete in athletics. Research has shown that obese children get twice as many infections as lean ones, probably because obesity reduces the ability of white blood cells to fight infection. These children have more leg pains when growing up and have a greater chance of developing arthritis later. Being overweight and physically inactive also increases the chances of developing Type II diabetes, especially in people with a genetic predisposition to the disease.

When we say "lean" we do not mean being thin or skinny. We mean having the *right amount* of body fat. Everyone can be lean. Not everyone can, or should, be thin. Ever wonder why some people can eat almost anything and stay lean and others eat less but carry around extra fat? That's because they have different body types.

Eat right for your type.

There are three general body types; we call them bananas (tall and lean), apples (medium or stocky), and pears (short and round). "Bananas" tend to burn calories. "Apples" and "pears" tend to store calories (and envy "bananas"). Whether your child is a fat-burner or fat-storer is hereditary. You can't change genes, but you can change eating habits. Apples and pears need to have more nutritious eating habits in order to be lean. They'll never be bananas, but they can become a leaner apple or pear.

So how do you keep your child from getting fat? Trying to control everything he puts in his mouth will backfire. Don't turn eating habits into a control issue — your child will eat more of the wrong stuff just to assert his own power. Studies have shown that parents who try to exert a high degree of control over a child's eating habits tend to produce children who are unable to control their eating on their own and who

eat more high-fat foods. (It's interesting to note that control issues are also at the center of eating disorders such as anorexia and bulimia, when adolescents and young adults use not eating to feel more in control.)

Better alternatives begin with modeling good eating habits yourself. For example; have nutrient-dense, low-fat foods available for snacks. These would include fruits and veggies, low-fat plain yogurt mixed with fruit and honey, and whole-grain breads and cereals. Don't use high-fat, high-sugar foods as rewards, and encourage your child not to go overboard with them. Most kids recognize that a second piece of cake or another piece of pizza will leave them feeling uncomfortable.

The best way to keep children lean is to set them up to get plenty of exercise. Couch potatoes, especially those who snack on potato chips, are the ones who get fat. The kids who are running around the soccer field, swimming laps

---

RESOURCES FOR KEEPING CHILDREN LEAN: THE L.E.A.N. PROGRAM

The L.E.A.N. Program (lifestyle, exercise, attitude, and nutrition) is one we have developed to help overweight and underfit children and parents in our pediatric practice. You can find information on a complete weight-control and fitness program for every member of the family in the following three resources:

- www.leanprogram.com
- www.leankids.com
- "Trimming the Family Fat" in *The Family Nutrition Book,* by William and Martha Sears (Boston: Little, Brown, 1999).

at the pool, or just tearing around the neighborhood on their bicycles not only burn more fat but have better control of their appetites and fewer opportunities for stuffing themselves with snack food. Get your kids up and moving — and get out there with them!

5. Give Your Child a Brainy Breakfast

Power breakfasts are not just for Wall Street executives. Breakfast could be called "the success meal." Eat a good one and your whole day will go better. Proteins tend to perk up the brain, and complex carbohydrates tend to calm it. A breakfast with the right balance of both helps a child learn and behave well all morning long.

So what's for breakfast? Here are some examples of brainy morning meals that contain a balance of proteins, complex carbohydrates, and calcium:

- Whole grain cereal, yogurt, and fruit
- Eggs, whole-grain toast, and 100 percent orange juice
- Whole-grain pancakes topped with fruit and a glass of milk

Notice that all of these menus emphasize high-fiber foods — the complex carbohydrates in whole grains and fruits. High-fiber foods are digested more slowly, and the sugars produced by digestion are released more steadily into the bloodstream. Breakfasts of doughnuts, sugary cereals, or packaged pastries lead to mid-morning learning slumps, caused by the drop in blood sugar that follows quick digestion and the release of too much insulin. Teachers will tell you that "morning tune-out" occurs between 10 and 11 A.M., which is one of the most difficult times of the day for children to learn. A better breakfast could help.

If your morning rush hour is like ours — sleepy children and busy parents — you probably can't imagine sitting your family down for a balanced breakfast. Here's an alternative from the Sears family kitchen, a smoothie I developed after months of experimenting. It has just the right balance of complex carbohydrates, proteins, fats, fiber, and calcium, yet it's tasty enough that our children will drink it. We call this School-Ade:

> 2 cups of milk or soy beverage
> 1 cup yogurt
> 1 tbsp. flax oil or 2 tbsp. flaxseed meal*

Because fiber steadies the absorption of carbohydrates, and therefore contributes to a steady blood sugar, flaxseed meal provides the healthy fat calories, plus fiber, but gives the mixture a more grainy texture, unlike flax oil, which has a smoother consistency.

SCIENCE SAYS:

Breakfast affects how children behave and learn.

Here's a big bowlful of what recent research has shown about brainy breakfasts:

- Breakfast eaters generally earn higher grades, pay closer attention, and manage complex academic problems better than breakfast skippers.
- Breakfast skippers are more likely to show erratic eating patterns throughout the day, eat less nutritious foods, and binge on junk-food cravings.
- Children who eat a breakfast containing calorically equivalent amounts of complex carbohydrates and proteins tend to perform better academically than children who do not eat such a balanced breakfast.
- Children who eat high-calcium foods for breakfast (e.g., dairy products) show enhanced behavior and learning.

1 banana
½ cup each of one or more of your favorite
fruit, frozen (e.g., papaya, blueberries,
strawberries)
1 serving of a multivitamin/multimineral
high-protein powder (chocolate or vanilla)
1 tbsp. peanut butter

Blend until smooth. Serve immediately after
blending, while the mixture has a bubbly
milkshake-like consistency. This recipe makes
about 32 ounces (enough for one adult and a
couple of small children). Enjoy!

Optional ingredients:

1 serving of soy protein powder
4 ounces of tofu
1 tbsp. oat bran or wheat germ
Whatever else your child needs to eat but
won't can often be disguised in a smoothie.

6. Give Your Child a Right-Fat Diet

Low-fat diets are not for children. Most adults
in our country need to cut back on the amount
of fat in their diet, but this doesn't mean that
parents should start counting fat grams for their
children. Growing brains and bodies need fat,
but they need the right kind of fat.

How much fat at what age?

During the first year, infants need to get around
40 percent of their daily calories from fat. Science
has learned this from studying the composition of
mother's milk, in which 50 percent of the energy
is in the form of fat. For most children and teens,
30 percent of their daily calories coming from fat
is enough. For adults 20 to 25 percent is plenty.

Right fats versus wrong fats.

The best fats for growing bodies and brains are
those that are high in omega-3 fatty acids.

These fats are actually considered "health
foods" in Asian cultures. In fact, the intellectual
benefits of breastfeeding have been attributed in
part to the amount of these healthy fats in human milk, particularly the omega-3 fatty acid
called DHA. Research is beginning to show
that some children with learning and behavioral
problems have omega-3 deficiencies.

Here's a guide to what fats are best to eat:

Best fats

- Fish (especially cold-water fish, such as
  salmon and tuna)
- Flax oil and flaxseed meal (ground flaxseeds)
- Vegetable oils (olive and canola oils)
- Seeds (sunflower and pumpkin)
- Soy products (soy milk and tofu)
- Nuts
- Avocados
- Peanut butter
- Wheat germ
- Vegetables

Good fats (eat in moderation)

- Yogurt
- Milk
- Eggs
- Lean beef and poultry
- Cocoa butter

Bad fats (little nutritional value, but lots of potential harm to your health)

- Hydrogenated (or partially hydrogenated) fats
- Lard
- Tallow
- Cottonseed oil
- Hydrogenated shortenings

Foods that add right fats to your child's diet

- Fish, such as salmon and tuna, at least two
  times a week

- Tuna fish salad made with canola oil, mayonnaise, and hard-boiled eggs
- Peanut butter sandwich on whole-grain bread
- Sunflower seeds (for children over three — small children can choke on them)
- Flaxseeds and nuts (for children over three — small children can choke on them)
- A tablespoon of vegetable oil as a dressing
- Flax oil (include in smoothies)
- Avocado and yogurt dips
- Hummus (a spread made from pureed chickpeas and olive oil) in salads or as a spread on whole-grain bread and crackers

7. Take Your Child Shopping

The supermarket is one giant nutritional classroom. Take advantage of it. Our children have enjoyed playing nutrition games in the supermarket, which not only keeps young shoppers occupied, but gives them small, frequent feedings of good nutritional information. Here are some of our favorite games:

Color games. Send your children on a color-finding mission down the produce aisle. Tell them to pick out two yellows, three greens, and two reds. Concerning fruits and vegetables, the more variety of colors, the more balanced and healthy their nutrition. Teach children that the deeper the color, the more nutrients there are in the food, such as deep green spinach instead of pale iceberg lettuce and pink grapefruit instead of white grapefruit. Talk about the nutritional value of the *yummy yellows* and *great greens*.

Find the missing word. Our eight-year-old, Lauren, loves to play "find the missing word on the label" game. She would learn to read bread and cereal labels and notice that the missing word was *whole* — as in whole grains. She would then find the breads or cereals that contained whole grains as the first ingredient. These were the "good words."

Find the bad word on the label. Lauren learned that *hydrogenated* was a bad word on cereal boxes. Soon she realized there was one aisle in the supermarket that we "just don't go down." That was the "hydrogenated" aisle full of all the "bad fats." She could then associate the hydrogenated aisle as a bad aisle and the "grow food," or produce aisle, as the good aisle. Take a stroll down the "bad food" aisle and notice all the fake fat (partially hydrogenated oil) in many of the packaged goods. Manufacturers add this factory-made fat to foods because it is cheap, has a long shelf life, and has a oily mouth feel that makes children want to "eat more than one."

In the supermarket, we learned to shop the perimeter.

8. Feed Your Child's Immune System

Good nutrition can boost a child's immune system, and poor nutrition can weaken it. Nutrients that are important to the immune system include

- *Vitamin C.* This nutrient increases the production of infection-fighting white blood cells and antibodies. Good sources of vitamin C are sweet peppers, guava, chili peppers,

---

DR. BILL'S FAT ADVICE FOR TEENS: Eat More Fish and Fewer Fries.

Because of pressures and worries about body image, adolescents often cut way back on fat in their diet, but they also cut out healthy fats. Other teens — the junk-food generation — eat too much unhealthy fat and not enough of the right kind.

SMART IRON

Studies have shown that infants and children who have prolonged, untreated iron-deficiency anemia score lower on tests of mental and motor performance. Iron is an important nutrient for growing bodies and brains. The best sources of iron are breast milk, iron-fortified formula, beef and poultry, seafood, lentils, beans, potatoes with their skins, pumpkin, tomato paste, iron-fortified cereals and pasta, prune juice, tofu, and dried fruits (apricots, figs, peaches, raisins, prunes).

papaya, strawberries, kiwi, oranges and orange juice, cantaloupe, grapefruit, and broccoli. It's better to get vitamin C from foods than from supplements, since when you take a huge dose of vitamin C in the form of a supplement, most of it will be excreted in the urine.

- *Vitamin E.* Good sources are sunflower seeds, vegetable oils, almonds, peanut butter, wheat germ, tomato puree, avocados, peaches, oat bran, and whole-grain fortified cereals.
- *Beta-carotene.* Good sources are yellow-orange and dark green fruits and vegetables: dried apricots, sweet potatoes, carrots, cantaloupe, peaches, pumpkin, kale, winter squash, and mangos.
- *Zinc.* Best sources that children will eat are zinc-fortified cereals, seafood (such as crab and oysters), beef, turkey (dark meat), and beans.
- *Omega-3 fatty acids.* Rich sources are oily fish (such as salmon and tuna) and flax oil. (See also page 103.)
- *Selenium.* This mineral found in seafood, whole grains, vegetables, egg yolks, poultry, sunflower seeds, and nuts can boost infection-fighting cells.

Feed fantastic phytos.

Phytonutrients are the chemicals that account for the color in fruits and vegetables. We tell our children that the same "phytos" that keep the plant healthy help keep our bodies healthy. Phytos help cells repair themselves by stimulating the release of protective enzymes. Phytos fight infections and prevent cancer. They boost immunity and contribute to the health of all the vital organs. Phytos are another great reason to encourage kids to eat fruits and vegetables. Sometimes we would ask our children, "Have you had your phytos today?" — meaning an array of colored fruits and vegetables.

HEALTH FOODS

These family foods are our top twenty picks for their health-promoting nutrients:

- Almonds
- Blueberries
- Broccoli
- Cantaloupe
- Chili peppers
- Flax oil, flaxseed meal
- Kidney beans
- Lentils
- Olive oil
- Papaya
- Pink grapefruit
- Seafood (salmon, tuna)
- Soy foods
- Spinach
- Sunflower seeds
- Sweet potatoes
- Tomatoes
- Turkey
- Whole grains
- Yogurt

Top phyto foods are soy foods, blueberries, broccoli, cantaloupe, chili peppers, flaxseed, garlic, pink grapefruit, red grapes, sweet potatoes, tomatoes, and watermelon.

Avoid sugar overdose.

Junk sugars (e.g., table sugar, icings, cookies, and pastry fillings) can depress immunity. Eating or drinking 100 grams (25 teaspoons) of sugar, the amount in two and a half 12-ounce cans of soda, can suppress a child's immune response system. Complex carbohydrates don't do this.

Reduce stress.

Stress hormones also depress the immune system. Ever wonder why your child gets sick *after* an episode of family or school stress? His body can't fight germs as well after a tough week at home or school. Ongoing and unresolved stress is especially hard on the immune system.

9. Model Healthy Eating Habits

The food you buy, your children will eat; the food you serve, your children will eat; most important, what you eat, your children will eat. You are your child's first nutrition teacher, and you make your biggest impression with your example. Studies have shown that children are quick to pick up on their parents' eating habits.

I knew my child was learning a lot about healthy food when she complained that the sandwiches I packed in her school lunch were so healthy that her friends wouldn't trade with her.

The "we" principle that parents use to shape values applies to nutrition as well. (See the use of "we" in behavior shaping, p. 230.) When your child complains that you never buy white bread like her friends' moms do, simply say,

"We eat whole wheat bread in this family," "We eat more fish than hamburgers," or "We eat our salad before dessert." This lets children know what you expect from them and what the norm is in your house. Your child is going to be exposed to less-nutritious eating habits at school, restaurants, and friends' homes. She may experiment with these foods as she becomes more independent, but at least she'll carry with her the nutrition model she learned at home. Chances are, she'll follow it at least some of the time.

We've gotten a lot of mileage out of the term *grow foods*. Children as young as four can learn that "grow foods" are good for the body and that other foods do not help them grow as well. Four-year-old Matthew, a child in our pediatric practice and the child of a "pure mom" who seldom lets her child eat junk food, sadly said to his mother one day, "I'm worried about my friend next door." "Why?" his mother asked. "I'm afraid she's going to get sick, because she doesn't eat her grow foods like we do in our home."

KEEP CHILDREN EXERCISING

Many American children are overfed and underfit. The National Health and Nutrition Examination Survey (NHANES) covering the years 1988 through 1994 showed that older adolescents eat too much and, more disturbing, that children don't exercise enough. The researchers felt that not getting enough exercise is a greater contributor to childhood obesity than overeating. Why are children less active than they used to be? A lot of it has to do with the change in the ways children entertain themselves. TV watching, video games, and computer time burn a lot less calories than playing baseball or working at an after-school job. In fact, television has a "double whammy" effect on kids' weight and fitness. A child's metabolism slows way down when he watches TV, so he burns fewer calories. He also is more likely to mindlessly snack on junk food while watching TV, putting on more weight. (We've found it helpful to put an exercise bike and a mini-trampoline in front of our family television.)

Healthier bodies.

So, are fit kids more successful? Yes, they are — though this should not come as a surprise. Exercise has been called "nature's smart drug," and when done sensibly, all the side effects are good ones. Exercise boosts special infection-fighting white blood cells called "killer cells" and increases the body's production of natural antibodies, which fight germs.

Exercise helps children grow by increasing how efficiently oxygen is transported through the body and into the cells. When the oxygen arrives at the cells, exercise increases the efficiency with which muscles use this oxygen.

Exercise is one of the best ways to stay lean. Exercise helps your body burn fat rather than store it. Like turning up the idling speed on your car engine, exercise increases your resting metabolic rate, causing the body to burn more calories after your workout is over.

You've probably heard the saying "Lift weights to lose weight." There is actually science behind this adage. Exercise builds muscle, and muscle burns more calories than does any other tissue. The leaner you are, the leaner you stay. To avoid injury to growing joints and muscles, be sure your teen has a professionally supervised weightlifting program.

One of the top health concerns among pediatricians is the increasing incidence of Type II (insulin-resistant) diabetes in adolescents. Exercise reduces the risk of developing this type of diabetes because it boosts insulin efficiency and reduces body fat. In fact, exercise is one of the best preventive medicines against this disease, even for individuals who are genetically predisposed to diabetes.

Livelier minds.

Exercise is as good for the brain as it is for the body. It helps kids feel right. Being able to maintain a sense of well-being is the hallmark of successful children. Exercise causes the brain to release endorphins, the feel-good hormones. These natural mood elevators counteract tension and account for the energetic but relaxed feeling most people experience after a workout. Exercise is also a good way to reduce stress. Kids who are fit handle all kinds of stress better — they're happier kids.

Pumping more blood to the brain also stimulates the release of neurotransmitters, the biochemical messengers the brain uses to think. Have a child or a teen whose brain doesn't wake up until mid-morning, hours after she has gotten out of bed? Maybe she should walk to school. That twenty-minute burst of physical activity might improve her performance in her first classes of the day.

Family fitness programs.

Children need at least thirty minutes of exercise a day. Don't assume that your children are getting this much activity during recess and gym class at school. A regular exercise routine (at least thirty minutes a day) gets a person into the habit of being active and feeling good mentally as a result. The wisdom of the body then begins to crave exercise. This is a healthy craving — cravings for nutritious food and a regular exercise routine are the perfect partners for health.

One of the best ways to help your children develop good exercise habits is to get off the couch yourself and be active together. Take family walks, enjoy family dancing, ride bicycles to-gether, or do something else you all enjoy. You want to give your child the message that being fit is fun, that doing something active is better than doing nothing. You also want your child to know that this is how "we" in our family take care of our health. Your own exercise habits are a model for your children, so get moving yourself.

NO SMOKING, PLEASE!

Almost everyone — smokers included — recog-nizes the health hazards associated with smok-ing. But did you know that parents' smoking affects their children's health?

Studies of children born to mothers who smoked during pregnancy have shown that smoking damages growing brains. Such chil-dren are at greater risk for learning difficulties, hyperactivity, behavioral problems, lower IQs, and decreased academic performance scores in school. Though there are no comparable studies of the effects of parental cigarette smoking on brain development after birth, it seems to me that exposure to cigarette smoke during any time of rapid brain development, including the first years of a child's life, has the potential to cause harm. We do know that after birth, chil-dren of parents who smoke have three times the number of doctor visits for respiratory illnesses and ear infections.

Suppose you were about to enter a room with your child and you noticed a sign that read: WARNING! THIS ROOM CONTAINS POISO-NOUS GASES THAT INCLUDE APPROXIMATELY 4,000 CHEMICALS (including carbon monoxide, benzene, ammonia, hydrogen cyanide, formaldehyde, and nicotine), SOME OF WHICH HAVE BEEN LINKED TO CANCER AND LUNG DAM-AGE AND ARE ESPECIALLY HARMFUL TO THE GROWTH AND DEVELOPMENT OF INFANTS. "I certainly won't take my child in there," you would say as you turned around and walked quickly in the other direction. Yet that's exactly what your child is exposed to when he is in a room with people who smoke.

Use the "we" principle.

If you smoke, quit. It's not easy, but you will be giving both yourself and your children the gift of better health. You'll also be setting an exam-ple for your children to follow: "We don't smoke in our family." You don't want your child to grow up thinking that smoking is the norm or that it's glamorous, tough, or cool. Early on, teach your child that smoking is bad (though smokers themselves are not evil). Obviously, children will be exposed to people who smoke cigarettes. Use these occasions as teachable mo-ments and be graphic. Once, when we were sit-ting in a "non-smoking" area in a restaurant (though trying to keep cigarette smoke out of half a restaurant is like trying to chlorinate half a swimming pool), we noticed people smoking in the smoking area. I took this opportunity to explain to my children how smoke affected their bodies from head to toe: "The cigarette smoke gets into the person's lungs and damages them and rots them, which makes smokers cough a lot and wheeze so they can't run fast. Eventually they get cancer. Smoke also damages the heart, leading to heart attacks. It damages the blood vessels, so that smokers get sore legs and can't walk and run as fast."

When explaining health hazards to children, relate them to the effects on their everyday activ-ities. Children, especially adolescents, believe that they are immortal, so the probability of get-ting lung cancer or heart disease in the distant future may not be enough to motivate them to avoid cigarettes now. Include the more immediate consequences of smoking — effect on athletic performance, expense, smelly smokers' breath — to give your message maximum effect.

Reduce your child's exposure to other environmental pollutants.

Do your best to minimize your child's exposure to automobile exhaust; construction dust from house remodeling; and fumes, hairsprays, and other chemicals in the air. While it's well known that these pollutants increase children's chances of respiratory infections, little is known, or appreciated, about the possible effects on growing brains.

WORKING WITH YOUR DOCTOR

Parents and pediatricians are partners in the process of keeping kids healthy. Your child's doctor can be a valuable resource when you have questions about nutrition, development, and the ordinary and not-so-ordinary illnesses of childhood. This is why it's a good idea to schedule regular checkups for your child, starting in infancy.

At well-baby checkups during the first two years, your doctor monitors your child's motor and mental development, along with his growth and health. After your child's second birthday it's wise to see the doctor for a thorough medical examination once a year until age five and at least every two years thereafter. During these exams your pediatrician will be sure that your child's immunizations are up-to-date. He will also discuss your child's development with you, her diet, and her good health habits. If your child needs a pep talk about certain health habits— hand washing, eating more fiber — make the most of the doctor's influence. Tell your child, "Let's talk to the doctor about it at your checkup." After he has talked with your child about

this issue, you can use "the doctor said" as a reminder to practice better health habits at home.

It's important for a child to have a consistent, familiar health-care provider. Regular checkups are a time for establishing a good working relationship between you, your child, and your doctor. Your doctor will be able to do a better job of caring for your child when she is sick if he knows what she's like when she's healthy. Physicians recognize and value parents who work hard at raising good kids.

Lots of children have special needs of one kind or another. (Actually, all children are special, with their own unique needs.) If you have concerns about any area of your child's development, be sure to talk them over with your pediatrician. A physician can refer you to resources in your community that can help you help your child. Consult your pediatrician if your child is having problems at school. A thorough checkup is an important part of evaluating a learning or behavioral problem.

When a child has significant health, learning, or behavioral problems, parents are an important part of the team of health-care professionals and/or educators caring for the child. Working with all these people who seem to know so much can be intimidating for parents, but remember that you know your child better than any of them. They may be experts in their field, but you are the expert on your child. Involved parents who listen carefully, ask questions, provide relevant information, and help develop solutions are the key to getting a child through hard times and back on the road to success. I have noticed that children of parents who practice attachment parenting can overcome all kinds of significant challenges.

At the end of the school year the teacher recommended that our daughter Lauren repeat kindergarten, as she still hadn't accomplished any of the skills needed for first grade. This didn't feel right to me, but I had noticed at home that Lauren couldn't accomplish most of the tasks her elder siblings had been able to do at her age. So I asked for her to be tested further. The teacher and school counselor weren't sure that was necessary, as Lauren wasn't a problem in class.

Her teachers and counselor were shocked when testing revealed that Lauren had severe learning disabilities. We were told that Lauren would need special-education classes the rest of her educational years and probably would never be able to read. Lauren's first day of special ed required her to ride a bus from her previous school to the "special" school. As we watched the children get on the bus, I could hardly breathe. What would happen to my daughter?

Well, let me tell you what happened. Lauren graduated from high school, lettering on the swim team and participating in drama while maintaining a B average. She was mainstreamed in high school, although she always needed additional help. She took her SATs (extended time for disabled students) and was accepted to two colleges. She is working toward her degree in recreation technology.

Most children with learning disabilities as severe as Lauren's also have emotional problems due to their many failures to succeed. Attachment parenting helped us to find ways for Lauren to succeed and feel successful at home and at school. At every assessment (every two years until age twenty-one) her emotional stability and development have been mentioned.

II

NURTURING THE TOOLS OF SUCCESS

In Part One you learned how to get connected to your child. Learning to form connected relationships is the basic tool your child needs for success in life. In Part Two we discuss additional tools for success and how to put them into practice in real life. When a child has learned to trust caregivers and to be sensitive to others, learning to use these additional tools follows naturally. We believe that among these tools, empathy is the most important. A child who is comfortable getting behind the eyes of another person and considering the feelings of that person before he acts will be able to use other success tools more skillfully. He has a head start in making wise choices, living as a moral child, being a responsible child, and being a good communicator. In this section we discuss how to raise children of character, which means helping children develop the wisdom to know what is right, as well as the courage to do what is right — no matter how high the cost.

Becoming success-full doesn't mean your child will lead a problem-proof, mistake-free life, yet by using these tools, he is likely to experience more success than failure. Even when he experiences failures and makes mistakes, your child will learn valuable lessons from them. It's never too late or too early to find ways to get connected to your children, be empathic with them so that they can empathize with others, or teach them how to communicate better and make responsible choices. You may wish you had done some things differently when your child was younger, but try not to worry about it. There are many ways to give children the tools they need to succeed in life. If you've missed earlier opportunities, you have a chance to make up for it now.

7

The Compassionate Child

HOW TO TEACH EMPATHY: FROM INFANCY THROUGH ADOLESCENCE

We have always used the adage "Treat people how you would wish to be treated yourself." We would remind our children that if they witness someone being treated badly, it could just as easily be them.

THANKS TO FAXES, CELLULAR PHONES, voice mail, e-mail, and the World Wide Web, communication these days is lightning fast. Modern parents want their children to be familiar with all of these electronic ways to share information, but high-tech devices cannot do the real work of staying in touch. Human beings need to connect with and understand one another, and how well they do so has nothing to do with buttons, beeps, or the Internet. It has everything to do with compassion and empathy.

The words *empathy* and *compassion* both have roots in Latin and Greek words meaning "to suffer with." Empathy means getting behind the eyes of another person, identifying with him, and understanding why he feels and acts the way he does. Having compassion causes you to help someone feel better because you understand that the person is suffering. Children learn these qualities, necessary for successful re-

lationships, at home. A step up from *sympathy*, which is an attempt to share another's feelings, empathy seeks to understand them.

No matter how well educated or computer-savvy children are, their success as adults will not be determined by these skills. Happiness comes from loving relationships. It is difficult to raise compassionate children in a society such as ours, which puts a high premium on individualism and encourages people to get whatever they can out of life, without regard for others. This "me first" philosophy influences even the simplest interpersonal transactions. A mother in our practice told us that her seven-year-old daughter would check the telephone's caller-ID screen before answering phone calls. "Molly told me she did this in case it was a friend she did not want to speak to." This mother was rightfully concerned about her child's attitude toward others.

The real world may very well reward children for avoiding certain friends. This unkind act may raise a girl's status in the class social pecking order. Ignoring inner nudges to help others leaves a teenager with more time to study or hang out with buddies. It is a challenge to nurture connectedness in a disconnected world, especially when parents' days are already filled with kids, career, chaos, and commitments. Although parents strive to live as compassionate adults, we often fall short of our own ideals regarding empathy, even within our own families. Yet raising kids who care is critically important — for the sake of an apathetic world that desperately needs people who care about more than just themselves and for the sake of our kids themselves. It has been said that we make a living by what we get out of life, but we make a life by what we give.

Setting compassionate goals.

Parents may wonder how to instill the qualities of empathy and compassion in their children. Although at times children show that they care profoundly about others, they are also capable of surprisingly selfish behavior. Some of this goes along with the egocentrism that is a necessary part of a child's developing a sense of self. But what can parents do to shape their children into more compassionate human beings who believe that giving to others is important and rewarding?

Our interviews with parents of successful, caring kids showed us that compassion and empathy are traits parents value and want to instill in their children. These interviews, our own experience as parents, and research on child development all suggest that parents are the first and most important teachers of these core values and that their foundation is laid early in a child's life.

Consider the story a mother tells of a birthday party incident:

During the party my young daughter tripped and hit her forehead on a rock on the sidewalk. Her forehead was bleeding, and she was terribly shaken and crying. I carried her over to a picnic table to cuddle and nurse her, which I knew was about the only thing that would comfort her at this time.

The other children stopped everything and gathered around her. I was fascinated by the different ways the children responded to the situation. Some gathered close and stroked her head, held her hand, and looked upon her with faces expressing such concern and compassion. A couple of the children left the circle to find salve and bandages.

Providing a striking contrast were a few others standing right next to her, with a blank sort of look on their faces. They were nearly shoving each other to get close enough to look at the blood on her forehead, making comments like "ewwww" and "gross."

The difference between their reactions and the responses of the other children was striking. It felt like the scene of an accident, and some of the children were onlookers just staring at what happened, whereas other children were Good Samaritans who stopped what they were doing to help the person in need.

What made the children at this party respond so differently to the same situation? What kinds of previous experiences influenced their reactions? Did the ones who reacted in a caring way learn such behavior from their parents? Probably so. And what about the children who just stood and gawked? What kept them from being more empathetic? What hadn't they learned, or what emotional resources did they lack?

In this chapter we share what we've learned from parents who have raised empathetic, compassionate children. There are no secrets to accomplishing this task, just the hard work of helping children understand others and setting a good example.

PLANTING THE CAPACITY TO CARE: HOW INFANTS LEARN EMPATHY

Plant the seed of empathy in infancy, nurture it throughout childhood, then watch this beautiful

TEACHING EMPATHY AND COMPASSION

- Respond to your child's cries with loving attention.
- Read your child's cues and respond to them appropriately.
- Respond according to your child's unique personality and temperament.
- Understand that children learn life skills through play.
- Point out to your child how others' experiences are similar to his.
- Model caring behavior.
- Encourage children to think about how others are feeling.
- Help children become aware of other people in the course of their everyday lives.
- Teach your child that it's okay — even commendable — to do something appropriate about an unfair situation.
- Correct your child's mistakes and poor judgments with courtesy and kindness.
- Respond to your child's emotions with empathy and sensitivity.
- Discourage judgments based solely on a person's appearance.
- Normalize differences by pointing out how all people are alike in many ways.
- Incorporate cultural diversity in your everyday life.
- Teach children about world social issues.
- Involve the whole family — particularly the children — in volunteer efforts.

You can lay the emotional groundwork. Infants learn to care by how they are cared for. Parents teach the skills needed for empathy by the way they empathize with their baby. Parents who approach their infant as a unique human being, someone with feelings that ought to be respected, are showing their baby how to be compassionate. As they respond to their baby's needs and help him interpret his emotions, they are setting him up to be sensitive to both his own needs and those of others. Being able to empathize begins with an understanding of human emotions. Babies learn about feelings in their first nurturing relationship with Mom and Dad. When baby cries and Mom responds with a tender touch and a caring "there, now," baby learns that distress is followed by comfort, that feeling sad is okay, and that feelings can be mastered and transformed. Baby learns that the world is a compassionate, loving, and predictable place.

Our youngest child, Connor, is only two and already shows a sophisticated level of empathy and compassion toward others. As an example, he and his friend Christian were standing on a chair together. They both fell off; Connor landed on top of his friend. Christian began to howl, and Connor immediately began to hug him, saying, "I'm sorry. I'm sorry." I've never seen a child of two display such concern. I believe that he is this way because he has always been given empathy and love when he cries. He's never been left to "cry it out" in a dark room. He's never been told to "just be quiet" when he cries. His injuries, his pain, his fears, are dealt with sensitively. Since he has experienced such loving concern for his emotions, he has been able to show that same concern toward others.

When an infant receives, he learns how to give. Children who are on the receiving end of sensitive parenting become sensitive themselves. When parents respond sensitively to

trait blossom in adolescence and adulthood. More than any other trait that defines a successful child, the ability to be empathetic is built upon a foundation laid during infancy. Can you really teach a baby empathy and compassion?

their infant's cries, wear their baby and keep her close to them, and understand and respond to baby's noncrying communication, baby learns that people help one another. These are baby's first impressions. This sense of how the world works will become part of her character. Caring, giving, listening, and responding to needs become the family norms, and these qualities become part of the child. This is how parents teach children their first lessons in empathy. These lessons are learned at a time when baby's growing mind and brain incorporate these lessons into her developing personality at the most basic level. Mothers (and fathers, too) who practice attachment parenting (described in Chapter 2) naturally model empathy to their infants by a process called *attunement*, when parents and baby are in emotional harmony with one another. They "feel" for one another.

Parents who are less responsive to their infants are less likely to raise an empathetic child. When a mother or father tries to make the baby conform to rules and schedules, instead of following baby's cues, the child's feelings are disregarded or subordinated to the parent's expectations of "good" behavior. The baby doesn't learn how to interpret the emotions within himself, nor does he know what to do about them. Without these skills that are learned early in life from interacting with consistently responsive caregivers, the child will have difficulty understanding his own feelings and those of others. Also, baby comes to believe that the world does not really care about his needs and that he can't depend on others for food, comfort, or company. His life experience tells him that he is alone in an unfriendly world. To protect his own well-being, this baby or child focuses on meeting his own needs independently of anyone else. His earliest impressions, therefore, are of an egocentric world in which he learns to settle for less and trains himself to care for himself.

The feeling that people should help and care for one another is not built into this child's personality. He might be taught this principle later on, but it will be harder to put it into action then, since the earliest emotional patterns imprinted on his brain tell him to look out for himself first. When a teammate is injured in the middle of a soccer game, he won't feel bad for the other child. He'll worry only about how this incident affects him — the delay in the game, how this affects the team's chances of winning. Fast-forward this child into adulthood and picture him making business decisions. He thinks first of his own career or the company's bottom line, caring little about how the proposed downsizing will affect his employees and their families. This adult person is reaping the seeds of selfishness that were sown in infancy. As long as his own job is protected, the decision feels okay to him. After all, that's how the world works, isn't it?

A child's relationship with the world at large parallels the relationship she has with her parents. In the early months parents are the baby's world. She'll use the information she gathers about this world to understand the larger world she lives in later.

We've always made sure our babies had lots of company, and we didn't ever let them cry. We've always figured that babies cry because they can't talk, not because they're trying to be manipulative or bad. We wanted our children to feel safe in the world.

Even babies younger than one year old seem to have rudimentary neurochemical pathways for empathy. An infant may start to cry when he sees or hears another infant crying. Or notice how a baby cries when seeing his mother cry.

The high-feeling, high-responsive style of attachment parenting may in fact reinforce these empathy pathways in a baby's rapidly developing brain. As we discuss in Chapter 11, empathy is the root of moral living. Criminologists believe that some psychopaths and hardened criminals may actually lack empathy pathways in their cerebral emotional circuits — hence the term "criminal brain."

Over the years I've observed how the quality of empathy stands out among attachment-parented kids. A group of mothers in my practice formed an attachment-parenting support group and invited a Holocaust survivor to come to their meeting to tell her story. After the guest had been around this attachment group for a while and saw how these parents cared for their children and how the kids cared for one another, the survivor concluded her talk: "Because of children like these, this tragedy will never again happen."

GET BEHIND THOSE LITTLE EYES WHEN BABY CRIES

As an exercise in empathy, try to see the world from your baby's viewpoint. Try to imagine the feelings behind those parent-penetrating cries. What is your baby trying to tell you? How your child learns to get behind the eyes of another person depends on how your child experiences you doing this for her. Being sensitive and responsive to baby's early-communication cries is your earliest lesson in empathy.

NURTURING THE CAPACITY TO CARE: TEACHING EMPATHY TO TODDLERS AND PRESCHOOLERS

My nineteen-month-old's little friend was visiting and they were taking each other's toys, as all toddlers do. When the other child would cry after my son took her toy, he would give it back to her and give her a kiss.

Learning to share — an early lesson in empathy.

"It's mine!" These are probably the two words a toddler uses most frequently when playing with friends. *Mine* is a powerful word, one that may be applied even when the toy in question belongs to someone else. Yet understanding what is "mine" and what is not is the first step in learning to share.

Children naturally want to protect their own things, and the toddler's classic refusal to share is a natural reaction. On the surface, sharing is about manners; on a deeper level, however, it is also about simple consideration for others' needs. It is no small task for a toddler to step beyond his own wants and needs to respect those of others.

A young child is unwilling to give up his toys because the things he plays with are almost a part of him. If he lets another child play with his toys, he is not sure that they will still be his and that he will get them back. The process of sharing demands new kinds of emotional and intellectual awareness.

Each stage your toddler or preschooler passes through enhances his ability to share. Let's look at the elements involved in this developmental process:

1. *He has ownership. "It's mine!"* The young child must first feel that he owns things. These possessions are an extension of

him. A child must have this feeling of security in possessing personal items before the giving and sharing process can begin.

2. *His world broadens. "It's yours."* The child begins to realize that not all of his surroundings belong to him. He has a new awareness of others. You hear him begin to repeat phrases such as "Mommy's keys," "Daddy's car," or "Jenny's skates." He understands that some items are "mine" and some items are "not mine."

3. *Time is important. "Mommy, how long?"* Whereas his day used to be an eternity, the child now understands terms such as "for a few minutes" or "while I count to ten." This initial understanding of time enables the young child to part with his prized possessions for short periods — sometimes hesitantly — knowing that the item will be his again.

4. *Friends are vital. "Somebody come and play."* Toddlers and three-year-olds tend to play alongside each other (called parallel play) but seldom play cooperatively together. Older preschoolers begin to desire friendships. As children develop their own social world, they begin to understand the rules that surround concepts such as fair/unfair, giving/receiving, and right/wrong. They learn the give-and-take of social interaction. The young child realizes that although the toy is hers, it may also please her friend. She also understands that the friend will use the toy for a while, and then she will get it back again.

Sharing at this stage of development is evidence of an awareness of others. Children whose needs and personalities are respected when they are small become less self-centered as they get older. Your four-year-old child finds more pleasure having friends and playing together than she does in holding the toys just for herself.

Teaching children to share.

You can't force a child to share, but you can create attitudes and an environment that encourage your child to be generous to others. Keep in mind that in toddler development, selfishness comes before sharing; toddlers need parents to respect what they mean when they say "mine." But you can set the stage for sharing by showing toddlers how it works.

• *Model generosity to your children.* Monkey see, monkey do. Share your "toys" willingly. Tell your child how Mommy is sharing her cookbook with her friend. Share with your toddler: "Want some of my cookie?"

• *Play sharing games.* Our kids loved to play "share Daddy." The two-year-old sat on one knee and the four-year-old on the other, so they could both learn to share me. Take advantage of those snacks that are made to break into four or more pieces. As we gave the snack to our three-year-old, Lauren, we had her break off a square at a time and pass them out to her brothers and sisters.

• *Time-share.* How you settle toy squabbles is an early lesson in teaching children compassion and fairness. If two children want to play with the same toy, set the timer. (Two minutes may be the limit of some children's ability to wait.) When the timer goes off, the toy goes to the second child for the same amount of time.

• *Use elder children as models.* Hand your five-year-old two cookies with the condition that he give one to the three-year-old. The younger child learns from the elder one that giving and sharing is the right thing to do.

SHARING EMOTIONS

A three-year-old is less egocentric than a toddler, and she realizes that there are people in the world who are as important as she is. This budding sensitivity can work to a caregiver's advantage in getting a child to do what's expected of her. Whereas a two-year-old notices her parents' emotions, a three-year-old gets involved with them. An entry from the journal Martha kept when our son Matthew was three years old noted the following event:

I asked Matt to pick up his wooden blocks as part of our daily "kids pick-up time." Matt balked and then I noticed him slyly letting his older sister do all the work. Irritated, I yelled that I was unhappy with Matt's not obeying, but then realized he needed time to reconsider his behavior. I backed off for a few minutes, and Matthew then willingly did his job. As he was picking up his blocks he said, "Do you still love me?" I reassured him, "Even when you cry and yell and disobey, I love you." Matt persisted, "Do you like me?" I answered, "Yes, I like you, but I don't like it when you don't listen and help. I like it when you make the right choices." Job done, Matthew came over, hugged me, and said, "I'm sorry, Mommy." I hugged him back and said, "I'm sorry for yelling." A few minutes later he said, "Are you happy to me?" This is the depth of emotional exchange you can expect between three and four years of age. They really want to make you happy. You will find living with children much easier if you give them many opportunities to please, and acknowledge their efforts.

Learning empathy through play.

Toddlers often demonstrate their understanding of human relationships as they play. Toddlers may first act out generosity by caring for a doll or stuffed animal (a companion who is far more predictable than another two-year-old). Parents can encourage this learning process by entering into the child's play and finding ways to expand upon it. "Teddy's hungry. Would you share your cracker with him?"

As children begin to play with others, they learn how to cooperate. By interacting with others, they learn that friendship requires give-and-take — no one child should be the boss all the time. (If your child is a born leader, be sure she plays with other leaders and not just followers.) They experiment with terms such as *mine, yours,* and *ours.* The child learns that there are benefits to sharing and to being patient. He also learns to cope with frustrations that arise when situations do not go his way.

Setting an example.

During the toddler and preschool years, a child continues to learn about empathy and compassion from the way others respond to him. (Even as adults we continue to learn from the compassion of others.) Yet this learning happens differently from the way babies learn about needs and emotions.

Two important abilities kick in about age three: the ability to *internalize* and the ability to *generalize.* Internalizing means that children make the prevailing way of doing things part of their own inner operating code. The way the family lives out values becomes the way the child behaves as well. Generalizing means that lessons learned within the family are applied to other relationships. If the teacher hugs him and looks directly at him when he talks, the four-year-old may think, "This is how Mommy and Daddy treat me, and they love me, so my teacher must love me, too." If the teacher lets him pass out papers or serve as line leader, he may think, "She thinks I'm important, just like Mommy and Daddy think I'm important when they give me jobs at home." Because of the ability to generalize, your child learns to trust other caring adults as he trusts you.

Home is the first place children practice their empathy skills. The ways we allow children to treat one another, us, their relatives, and even their pets let them know what behaviors we expect them to adopt as their own. Asking children to help Mommy set the table for dinner, pick up the Legos so that the baby doesn't swallow them, or pour food into the pet's bowl conveys the expectation that caring for others is important.

Consider the message you are conveying to your young child when you allow him to scream at his sibling, hit the family dog, or shout at you when he doesn't like the family's rules. Make sure you intervene during these times, firmly and lovingly letting the child know what is appropriate and what is not, emphasizing the importance of caring for others. Let your child see you interact compassionately with his siblings, your spouse, or grandparents who need a helping hand. Of course, busy parents who are called on to fix meals, drive the Little League car pool, clean up spilled juice, spell words out loud for first-graders, and field phone calls from in-laws and neighbors can't be paragons of compassion all the time. We all blow it occasionally. Remember that your children learn from the prevailing attitude in your home — and also learn how to handle mistakes from the way you handle your own.

EMPATHY GAMES

Empathy comes naturally to some children, but others need a bit of parental guidance to help them learn to get behind the eyes of another person. To help your child become more comfortable with looking at feelings from another person's point of view, try these empathy builders:

Switch places. One day your two sons, Jimmy and Bobby, are squabbling and Jimmy says to Bobby; "You're dumb!" Enter parent empathy director: "Jimmy, put on Bobby's hat [place one of Bobby's hats on Jimmy's head], and now I'm going to say, 'You're dumb. . . .' How does that make you feel?"

Imagine that . . . Your child has made his own birthday card for his grandmother. As he shows it to you, help him look ahead: "Imagine that you are Grandma and you are reading your nice card. Imagine how great Grandma will feel after reading your card."

Share feelings. To help your child learn to translate what he does into how others feel when he hurts himself, quickly say, "Ouch!" If he hits his brother, issue a reminder, "Ooh, that must hurt. . . !"

Teaching children that others have feelings, too.

Small children can begin to understand that other people have feelings, too. As children gain knowledge of who they are and how they are separate from Mom and Dad, they begin to move away from a self-centered existence. They realize that other people feel sad, angry, and happy at different times.

The other night, I was upset about something, and my two-year-old son came up beside me. He gently patted my arm and said, "It's okay, Mummy, Thomas is here." He was clearly mimicking all those times that I've comforted him by saying, "It's okay. Mummy's here."

"How would you feel if . . ."

Parents and other caregivers can help a child get behind the eyes of another child and imagine how he feels. Your three-year-old pushes another child and grabs his toy. Enter the parent-referee. Instead of saying, "Sean, give that back and go to your room," Dad tries this approach: "Sean, how would you feel if Jason pushed you and took your toy? You would be angry, and you might not want to play anymore." If a visiting friend is crying because she left her favorite toy at home, a parent might say to her own child, "Remember how sad you were when we went to Grandma's and forgot to bring Bunny? That's how Lindsay feels right now." The parent

is thus able to help the child understand her friend's pain.

Children who have experienced attachment parenting and are securely attached to their parents seem to be more empathetic, apparently following the example of their parents. Nancy Eisenberg, Regents Professor of Psychology at Arizona State University, has demonstrated that parents who respond to their children's emotional needs with acceptance have children who display more compassionate behavior. She has also found that parents who reinforce their children's sympathetic reactions tend to have children who are sensitive and helpful to others.

I was with our son, Michael, who is three years old, on one of his first dentist appointments. While we were in the waiting room, a technician came in and took a little boy about Michael's age back to an exam room to get his teeth filled. His mom waved good-bye and stayed seated in the waiting room, reading her magazine. We could see through the slightly opened door that the boy was beginning to cry and looked very scared. Michael was noticeably disturbed. He said to me that the boy was scared and his mommy should be with him to take care of him. I agreed. Michael then got up and walked over to the mom and said, "You should be with your boy. He is scared. You should go in there and be with him." Michael had a very intent look on his face. He was pointing to the boy behind the door.

The boy's mom said, "Oh, he'll be fine." She then went back to reading her magazine. Michael was looking even more disturbed now. He came back to me and asked me what we could do to help the boy. I sadly said, "Nothing." I explained to Michael that not all parents treat their children the same, that I did not agree with what the mom was doing and I also thought she should be with her son to support him. I told him that our family does things differently than some other families, and what we can do is be supportive of one another in our family. I feel that our attachment-parenting practices influenced Michael's sensitivity in this situation.

TEACHING SCHOOL-AGE CHILDREN TO CARE

We don't allow name-calling in our family. We have explained to our children that it hurts other people's feelings and that we should never choose to hurt another person. When our son was on his first tee-ball team, we watched him demonstrate his compassion one day at a game. A little boy was at bat and after many swings and misses, all of the other kids were making fun of him. Our son spoke up and told them to stop. He said that they should never make fun of a teammate. I could see that even the coach felt embarrassed. From then on, all the kids cheered for one another instead of laughing at their mistakes.

A child's ability to walk a mile in another's shoes increases with age. During the elementary-school years parents can encourage children to stretch their thinking and imagine how other human beings think and feel. You don't have to go far from home for these lessons. In fact, it is difficult for a child to imagine what it must be like to be starving in Africa or even homeless in America. You can start to build children's awareness of others by helping them see the people they meet every day in a different light.

Encourage understanding.

A store clerk who waits on you is rude and short-tempered. Instead of subjecting your child to a tirade about poor service as you walk back to the car, why not encourage compassion by discussing the reasons the clerk may have acted this way? Could she be ill, suffering from a cold or headache? Maybe her child is sick and

she didn't get much sleep last night, or her dog just died. When we teach our children to think compassionately, we open up a whole new world to them, a world full of real people who have needs, pain, and troubles. (Be sure to also explain that there are not always "excuses" for unpleasant behavior — that perhaps the clerk just needs to learn better customer-service skills!)

When the opportunity arises, I try to assume the role of a facilitator, helping my children glean from life's experiences some lesson they otherwise wouldn't glean for themselves.

Encourage empathy.

Make your children more aware of what is going on around them. When you drive by a construction crew working in the rain, comment on how difficult that job must be in inclement weather. When you spot a wheelchair-bound person going the long way around to get into a building, mention how frustrating it must be when there isn't a ramp closer to the front door. Look for teachable moments, lessons from real-life situations that can make an impression on your child.

When your child comes home from school with complaints about another child's behavior, ask her to think about the situation from the other child's point of view. "Why do you think she said that? What made her so angry?" Encourage your child to look beneath the surface. "Yes, so-and-so is hard to get along with. He gets picked on by the other kids so much that he's forgotten how to be friendly. How could you be his friend?" It isn't always easy to empathize with peers, but a child who brings compassion to the classroom or playground can make a huge difference in a classmate's life or in the way the whole group of kids gets along with one another.

My son is fourteen, and it seems like everyone is his friend. Girls call him, boys call him, they all call to talk about their problems. He listens well and seems to understand everybody. Partly this is his generous and observant nature. Partly this is the way he's been treated. I always try to listen to his side of a controversy, but I ask him to tell me about the other side as well. Sometimes when my friends are struggling to understand something about their kids' social lives, I go to my son for insights to share.

◆

When my seventeen-year-old son was in Cub Scouts, he won the Pinewood Derby Race over all the boys in the pack, most of whom were a few years younger than he. As he was handed his trophy, he noticed that the boy who came in second place was crying because he hadn't won. My son got upset and wanted to give the other boy the trophy. He wasn't able to enjoy winning, knowing that someone else was a "loser." As you can imagine, he is liked by everyone he meets.

Encourage compassion.

If Grandma is frustrated by arthritis in her hands (or a schoolmate has cerebral palsy), try this learning technique to help your child understand how others' physical limitations affect their lives. Put a large rubber band around your child's fingers so that it is difficult but not impossible to bend them. Give him a bowl of cereal and a spoon. Ask him if it is difficult to eat with such poor mobility of his hands. Then give him a pen and piece of paper, and ask him to write his name or draw a picture. It's almost impossible! Tell him that those are the limitations many people have. He'll be quick to help Grandma or his schoolmate whenever he can.

I have always taught my children that while people have many differences, they are all human beings to be treated with respect and caring. When my son was at a new school in third grade, he noticed that there was an older boy who was the victim of much teasing. My son came home to me one day and said, "Mum, there is a boy at school who everyone teases because he talks differently." When I asked what he meant, he said, "Well, he has trouble saying the words sometimes." I explained that sometimes people have what is called a stutter, which makes it hard for them to talk. He said, "Mum, his name is Shane, and I like him a lot. He is really nice; I don't care what anyone else says about him. He's my friend." When he said this, tears welled up in my eyes. My son had demonstrated not only that he understood that all people should be treated with compassion but that he would live this.

Encourage children to make a positive impact on the world.

When children have a feeling that something is not right, they look to their parents for clarification and for permission to do something about that feeling. Parents must teach children how to intervene respectfully in situations that disturb their sense of fairness or rightness.

There was a child in our seven-year-old's class who was always getting into trouble, and the teacher seemed to always be on his case. One day the usual troublemaker did a very kind act toward another child. My son noticed this, but the teacher didn't. My child went out of his way to be sure the teacher noticed that the boy who was constantly doing the wrong thing did the right thing.

Like most other lessons in values, this one is first taught at home through example, as parents handle sticky situations. When children are the recipients of gentle corrections and when parents show them courtesy and kindness even when they make mistakes or exercise poor judgment, they learn that there are tactful ways to point out other people's mistakes. Remember, too, that children are listening and watching how you handle difficult situations with others. If you laugh when a friend makes a joke at another's expense, your children learn that this is okay. If you defend the other person in conversation, your children will be more likely to do the same within their own circle of friends.

Teach children to see all people as equal.

At an early age children need to learn that being different doesn't make someone less of a human being. During the elementary-school years children become very aware of appearances and differences between themselves and others. At first this is simply a sign of their expanding awareness, yet the next step may be to attach meanings to those differences. A child who hears a parent or caregiver make derogatory remarks about a person based on gender, color, or outward appearances easily may assume that *all* people who look that way fit the negative description. On the other hand, children readily accept differences in people when parents teach that while human beings may look different on the outside, we are all the same on the inside.

My two daughters have dark skin and black hair; I have a very fair complexion and blond hair. So I am used to people looking at us questioningly. One day we were standing in line at a movie theater and the teenage boy in line behind us kept staring at us. Finally he asked, "Are those your kids?" I have yet to come up with a clever answer to this question, so I just said, "Yes." To my complete surprise, he answered, "Wow. You don't look old enough to have kids." I guess he's from a generation that's more accepting of ethnically diverse families.

Another way to broaden children's view of the world is to provide them with books, toys, games, and movies that show people of different races, ages, genders, and abilities as capable individuals involved in all kinds of activities. You can also expand your child's worldview by visiting culturally diverse places within your community, such as ethnic food stores, restaurants, and theater.

Talk about disabilities.

When a child notices something different about a person and brings it to your attention, turn it into a teachable moment. Suppose you are in the supermarket with your daughter and she says, "That man has only one leg." Don't just hush her up and tell her not to stare. Make a point of acknowledging what your child has seen, and share some insight. "Yes, I see, and he uses a wheelchair to get around. I bet that makes shopping a challenge when he has a lot of groceries to buy." Also address your child's fears: tell her that it's very unusual for someone to lose a leg and that it rarely happens to children. You can normalize awkward situations with your insight and teach your child important values about acceptance and empathy: children need to learn that people with disabilities are just like the rest of us (they go shopping, too) but that they do have challenges to face (being in a wheelchair).

Studies by Drs. Janet Strayer and William Roberts found that the more empathy a child feels for another person, the more similar that person seems. "When we are empathetic with somebody, it makes our dissimilarities similar," says Strayer.

How you talk about people being "handicapped" or "disabled" affects how your child thinks about them. Teach your child that people with disabilities are people first. They are more *like* people without disabilities than they are different from them. Avoid referring to people with disabilities by their medical diagnosis — "the retarded child" or "Grandma's blind friend." This devalues them. Instead, say "the child with Down syndrome" or "Grandma's friend Anna, who can't see." Even *disabled* is not the best of terms. When a traffic reporter describes a traffic jam, you'll often hear that "there is a disabled vehicle on the highway," as if being "disabled" were synonymous with "broken down." People with disabilities are not broken! Try "differently abled"!

My son Benjamin is an eleven-year-old. He loves the Lone Ranger, ice cream, and playing on the computer. He has blond hair, blue eyes, and cerebral palsy. His disability is only one small piece of his life. When I introduce myself to people I don't tell them I'll never be a prima ballerina. Like others, I focus

---

TALKING WITH A PERSON WHO HAS A DISABILITY

Many children feel uncomfortable around a person with special needs because they're afraid they may say or do the wrong thing. In its booklet *Tips for Disability Awareness,* the National Easter Seals Society offers excellent advice on talking to people with disabilities and using People First Language:

- Speak directly to a person with a disability, rather than through a companion.
- Don't be embarrassed if *you* happen to use accepted, common expressions, such as "See you later" or "Got to be running along," that seem to relate to the person's disability.
- To get the attention of a person who has a hearing disability, tap the person on the shoulder or wave your hand. Look directly at the person and speak clearly, slowly and expressively to establish if she can read your lips. Place yourself facing the light source, and keep your hands and food away from your mouth when speaking. Shouting won't help. Written notes will.
- When talking with a person in a wheelchair for more than a few minutes, place yourself at the person's eye level to spare both of you a stiff neck.

- When greeting a person with severe vision loss, always identify yourself and others who may be with you. Say, for example, "On my right is Penelope Potts." When conversing in a group, give vocal cues, such as identifying the person to whom you are speaking. Speak in a normal tone of voice, indicate when you move from one place to another, and let it be known when the conversation is ending.
- Give whole, unhurried attention when talking to a person who has difficulty speaking. Keep your manner encouraging, rather than correcting. Be patient; try not to speak for the person. When necessary, ask short questions that require short answers or a nod or shake of the head. Never pretend to understand if you are having difficulty doing so. Repeat what you understand. The person's reaction will clue you in and guide you to understanding.

Using the above tips helps you sensitively focus on who the person *is* rather than what the person *has.*

on my strengths, the things I do well, not on what I can't do. Don't you do the same? I don't say, "My son can't write with a pencil." I say, "My son uses a computer to do his schoolwork." I don't say, "My son can't walk." I say, "My son uses a walker and a wheelchair." And Benjamin isn't "wheelchair bound." When he uses it he's free to go when and where he wants to go!

We have noticed that connected kids seem better able to see the human beings inside those who are disabled. Different physical appearances do not seem to bother them as much, or perhaps their own self-confidence helps them be more accepting of a wide variety of people.

Don't pass on prejudice.

Prejudice is contagious, and children can pick up on subtle distinctions. They will notice if you avoid contact with a person of a different color at a party or if you refer to an ethnic group using derogatory labels such as "those people." If all your friends and acquaintances are of one race or culture, your words about "all

---

TEN WAYS TO TEACH CHILDREN ABOUT DIVERSITY

1. Explain empathy — the ability to share in another person's feelings. Ask, "How would you want to be treated if you were somehow different from a group of friends?"

2. Check out books from the library that show differences in people — different nationalities, different ages, different abilities. Talk about how boring the world would be if we were all the same.

3. Visit people in a nursing home or rehabilitation center. Talk with these people so that your child sees how much they are like him.

4. Volunteer to help in your child's class and let your child see you hugging and accepting all children.

5. Check out books from the library on different ethnic customs. Talk about them with your child and incorporate a new custom into your next holiday celebration.

6. Check out books from the library on sign language for the deaf. Learn some signs (try "I love you") and use them throughout the day.

7. For younger children, use everyday activities to talk about similarities and differences. For example, make a fruit salad, letting your child help slice the fruit. Talk about the different colors, tastes, and textures of the fruit.

8. Have your child cut out pictures of people from magazines. Talk about the differences — sizes, colors of hair and skin, ages. Affirm that there is enough love for all people.

9. Volunteer your family for a job at a local shelter or other agency that serves the less fortunate. Talk about the people you are helping. Maybe you can get to know one or two families and correspond or meet periodically for lunch.

10. Talk about the diversity in heritage among your family. You might say, "I'm part Dutch, German, Swedish, and Scottish. Daddy is half German and part Scotch-Irish and Austrian. You are part Dutch, German, Swedish, Austrian, and Scotch-Irish."

people being equal" won't ring true. If your children never have the opportunity to socialize with people outside your own ethnic group or culture, they will tend to see others as "outsiders," people who are not like them. Seek out opportunities to get to know people of all races and cultures, because the more you expose your children to the many different types of people in our world, the more likely they will be to accept these differences.

My eight-year-old son, a blue-eyed, fair-haired kid from the suburbs, plays in a Saturday morning basketball league made up mostly of African American kids from the city. He enjoys their unique qualities — the seven-year-old kid who can shoot amazing three-pointers, the six-year-old flashy dribbler. They respect him for his rebounding ability and his height. (In kids' basketball, being one of the taller kids matters.) He's very comfortable on this team. And all the other parents cheer for him, which is great for him.

◆

We have moved around a bit and we've always had friends of many races and beliefs. This has given our children the understanding that people may look different, but this means no more than that — they are all just people with differences.

Begin empathy at home.

You can talk to school-age children about compassion and empathy and they will understand what you mean, but your example is still the most powerful teacher. When you try to get behind the eyes of your children to understand how they feel, you model for them that this is the way people should treat one another. If you make it a habit to talk with your child about why he does what he does, instead of just blowing your top when he misbehaves, he will apply this lesson to other relationships. Talking about

feelings, naming them, and understanding how they affect behavior are valuable life skills, ones that cost thousands of dollars and months of time to learn in therapy as an adult. When you sensitively understand your child's feelings, you help him understand himself. If your child understands himself and knows what it's like to be understood, he will make a greater effort to understand another's feelings.

Practice empathy identifiers.

These are little phrases that show and tell your child that you understand and care about her feelings:

- "Ouch! That must hurt."
- "You must feel very sad that your goldfish died."
- "That really hurt your feelings when your friend didn't invite you to her party."
- "Wow! You must feel happy making an A on that test."

These little phrases will help your child connect with others in the years to come. From your example she'll learn to say, "You must really feel sad that your mom died" or "That was a great effort on that project. You must feel proud!" By teaching your children to recognize and respect others' feelings, you are giving them a valuable tool for improving interpersonal relationships.

Model empathy and compassion.

Watching you care for others, especially their siblings, shows your children how people care for people. One day our youngest child, Lauren, then three years old, was playing with her elder brother, six-year-old Stephen. Lauren hurt her finger — or thought she did. Her reaction went way beyond the seriousness of her actual injury. She held her finger up to me, pleading,

"Daddy, kiss owie!" I realized that this very healthy-looking finger was not the issue. Though my first impulse was to say, "Come on, you're not hurt," I knew that Lauren thought differently and that I had to acknowledge her strong feelings. "Show me where it hurts," I said as I looked into her eyes and then carefully examined her finger.

Stephen watched this scene skeptically. He knew that Lauren was not badly hurt and that his sister was overreacting. Nevertheless, he watched me empathize with her and offer a compassionate response. He learned from my example that we offer compassion to anyone who is hurt — or anyone who feels that she is hurt. We don't make fun of her or call her a baby, because her feelings are real, even if the injury is not. "Let's make it better," I said, and Lauren and I went to the kitchen to get the "boo-boo bunny" (a cloth container for ice cubes) out of the freezer. Stephen came along to help.

Show that choices have consequences.

Children are often egocentric and do not understand that their deeds have consequences for people besides themselves. This is particularly true of impulsive children, those who tend to act without thinking.

One day my eight-year-old son and I were out in the backyard when we saw two ten-year-old boys perched on the hillside next door, ready to toss water balloons onto cars passing below. I nabbed them before their mischief began and sat down to talk with them. I asked them to imagine what it would be like to be driving a car and have a water balloon suddenly explode on the windshield. They needed to put themselves in someone else's driver's seat.

"Jason, what do you think might happen when the water balloon hits the car?" I prodded.

"It would splat all over the car," Jason responded.

"Imagine if you were the driver. How do you think you might feel?" I said.

"I dunno," Jason mumbled.

"Do you think it might scare him?" I persisted.

"Yes. I guess so," admitted Jason.

"He might be so startled that his car could go out of control. The driver might run up on a sidewalk and hit something — or someone. Isn't that possible?"

"I guess so."

"You would feel pretty bad if that happened, wouldn't you?"

I wanted these children not only to find a better target for their water balloons but also to learn to see their deeds through the eyes of others. They had been totally focused on their own immediate fun and had forgotten that the cars they planned to use as targets contained real people.

Besides my desire to protect passing motorists, there was another reason I intervened. I had tried the same irresponsible prank when I was their age. I still remember the driver of one of the cars pulling over and impressing on my eight-year-old mind the potential consequences of my actions. Because this driver took the time to talk to me about the repercussions of childish pranks, I knew I had to do the same for the neighborhood boys.

Model sensitive listening.

Listening is an important ingredient in empathy. Often what people need most, whether they are happy, angry, or sad, is someone who is willing to listen — just listen. This is not a passive activity. Good listeners affirm and reflect feelings as they listen. They ask questions to help them understand what the other person means. Sometimes they offer useful information, but they don't take over the conversation, don't offer advice, and don't try to solve the speaker's problem for her.

Anger overrides empathy. When a person is angry, the nerve pathways for the emotion of anger override those for empathy. Before there can be a transfer of feelings between two people — say, a parent and an angry child — it's first necessary to calm both the angry talker and the angry listener.

It isn't easy for parents who are older, wiser, and more experienced to just listen as a child vents her feelings, but listening is how you show children that you respect their viewpoint, even if you're itching to disagree or fix the problem. Often, letting a child talk enables her to calm herself down or talk herself out of a ridiculous idea. Until she has a chance to talk through her feelings, she probably won't be able to hear any solutions.

In planning a family trip, we had carefully chosen a seat on the airplane for our eleven-year-old daughter, Erin, that would give her a good view of the movie. When she got on the plane, she began complaining because she wasn't sitting next to us. She was truly upset. Martha and I said nothing but listened attentively. As she was winding down, we carefully mentioned, "You can see the movie better from the seat you are in, but one of us will trade with you so that you can sit in whichever place you'd like." She considered her options, and given the face-saving opportunity to make a choice, she chose the original seat with a better view of the movie. She made a good decision because we didn't try to argue with her or impose our ideas on her.

Use similar strategies to help children work through their feelings. Give your child the opportunity to present his whole story. Listen attentively and pay attention to the emotions behind the words he uses. Don't jump right in with advice or scolding. If you are busy mentally constructing your own reply while the child is talking, he'll feel that you don't really care about his point of view. Knowing when not to speak is an important part of good listening. Teach your children how to listen to others by the way you listen to them.

Avoid trying to cover up uncomfortable feelings.

One day Erin's bunny died. She was heartbroken, but I was busy when she shared with me the news about her tragic discovery. "We'll get you another bunny," I said, a lame response to Erin's sorrow. I didn't want to deal with deep feelings. I offered a quick remedy so that I could go back to doing whatever it was I was doing. Later I learned from Martha that besides feeling sad that her rabbit had died, Erin was also feeling guilty because the bunny didn't have enough water when he died. Giving the bunny water had been her responsibility. Though I had missed my original opportunity to help her with these complicated feelings, I talked to her later and helped her work through her grief.

Most parents would rather not have to talk about many subjects with their children. Death, sex, divorce, and money are only the beginning of the list. Yet it's important for children to learn that people can and should talk with each other about even difficult topics. To raise children who feel deeply for others, you have to give them experience with painful emotions as well as joyful ones. Besides, when parents struggle with financial, marital, or health problems, children sense the difficulties and need help in understanding what is happening. When your child is feeling sad, guilty, or angry, don't try to dismiss those feelings. (They won't go away.) Ask your child to share his sadness or his troubles with you, and listen — respectfully and attentively. Similarly, when you are feeling angry

FEELING PROPS

It would be great if you could ask your kids, "How do you feel?" and they would answer honestly and directly. In reality, children often clam up when asked to talk about fears and feelings.

Young children may be more willing to confide in a favorite doll, a puppet, or even a make-believe friend whom they know will listen and not talk back. Parents can use these props as go-betweens. Play puppets with your child and ask him, in the puppet's voice, what he is worried about or scared of. Or ask the child to play both parts and have two puppets, dolls, or stuffed toys talk to each other. Children may express in this kind of play feelings that they are unable to talk about directly.

or worried, explain your feelings to your child in age-appropriate terms he can understand.

Try empathy before explanations.

Empathy includes seeing a problem from the other person's viewpoint. When you empathize, you accept that person's understanding of reality. By dealing with the feelings first, you earn your child's trust. Then build on those feelings.

TEACHING EMPATHY AND COMPASSION TO TEENS

During the preteen and teen years, children expand their empathy and compassion beyond home and friends. They can think and learn about bigger world issues, such as hunger, poverty, and homelessness. What adolescents learn about social issues may shape their thinking for the rest of their lives.

I want my children to know that being concerned about others' welfare and being helpful to those people is part of being a caring world citizen. I try to teach these values to my kids on a practical level. So we began Kids Care Clubs, which provide children with meaningful opportunities to help others in their communities. We call it "hands-on love." I believe most kids have a hunger to define themselves by what they can contribute, not what they wear or what they look like, and it is up to us adults to get them started in the right direction.

Do something!

Teens' pronounced sense of right and wrong, combined with their idealistic view of the world, often makes them determined to change things. "We must do something!" they may say. Older and more cynical adults shake their heads at this youthful idealism, but this enthusiasm for fairness need not be seen merely as a stage to be outgrown. Here is where parents can make a big difference. A parent's response to a child's interest in making things better can either nurture that desire or cause it to disappear.

When John Holland-McCowan of Los Gatos, California, was four years old, he discovered that some underprivileged kids didn't have any toys at all. He cried about it and insisted, "That's not right!" He asked his mom a powerful question: "Why can't kids help kids? Kids can make a difference." He began to save his allowance to buy toys for needy children. His mother, Anne, arranged for him to meet a boy from a homeless shelter and not only give him toys but play with him. When John was five, he was still expressing concern about children without toys or friends, so his mother helped him form Kids Cheering Kids, which organizes young volunteers to play with kids in shelters and pediatric units in hospitals and to tutor children who are struggling academically. Kids

Cheering Kids literature says, "These times of sharing provide the foundation for building relationships; they open eyes and hearts to better understanding, thoughtful communication and to the importance of unselfish contributions to their community."

Eleven-year-old Aubyn Burnside of Hickory, North Carolina, discovered that foster children who were moved from home to home often had to carry their belongings in trash bags. She was dismayed that these children who owned so little had nothing to carry their stuff in. "I thought it was horrible," she says. "I wanted to make them feel special by giving them something of their own to keep. I tried to put myself in their place and think how I would feel." The following year Aubyn, with her family's help, organized an effort to collect, clean, and distribute thousands of suitcases. A foster child who was en route to his seventh foster home was ecstatic to receive two huge sports bags to call his very own. The program, Suitcases for Kids, has now spread to all fifty states and Canada.

Endowed with the fresh perspective of youth, preteens and teens may see solutions to problems that we adults have long since stopped noticing. But awareness is not enough. A child may have the empathy and compassion to help others, but not the knowledge or ability to put his emotions to practical use. That is where his parents must step in.

When a child shows concern about a social issue, it's certainly easier for a parent to express dismay about the situation and then move on to something else without a second thought. A parent who is willing to spend some time and energy can help a child take positive action. Arranging for a child concerned about homelessness to help out at a soup kitchen teaches that child more than television news stories, books, or parental diatribes could. Taking a child who

cares about the environment to a park cleanup event shows him that others share his concern, that they are willing to do something about it, and that when we join forces with others, we can make a tangible difference.

One day I was driving with our eleven-year-old daughter, Erin, when we passed a person on a street corner holding up a sign that read: NEED FOOD. Ah, another teachable moment, I thought. I discussed with Erin why I felt it would be unwise to give this person money and asked her to come up with other ideas for how we could help this person. She suggested that we ask him what he likes to eat and then go to the store and buy him some food. That is exactly what we did, and we both felt good about helping someone in need.

Help your child take small steps.

Rare is the child (and family) so impassioned about a cause that she creates an organization like Suitcases for Kids. Instead, encourage your child to get involved in a variety of causes to remind him that he has a responsibility to contribute to society. A child can take his old jackets to a clothes drive, give toys to charity, and participate in school fund-raisers. All these small efforts come together to help a child define himself in a way that says, "I care about my community and I do things to help."

Demonstrate charity at home.

It's one thing to *talk* to children about making a difference in the world. Putting actions behind those words is quite another. If your idea of public service is donating canned food to the food bank during the holidays, you may be doing your children a disservice. We must convey to our children that *truly* giving of ourselves means more than pulling a couple of cans out of the pantry. Benevolence involves sharing

FIVE GIFTS OF VOLUNTEERING

You've done it. You've convinced your children to spend some time at the local food bank, school fund-raiser, or neighborhood cleanup project. You're proud that they're getting involved in a good cause — and giving back to the community. But you may not realize what they're getting from this experience:

- **The joy of giving.** Children may agree to become involved in a community project because they feel they should or because it sounds fun. Once engaged, however, they discover how wonderful helping someone else feels.
- **A feeling of value.** When children use their skills and talents to help others, their feelings of personal worth and self-esteem grow.
- **Skills for life.** In the course of volunteer work, children gain real-life work experience. They learn new skills and can cite accomplishments and tasks that may help them get ahead in whatever field they pursue.
- **A sense of accomplishment and teamwork.** Whenever a group comes together for a good cause, all participants unite toward a common goal. The group of individuals becomes "we," and each member is accepted and acknowledged as part of the unique family that group has become. Adding her one small part to a project — whether it's a single gift among a large pile intended for needy families or a tree planted in the local park — gives a child an unparalleled feeling of contribution and success. She can feel pride both in herself as part of a group and in her *self*, standing for what she believes in.
- **A feeling of power.** Your child has noticed that there is a need, suffering, or loss. Then he sees that he has in some way made things better. He comes to realize that even one person can make a positive impact on the world and that he has the power to be that one person. Psychologists have identified control over one's environment as a key factor in happiness; a child who learns that he can change the things he sees as wrong gains the key to lifelong satisfaction.

My five-year-old tells me stories of how he helps someone with carrying stuff or giving his last cookie to someone who didn't have a dessert in his lunch that day. He says he gets tears in his eyes when he does nice stuff like that.

We consider empathy the primary tool, a sort of root for all the other success tools. Empathetic children tend to be more moral children. Kids who care tend to experience more social and academic success. Empathetic children are the best communicators since they astutely read what the person feels behind what that person says. Finally, they make better mates. After all, mutual loving is mutual feeling for each other.

time, energy, and money. It means being involved in community organizations, schools, churches, and charities. Parents who volunteer in the community should explain to their children what they are doing and why. Bring them along when there's work to do. Teens like being given this kind of responsibility. (Many high schools actually require teens to accumulate community-service hours in order to graduate.) Make helping out your family norm. And take children's contributions seriously — be it a four-year-old's crayon picture for a child at the hospital or a sixteen-year-old's Eagle Scout project.

We have always found ways to volunteer our time in the community as a family. We've tried to teach our children how to show compassion for other people's needs. We realized what an impact we had made on our children when our daughter donated her birthday gifts to the children who had lost things in the Northridge earthquake in 1994. She was awarded Child of the Year by the Salvation Army, but I believe the greatest reward is that she has become a valuable, compassionate addition to our society.

Stay connected during adolescence.

Teenagers naturally try to establish their independence from Mom and Dad. As they work at this process of individuation, it may seem that they don't seek your understanding and don't much care if they have it. But, of course, they still need parents who treat them with empathy and respect. If you can see the world though your teenager's eyes, you'll be able to communicate with her more effectively and know when something is troubling her. If the two of you have a strong connection, she might just pour out her heart when you ask, "Would you like to talk to me about something?"

Other teens may resist answering direct questions about their feelings. This is especially true of adolescent boys, who often have to downplay feelings in order to maintain their masculine image among their friends. Kids are more likely to open up and talk to you while sharing some other activity, maybe while cooking or cleaning up after a meal or shooting baskets in the backyard. They're more comfortable talking about friends and feelings if they're not in the glare of a parent's concentrated attention. Many parents find that older children and teens will talk to them about all kinds of sensitive subjects while riding in the car. You can't always plan these moments, but you can take advantage of them when they happen!

Kids may not have the language needed to describe what's bothering them, or they may not recognize their feelings for what they are. You can help them acquire the understanding they need to talk about feelings and to understand the feelings of others by describing your own emotions in different situations, by discussing the reactions of characters in movies and television shows, and by talking about the feelings of friends and family members.

The "empathy first, explain later" approach is particularly valuable for older children. Before you can get them to think about their problem in a new way, they first have to believe that you truly understand their viewpoint, even though you may not necessarily agree. Nothing bugs a preteen or teenager more than parents who don't understand and who don't try to understand. But if you want your teen to take empathy and compassion with him into adult life, you must model these qualities for him even during the most exasperating moments of his adolescence.

8

The Ability to Make Wise Choices

"It is our choices, Harry, that show what we truly are, far more than our abilities."
— *Headmaster Dumbledore to Harry Potter, in* Harry Potter and the Sorcerer's Stone

THE HEADMASTER OF HOGWARTS is wise in more than just the ways of wizardry. Making choices — the right choices — is crucial to happiness and success in life, and character is nothing more than the sum of the choices we make. In our busy and rapidly expanding society, daily living presents an almost overwhelming number of choices: some we make consciously and some we are not even aware of. For most people, their happiness depends on the choices they make and on believing that they do, indeed, have choices. Most of the sadness in life is due to making poor choices, or not making choices at all. One of the most valuable life skills you can give your child is the ability to make wise choices.

Children make choices — some that are disastrous — every day, as evidenced by these alarming statistics:

- The leading causes of death in young people ages fifteen to twenty-four are car accidents, homicide, and suicide.

- A study in 1999 showed that 22 percent of eighth-graders and 50 percent of twelfth-graders used marijuana.
- Fifty-two percent of eighth-graders and 80 percent of twelfth-graders drank alcohol.
- Forty-four percent of eighth-graders and 64 percent of twelfth-graders smoked cigarettes.
- Nearly two-thirds of U.S. teenagers reported having had sexual intercourse prior to high-school graduation.

Wise choices, foolish choices, and probably in many cases choices made with little thought or deliberation — these decisions affect the child's life, learning, and relationships and become part of a child's adult identity. Choices show who we are and determine who we become. What's more, our individual choices collectively determine what kind of a society we live in. This chapter is about how to equip your child to live a life of healthy choices.

AGES AND STAGES OF DECISION MAKING

Children learn the decision-making process in stages:

- First, they learn that they have the capability to make choices and that making choices makes them feel important.
- As they practice decision making, they discover the joy of making wise choices, and the difficulties and sadness that follow unwise ones.
- With freedom comes the responsibility to make wise choices.

Younger children can apply these developing skills to simple, everyday decisions. Just recognizing that they have the ability to make a choice helps children begin to make good decisions. "Do you want to wear your red shirt or your blue one?" you ask, showing both to the deliberating two-year-old. Most children make these early decisions based on impulse and ever changing notions about what they like. The toddler doesn't really have the ability to think these minor decisions through, but she's practicing. As she gets older, she'll learn to recognize when she has a choice in front of her and she'll be able to make more important decisions for herself. Here's how you can help your child develop good decision-making skills as she matures.

Respect baby's first choices.

A baby who is just a few days old can communicate a preference. She knows that she wants to be fed now or that she wants to be held in your arms rather than left lying in her crib. When you honor a baby's first choices, you give her positive feedback about her ability to make her needs known. You're also telling her that she has control over what happens to her.

Consider the process of starting your baby on solid food. You sit with a wonderful little bowl of rice cereal and another one of mashed bananas. Your baby's eager acceptance of the bananas tells you that he's enjoying them. However, when he turns his head away or spits out that bland rice cereal, he is saying, in the only way he can, "Thanks, but no thanks." Don't scold your baby for making a mess; respect his right to decide what he likes.

Playtime is a good time to offer your baby choices. Instead of just popping a toy of *your* choice in his hand, hold up two different items. Watch your baby's facial expression, where his eyes linger, and which toy makes him smile. Even if he's too young to reach out and grab the toy, he is still communicating a preference. Be sure that when you play with your baby, you give him many opportunities to lead the games.

Respect toddler choices.

As a toddler's world begins to expand, she begins to assert her independence. Within her home she discovers that her clothes, food, and bedtime stories are increasingly subject to her preferences, though Mom or Dad may have the final say-so. She begins to decide which bugs to chase and which ball to kick and in what direction. As she matures she takes more control over her life, enjoying the power of her free will, simple though her choices may be. Wise parents allow their young ones to make some small decisions in order to satisfy their growing desire for autonomy. You can offer kids opportunities for choice in many arenas. Milk or juice? Toast or cereal? Red pajamas or blue ones? You zip it, or shall I? *Goodnight Moon* or *One Fish Two Fish Red Fish Blue Fish*? Blocks or cars? Slide or swing? Walk to the car or hop? By offering your child choices in these small daily events, you help her learn how to think critically about her actions. The more practice she has now, the easier it will be for her to make bigger, more important decisions later in life.

Another huge advantage of offering young

children choices is simply this: they love it! Children, like adults, thrive in environments where they feel they have some control over their lives. They feel capable and important, which builds self-esteem. Even a three-year-old child needs to feel in control of her life; she needs to feel she has some say over what happens to her, especially in bodily functions such as toilet training.

Make choices for your children until they are able to make choices themselves.

Obviously, little ones can't have choices about everything. Spitting out rice cereal is one thing, spitting out a spoonful of medicine is another. But when parents must make a decision for a child, it's wise to explain the *why* behind it so that children learn from parents' actions. Being calm, firm, brief, and gentle with these explanations communicates the thoughtfulness behind a decision, even to a child who is not yet verbal. Children derive a sense of security from trusted authority figures' helping them make wise choices. Too much freedom overwhelms a growing child; it won't teach good decision making. By setting limits and providing simple explanations, children learn about what is right and wrong, what is wise and what is foolish. Provide parameters within which children can make choices that are acceptable. By making decisions for them and then with them, parents teach children what they need to know to guide their independent decision making.

With our children, we have used *reminders* as a tool to prompt them to make wise choices. These cues get a floundering child back on track. A reminder may be something as subtle as a look that tells the about-to-go-astray child "You know better" or a gentle verbal cue that makes a child more aware of his actions: "Where does that bike belong?" Reminders put

the child on track to make a better choice. They also establish a pattern of association within children's minds so that they learn to remind themselves — and need less outside help. (See "Remind + Rewind," p. 46.)

Little children, big ideas.

If you want your children to be independent — or, a better term, "self-dependent" — you must respect the choices they *do* make. Children often have grand ideas, and when Mom or Dad shoots those ideas down as being impossible or foolish, they feel deflated, the magic goes out of their world, and they hesitate the next time they are called on to be creative. Responding to these grand ideas with enthusiasm and support encourages creativity while helping children develop their ability to think. Respecting a child's ideas reinforces the belief that she really can affect the world around her. Children must believe this if they are going to make good decisions in the future.

Thomas is only three years old but is able to reason things through, and we encourage this. He often says to me, "Mummy, I have a plan!" Usually it is something very reasonable indeed, and even if it isn't, I treat it with respect and thank him for thinking of it.

Decisions for School-Age Children

There are many different *areas* in which elementary-school children can make their own choices. The small, daily maintenance issues are great places to allow children to practice their decision-making skills, such as food, clothing, and playtime activities. Within these areas there are a variety of *ways* to give children choices. You can give simple options, both of which are acceptable to you: "Cereal or toast?" "What do you want to do first, your homework or the dishes?" "Do you want to clean up your room now or after lunch?" You can offer choices of *how* something can be done or *where* it can be done.

To help our children make wise decisions in their lives, we have always given them the freedom of choice. They make their own decisions regarding a number of things: who their friends are, what activities they do away from home, how they will approach a large homework assignment. We always discuss possible consequences of their actions and let them know how we feel about what they are doing. But in the end, the decision is theirs to make. As well, the consequences are theirs to learn from.

Ignore the smallies; concentrate on the biggies.

Interestingly, when you give your child freedom to choose, you may find yourself facing some difficult decisions about your child's freedom of choice. Ask yourself this question: What is the worst thing that can happen if he makes the wrong choice? If the consequences are minor, something that you can live with, then let your child make his own decision. For example, if your child wants to choose his own clothes for school, what is the worst thing that can happen? Perhaps he'll choose to wear shorts and a T-shirt on a rainy, cold day. What would be the result of that? He may get chilly on the way home from school. Can you live with that? Probably you could, so allowing the choice of apparel would be acceptable. When you can live with several options and the result of a poor choice is not disastrous, it's a good time to tell your child, "You decide."

If they want to get a really dumb haircut — let them. (Hair grows back.) A dirty sock on the floor won't kill you. (Wearing dirty socks to school will encourage them to use the hamper next time.) Earned *money spent foolishly teaches a good lesson. (Don't just give them more money.) None of this is life-threatening, but having your child grow up to be a person who can't make a reasonable decision as an adult — now that will break your heart.*

As parents of eight children, we define *discipline* partly as doing whatever we need to do to *like* living with our children. One thing that has saved our sanity is dividing children's misbehaviors into *smallies*, nuisances and annoyances that are not worth the wear and tear of getting upset about, and *biggies*, transgressions that include hurting oneself or others, showing disrespect, and otherwise acting in ways that demand we intervene. We selectively ignore the smallies and regard them as childish irresponsibilities that will self-correct with time and maturity. This leaves us plenty of energy and authority to focus on the biggies, choices of real consequence. (The more you practice selective ignoring in the early years of a child's life, the more prepared you will be for the challenges of the teen years, when you will be called upon to ignore a lot: sloppy clothing, unconventional hairstyles, annoying music, moody behavior, and a phone permanently glued to an ear. In an otherwise good kid, these are all smallies.)

HELPING YOUR CHILD DEVELOP DECISION-MAKING SKILLS

As they mature, children become aware that they have free will, which is a powerful tool — and an enormous responsibility. Freedom is wonderful, but children must learn to use it wisely. To do so, they need decision-making skills — and lots of practice. By learning how to make decisions when they are young, children prepare to make good decisions when the stakes are higher, such as in the choice of a college, career, or mate. They also learn skills that help them make wise choices about alcohol, drugs, and sex as teens and young adults.

It's important to understand that children are "works in progress." They have much to learn about life, and many of these lessons cannot be self-taught. As children grow and develop, it is up to the adults in their lives to give them proper direction. It is also up to adults to teach children to evaluate their own behavior to determine if they are making the best decisions.

PRETEND CHOICES

Here's a technique to teach your children when they are having trouble making an important decision. Have them make a "pretend" decision one way or the other and imagine living with that decision for a while. If this decision continues to feel right to your child after a couple of days, then they can make this their real decision; otherwise encourage them to try a different one.

For example, your child is trying to decide whether to participate in summer soccer or baseball. You've helped her evaluate the pros and cons of each sport, but she is still undecided. She needs to make a decision by next week. She makes a pretend decision to "choose soccer." During that week she imagines herself going to soccer practice, playing games, and going through all the other fun — and commitments — of that sport. Each day she remains happy with her decision, so when next week arrives, the final decision is much easier for her.

Here are some of the ways the parents we interviewed for this book have taught their kids to make wise decisions.

We use a Stop/Go paper to teach our children to review their behavior and to grow from the experience. If there is a situation of misbehavior that we want them to learn from, we give them a piece of paper with the top half labeled "Stop." They write in a description of the misbehavior. The bottom half of the paper is labeled "Go." Here they write what they need to learn to do instead. From this exercise, they can improve their actions.

♦

We taught our children to make a decision by counting the negatives on their left hand and the positives on their right hand, and then comparing the two.

♦

I help my child learn to make wise choices by giving him the chance to practice in big and small ways. Sometimes he makes good choices and other times not, but I think the more practice he gets, the more likely he is to make better decisions. When there is conflict, we talk about the choices involved, since this is a way to help him learn how to make wise choices. He can see that with behavior, there are always choices. For example, he can continue to talk back after being asked to stop, making a situation worse; or he can reevaluate the conflict and find a more respectful way to solve it. It's always his choice, and more often than not, he makes the wise choice. I think helping my child make wise choices is one and the same as helping him learn to be responsible.

♦

I have always helped my daughter make choices by pointing out her options. The middle-school years gave us some wonderful opportunities because of peer pressure. Many of the girls in her school dressed very well and often purchased expensive clothing. We didn't have unlimited funds to purchase all the latest fashions. I gave my daughter a choice when shopping for school clothes. I would give her a clothing allowance: she could buy one pair of really expensive jeans and then have only one pair of jeans, or she could purchase less expensive jeans and have enough to purchase two pairs of jeans with money enough to add two shirts. She realized quickly how she could look good and have more for her money. We always guided her in her decisions in this way. We would point out the positive things and the negative things but allow her to choose. Sometimes our positive approach to choices gave her the room to make some poor choices, but now, at age twenty-two, she has demonstrated that she has learned how to make good life decisions.

Use problem solving to teach decision making.

When a child faces an obstacle or a major decision, it's a great time to teach him the following formal problem-solving procedure. Though it might seem much easier and quicker just to provide a solution to his problem, involving the child in the process of finding a solution teaches important life skills. Here's what to do:

- Sit down with your child in a quiet place where you won't be interrupted. Have a pad of paper, pen, snacks, and something to drink.
- Begin by defining the problem as specifically and unemotionally as possible.
- Brainstorm and come up with as many solutions as you possibly can. Write them all down — the reasonable and the not-so-reasonable.
- Review the options, discussing the possible outcome of each one.
- Decide together on the best course of action and set a plan.
- Follow through to make sure the plan is carried out and that it works as effectively as you both hoped.

When our children are faced with a dilemma, we discuss the issue and provide them with examples of how things will turn out if they choose certain pathways. We encourage them to review all their options before making a final decision. We also make them aware that life is not always fair and therefore help them to develop the ability to be accepting when things don't always go according to their plans.

Encourage children to ask questions.

As children experience life, they will have questions about what they see and hear. When parents encourage children to voice these questions, and then take the time to answer them, children gain information they need to make future decisions.

Children's questions may often seem silly or unimportant, but each one means something to the child who is trying to put into place one more piece of the puzzle. When Mom or Dad says, "That's a good question," the child lights up inside: his thoughts are valuable and he's on the right track, thinking things through. Honest, age-appropriate answers provide a child with facts that he can add to his personal data bank. All the little pieces and parts of life are added together to create a complete picture of who he is and how he fits into the world. As children absorb more details, they are able to make better decisions.

Think out loud.

At times, a child asks a parent a question and the parent makes a decision after thinking it through. The child benefits from hearing the thought process the adult uses to arrive at the decision. When the ten-year-old asks, "Can we go out for dinner tonight?" Mom might respond, "I don't know. Let me think. We just went out for lunch yesterday, and I bought that hamburger that's sitting in the refrigerator. If we go out tonight, the hamburger might spoil and that would be a waste of money. But I suppose if I put it in the freezer, we could save it for Thursday. Hmm. Except Thursday we are having Grandma over for dinner and I don't think there's enough for her. Maybe when we're out, we can stop at the store and buy more hamburger. Okay. Let's go out tonight."

As you can see, a child who hears this monologue learns a lot more about the decision than if the parent answered with a simple yes or no.

Think through what you're about to do.

We believe these seven words portray one of the most valuable lessons in life. Impulsiveness is the enemy of good decision making, and most children are impulsive (at least at times). Teaching your child to "think through what you're about to do" is like installing an alarm system to warn against impulsive behavior. At first, children see only the tempting behavior — striking the match and setting a piece of paper on fire, climbing on the countertop to get the cookies down from the top shelf, riding the bike on the smooth surface of the street instead of the sidewalk, with its bumps and curbs. They don't think about what might follow these actions — a fire that can't be put out by an eight-year-old, breakables that tumble off that shelf to the floor below, cars that don't see kids in the street. You won't always be right there on hand to stop your child from trying out these tempting behaviors. You have to teach them thinking skills ahead of time. Tell your child to "push your 'pause button' that causes you to think before you make a fool of yourself or make an unwise decision."

This means that when you're lighting candles for a dinner party or lighting the barbecue fire, you talk to your six-year-old about the dangers of playing with matches. You don't just

say no; you give him reasons for why children are not allowed to play with fire. You talk about what you are doing to safeguard yourself and your house from fire. You tell and show your child how he could hurt himself using matches or a lighter. Maybe when he's a little older, you supervise as he carefully lights the candles on the birthday cake. Someday, when a group of kids tries to entice him into a match-burning episode out in the driveway, he'll recall everything you've told him about the consequences and will decline. You've given him the information he needs to think through what he's about to do. You have modeled thoughtful behavior for him.

Example is the best teacher. If my children are about to make a bad decision, I ask them, "What might happen if you do that?" When they respond, I continue, "Is that a good thing or a bad thing?" Then follow up with "So, should we do that or not?" Most people these days don't seem to ever think about the consequences of their actions. I don't want my children to be that way.

Fast-forward to this same child as a teen who has been taught in similar fashion about the temptations and consequences of using drugs. He's offered some marijuana at a party. Even though adolescents are notorious for focusing mainly on immediate gratification, he is able to refuse, because he knows that this behavior has consequences that extend beyond a few minutes of euphoria.

Teach children that choices have consequences.

One of the most lasting ways to immunize your child against bad choices is to let him experience the natural consequences of his actions. Experience is the best teacher: when a child is careless, she falls down; he leaves his bicycle in the driveway, it gets stolen; when she doesn't finish her homework, she misses her favorite TV show. Wise parents protect their children enough so that they don't get seriously hurt but do not overprotect them to the extent that they don't learn the consequences of their folly.

I reinforce the choices he makes and point out where we might have done something differently. For example, if he tries to fill up his cup and it spills on the carpet, I might say, "Next time we should keep that cup in the bathroom and put the lid on in there, so it doesn't spill." Later, when he does make that wise choice, I tell him what a great idea it was and point out how and why he was successful.

Expect children to make unwise choices on the way to becoming responsible adults. Children, like adults, must experience the consequences of their actions to learn from them. Let your toddler explore, fail, bump, and learn — within reason. Some bruises and scrapes along the way are both unavoidable and educational. Expect your preschooler to help clean up his messes. Don't interfere when your school-age child must suffer the penalty for not completing his homework on time. Experiencing the natural consequences of their behavior is an effective way for children to learn about the importance of making good choices. Consequences teach children to be responsible for their own behavior. After years of small inoculations of consequences, children gain at least partial immunity against bad choices.

Children learn better from their own mistakes than from your preventive preaching. When they are allowed to make their own mistakes in small matters, they can learn valuable lessons that will enable them to make better big decisions. By the time your child is an adoles-

cent, the consequences of wrong choices become more serious. The child who has learned from mistakes made as an eight-year-old is more likely to be successful with decisions made at age sixteen. (This child may also be more willing to listen to advice from sympathetic adults.) As a parent, you must strike a balance between overprotecting your child and being negligent, between guiding your child and allowing him to be independent.

We help our children make wise choices by avoiding the temptation to run interference when they make mistakes. They learn a lot from small mistakes, and I think it has helped them avoid making big mistakes in their teenage years.

The overprotected child enters adolescence unable to handle frustrations and risks and too scared to make choices. Many parents are so intent on protecting a child from poor decisions that they make all of the decisions *for* him. The child never gets to exercise his decision-making muscles. When he eventually heads out into the world, weighty decisions bombard him at every turn and he is often unable to respond without making mistakes. We've all heard of people who wasted their first year or two of college making frivolous choices, some of which ended their college careers altogether.

On the other hand, the child of parents who grant too much independence too soon may feel as if no one cares. Sometimes the wisest solution is to state your opinion and offer some guidance but then back off and let the natural consequences of a decision show your child whether she made the right choice.

Make the most of teachable moments.

When your child makes the wrong choice, turn the experience into a teachable moment — an

CHOICE VERSUS CONTROL

Controlling parents can cripple a child's ability to make choices, yet not helping a child to develop decision-making skills is like sending a child out to sea in a boat without a rudder and without sailing lessons. Rather than controlling their children, wise parents think in terms of shaping their children's behavior. Here's a way of understanding the difference.

A wise parent is like a gardener. The gardener can't control the characteristics of plants in the garden — things such as color or when a flower blooms. Yet the gardener can pick weeds, prune the plant, and fertilize so that it will bloom more beautifully. There are flowers and weeds in every child's temperament and personality. Throughout this book we give you "gardening tools," which are techniques we call *shapers,* that we have learned in our years of parenting and from interviewing parents of kids who turned out well. Years of shaping help children build self-control, the ability to make their own wise choices.

With the controlling type of discipline, children behave more out of fear of punishment than out of the desire to please.

As a result, they develop few inner controls. Once the controllers' backs are turned, the controllees are out of control. These children grow up lacking the inner discipline needed to motivate and control themselves.

Controlling parents often perceive a more sensitive style of discipline as "losing control" or "feeling manipulated," or they protest that they are "giving up their authority." These parents confuse being in charge with being in control. Instead of trying to control children, wise authority figures shape situations in order to make it easier for children to learn to control themselves. (See related section on setting limits and providing structure, p. 44.)

The phrase you frequently see in headlines — KIDS OUT OF CONTROL . . . — does not mean that the parents didn't control their children but that the children never learned to control themselves. Instead of trying to control the child, wise parents will "control," or rather limit, the choices the child has, while leaving the child in control of the final choice. Give a child a list of wise choices and leave the rest to the child. It's a win-win situation.

opportunity for learning. We call these experiences teachable moments because real-life experiences are great opportunities to learn lessons that will have a significant impact on a child's future behavior. When a child learns something primarily through experience, he gains in-depth understanding. Parents can build on this by calling the lesson to his attention.

How do you take advantage of a teachable moment? Don't scold. Resist the temptation to say, "I told you so," or "If only you had listened

to me." Otherwise, your child will shut you out, because you've made a point of reminding him that you are smart and wise in the ways of the world and he is not. Instead, be sympathetic as you talk over the situation and gently point out (or ask him) what he might have done differently.

When our children make poor decisions — smallies — we often play the "rewind" or "replay" game. For example, you tell your child not to run on slick, rain-soaked pavement; he refuses to heed your warning, falls, and bruises his bottom and his ego. Take your child by the hand and in a caring way say, "Let's replay that!" or "Wait a minute! Rewind!" (Children understand the concept of "replay" or "rewind," from pushing buttons on the VCR.) Then take the child by the hand, walk backward, and then forward, slowly, *around* the puddle. You're giving the child the opportunity to compare his decision and the consequences with the choice recommended by someone older and wiser. He'll figure out which one is easier on his body and him.

At other times it's best to let the consequences speak for themselves: the child spills her soda and there is no more soda; she insists on wearing her favorite sweater even though it's eighty degrees outside and she's uncomfortable; she snubs a friend and the friend snubs her back. Most children learn from these consequences without your saying a word.

Positive consequences also leave impressions. The child who takes good care of his hand-me-down bicycle gets a new one for his birthday. The child who finishes her homework on time gets a star. Be sure that your child receives lots of appropriate positive reinforcement. Positive consequences usually have a more lasting impact than negative ones. By letting children experience both good and bad consequences to their actions, you encourage them to take responsibility for their behavior.

Take advantage of lessons the media offers.

Not everything in the media is bad. In fact, newspapers, television, and magazines offer many opportunities and much raw material for teaching children about the power of wise choices and foolish ones. When you read an interesting article, share it with your child. Talk about the choices made by the person on the television show, and ask your child why she

thinks that character made that particular decision. Talk about the alternatives and hypothesize what the outcome would have been had the person chosen a different path.

We talk about news or magazine articles that bring poor life choices to the forefront. We talk about how the choice will affect the person's life. I think our kids take pride in knowing that they understand the long-term influences of these bad choices and are happy knowing they have a handle on it before they run across a similar situation. We teach from the very beginning that life is real. Sometimes that means being left out, forgotten, ignored, not winning the prize, coming in last. We teach our kids to look to the future. There will always be other times, other contests, more chances to practice.

Teach that bad decisions aren't the end of the world.

All of us, no matter how sensible or wise, make bad decisions sometimes. All of us face problems. When our kids make poor choices, they often feel stupid or foolish. Teach them that human beings are not infallible and that all people make mistakes — and through these mistakes, we grow and learn.

I've taught my children that choices do deserve forethought, but that no matter what one decides, every day is a learning experience. Character development comes through experience. To do the best with one's life requires a willingness to make changes and to stand strong against the crowd. We encouraged our children to keep an open mind and not rush into decisions. Each time a child encountered a challenge, we would point out any real dangers we might want to warn them about and then encourage them to go ahead and try, if they felt it was the right choice. If they should fail, our role was then to help them pick up the pieces and start over. They always knew we were there when they needed us, but each of them found their own inner resources and ability to solve problems, no matter how daunting. They are now dealing with the next generation in the same way, so we have a host of brave young grandchildren doing their part to build the world.

We send a message about perfection to our children every time they err. If you find yourself jumping in with a negative comment such as "Why can't you be more careful?" or "I told you not to do that!" you're telling your child that mistakes are bad, that he should have known better, and that he should never fail. On the other hand, if you encourage your child to clean up his mistake, find a solution, and move forward, you send a more constructive message of hope. You tell your child, through your words and actions, that he is normal and that he can learn valuable lessons through his mistakes — lessons that will benefit him in the future.

I always try to be a positive person, even in the face of adversity, and have set this example before my children. If something bad happened, I would say to them, "When life gives you lemons, make lemonade," or "When God closes a door, he always opens a window." I would teach them to smile and shrug off problems. Now when the kids have disappointment to deal with, they are more apt to look for the rainbow instead of complaining about the rain.

Teach that choice is a privilege.

Particularly in the United States, we live in a world rich with freedom. Many of us take for granted the options in our lives. We should teach our children to appreciate the wondrous opportunities they have.

I'm a mother of a child with severe disabilities, so I have learned that choices are a privilege. Not *everyone has a choice. Many children with disabilities are limited to what choices they can make in their lives.*

TEACHING THE MORAL DIMENSION

Parents of successful children have told us that they did not try to control their children's choices. Rather, they taught their children from an early age to evaluate all possible courses of action, look at the consequences, and consider the effects on themselves and others. When making decisions, children should also be encouraged to consult their own developing "moral compass."

Teach "inner listening."

Each human being has a conscience that influences behavior and choices. Sometimes we listen to that inner voice, and sometimes we choose to ignore it, but no matter what we do, it is there. Children begin to develop that inner voice, but they need help. Parents and persons of significance in a child's life exert a powerful influence on what that inner voice says to a child and on whether or not she listens. (See Chapter 11, "Raising a Moral Child.") A well-developed conscience signals to a child that she is headed in the wrong direction, as long as she can recognize the signals. Maybe it's a stomachache; maybe it's a cold sweat; maybe it's just a vague, "icky" feeling. In any case, kids must learn to analyze their choices based on these important messages.

Delay instant gratification.

We live in a world that encourages instant gratification: fast food, fast computers, fast travel, easy answers. Parents inadvertently add to the pressure when they grow impatient while a child weighs a decision. Learning to be deliberate in their decisions is of enormous benefit to children, as hasty, impulsive choices often result in bitter endings. This may mean ten more minutes in the toy aisle at the department store, but the long-term gains are worth the time spent. When parents help children learn how to look before leaping, they are giving kids the ammunition needed to fight the war against short-term pleasure and its long-term price.

When my daughter was five years old, I took her to the store with me because she had received birthday money from her grandmother and, of course, immediately wanted to spend it. After I had collected a few groceries, we got in line at the checkout stand and I noticed that she had nothing in her hands. "Weren't you going to buy something?" I asked. "I just can't find anything good," she responded dejectedly. "How about one of these candy bars?" I offered, trying to be of some help. She agreed that it was a good idea and made her choice. But then a very thoughtful look came over her face. Suddenly her eyes lit up, she returned the candy bar to its place on the rack, and said, "I'll be right back!" Soon she returned, her face beaming, proudly displaying a book she found. "Why did you decide on the book instead of the candy bar?" I asked. She explained, "Well, I like candy bars, but it would have made me happy for only a minute. I wanted something that would make me happy for a long time." I gave her a hug as I realized she was well on her way to understanding the eternal nature of true happiness. My daughter is now fifteen years old and I see her continuing to make good choices in her life.

Consider the impact on others.

Thinking through what you're about to do includes considering how your decision will affect others besides yourself. Being able to do so begins with empathy, which we discussed in the previous chapter. When making choices, most people (especially children) first consider how a choice will affect them personally. Yet making moral decisions must also include considering how a decision will affect other people. Helping your child develop empathy — the ability to imagine and understand how others feel — helps her think through the impact of her choices on others. This ability is a valuable life skill, one that is needed for success in personal and professional relationships.

Monitor outside influences.

Children place a great deal of value on their friends' opinions, and many of those friends make bad decisions. Kids watch a lot of television in many households and are easily influenced by the bad decisions so often and so glamorously portrayed. That's why it's important for children to learn that what's wrong is never made right just because "everyone else" is doing it or because "everyone else" thinks it's acceptable. Children need to trust their own inner value system so that they learn how to make the right decisions regardless of what the rest of the world is doing. Parents can help them do so by praising good decisions and reminding kids that sometimes it takes courage and strength to make a right decision, but going along with the crowd is cowardly and weak.

I received a phone call from my fifteen-year-old son who was visiting a friend. He seemed very disturbed about something. He told me that he didn't want to come home right away and didn't know why I wouldn't let him stay longer. Since I had said no such thing, I immediately caught on that something was wrong and headed right over to pick him up. In the car on the way home, he told me that the boy's parents weren't at home and that several of his friends were drinking beer they had found in the garage. I was very impressed with his ability to find a way out of the situation and for keeping his values in the right place. We made a pit stop for an ice-cream sundae on the way home, and I praised him for his smart decision.

The final test of a child's values are the decisions he or she makes. To the growing child, the world is a jungle, and morality is the machete that cuts through it all, though it's not always an easy or light instrument to carry. Morality is another of the necessary tools our children need in order to make wise decisions. We should not send teenagers out into a world filled with risky choices armed with only a few last-minute instructions and some dire warnings. If we expect them to make the right decisions, we must help them learn to judge what is right and wrong. It's also parents' responsibility to provide children with a strong moral example.

LEARNING TO LET GO

Elizabeth says: *I remember one evening when my son, David, was barely five years old. I made a typical request on a typical evening: "David, please go get ready for bed." Ten minutes later I found him in his room, constructing a fanciful Lego castle. Respectful of the creative process, I marshaled some patience and gently reminded, "Honey, please put on your pjs and brush your teeth."*

Twenty minutes later David was still not ready for bed; rather, he was up in his Grandma's room, chitchatting with her about his day. Loudly I implored, "GO! Get ready for bed!" Motivated now, he ran off to his room and I, to mine. After putting on my own pajamas, I looked up to find him standing there in my doorway, his five years of experience flushing his face with confidence. With tiny fists perched on equally tiny hips, David took a deep breath. In a deliberate,

solemn tone, he announced, "Mommy, I want to tell you something. I'm the only one who's in charge of me!"

As I was picking my jaw up off the floor, I saw Grandma standing behind David. By the look on her face — half amused, half horrified — I surmised that she'd heard his proclamation as well. She gathered her wits faster than I could (perhaps owing to experience parenting me?) and began Famous Grandmotherly Lecture #124. "Now, David. Even though you are in charge of your own behavior, there are times when you have to listen to Mommy. There are times when you have to do things in your life, even if you don't want to."

"Well said!" I thought.

"Like when?" asked David. "Well," Grandma began, pausing as an example took shape in her mind, "like when you're riding your bike. If you are going on a road, and you suddenly come to a cliff. You would have to stop."

David's face scrunched into thought briefly before he lit up with a sudden realization. "No," said he, "I might choose to go over the cliff."

As five-year-old David clearly demonstrated, no matter how consistent and effective a parent you think you are, *your child is separate from you.* In the end, he will make his own decisions. Your job is to use every opportunity you have during his youth to teach him how to make good choices — and why. Helping children develop the inner voice that guides them to become capable, responsible people is one of the most important jobs parents have. You are teaching your child to "be in charge of me" in a way that is thoughtful and wise. This is the essence of being a mature adult. Many parents we interviewed showed us that the keys to developing children's ability to make wise decisions are self-respect and love: children

INFLUENCING CHILDREN'S CAREER CHOICES

Although many factors (such as talent, exposure, resources, interests, teachers, and gender) influence a child's career choice, parental guidance and expectations are particularly high on the list. Parents set an example and also offer children some general guidance. Here is what we have done in our family as our children have planned for higher education and careers.

One of the reasons our first three children went into medicine is that they saw that I enjoyed it. They saw excitement and satisfaction in my profession. In fact, many times I would advise them: "Do what you enjoy and what you're good at." I also impressed upon them the importance of having a sense of personal satisfaction, a good feeling at the end of the day, knowing that what you have said and done has made people's lives better. This is what I believe is the true test of a successful person.

Another message we try to give our kids is "Whatever you do, do it well — and be sure that what you're doing is worth doing." We want our children to have higher ambitions than monetary ones. We want them to make the world a better place to live.

Nevertheless, money is important, though we have tried to teach our children that money is a means to an end, not an end in itself. If you make more money per hour, you can work fewer hours to make a living and have more time with your family and your hobbies. Others might choose a less stressful job so that they have more energy left for their family and other interests at the end of the workday. Working long hours or juggling multiple jobs may make ends meet, but it also deprives your family of your presence.

What kind of career teens and young adults choose to pursue is also a determining factor in success. Spending eight hours a day, five days a week, doing something you don't enjoy does not contribute to personal happiness. The fact is that children who achieve higher academic and social success also tend to earn higher incomes as adults. But while having enough money is important to happiness, ultimately it's personal worth, not net worth, that leads to true success.

---

determine their own futures and affect others' as well. A child who loves and respects himself will care enough to make better choices.

Think long-term.

In the daily hum of life, "parenting for the moment" — for the peace, for the quiet — is a dangerous though easily acquired habit. But short-term solutions may not produce the best long-term results. Give a hungry child a cookie shortly before lunch and you may prevent the public temper tantrum — to the relief of all the onlookers at the grocery store. The better long-term decision, however, is to teach the child why he should have lunch first (if he's old enough to learn this lesson) and why some foods are more important to good health than cookies are. You may have to endure the complaining, but eventually, helped along by parental consistency, the child learns to make the right decision, even when it's the harder choice.

We have such a short time to teach our

children the skills necessary for success —
about eighteen years (or less, considering a
teenager's reluctance to listen to parental advice)
in which to demonstrate good decision-making
processes. We have learned that we can't force
children to want to do anything but that they
can learn to determine for themselves why a
given course of action is more desirable than
another. But finally we must let them go — and
hope they'll choose *not* to go over that cliff.

*Destiny is not a matter of chance, it is a matter of
choice; it is not a thing to be waited for, it is a thing
to be achieved.*

— *William Jennings Bryan*

Parent's Action List — Wise Choices

- Make long-term decisions when teaching
  your children.
- Respect baby's first choices.
- Every day give children simple choices.
- Explain the *why* behind your rules.
- Help children evaluate their own behavior.
- Tell your child, "You decide," whenever you
  can live with any of the options available.

- Ask questions to guide your child's thinking
  process.
- Point out the possible repercussions of choices
  by helping kids remember past situations.
- Teach how children's choices affect other
  people.
- Create opportunities to get kids involved in
  decisions about their own lives.
- Help children pause before making a choice
  and weigh the pros and cons first.
- Let your children learn by experiencing the
  consequences of poor decisions.
- Teach your children a formal problem-solving
  procedure.
- Respect children's questions and take the time
  to answer them.
- Talk about what you see on TV, at the
  movies, or in the paper.
- Help kids know that mistakes are normal and
  that they are valuable keys to learning.

Don't take all the credit or blame for the
choices your children make. The best you can
do is to help your children make informed and
responsible choices. The rest is up to them.

9

Teaching Children Communication Skills

S ANY PARENT KNOWS, communicating with children is not always easy. There are days when your child seems to be listening attentively to your instructions, yet later remembers nothing about the conversation. There may be days when your child talks incessantly, then accuses you of not hearing a word she said. Children communicate differently at different stages of development. Your five-year-old chatterbox may turn into a fourteen-year-old who answers your questions with only one syllable: "How are things going, dear?" you ask. "Fine," he grunts. "What did you do today at your friend's house?" "Stuff."

As parents of eight children — some very outgoing — some more reserved, we know that every family has its communication gaps. Children go through stages in which they are very open about their feelings, and times when they are quieter and keep their thoughts and emotions to themselves. But communicating with kids is important all of the time. Staying connected depends on good communication.

Children who are good communicators are more likely to be successful. They will talk — and listen — their way into friendships, a quality education, jobs, and marriage. They will negotiate their way out of jams and into fruitful

relationships. How kids learn to exchange information with others will influence whether they do well in school, whether they make and keep friends, and whether they close the sale or convince Ms. or Mr. Right to say, "I do!"

The way you talk and listen to your children greatly influences how they communicate with others. Parents of kids who turn out well usually communicate well with their kids. Over the years, we have noticed that attachment-parented children speak in a way that conveys sincerity and caring. It's not so much what they say as how they say it and the body language they use. They seem comfortable making appropriate eye contact with adults and make you feel that they are truly interested in what you have to say.

As these children know almost instinctively, communication is much more than just the words that come out of your mouth. Communication is also the body language that accompanies these words. Good communication is knowing when to speak and when to keep silent. It's being able to understand what your words may mean to another person, and to be a good listener. Being able to communicate well is related to other qualities associated with kids who turn out well: self-esteem, empathy, sensitivity, kindness. Poor communicators not only have difficulty getting their point across, they frequently don't understand why they are misunderstood: "I really didn't mean to act that way," pleaded the child whose peers had tagged him as "bossy."

Communication style depends largely on a child's temperament and personality. For some people, communicating is a total body experience — they simply have to move their hands when talking. Some people chat with friends nonstop; others are more selective about what they say. All of these variations in communication style can be effective. How well you communicate actually depends on other factors. Good communicators

1. listen attentively
2. listen empathetically
3. think before they speak
4. also communicate with body language
5. speak appropriately and tactfully
6. practice self-control so that their tongues don't get them into trouble

In this chapter we talk about how connected kids acquire these important communication skills. As with other interpersonal skills, the ability to communicate is shaped first by a child's relationship with her parents. Communication skills are learned at home, beginning in infancy.

THE GOLDEN RULE OF COMMUNICATION:

Talk to your children the way you want them to talk to others.

HELPING YOUR BABY COMMUNICATE

The word *infant* comes from a Latin word that means "a child not yet speaking." However, babies learn about communication long before they can talk. Attachment parenting helps to lay the foundation for good communication already in infancy. Babies who spend the first year in arms, at breast, and in touch with their parents learn that communication is a two-way street. Here's how some of the Baby B's of attachment parenting prime the infant for understanding the complexities of human communication.

Believing in the signal value of baby's cries.

A baby's cry is her earliest language, her earliest communication skill. When caregivers recognize a baby's cries as communication, the baby learns that these cues of hers have value. She learns the basic pattern of communication: "I give a signal, someone responds." Getting a response motivates her to communicate again.

Does this mean that babies whose parents respond to their cries learn to cry more? No. Actually, they learn to cry *better*. Parents' ready responses teach babies that their cries are heard, usually well before the crying has grown desperate and annoying to adult ears. Babies then begin to experiment with more subtle signals — other sounds, body movements, eye contact — to tell Mom and Dad what they need; because Mom and Dad are paying attention, these subtle signals also get responses. Babies' communication styles grow more varied, and so do parents' answers. Even before they are using words, babies develop a rich and interesting language in which they communicate with caregivers. This makes them a joy to have around, which ensures that parents continue to be responsive to their needs.

Sometimes parents are led to believe that responding to babies' cries only encourages them to cry more. Advisers from the "cry it out" crowd who pass along this idea don't give babies enough credit for being able to communicate. Babies whose cries are often ignored may eventually learn to cry less and become "good" babies, but they miss out on important opportunities to develop their communication skills. Because they learn that their cues have little communication value, they clam up. If blessed with a persistent personality, they may keep trying and learn to yell louder — but then caregivers get crabby and may shut out baby's cries completely. These babies do not learn that communication is a two-way street. Instead of sharing their feelings, they eventually learn to keep them bottled up inside.

Elizabeth says: Our lucky fourth child, Coleton, has had an entire family responding to his every call. I remember one day, when he was a newborn, I had put him asleep in his cradle for a nap. A few minutes later his thirteen-year-old sister, Angela, came into the room, carrying him. "Oh, was he crying?" I asked. "No," she responded, "he just didn't look happy." These days, now that Coleton is a toddler, he rarely cries. Even when he wakes from a nap, he doesn't cry. We listen on the monitor as he says the names of everyone in the family — Mommy, LaLa, DaDa, Nenna — until someone shows up. He's learned that someone always responds to him, so he can patiently wait.

When you respond to baby's cues — cries, babbles, or sighs — you are letting her know that these noises correspond to feelings inside of her. How do you respond?

- She cries. You cuddle.
- She fusses. You comfort her.
- She babbles. You smile.
- She sighs. You hold her until she drifts off to dreamland.

Mothers are naturals when it comes to communicating with infants, instinctively adopting the upbeat tones and facial gestures of "motherese." They raise their pitch, s-l-o-w the rate, and E-X-A-G-G-E-R-A-T-E vowels and main syllables when addressing baby. ("Ohhhh, whahhht's wrooong?") Their faces also become more animated. All of these changes help baby focus on what mother is saying.

Mothers talk in slowly rising crescendos and falling decrescendos with bursts and pauses, allowing their babies some time to process each short vocal package before the next message arrives. Though it might seem that talking to a baby is really just Mom doing a monologue, mothers speak to babies as if they are part of a dialogue. Video analysis of the fine art of mother-baby communication shows that mother behaves as if she believes baby is "talking" back. She shortens her messages and elongates her pauses to coincide with the length of the imagined response from the baby, especially when talking to the baby in the form of a question. In these early speech lessons, mother is shaping baby's ability to listen and respond. The infant stores away these patterns and uses them in future communications.

Observe stop signs. It's important to "listen" to babies in addition to talking to them. Listening to a baby involves observing facial cues and body language as well as heeding the sounds baby makes. Even two-day-old infants can give you cues that say they've heard enough. Babies protect themselves against sensory overload by closing their eyes or breaking eye contact. When a baby's expression starts to go blank or she turns her head away, it's time to change communication strategies. It may be time to stop revving up baby and do something more soothing.

Babywearing.

Imagine everything baby hears and observes when held close to mother in a sling for several hours a day. He hears everything she says; he can watch every move of her mouth and every expression on her face. He's intimately involved when Mom talks to Dad, to siblings, or to friends. We have noticed that sling babies are very attentive during adult conversations, their heads moving back and forth as if they were following a tennis match. Early on, baby learns that communication involves taking turns speaking and listening. We have also noticed that mothers who wear their babies in a sling talk to them as they go about daily life, chatting about food purchases while walking through the supermarket or about who wears what as they sort laundry. Mother's chatter makes the unfamiliar familiar and the familiar more fun. It also provides baby with his first language model.

As a speech pathologist, I believe that practicing attachment parenting, especially wearing our babies in a sling, has greatly contributed to our children's ability to communicate. When they were able to sit upright in the sling, they began watching speakers use turn taking to communicate. They learned about expressing feelings such as happiness, sadness, frustration, etc., from the sound of the voices they heard. By viewing the speaker's mouth up-close, they learned to imitate correct speech movements for accurate articulation patterns. Because they had been attachment parented, our children started practicing words and sounds at an early age. When language is developed early, children have the ability to store many more memories at an early age. I believe the sling and other components of attachment parenting are the

reason our children speak so well. Our six-year-old is bilingual and would like to add a third language. He recently told me he wanted to learn French so he could "talk to even more people."

Babies who are worn spend more time in the state of *quiet alertness* (also called *attentive stillness*), the behavioral state in which infants are more attentive to their caregivers and better able to learn from them. Babies who are carried more also cry less, which allows them more stress-free time to listen and learn.

Breastfeeding.

Breastfeeding teaches mothers to read their babies better, since they must watch baby's body language for cues that he's hungry or needs comforting. Breastfeeding helps mothers communicate better with their babies, and mother's sensitive responses encourage baby to communicate better as well.

Breastfeeding has other advantages that relate to the development of language and communication skills. Children with frequent ear infections often experience delays in acquiring language skills, because of the effects on their hearing at critical points in development. Breastfed babies have fewer ear infections and thus are less likely to have hearing problems in infancy. The sucking action used in breastfeeding uses more muscles than bottle-feeding and contributes to better development of the facial muscles, jaws, and palate. The tongue-thrusting action bottle-fed infants use to control the flow of formula can contribute to childhood speech problems. Not only are breastfed babies likely to hear better, they are likely to talk better.

Watching communication skills grow.

Babies' language skills grow daily. Receptive language (what they understand) develops more

EIGHT WAYS YOUR BABY COMMUNICATES

1. Crying to communicate fear, sadness, pain, discomfort, loneliness, and hunger
2. Laughing to communicate happiness, contentment, pleasure, and joy
3. Cooing or babbling to communicate feelings and thoughts
4. Closing his mouth to communicate a dislike for a certain food or that he's no longer hungry
5. Yawning or sighing to communicate tiredness and a need for rest
6. Opening his arms to communicate the need to be held or picked up
7. Fussing to communicate boredom or tiredness
8. Using pre-cry signals (rooting or grimacing) to signal needs

Life gets easier for everyone as toddlers and preschoolers' expressive language skills grow and they begin to use words to tell you what they need. This new skill is entertaining but can also be frustrating as parents struggle to understand just what "ma-moo" or "goo-bah" really mean! Be patient and keep trying to understand. Try to imagine what your child might want to tell you and observe his body language carefully if those funny toddler words have you befuddled. Try getting down to his level and looking into his eyes. Be attentive, nod your head, and make eye contact even when you don't quite understand what your toddler is trying to say. Encourage him: "Tell me again what you want." The more you work at understanding your child's language, the more effort he will put into communicating with you.

Part of learning to talk is trying out different noises and intonations, to give expression to feelings. Toddlers screech and squeal, yell and jabber. Sometimes this is pleasing to your ears, other times it's nerve-racking. Language gives expression to feelings. A feisty "no" from your formerly agreeable child can raise your eyebrows. (Wonder where he heard that word!) Help your child learn words to go along with these emotions: "Oh, Sam is angry," or "You are so excited!"

Giving simple directions.

When parents give directions and their toddler does just the opposite, they often wonder, "Can she really hear, or is she being stubborn or ignoring me on purpose?" On average, at fifteen months a toddler can begin to follow one-step directions, such as "Get the ball" or "Bring the book." Toddlers can definitely understand the meaning of "no" or "stop," but the word alone is not enough to keep them away from trouble. Parents must follow through and remove the child physically from the hazard facing her. Add

quickly than expressive language (what they can say). Between eighteen months and two years, children may say little but they understand a great deal. You can gain toddlers' cooperation by telling them what's going to happen: "Mommy is going to give you a bath," or "Daddy is going to put your coat on because it's cold outside."

At eighteen months, an average toddler has a vocabulary of fifty words. By twenty-four months, the average toddler can say about two hundred words and starts putting these words into sentences of two or more words. By age three, the preschooler's vocabulary increases to about five hundred words, and most of her speech is coherent and understandable. By ages four and five, preschoolers speak clearly and can describe events in long and detailed sentences, though there may still be a few sounds that are difficult to articulate, such as *r* or *th*.

an explanation of why you said no. If she were reaching for a cup of hot coffee, you'd say, "No! Hurt baby," and grab her hand and move the coffee out of her reach. Toddlers have to be told the same thing over and over again. Children younger than two have difficulty remembering rules and generalizing them to other situations. At your house you might tell your toddler that the bathwater is hot, but don't expect him to apply that information to bathwater at Grandma's.

ASK A GOOD QUESTION

What's the single most common answer to the question "What did you do at school today?"

"Stuff."

One-word answers are common in children of all ages and at all stages. How you ask a question can mean the difference between a one-word answer and an extended joyful dialogue. To start a conversation, choose a topic that you know your child gets excited about. Ask questions that require more than a yes-or-no answer. Ask for specifics. Instead of "Did you have a good day at school today," try "What was the most fun thing you did today?" A great way to get your child talking is to base your question on something you already know. This shows your interest and attention to your child's life and encourages him to tell you more. A question such as "Did you finish your clay animals in art class today?" will get your child started on a familiar topic, and will most likely spread to other topics as well.

MODELING COMMUNICATION SKILLS

Communication skills are more easily caught than taught. Children are the world's best mimics and copycats. They say what they hear, and gesture the way they see others move. What comes out of your mouth, the way you use your hands, your facial expressions, and your tone of voice will powerfully influence your child's communication skills in the school-age years. You are your child's first and most important speech teacher.

Narrate your living.

Parents of kids who communicate well make a point of conversing with their kids — even before their children understand them. Don't diaper your infant in silence. Chat about what you're doing and imagine that your infant is listening to you. (He is!) "Now Daddy is going to take off your diaper . . . and pat your bottom . . . and put a nice clean diaper on." You might feel a bit silly talking to someone who can't reply, but you'll soon realize that baby enjoys your running commentary on life — and understands more than you may realize!

Keep up the commentary as your child grows. Tell him about the family's plans for the day or about the sights you see when you're out for a walk. Talk about what you'll cook for dinner or what you're looking for at the hardware store. As your child gets older, your conversations will grow more varied and more interesting. Ask him what he thinks about his new teacher or where the family should go on vacation. One of the rewards of having children of your own is discovering that they make delightful companions. The more you talk and the more you listen, the more you will enjoy each other. Your child's world will expand in these conversations because of what you tell him and because of the way your listening affirms what he tells you. Did you ever notice how some people's children sound so much like their parents? You can bet that these kids with the grown-up-sounding speech spend a lot of time conversing with Mom and Dad.

Use brief sound bites.

The younger the child, the shorter your sentences. Try what we call the one-sentence rule: Put your main point in the opening sentence. It may be the only one your child listens to anyway. The longer you ramble, the more likely your child is to develop "selective hearing."

Many years ago, in preparation for some television shows, I (Bill) took a one-day course on how to communicate. The course emphasized talking in short sound bites — the kind of quotes that are easily plugged into a story on the local news. By the end of the day I thought, "Why, this is just like communicating with children." To keep kids' attention, use short sound bites and an animated way of speaking. Make your point quickly. Ask your child to repeat your request back to you. If she can't, your request was too long or too complicated.

Keep it simple, make it fun (KISMIF).

KISMIF is actually a Cub Scout leader's motto. "Keep it simple, make it fun" is how you hold kids' attention during pack meetings. As a scoutmaster, I found this technique valuable. It's also a useful communication principle. Simple, short sentences are the most effective. Don't use big words. Don't ramble. When children get that glazed, uninterested look in their eyes, they are no longer paying attention to what you are saying. Also, too much talking gives children the feeling that you're not quite sure what you want to say. Consider your child's level of understand-

ing. Instead of asking a three-year-old, "Why did you do that?" try, "We don't throw food!"

Kids love to have fun with words and rhymes. We have found *rhyme rules* a hit in our home: for example, "If you hit, you must sit." To make these rhymes stick, get your child to repeat them. There are lots of other ways to have fun with language when you are communicating with your children. Try a funny accent or a different language, or become a different character.

Speaking comfortably is more important than speaking correctly.

One of the most important speech lessons you need to convey to your children is that communicating is *fun*. A beginning communicator needs to be able to speak naturally, spontaneously, and from the heart. Children's early speech is impeccably honest. As the saying goes, "Out of the mouths of babes . . ." Tact and grammatically correct sentences come much later. There are solid developmental reasons for this, so don't interrupt your child's narrative to correct grammar or even to suggest a more delicate way of stating what is obvious. Correct speech is caught, not taught. The fine points of politeness are best learned from parental example — not parental lectures. However your child talks to you, speak "adult talk" back to him. He'll pick up your cues as his developing brain is ready to do so. Trying to get a child to use consistently perfect grammar too soon can lead to speech problems, such as stuttering, or contribute to a reluctance to communicate at all.

Study your child.

Again, those three magic words of parenting. As your child watches and listens to you, observe her natural way of communicating, her "special something" — the way she gestures, moves her eyes, nods her head, makes facial expressions.

Some persons are in-your-face, eyeball-to-eyeball, hand-on-shoulder communicators. Others are more comfortable communicating from a distance. Encourage your child to develop and refine her own natural way of communicating — one that reflects her own personality — rather than inflicting a lot of rules on her. The more you observe her, the better you'll be able to read her mood and understand the meaning behind her words and manner.

Young communicators show occasional twitches, wiggles, and other quirky mannerisms on the road to refining their communication skills. Kids are like that! If you see a mannerism developing that you perceive could work to your child's disadvantage, help him work these quirks out of his repertoire, mainly by your own example. Drawing attention to the way your child always says "it's like" or "uhhh" will only make him self-conscious.

Address your child by name.

Here's a good communication habit to model for your child: Use people's names often in conversation. When you ask a child to do something, begin your request with the child's name, "Lauren, will you please . . ." When addressing other people, let children hear you use the person's name at the beginning of the dialogue and frequently during it. By doing so, you prevent having to repeat yourself because you didn't have the listener's attention up front. Saying a name first lets that person know you are about to speak to him.

Early in my childhood my grandfather impressed upon me the importance of using a person's name in conversation as a way to convey to listeners that you are interested in them and that they are important enough for you to use their name. Years later this advice helped land me a summer job as a traveling sales rep for the Lipton Tea Company. (It was a time in my life when I was trying to earn tuition for medical school.) I had been one of a dozen candidates, most of them business majors. Later I asked one of the interviewers why I, a pre-med student, was chosen for a sales job. He told me, "Because you used our names in the interview. That made a good impression."

Using someone's name tells him that he is important to you, that he is worth mentioning by name. It's a wonderful way to connect with other human beings. You can also teach your children how to politely learn someone's name. Teach them phrases such as "I'm sorry, I didn't catch your name." Many people don't learn this technique and instead avoid calling their conversation partner anything at all for fear of using the wrong name.

Practice give-and-take.

Give-and-take family conversations let children practice stating their opinions and standing up for what they believe to be true. Some families call this type of communication argumentative. In our home we call it exhausting! But we firmly believe that the family should provide a safe testing ground for children. By asserting their opinions in family conversations, children can test their personal beliefs and learn how to persuade others to their point of view. Children need to be allowed to state their viewpoints during family conversations. This does not mean that you must allow them to follow through on every plan or opinion they propose, but you should be prepared to give good reasons for your decisions. Teach your children that it's acceptable to voice their opinions, and then teach them how to do so politely. It's often the words they choose and their tone of voice that mean the difference between opinion and argument.

Monitor communicators outside the family.

Remember, communication skills are contagious. Your child catches them not only from parents but also from other persons of significance. Set up your child to learn communication techniques from worthy examples. Observe the messages that your child receives from peers, teachers, coaches, etc. Ask yourself, "Are these the messages and communication skills I want my child to use in her life?" A child who often hears discouraging words; loud, angry voices; and inconsiderate put-downs concludes that this is the way people talk out in the real world. Steer her to better role models and draw her attention to what is wrong with what she hears from poor role models.

Talk about undesirable language.

"We don't talk that way!" may be your initial reaction when you hear offensive words or expressions come out of your child's mouth. It's inevitable that your child will pick up speech habits that are less than desirable, to say the least. You can handle the problem in two ways. Try the "we" messages (described on p. 230) so that your child learns that this way of communicating is not the norm and will not be tolerated in your home.

Another technique for combating offensive language is to turn it into a teachable moment. When you and your child are the audience for atrocious language, turn this awkward situation into an opportunity, a teachable moment: "Do you enjoy listening to that person? How does that kind of talk make you feel? What do you think of the person who's talking?"

POSITIVE SPIN: USING "I" AND "WE" MESSAGES

"You'd better do this" or "You should have done that." "You" messages can put a child on the defensive, causing him to argue or refuse to cooperate. "I" messages don't accuse, nor do they imply that the listener doesn't know anything. Instead of "You have to take out the garbage before you go outside to play," try "I would like you to take out the garbage first." Instead of "You never remember to shut the door," try "I am so pleased when you close the back door behind you."

"We" messages (as discussed in more detail on p. 230) imply that the expected behavior is not optional and that it is the family norm or simply the way people behave. Instead of "You need to clear the table," say, "We always clear the table after eating." Instead of "Don't throw your coat on the floor," try "We always hang up our coats." Using "I" and "we" messages turns negative requests into positive ones. Instead of "No running," try "Inside we walk, outside we run."

Another way to turn a negative message into a positive one is to plant an idea in a child's mind and let him complete the thought so that he gives instructions to himself. Instead of "Don't leave your soccer stuff on the floor," try "Matthew, think of where you want to store your soccer stuff."

UNDERSTANDING NONVERBAL COMMUNICATION

Body language often speaks louder than words. The expression on someone's face, the tension in a person's body, posture, even the way a person is breathing all convey meaning. What body language says may reinforce what is being said verbally or can contradict it. Body language is the key to the feelings behind the message. As such, it's an important ingredient in communication.

Families use all sorts of signs, movements, smiles, and gestures to express caring and love. Other signs and gestures express distrust, disgust, and anger. Context matters. Smiling at the wrong time — say, during a heated discussion with your spouse — can cause as much emotional havoc as not smiling when you should have.

Parents and children who are connected are usually very good at reading one another's body language. They may not realize exactly what it is that is telling them that the other person is angry, scared, worried, or excited, but they get the message nevertheless. Here are some of the signs parents and children pick up on:

- downcast eyes
- tight mouth
- lots of eye contact, or very little
- slumped shoulders
- restlessness
- pouting lower lip
- clenched fists
- happy grins
- arms swinging freely from the shoulders
- head tilted to one side
- leaning forward
- pulling away

You'll notice many more body-language cues as you become more consciously aware of the physical and visual aspects of communication. Albert Mehrabian, author of *Messages: The Communication Skills Book* (Oakland, Calif.: New Harbinger Publications, 1983), found that spoken words account for only 7 percent of the information people receive through interpersonal communication; 55 percent of the message is communicated through body language, and 38 percent through the tone of voice. This explains why children are so profoundly affected by the moods and attitudes of their parents, siblings, and other persons of significance. We have learned to apologize for having a "bad day" so the children won't take our attitude personally, such as the stressed look on Mom's face that sends out a message she really doesn't intend.

Talk with your child about body language and help her assess the message she may be sending to others. Explain that the way she sits or stands, crosses her legs, gestures, or smiles while listening affects how the other person perceives her. Poor posture makes her look uninterested. Standing too close makes others feel edgy. A person's facial expression can reflect confidence and conviction or uncertainty and hesitation. An affable, responsive face can be a tremendous asset in communicating with others. Though we can't always control our body language, our real feelings have a way of coming through, whether we want them to or not. Yet there are times when being conscious of body language will help your child put her best self forward.

COMMUNICATING ABOUT FEELINGS

Give children time, space, and the freedom to express their feelings. This is a wise long-term

TALKING TO TOTS

Usually neither parents nor children are conscious of what their body language is saying. But since children are so good at mimicking adults, your example will influence how your child uses his body to communicate. Here are some ways to improve your own body language and provide a good model for kids to follow:

Sign it.

Babies and toddlers often know what it is they're trying to say but are unable to form the necessary sounds to make the word or concept understandable. Teach your baby some simple, practical signs. For example, you might teach your one-year-old the sign for drink (pretending to hold a cup to your lips and tipping it) or eat (fingers drawn together touching the mouth). This will enable her to tell you when she's hungry or thirsty. She'll learn about the power of language, and she'll get to feel more grown-up. Signing with small children is lots of fun. To learn more, see the book *Baby Signs,* by Linda Acredolo and Susan Goodwyn (Chicago: Contemporary Books, 1996).

Connect before you direct.

Before giving children directions, get down to their eye level and engage them in eye-to-eye contact. Doing so gets their attention and lets them know that the information you are about to share is important. Teach children how to focus by saying, "Trisha, I need your eyes," or "Samuel, I need your ears." Offer the same kind of eye contact when listening to your children. Notice that eye contact is usually most comfortable when it is not constant. When speaking, and especially when listening, we tend to look away from time to time and then look back. If you never take your eyes off your child as you are speaking to her, she may perceive that you are trying to control her rather than connect with her.

Legs first, mouth second.

Instead of hollering from the kitchen, "Turn off the TV, it's time for dinner!" walk into the family room, join in with your child's activity for a few minutes, and have your child turn off the TV. Your presence conveys that you're serious about your request, but you also respect what the child is doing. When you yell from another room, you don't really connect with the other person.

Connect physically when speaking.

A hand on her shoulder or an arm around your child's waist lets her know that you care. It's a tangible sign of your attention and will help her relax and say what she needs to say.

Don't forget to smile.

Be aware of your facial expression when you are talking to your child. A smile isn't always the appropriate accompaniment for what you're saying, but most parents could afford to smile more than they do. We are often busy and involved in maintenance conversation (do this/don't do that), usually with too serious a face. A smile conveys the pleasure you feel in your child's presence. Being reminded that parents like to be with them makes kids feel good.

COMMUNICATION STUMBLING BLOCKS

Certain phrases and attitudes are bound to block communication. If you hear these words coming out of your mouth, stop and think again.

Negative thinking	*You'll never be able to do that.*
Personal biases and prejudices	*This is the only answer that works.*
Absolutes	*You always forget to do it. You never . . .*
Clash of positions	*I'm sure this is the best way.*
Rigid expectations and rules	*I do not believe in that.*
Pointless questions	*How many times do I have to tell you?*
Automatic thoughts	*I've heard enough, now drop it.*
Judging, criticizing, blaming	*Isn't this typical of your behavior.*
Assuming the worst	*You two can never get along.*
Moralizing	*I told you that would happen.*
Threatening	*If you ever say that again . . .*
Ridicule	*You would say something like that.*
Avoidance	*I don't want to discuss it further.*

investment of your parenting energy. If children learn at an early age that they can talk to you about what's bothering them, they're more likely to continue to share their troubles down the road. You may spend a lot of time discussing seemingly trivial matters, but doing so ensures that your kids will come to you with their big, important problems as well. Talking with toddlers requires patience and creativity, even when their problems are small. But what is really frustrating and emotionally draining is a teen who won't share her feelings with you. You worry about what you don't know, and your teen doesn't get the benefit of your adult judgment. Now *that's* a big problem — one that might have been avoided if you had been more accepting of her feelings early on.

Communicating about feelings isn't easy. Sometimes parents' responses give children the impression that it's better to stuff their feelings inside than to share them. When you respond to your children's emotions with anger, judgment, or adult logic, they sense that you don't want to deal with their real feelings, so they clam up. This is a lose-lose situation. Your child misses out on the benefits of sharing feelings with an empathetic parent, and you lose out on opportunities to connect with your child. In the long run, your relationship suffers; your child not only doesn't trust you with her emotions, she doesn't trust herself.

Suppose your child's goldfish dies and he comes to you, holding the bowl with his dead fish sloshing around belly-up. Consider these two responses:

"Well, what did you expect? You haven't cleaned the bowl in two weeks."
"Oh, how sad. You're going to miss Goldie!"

Which response encourages your child to share more of what he is feeling? Which one says that his feelings don't matter? Below are some examples of statements that are "feeling stuffers" and others, "feeling expressers," that encourage your child to tell you more about what she's experiencing.

Women tend to be more comfortable expressing their feelings than men are. A woman with a problem talks about it over coffee with a friend, while a man with a problem goes and watches a football game or works out at the gym. This is why mothers often have an edge when it comes to talking with children about feelings.

Early in our parenting careers, Martha and I responded to our children's emotional outbursts differently. When a child came running to me with a "boo-boo," I would immediately assume my doctor role and make an objective assessment of how badly the child was hurt. This took care of the medical problem, but it was less effective at easing pain and stopping tears. Martha, on the other hand, first tended to the child's emotions. If the child's distress registered a 10 on the boo-boo rating scale, Martha's empathetic response would be equally intense. She would meet the child where he was, then help him calm down. As Martha toned down her response, the child would wind down and soon realize that the scrape was not life-threatening. If the injury turned out to be no big deal in Mommy's eyes, it was not worth wasting energy on and he would go back to his play, happily sporting a Band-Aid.

Logical responses do not take the place of talking about feelings. Children are not logical. You can say that there's no such thing as a monster in the closet, but as long as your child thinks there is, your logical explanation will do no good. Deal with the feelings first and your child will be more likely to trust you when you bring in your logical, adult wisdom.

In healthy families, children discover how to balance those feelings that need to be expressed with those that need to be suppressed. Every little emotional twinge doesn't have to be examined and acknowledged with the same care, but families do need to talk about the big issues. One sign that a family is not functioning well is that there are significant subjects "we just don't talk about." When children suppress feelings about family problems or their own difficulties, bad things happen. They blame themselves for situations they can do nothing about. They lose touch with their own feelings. They worry and feel scared and lonely.

FEELING EXPRESSERS	FEELING STUFFERS
"Are you afraid?" "That must have hurt. I would have cried, too!" "That must make you angry." "Are you feeling lonely tonight?" "Tough loss. You must be disappointed." "I bet you are so excited!" "Ouch! That must have hurt."	"You're being a big baby." "I'm not in the mood to hear you whine." "You are not thirsty [or hungry, cold, etc.], now get to bed." "You are acting like a brat, now be quiet." "You don't need my help." "Stop that crying. You're not hurt."

My husband has been struggling with depression lately, and this is puzzling to the kids. When they ask questions or complain about Dad "acting weird again," I am careful to let them express their frustrations. My husband was yelled at and shamed for expressing angry feelings as a child, which has made it more difficult for him to understand his feelings as an adult. I want my kids to know that it's okay to be angry or sad. Fortunately, they trust me to respect their feelings and opinions, which has helped them stay emotionally healthy through challenging times. Attachment parenting isn't just for perfect families and perfect parents. I think it can be a family's saving grace when relationships are strained or troubled.

Children may not know how to communicate their feelings. When a child stomps her feet or storms off to the bedroom crying, parents know something is wrong, but it may take some digging to find out what.

"It's not fair," shouts the little brother. "I never get to go anywhere."

"Where would you like to go?" says Dad.

"I don't know. Somewhere."

"Your big brother is playing at his friend's house. Do you wish you could play there, too?"

"No, they're stupid!" cries the little brother.

"But you're here all by yourself."

"Yeah, and there's nothing to do!"

"Are you lonely? Do you miss your brother?"

"Yes," wails the little brother. "He's the only one who will play cars with me."

"Oh," says Dad. "Do you want me to play cars with you?"

"No, you don't know how."

"What if we go outside and play catch? We could do that together."

"Okay," sniffles the little brother. "I just don't want to play by myself."

When this child yelled, "It's not fair," his father could have reminded him of all the times he had played at the homes of friends. He could have told him not to call his sibling "stupid." Instead, he kept asking questions and commenting on the situation, trying to think about it from his child's point of view. Instead of telling his son not to feel the way he felt, he helped him explore his emotions until they discovered that he was feeling lonely and left out. Children often cannot answer direct questions about their feelings, but parents can help them interpret what is going on inside their minds and hearts.

Positive self-esteem helps expressiveness.

Communicating well starts with self-esteem. Children must feel that they are valuable and that what they say is worthwhile if they are going to express themselves well. One of the greatest ways we parents can help children learn to express their thoughts and feelings is to let them know that we love and respect them. Children must know that whether they are gregarious or reticent, they are real people and important to someone. A young mother in our practice tells of how making children feel "real" is crucial for self-esteem.

I arrived early at our mother's play group, getting ready to take care of the six toddlers and preschoolers. A four-year-old came into the room with her grandmother.

"Good morning," I said.

The grandmother nudged the tiny girl, "Say good morning, Kristin dear."

Kristin stood with a timid look on her face, so I continued to try to engage her in conversation.

"Would you like to help me put the puzzles on the table?" I asked.

Again Grandmother responded for her. "Oh, yes. Kristin is such a good helper."

Kristin opened the box of puzzles and put one at each place. I decided to encourage communication one more time.

"Kristin." I looked directly at her eyes while I spoke. "Did you bring something to share with your friends today?"

And one more time, Grandmother interrupted her by saying, "Oh, no. Kristin forgot to bring something today."

But as Grandmother was speaking, Kristin's face lit up and she said, "I did bring something!" She reached into her pocket and put some tiny purple flowers on the table. Then she looked up at her grandmother and said, "Grandmother, my teacher thinks I'm real."

Respect your child's viewpoint.

Studies by Dr. Stanley Coopersmith, author of *Antecedence of Self-Esteem* (New York: Freeman, 1997), have shown that children with high self-esteem had parents who were approachable, listened without judging, and respected their children's opinions. What's least important to your child is whether you agree with her. Wait till she's had her say before you offer advice or other options. Reflect for a moment on the people you enjoy conversing with — people who respect your opinion and allow you to state it, even though they may disagree. They will listen and nod, acknowledging that you have a point. By doing so, they get you to respect their opinions as well and perhaps come over to their way of thinking. You're more likely to change a child's mind if you respect her feelings and use them as a starting place for offering advice.

Preteens and teens are particularly sensitive to listeners who pass judgment before they have all the facts. Teens believe that most adults are not interested in what they think. Before you can get through to adolescents, they first have to believe that you truly understand their point of view, even if you don't necessarily agree.

You have to wait for the right moment to talk to teenagers. Watch for openers. If your child is kind of hanging around while you're busy on the computer, he's probably waiting to see if you're approachable. Acknowledge your child. Turn toward him and give him your undivided attention, even if it's for only a few minutes. This conveys to your teen that he and what he has to say are important to you. Even if you can't spend half an hour talking right then, take time out to focus on your child.

Teach tact.

Although you want your child to be able to express her feelings spontaneously and honestly, children also need to learn to be tactful. Tact means knowing the right thing to say (or not to say) to avoid offending another person. In the preschool years children say what's on their mind, and to a certain extent can be allowed to, since they are not able to understand that there are many sides to a situation. Between the ages of five and seven, children are old enough to think before they comment, and it's up to parents to help children be sensitive to the feelings of others. ("If you were working hard to lose weight, how would you feel if someone called you fat?") As children naturally learn to be more empathetic, they usually learn to be more tactful. They will find a time and a place to express their feelings and beliefs without offending listeners.

LISTENING TIPS

Listening is the single most important activity in communication. You can't learn anything new if you are the one doing all the talking. When a parent and child are trying to communicate, they both need to learn about each other. You as a parent should listen at least as much as you lecture. The way you listen to your children tells them how you want them to listen to you and others.

Listen attentively.

Give your child your undivided attention. Keep your eyes on her. Nod your head appropriately, smile when she smiles, and laugh when you're supposed to. Use your facial expressions to let the child know that you understand what she is saying and that you're mulling her words over in your mind.

Listen empathetically.

Good listeners chime in with brief comments that show they are feeling what the child is communicating: "I understand," "Wow! That's tough," "You must really be angry," "That's great."

Listen patiently.

Children can sense when you are not really paying attention to what they're saying or when you're just waiting for them to finish so that you can rush in and fix the whole problem with your advice.

Don't interrupt.

Instead, wait for the child to invite you to respond. This invitation may be in the form of a direct question ("So what do you think?") or other cue that reveals the child is ready for your response (". . . and that's about it").

Listen to the main message.

While someone is talking, mentally underline the main point of the message. Ask yourself, "What's the real issue here? What's the problem?

How can I help?" This is especially important when you are talking to someone who tends to ramble and you're trying your best to figure out what point you're supposed to address. When your teen is done talking, sum up what he has said: "It seems to me your main concern is . . ." You're not only clarifying the issues, you're also demonstrating that you really do understand. This will win you points with your teen!

Allow children to let off steam.

Even when someone is wrong and you desperately want to set her straight, you need to listen attentively, empathetically, patiently, and often silently while the person vents feelings and unloads everything. Let the toddler's tantrum run its course. Let the overdramatic teenager play her scene to the finish. Nothing sinks in when a child is an emotional wreck. Tears enable children to get in touch with their thoughts and feelings and express them openly in an atmosphere of support, without fear of reprimand.

When your child yells, respond quietly. When your child is out of control, it's important that you stay calm and help him manage his emotions. Sometimes letting a person ramble on and on enables him to talk himself out of a ridiculous viewpoint, without your having to say a word. In this case, the child who is upset needs a soothing touch and a caring tone of voice more than he needs your words of wisdom. Once the dust has settled, you can offer additional information or another opinion. People usually aren't ready to listen when they are an emotional wreck.

COMMUNICATING THROUGH TOUCH

Science has shown that human touch is crucial to human development. In the 1940s researchers found that homeless or orphaned infants who were placed in institutions wasted away from the lack of human touch, despite being well fed. Researchers also found that talking, maintaining eye contact, and stroking helped these hospitalized babies grow and mature at the same rate as babies raised in their natural birth families.

Touch helps us be genuine and real with our children. Offering extra strokes and hugs, especially when their behavior is not so lovable, sends a caring message that is felt deep within. A pat on the shoulder, a hug, a firm handshake, or other forms of touching often generate a stronger sense of love and concern than spoken words alone. Touching and hugging are some of the most joyful forms of nonverbal communication. Enjoy these tips:

1. Try hugging your child after you have reprimanded him. Somehow, all the anger you felt toward the child is eased as you hold him close and express your love with a gentle hug.

2. Some children seem to "run" from hugs. Continuing to give and receive this type of affection as they mature can enable them to stay in touch with their true feelings. Find times during the day to give your child a big bear hug. Lift him off his feet! Let him know that it is okay to hug someone he cares about.

3. Kiss and hug your children at regular times throughout the day — when you send them off to school, when they get home, at bedtime. These rituals will help you stay in touch even when life gets hectic or they get older.

4. Enjoy other kinds of physical contact with your kids: tickling, roughhousing, back rubs, stroking their hair, or rubbing that buzz-cut head. Cuddle up on the couch when you watch television or read stories together.

5. Group hugs or family hugs get everyone involved — even that preteen who is reluctant to initiate hugs on her own.

Communicate the rules about "good touches–bad touches." Let your children know that no one should ever touch them in private places — the parts of the body that are covered by a bathing suit. Especially if your child is away from you and in the care of other adults, this point needs to be addressed. Let your child feel comfortable coming to you and talking if he is ever concerned about this subject.

HELPING THE SHY CHILD BLOSSOM

Shyness is a personality trait, not a fault, and it does not have to be a social handicap. Some

---

10 WAYS TO GET INTO THE HUGGING HABIT

1. When the child wakes up — good morning hug
2. After breakfast — "I love you" hug
3. Before school — "Have a good day" hug
4. After school — "I missed you" hug
5. Anytime — big, bountiful bear hugs
6. Before dinner — "Wash your hands" hug
7. After dinner — "I'm glad you're mine" hug
8. After chores or favors — a "thank you" hug
9. After homework — "I'm proud of you" hug
10. Bedtime — "Sleep tight" hug

KIDS' COMPLAINTS

Whining and complaining can grate on a busy parent's nerves. But if your child happens to be a chronic complainer, relax. Complaining is common among children. Of course they complain. They often feel powerless. They must compete with siblings at home and with peers at school to gain adults' favor. Without the opportunity to complain, the child's resentments and hostilities can smolder inside, creating obstacles to healthy communication. The way you handle your child's complaints can help turn complaining into more effective communication. Yes, there is hope for complainers!

Remain calm around complainers.

When your child comes to you with a complaint — whether about a teacher, a sibling, or even you — stay calm (even if you think you might explode!). Don't overreact and allow your emotions to control your response. Remember, this is a learning process for children; the fact that a child is asserting an opinion shows growing self-confidence. Complainers want to think, "I am important, and I have rights, too."

Get to the root of the complaint.

It is important to help the child define the goal of his complaint. Is he venting built-up hostility toward a new baby brother? Or is he calling for a change in his bossy elder sister's attitude? Does he complain when he does not get his way on the playground with peers? Maybe he complains because the school routine is too confining or the teacher is too strict.

Teach him acceptable ways to express his complaint.

If the complaints stem from anger, teach your child ways to "let off steam" in an appropriate manner, such as riding a bike or kicking a ball in the backyard. But if there are valid issues behind your child's complaint, really listen to determine what his inner needs are. Help him learn to state complaints and requests in a way that does not trigger resentment or cause defensiveness in the listener.

Showing empathy is important to change the complainer's style of communication. What underlying emotional needs does he speak of? Does he feel unimportant at home? Ignored or insecure around peers? Is schoolwork too difficult? If you can address the underlying issues, the complaining may go away on its own.

Use the Golden Rule.

Remember the Golden Rule — *Do unto others as you would have them do unto you* — when teaching children about communication. Once you understand what your child is feeling and where the complaints are coming from, engage him in role-play as you teach a more acceptable way to communicate. Teach your child to restate complaints using the Golden Rule as a guide. How does he like to be spoken to by parents? By siblings? By peers? By teachers? Can he reword the complaint so that it calls for action rather than resentment from the listener? Instead of complaining, "Why can't we ever have food I like for supper?" he could say, "I like tacos. Can we have tacos tomorrow night?"

After your child practices acceptable ways to voice an opinion without negative complaining, it is time to make a deal. Tell your child that you will listen to complaints only when they are stated without offending or threatening anyone, then follow through with this rule. When he has a negative complaint, say, "Can you restate that in a positive way that does not put down anyone or make them angry?"

We've learned that if you can patiently follow through with your end of the negotiation, in time children will learn acceptable, nonthreatening, and effective ways to ask for what they need.

people who are shy are simply private, quiet people. They are attentive listeners and exude a welcome presence without saying a word. The world is full of talkers. We need more listeners.

"Shyness" is what attracted me to Martha. We met at a fraternity party during my senior year of medical school. She was standing next to a bunch of my boisterous frat brothers. Everyone was talking but her. She listened. Her eyes met everyone else's. She smiled and made her quiet presence felt. She wasn't outgoing, but she made all the extroverts around her feel comfortable. I thought, "What a nice person to be around." I called her the next day, and the rest is beautiful history. After eight kids and thirty-four years of marriage to a hyperactive husband, Martha is not exactly "shy" any longer. But she's still a great listener who brings out the best in everyone she talks to. Here are some ways you can help your shy child blossom.

Frame your child positively.

Avoid apologizing for your child's shyness, especially in front of him. No one likes to be labeled, and your child will rightly perceive your explanation as a put-down. There are better ways to describe children who don't do a lot of talking. Shortly after Matthew started school, we had our first parent-teacher conference. The teacher said, "Matthew sure is shy, isn't he?" "Matthew is reserved," we explained. Later the subject came up again: "Matthew is very quiet." "He is very focused," we answered. As the discussion of Matthew continued, the teacher soon realized that we saw Matthew's traits as positive. By re-framing Matthew's shyness, we helped her see him in a different light, and during the school year the teacher grew to respect his quiet nature.

Most people equate being shy with having a problem. They believe a shy child must suffer from poor self-esteem. This is not the case. Many shy children have a solid self-concept. They also radiate inner peace, and their quiet ways help them protect their deep sense of well-being. Children like this are some of the most peaceful, happy children ever to live on the face of this earth. They are discerning about friendships, yet once they make a friend, it's for life. They are reserved and warm up slowly to new acquaintances, but once they are comfortable in your presence, they can be charming. They study potential friends to see whether the relationship is likely to be worth the effort. They are just nice persons to be around.

When shyness is okay.

Parents worry when their child is quiet in situations where other children are more outgoing. "Is he just shy, or does he have an emotional problem?" Here's how to tell. The shy child with healthy self-esteem makes eye-to-eye contact, is polite, and seems happy with himself. He is just quiet. His behavior is generally good. He is a nice child to be around, and people are comfortable in his presence. Children who are shy usually become more outgoing as they get to know people better.

When shyness is a problem.

Sometimes shyness is a red flag indicating that a child is struggling with inner problems. These children are more than just quiet, they are withdrawn. They avoid eye-to-eye contact and seem to have more than their fair share of behavioral problems. People are generally not comfortable in their presence. These children are often angry or fearful instead of peaceful and trusting. Some children hide behind the "shy" label to avoid revealing a self they don't like. They retreat into their protective shell and do not develop healthy relationships with others.

Try these shyness pull-ups.

You can't force a child out of shyness, but you can create a comfortable environment that lets his social personality unfold. Go slowly. Pushing a child too far too fast can backfire, and cause him to retreat further into his shell.

Never label a child "shy." On hearing this, the child feels that something is wrong with him and may even act more "shy." If you must use words to describe your child, frame him as *reserved, private, quiet, thoughtful,* and *cautious.*

Ease into strangers. When I meet new patients in my office, I am careful not to come on too strong, especially when I see a child lower her chin to her chest, put her thumb in her mouth, or dart behind her mother. I greet the mother and chat with her. The child takes her cues from Mom and, once I'm a Mom-approved person, soon feels more comfortable talking to me.

Avoid putting the little performer on the spot. The grandparents are visiting and you can't wait to have five-year-old Susie play the piano for them. While it's good to encourage your child's talents, give her advance warning and get her okay before you put her on the spot. Encourage her by focusing on how much Grandma will enjoy her playing — not on the performance itself.

Help him establish who he is. If your child is going to be visiting strangers or relatively new acquaintances, have her bring along a prop, such as a favorite board game, which can often act as a bridge for communication.

Avoid talking for the child. Laura, a private, polite, and approachable five-year-old, and her mother were in my office for Laura's school-entry exam. "Laura, this is *your* special checkup," I began. "Are there any pains or problems you'd like to tell me about?" Within a millisecond and before Laura could open her mouth, her mother interrupted, "She feels . . ." I asked Laura, "Is that how you feel?" Within another millisecond mother interrupted again, "And she also . . ." Soon this became the mother's checkup instead of the child's. The more mouthy the mother became, the more mousy the little girl acted. Her mother would say, "Now, Laura, don't be shy. Tell the doctor what bothers you." When Laura went with a nurse to another room for her immunizations, her mother confided, "Doctor, she's so shy. I don't know what to do." I suggested that if she became more reserved around Laura, her child might become more outgoing. During Laura's next checkup, her mother sat quietly behind her and nodded approvingly yet let Laura talk about *her* concerns.

10

Raising a Responsible Child

A S I LOOK AT MY SON, *now grown into a young man, I have to say that the thing I am most proud of is the fact that he is a responsible person. He achieves good grades at the university, he is a valuable employee at his part-time job, he volunteers tutoring time at our local elementary school, and he is dating a wonderful young woman. After what seems like a lifetime of guiding him, I can, at last, take a deep breath and know that he no longer needs my help. He is on the path to a successful adult life.*

Acting responsibly means:

- doing the right things purely on principle, not because someone else is forcing you to do them
- making wise decisions, after weighing all the options
- holding yourself accountable for your actions
- assuming ownership of your life as a productive member of society

> ## PARENT TIP:
>
> The ultimate goal of all the effort we put into parenting is to enable our children to live without us.

Part of being responsible is being independent, which means:

- being self-reliant and self-supporting
- having confidence in yourself so that you are able to make decisions without constant direction from others

Isn't this what every parent wants for his or her child? Parents of kids who turn out well realize that children learn responsibility in small steps, and healthy independence in adulthood begins with healthy dependence during early childhood. You don't teach children how to swim by throwing them into water over their head. Similarly, parents teach responsibility incrementally over time, helping children build on their success. Here's what we've learned about how parents raise responsible kids.

A RESPONSIBLE BEGINNING

Notice that the word *responsible* comes from the same root word as *response*. Someone who is response-able is someone who is accountable, is trustworthy, and does what is expected of her. In other words, someone who responds when called upon to do something. How do children learn to respond in a responsible way? Children's earliest lessons in responsibility come from parents who are responsive to their needs. Here again the keys to children's success are in parental *responsiveness.* That one quality is at the heart of so much of what we want to give our children and expect of them.

Parents who respond appropriately to their children are likely to raise responsible kids. Why? Responsiveness becomes the norm for their children: people should treat other people in a responsible way. Children whose parents understand and meet their needs are more likely to understand their responsibility to others and to themselves. To grow up learning to feel good about yourself, you must behave responsibly.

We carried our babies a lot and responded quickly to each cry. Despite every negative comment about creating clingy, spoiled babies, we now proudly accept every compliment about how responsible and independent they are. I believe that's because we have always met their attachment needs, so they are now able to move away from us with absolute confidence. Our children have a strong sense of self. I believe that by trusting their cues and responding to them, I am allowing them to blossom fully into the unique people that they are, rather than imposing my ideas of who they should be.

♦

When all of a child's basic needs are met, he feels secure, centered, and self-confident. It is a good foundation upon which to go out and explore the world around him. He becomes independent and responsible on his own time schedule.

In the early months, when babies require almost constant attention from their parents, they seem anything but responsible and inde-

pendent. It can be hard to understand how infants' dependency lays the groundwork for future self-sufficiency, especially when friends and relatives are telling you that "you have to get that baby used to sleeping alone" or "you shouldn't pick him up all the time — you'll spoil him and he'll be too dependent on you." However, when you respond to your baby's cues and cries, you are helping him learn to trust himself. You're affirming his assessment of his feelings and needs. This trust of oneself is the foundation of being trustworthy later in life. Being responsive to your child's cues also shows him that his actions have an effect upon his environment — he's not helpless, he can make things happen.

Toddler self-sufficiency.

"Me do it!" Those three magic words are a signal of a child's growing awareness of her individuality and ability to take care of herself. Wise parents take advantage of this desire for autonomy by letting their children practice their emerging skills as often as possible in a safe environment. Your role as a parent is to function as a facilitator. You're not the one who makes things happen, but you set up the situation so that your child can make things happen. (See meaning of "facilitator," p. 72.)

We let our children try new things and did not relay our fears to them. If the slide was high but they wanted to try it, we would encourage them all the way to the top of the stairs, while we stood close by to rescue them if necessary. It was their willingness to try that we would support. If they reached the top and were stuck, we would encourage them to slide down. If that didn't work, we would climb up the ladder so that we could slide down together, and then repeat the whole scene again! We wanted them to develop a "can do" attitude and know that if they needed us, we would be there. I have children who grew up to be gymnasts, adventurists, rock climbers — and one who wants to skydive!

Encouraging your child to try new things, fall down (safely), and then get up and try again is a lesson in responsibility. The child learns that his actions have consequences. He climbs impulsively and falls. With encouragement, he keeps trying until he learns to climb more adeptly and safely — more responsibly. Through trial and error, he learns that the consequence of not climbing safely is a fall and a bump and that it's his job to keep that from happening.

Babies and toddlers take giant steps toward responsibility and independence as they master their own bodily functions. They learn to sit, crawl, walk, run, jump, and feed themselves. They graduate to learning how to dress and undress, how to brush their teeth, and how to use the toilet. Although you can't force a child to master these skills, you can create the conditions that encourage your child to learn them. Give your child lots of opportunities to experiment with these skills, have appropriate expectations for her, and praise her for each new skill she masters. On their way to feeding themselves, brushing their own teeth, dressing themselves, and using the toilet, toddlers will make plenty of less-than-successful attempts. They will spill juice, get toothpaste all over their pajamas, run through the house naked, and have a few "accidents." Parents of kids who turn out well approach their children's development as an exciting journey from babyhood to childhood to adulthood. They enjoy the steps — and the missteps — along the way, as each new stage brings kids further up the ladder to responsibility and independence.

KIDS NEED CHORES

Chores develop a sense of responsibility. When we asked parents about teaching responsibility, almost every one mentioned chores as an important component of how their children learned to be accountable and helpful. Getting their children involved in household chores started during the preschool years. Expecting children to be responsible for certain tasks helps the child believe in herself (see Chapter 12, "Eleven Ways to Boost Your Child's Self-Confidence") and provides early lessons in responsibility. Here is just a sampling of the many comments we collected:

When our children were young, we would start them with simple tasks, such as bringing their plate from the table to the dishwasher and putting their dirty clothes in the laundry basket.

◆

At about age two, the kids started taking their Tupperware plates to the sink. They could barely reach up but would balance them on the edge of the counter in front of the sink and push! They were responsible for clearing the table of everything nonbreakable.

◆

I always felt that if they were old enough to take the toys out of the toy box, they were old enough to put them back.

Parents can create a positive attitude about chores. The word has unpleasant connotations — something boring and repetitive that housekeepers or farm children have to do but don't really want to. Early on, we learned that we got better cooperation from our children if we approached chores as a natural part of our everyday routine: "After you eat off a plate, you take it to the sink,"

"If you play with the toys, you put them away." In this way, children grow up regarding these tasks as normal things you do in family life.

It takes all of us to make this home run smoothly — so all of us are responsible for helping out.

Doing chores is also a survival tactic for large or busy families. Chores are what children need to do as part of living in a family. It's as simple as that. Having this matter-of-fact attitude helps children realize that chores are not optional. In fact, we seldom even use the word *chores,* as in "Have you done your chores today?" Call them *responsibilities* so your child learns to value this term. Being responsible for cleaning up after oneself is just part of daily life. Every action comes with strings attached — play with the toys, then pick them up; paint a picture, then wash the brush; change into pajamas, then put the clothes you were wearing in the hamper. You are creating good habits. A young child who is consistently encouraged to clean up after an activity learns that doing so is a normal pattern of behavior. On the other hand, a child who is never expected to clean up after himself assumes that he can do as he wishes and someone else will be there to tidy up after him.

One day while I was putting on my scrubs at the local hospital, I noticed that as some of the doctors changed clothes after surgery, they naturally put their scrubs in the dirty clothes basket. Others left them on the floor. Lessons learned in early childhood? One day it was clear that someone had had enough of this. A sign appeared on the locker room door: YOUR MOTHER DOESN'T LIVE HERE.

Match the chores to the child.

When you watch for particular talents in your children and help them apply these particular abilities to chores, you foster success, cooperation, and confidence.

At age three my daughter still has trouble with colors; given a pile of socks to sort, she'll throw them up in the air to see how they land, or jump in the pile to see what shape it takes. So the laundry room isn't the best spot for her to learn responsibility. She is fascinated with shapes, so one of her daily chores is putting away the silverware, sorting it into the appropriately shaped areas of the drawer. She listens as the utensils make different sounds when put in place, and talks about how each one is used.

As you observe your child at work and at play, think about how you can help her use her skills at each stage of development to handle chores. A child who loves to sort her toys can learn to sort silverware. A child who loves to touch and handle objects can dust them. Develop their skills in real-life situations.

I believe that it's very important to take your time to understand what toddlers and children typically can and can't do at different ages and stages. I learned early on that understanding what my child's capabilities are is the best prevention of discipline problems. Once I started to understand developmentally appropriate behavior, I stopped expecting them to be and do something they couldn't. Discipline was more a matter of us parents learning about our children rather than us trying to change them.

Children have an inborn desire to express their independence by doing things for themselves. If parents nurture this desire, children naturally become more and more capable and, therefore, responsible. By encouraging their children to tackle increasingly challenging tasks, parents help their children develop a "can do" attitude.

When my son was about six, he was in the kitchen creating concoctions of eggs, soy sauce, ketchup, and all my spices. He enjoyed the mixing, the creating, and the mess. So I bought him an easy cookbook and allowed him to experiment with foods for our family. His creative side was satisfied, and he also learned to cook!

THE FIVE BENEFITS OF CHORES

1. Chores are an investment.

Children who perform chores have an *investment* in the family home. Unlike guests, who enjoy the comforts of a home but are not part of what makes it function, children who do chores are personally attached to their home. Kids who wash the dishes, vacuum the floors, and clean the sink take on a real feeling of ownership, which leads to greater respect for the place where they live. Children who sweep the porch aren't likely to cross it in muddy shoes.

Our children didn't start doing chores until they were about eight years old. We really feel that we made a mistake in this area. They should have been doing much more, much earlier. Waiting so long made chores a very unpleasant issue in our home; the children felt put-upon anytime we asked for their help. They expected that we should do everything, and they didn't truly appreciate the things that we did for them. It took quite some time before we settled into a more pleasant attitude about chores, but at long last they are very helpful, with a proper attitude.

2. Chores foster skill development.

Parents can gradually increase the complexity and number of chores their kids are accountable for. As children master an array of tasks, they learn many new skills that help them in other areas of their lives.

Our daughter has her own vegetable garden. She first planted it years ago. We helped her quite a bit at first, but she has learned so much that she now tends to it all on her own. She loves it. She now decides who gets vegetables from it.

When parents take the time to teach their children how to do different jobs, the children *learn how to learn.* They find out that they can successfully take on new and different tasks. A child who learns how to run the dishwasher can transfer some of that knowledge to the washing machine. A child who learns how to sew a tear in a seam can easily learn how to hem his jeans. Learning how to follow a cookie recipe enables a young cook to follow a recipe for lasagna.

We would work with our children on a new job until they learned how to do it, then we would continue to supervise and teach. Just saying, "Go clean up your room," doesn't work, because children don't really understand what that means to the adult. Heck, some adults don't get that one, much less their kids.

3. Chores foster a sense of accomplishment.

Children enjoy a wonderful feeling of accomplishment when they look back at a job well done. Whether a freshly mowed lawn, a tray full of cookies, or a shiny, waxed floor, the fruits of a child's labor are sweet indeed. When children know that their contribution of time and energy has tangible results, they're motivated to do more. Smart parents give their children jobs that have visible results, and then comment positively on those results.

I would help my children pick up toys and walk with them to the toy box to put their things away after playing. Then I would point to the tidy room and give them hugs and tell them I was proud of them for picking up the toys and putting them away. After several months of encouragement, they began to pick up their toys on their own. We believe that doing household chores has given them a feeling of personal value. They know that their work is important to the family. It gives them the knowledge that they are capable of many things.

4. Chores give a feeling of pride.

Lots of encouragement and praise is important. Children may take a long time to complete a new job, and they may find the results less than gratifying. But given time, practice, and encouragement, they will keep adding skills to their growing list of abilities. When parents point out their successes, they feel proud and "big."

My daughter was included in my activities, even though it usually took twice as long that way.

5. Chores teach that everyone is expected to contribute to the family's well-being.

One thing was remarkably absent from parents' comments about chores: money. Paying children to do chores puts an entirely different slant on the issue. Payment tends to create the illusion that if children don't want the money, they aren't obligated to do the chores. Family chores should be seen, rightly, as a child's contribution to family life, not as an option. The rewards of being an important part of a family are much more valuable than a few dollars of allowance. Contributing to the smooth running of the family gives children self-esteem, confidence, independence, pride, accomplishment, and mastery of important life skills.

We've never paid our children to do the dishes, take out the trash, and perform their other household chores. After all, I don't get paid for making dinner and doing the laundry!

GIVE YOUR CHILD RESPONSIBILITIES

My children begin to do chores as soon as they are able. It gives them a feeling of value to the family.

Children's self-confidence grows when they complete tasks that are important to the family. By contributing to the running of the household, they see themselves as significant members of the family "team." In addition, as they master new skills, they feel competent, and this feeling of competence carries over into other areas of their lives. Children need jobs. Giving children household duties helps them feel more valuable and channels their energies into desirable behavior and skills. (See Kids Need Chores, p. 173.)

To make chores age- and stage-appropriate, try these tips:

Choose tasks the child has already shown an interest in.

Our two-year-old, Lauren, had a thing about napkins, so we gave her the dinnertime job of putting napkins at each place setting. A mother in our practice told us, "I couldn't keep our three-year-old away from the vacuum cleaner, so I gave her the job of vacuuming the family room. She kept busy and some cleaning got done." Between the ages of two and four, a child can learn the concept of being responsible for his personal belongings. The child needs to learn to pick up clothes, hang them on the hangers, and put toys in the appropriate place on the shelf.

Young children love to scrub.

By two years of age, the child can be taught to clean sinks and tubs using a sponge. Threes and Fours love to sort laundry into dark and white loads. By five years of age, the child can be doing dishes. Show and tell him exactly how you want them handled. Of course, breakable and valuable items are handled by adults. Between seven and eight, a child can be cooking or at least helping prepare one meal a week. A supermarket is a great learning experience for a child. When you shop with her, help her pick out the ingredients for a meal that she can help prepare. As a nutritional perk, children are more likely to eat what they make themselves.

Give special jobs.

You'll get a lot of mileage out of the term *special.* Whenever we add "special" to a request, it gets results. Perhaps the child concludes, "I must be special because I get a special job." To keep some order in our busy house, we assign "tidy time." Try assigning one room to each child to tidy up, probably his own. Children at all ages suffer a bit of work inertia, especially as tasks lose their fun appeal. Yet, to prepare them for real life, children need to learn at a young age that work comes before play. To jump-start your children, work with them.

Create job charts.

At a family meeting, list the jobs to be done and let each child choose what job he wants. Let them rotate jobs if they want. Between five and ten, children can make the connection that with increasing privileges come responsibilities.

Plant a family garden.

Our family garden proved to be a great learning experience for our children, as well as a lot of fun. Children learn that when they water the plants and pull the weeds, the flowers and vegetables grow better.

Do jobs along with your children.

Work side by side, doing such chores as washing the car, sweeping, and dusting.

Kids say: *One thing my parents did that really affected my life is taught me the value of hard work.* (age nineteen)

When children have jobs, they feel that they are contributing to the cause. They feel useful and needed, and it gives them tools that someday they will use to take care of their own home.

FROM BEING RESPONSIBLE TO BEING ACCOUNTABLE

Studies of kids who get into trouble show that they *lack accountability.* They don't understand what it means to be responsible for their actions and the consequences of these actions. They are quick to pass the buck and blame others for their misdeeds: "He made me mad, so I had to hurt him."

When a child is held accountable for her actions, she learns more than the fact that her behavior has consequences for herself and others. She also learns that people depend on one another, that they are interdependent. She is part of a social system that is bigger than she is, and her choices affect others besides herself. Being accountable is an important part of belonging to a family, to a social group, and to a community. Teaching kids that they are responsible for their behavior gives them a valuable tool for living with others. It also gives them a sense of belonging.

Teach children to accept responsibility early on.

Refuse to accept irresponsible excuses: "I forgot," "I didn't mean it," "I didn't know what you meant," "I can't," "I didn't hear you," and generally, anything that begins with the word *but*. Excuses are a sign of a child's immaturity, and you will hear plenty of them in your years as a parent. How you respond lets your children know that excuses are not acceptable.

A four-year-old knocks over a vase of flowers and when asked about it says, "The cat did it!" Of course, Mom knows better, but she also knows that blaming the cat is easy while admitting that "I wasn't supposed to be running in the house" is hard. A wise parent in this situation doesn't get into an argument about who knocked over the vase. Instead, she reminds the rambunctious four-year-old that this is why there are rules about running in the house and then helps him find a rag to wipe up the mess. The next time her son's behavior gets too wild for his surroundings, Mom reminds him of the vase.

When an older child makes excuses for a poor test score or forgetting to go to soccer practice, parents let the child know that these things are her responsibility and that failing to do them produces consequences. The new rule is that she must complete homework before spending time on the computer. Or she must face her coach and admit that she had no good reason for having missed practice.

It's easier for children to admit mistakes if they know they can trust their parents to respond with fairness and understanding. Refusing to accept excuses does not mean that parents should humiliate or ridicule a child for saying, "The cat did it." When you correct your child's misbehavior, your goal is to make her aware of what she has done wrong and what she must do to rectify it. Don't tear her apart. Let her know that you know she is capable of doing better — and then help her not make the same mistake again.

Our children learned from an early age that they were responsible for their own behavior. We would not allow them excuses for misbehavior. They were held accountable for their own actions.

Establish family rules and routines.

As children are developing the skills necessary to become responsible for themselves, it can be very helpful for them to follow routines. When certain tasks are always done a certain way, it's easier for children to remember how and when to do them. For example, if the routine is that homework is always done immediately after dinner, children will eventually remember to do their homework at that time, without a reminder from you.

Give children simple, commonsense rules to follow that teach them to be responsible for their own actions.

Expect accountability.

Expectations are a powerful motivator, especially the expectations of parents and other trusted authority figures. Early on, convey to your child that being responsible for doing the right thing and being accountable for the consequences of mistakes are not optional. This is what you expect; it's "the way we do things in our family." Children carry this attitude into the way they act in society in general. Their parents' expectations become part of themselves.

I sure had a lot of expectations for my children. I believe that children live up to things that are expected of them. I expected them to behave when we went out — they did. They were expected to have their rooms tidy — and they did. They were expected to be polite and mannerly — they were. I expected them to grow up to be good people — they are.

♦

My son is just over two years old. As he's been able to manage them, he's been given responsibilities. He helps me with household chores, cleans up after himself when he can, and knows that he must pick up what he's been playing with (although he is always free to ask us for help) before moving on to the next thing. It's not about strict rules, it's just "the way it is" in our household. There has been little need to enforce rules in our home, as the routines of responsible behavior have always been important. We expect our son to up-hold his responsibilities. They are just part of his life.

Catch children in the act of doing right.

As your children are learning responsible behavior, show them that you notice the things they are doing right. Praise and encouragement will motivate your children to repeat their positive actions. Pointing out what our children do right and letting them know how pleased we are with their behavior guarantees that we will see more of that behavior.

Even though my son was required to do his chores, I always said "thank you."

Children are happy when they can bask in the warm glow of the parental approval they are always seeking. They may be reluctant to cooperate sometimes, but knowing that their good behavior will be noticed and applauded allows them to feel proud. That pride is what helps kids develop their own high standards for themselves.

TEACHING CHILDREN TO THINK AND PLAN AHEAD

Wait is a word children hate to hear. "I want it, now!" What preschooler hasn't stomped his foot

and said these words? But part of developing a sense of responsibility as the child matures is learning to wait and to put in the groundwork needed to reap the richer reward down the road.

The ability to take the long-term perspective is critical in life. So many things require enormous effort and commitment before any results are seen: spending years in college to obtain a degree, saving for a down payment on a car or house, working at an entry-level job to move ahead. We need to equip our children to be able to look ahead and make sacrifices in the present in order to obtain a better future.

Here are some simple ways to encourage this patience:

- When a child is assigned a book report or a big project at school, you have an opportunity to demonstrate *forward thinking*. Sit down with the child and plot out the various steps needed to complete the project on a time line. Make a realistic schedule for what needs to be completed by when. This teaches kids that worthwhile results take planning and forethought. As the project takes shape according to schedule, children see the tangible benefit of this approach: a successfully completed project without a lot of rushing around at the last minute.
- The next time your child becomes enamored with the newest latest-greatest-gotta-have-it gizmo, resist criticizing him. Help him create a *financial plan* to earn and save money so that he can buy the object for himself.

Teach time-management and organizational skills.

Most adults have some kind of daily planning system (a computer program, a day planner, a written to-do list, etc.) to help them remember what they must do from day to day. Interestingly, though, many of these same people expect their children to remember their chores, schoolwork, sports, and extracurricular activities without such aids. While a child's list of things to do may seem uncomplicated, remembering all this stuff can be overwhelming. A child will feel more in control of his life when he has his own written to-do lists. They can be as simple as a chore chart and a place to write down homework assignments or as complicated as an actual daily planner book. The choice of system depends on the child's personality and the activities he needs to track. Regardless of its form, an organized reminder system can teach a child good time-management habits for life.

When our children were little, we began posting a large calendar on their bedroom walls. We would mark down all the important events: birthdays, holidays, and special events. As they got older, we added school assignments and sporting events. They have come to rely on their calendars to keep themselves organized. Our eldest has entered college, and one of the first supplies he purchased for college life was a large wall calendar.

With privileges come responsibilities.

As your child grows, let his responsibilities grow along with him. School-age children (especially preteens) should learn that as they are given greater privileges, you expect them to be more responsible. If they are allowed to walk to the park by themselves, they are expected to be home at the promised time. If they are allowed to use Mom and Dad's computer, they will be careful to save Mom and Dad's files.

Teens expect their parents to hold them accountable, and they get confused and lose respect for parents who are lax about conveying expectations. The teen needs to have a clear understanding of what you expect: you expect your teen to tell you where he is, whom he is with, what they're doing, and what time he will be home. If there is potential for misunderstanding your expectations, write them down, for both of you. You may have to produce this document later if your teen comes home an hour late and says, "But I thought you said midnight."

We rewarded responsible behavior with additional privileges. If our kids repeatedly came in by curfew, they were rewarded with more say in what their curfew would be. On the other hand, coming in late would result in an earlier curfew until they again proved themselves responsible.

Equip children with life skills.

By the time children leave home, they should have the skills needed to be self-sufficient. But they will never learn such skills without the opportunity to practice them. Parents of capable teenagers have had the patience to endure the early learning process that results in their children's ultimate competence.

Our children both know how to cook, clean, do laundry, shop, and perform other home maintenance. We know that they will head off to college or their own adult lives with the skills they need to run a household.

Parents teach life skills one at a time over many years, each learned skill bringing the child closer to successful independence. As you go about your day, pay attention to the many tasks you do, often without much thought, that your children would benefit from learning about: putting gas in the car, changing a lightbulb, resetting a tripped circuit breaker, unclogging a drain, putting new ink in the printer, calling in a catalog order, replacing a battery, or changing a tire. The list is endless; you have opportunities to teach your children life skills nearly every day.

We start each year with our children creating a list of goals — things they would like to learn. Then we focus on adding those skills to their already impressive lists of abilities. When our children leave home, they will take with them the skills they need to cook, clean, balance a checkbook, write a letter, sew, do simple home repairs, garden, shop, and do laundry. We've always believed that these life skills should be learned at home before you head out into the world.

SCIENCE SAYS:

Impulse control predicts success.

A Stanford University classic study on impulse control — dubbed the Marshmallow Study — showed that young children who practice delayed gratification are more likely to become successful teens. A group of four-year-olds were given two choices of marshmallows for a treat. The researcher said they could have one now or, if they waited twenty minutes, they could have two marshmallows. This experiment naturally divided the children into two groups: some grabbed a marshmallow immediately, others waited for the two-marshmallow reward for waiting. These two groups of children, those who acted on a whim and those who were able to wait, were tracked through the end of high school. The children who were able to delay their impulse at four tended to become more socially and academically successful. The researchers concluded that poor impulse control is a risk factor for poor success later on.

Model responsibility.

When parents take their own responsibilities seriously — when they show dedication to their jobs and their family — they send important messages to their children. How you view your own responsibilities in life has a tremendous influence on whether your children live up to their responsibilities.

We try to lead by example, as children are quick to copy.

Many parents inadvertently talk too much about job frustrations and family aggravations in front of their children. Children who hear too much of this negative talk assume that having adult responsibilities is difficult and unpleasant. However, when parents' conversation focuses on the positive aspects of their roles, children perceive responsibility as a normal, acceptable part of adult life — even something to look forward to.

We own a family business, so our work was always evident to the children. They learned by example that working hard can be very rewarding. Each of them was given opportunities to work along with us at various print-shop responsibilities, from collating to billing to editing and typesetting.

PUTTING TEENS TO WORK: WHY, WHEN, HOW MUCH?

Though I (Bill) have had a lot of jobs in my life, the ones I had as a teen particularly stand out in my mind. One thing I especially remember is how I was expected to pay part of my way at an early age. As a preteen I began as a young entrepreneur in my role as neighborhood grass cut-ter. Soon I learned that it was more efficient — and higher-paying — if I had a power lawn mower. So I saved up enough to buy a power mower (which was a luxury fifty years ago), which allowed me to mow more lawns in less time. Perhaps my relatives were trying out a bit of reverse psychology when they landed me less-than-glamorous summer jobs working for the city street and sewer department, on construction sites, and in glassworks factories and steel mills. After a couple of summers of hard work, I couldn't wait to get off the assembly line and into college. From these experiences, I learned how important it was to learn specialized skills or to train for a profession. To this day, I hold a special place in my heart for people who earn their living with hard physical work.

Should teenagers have jobs? This simple question comes with a complicated answer. The most important goals of childhood are healthy development and education. Yet an estimated 85 percent of American adolescents will have a part-time job at some point during their high-school careers. How do these jobs mesh with those goals?

Various studies have found strong evidence that employment during the teenage years has both positive *and* negative effects on the lives of young people. So the question about whether teenagers have jobs actually leads to more questions. Why *do* teens work, and why *should* they work? How does work affect their studies? What kinds of jobs should teenagers have? How many hours should they work? How do you decide whether working is right for your child?

Why do they work?

When your child first approaches you for permission to take a job, you should first find out about why he wants to work. Nearly 90 percent of American teenagers work to have money for clothes and personal spending. This finding

tends to support the growing concern of older adults about young people's materialism and their desire for instant gratification. The average child is bombarded by television advertising that uses sophisticated and powerful strategies to create and feed the desire for high-status material goods. Few teens work in order to contribute to the family budget. (Teens from middle-income families are more likely to work than those from low-income households.) The second most common reason that teens say they want to work is to gain independence. A surprisingly small number cited saving for a car or a college education as their primary reason for working. Very few said they worked to learn life skills.

Why should they work?

While consumerism may underlie a teenager's desire to work, the experience can nevertheless be beneficial. In urban and suburban environments, few children are involved beyond perfunctory chores in the daily activities necessary to run a household. Holding a job allows teens to gain skills and training that may contribute to their productivity within society. A positive work experience can teach a child much about responsibility, punctuality, teamwork, problem-solving skills, the complexities of customer service, and the realities of dealing with a budget and money management.

When fourteen- or fifteen-year-olds apply for their first jobs, routine, repetitive labor is most likely where they're going to start. They have to be realistic. I personally believe it's not a bad thing. Once the novelty of having a job wears off and it becomes boring, there are still a few benefits:

◆

1. It becomes a good time for parents to stress the importance of a college education. There's leverage here . . . so the point can really sink in. This experi-

ence can help with motivation for setting goals. After all, who wants to mop floors and clean toilets at McDonald's forever?

◆

2. There's something to be said for learning firsthand how to "climb the ladder" and "pay your dues." We all have to begin somewhere. It can be humbling and help us keep life in perspective. Also, after having "been there," hopefully these kids will remember what it's like to be the low guy on the totem pole, and maybe will be kind to others in that same position once they've moved on.

◆

3. The rewards of "starting at the bottom" and working your way up to a promotion (however small) can be empowering. Also it's a good time for parents to stress doing your best, no matter what job you have. This helps to instill a good work ethic.

◆

Remember how great it felt getting a job you like (even if it wasn't perfect), after leaving a job you hated? And how much you then appreciated that new job?

How does work affect their studies?

All the reports on youth employment agree that the more time adolescents spend at work, the less time they spend studying. Students who work more than twenty hours per week show high levels of stress and a diminished investment in their education.

Too many times I've had kids come in to school at 10:30 A.M., saying they had to close up at work the night before. Students find it harder to say "no" to their bosses than to the school. Fatigue and missed assignments aren't the worst of it, either. Too many kids are missing that quality time with their family. When the parent gets home, the child goes to work. When the child gets home, the parents are asleep.
— *"A Week in the Life of a High School,"*
Time, October 1999

Whereas working more than twenty hours per week is probably too much, studies do show that teenagers who work between fifteen and twenty hours per week have higher grade point averages than their nonworking peers. It's unclear whether this finding is related to the type of students who take on jobs or to the resulting sense of responsibility that a job engenders, or whether it's living proof of the adage "If you want something done, ask a busy person."

What kinds of jobs should teenagers have?

According to the National Institute for Occupational Safety and Health (NIOSH), about seventy teens die annually from work injuries in the United States. Another 70,000 get hurt badly enough that they go to a hospital emergency room. Injury rates are almost twice as high for adolescents as for adult workers. Teens are often injured on the job because they do not receive adequate safety training and supervision. Teens are also lacking in the wisdom that comes with age and can make mistakes due to poor judgment. Teens are much more likely to be injured when working in jobs that the law prohibits them from holding but in which they are nonetheless employed. Obviously, the type of jobs held by a teenager affects the risks and benefits of working. An important consideration in deciding whether a teen should work, then, is the actual work the teen will do.

How many hours should they work?

Federal and state laws protect teens from working too many hours, too late in the day, or too early in the morning. However, unless teens and their parents know these laws, their child may be asked to work beyond legal limits.

According to the *U.S. Department of Labor Safety and Health Standards for Nonagricultural Child Labor* (December 1999):

- Youth ages fourteen and fifteen may work outside school hours in nonmanufacturing, nonmining, nonhazardous jobs for no more than three hours on a schoolday, eighteen hours in a school week, eight hours on a nonschool day, or forty hours in a non-school week. They may not begin work before 7 A.M. nor work after 7 P.M. except from June 1 through Labor Day, when evening hours are extended until 9:00 P.M. (Approved work experience programs have separate rules.)
- Youth ages sixteen and seventeen may perform jobs not declared hazardous by the secretary of labor for unlimited hours.

The laws for fourteen- and fifteen-year-olds are in accord with the research demonstrating that students who work more than twenty hours per school week suffer negative effects ranging from poor school performance and attendance to poor diet, lack of exercise, erratic sleep patterns, high levels of stress, and an increased likelihood of engaging in criminal activity, sexual activity, and drug use.

Research shows that students who work fifteen to twenty hours per school week are at less risk of these dangers, though they may still be an issue; it all depends on the job and the child. A healthy work experience that allows for balance among school, work, and leisure-time activities can have positive effects, including a healthier parent-child relationship; good school performance; healthy patterns of diet, exercise, and sleep; and healthy self-esteem.

My daughter, Sarah, works sixteen hours a week, and we think that's just right for her. Sometimes I think she might like a little more time with her friends, but she does like working and she likes her job. But, you know, even good decisions that benefit you in the long run still require a certain amount of sacrifice. It is, of course, her decision to work or not, and she has chosen this path. We told her when she started that if her grades suffered or if we felt she was just getting too stressed, she would have to quit, but so far things are going very well. We also discussed time management and setting priorities, and we helped her with ideas on how to juggle those things until she "got her own rhythm." She really does quite well on her own now. Because we've made a careful, thoughtful decision, this is turning out to be a great experience as her first step into the real world.

One point missing from the research regarding the number of hours teenagers should work is an analysis of how teens spend their free time when they don't have jobs. Surveys do tell us that the average American twelve- to fifteen-year-old spends an average of seventeen hours a week watching television. Other favorite teen activities, such as hanging at the mall with friends, occupy nonschool time as well. Clearly, if TV time or unstructured idle time gets the boot when a teenager gets a job, then the job is a good thing, indeed.

Though many obstacles and disappointments have been laid in front of her, she has always bounced back and continues to achieve. Instead of whining, she keeps a positive attitude, knowing that hard work will pay off eventually — and it always does.

Teach them early, then trust them later.

Raising a responsible child requires high doses of patience and commitment, but it is one of the best investments you'll ever make. You're going to put your time in at one end of childhood or the other, either by preparing your child for adulthood or by worrying about him constantly when he's out on his own. Trust us, as parents of many kids, when we say that you'll have far fewer anxious nights if you invest your time in raising a responsible child right from the start.

TO WORK OR NOT TO WORK — HELPING YOUR TEEN DECIDE

How do you decide whether working is right for your child?

Every child is different, and every work opportunity is unique. This is a situation that requires a thoughtful approach involving both parent and child. Consider what your teen will be giving up in order to work and what she stands to gain from the job, what her daily schedule will be like, and the effects on her schoolwork and her leisure time with friends and family. Is she ready for this kind of commitment? Use these questions as guidelines in making the right decisions:

What will the teen be giving up in exchange for work time?

The answer to this could be as varied as "her favorite TV sitcoms" or "her chess club and debate team." Clearly, the answer to this question is a vital component in the decision.

Is the job safe in all aspects?

This may require a visit to the workplace and an in-depth assessment of the job. While being a janitor at the local bowling alley may sound good, you may discover that your child would be working with toxic cleaning chemicals and that he would be opening the building, alone and in the dark, on Saturday mornings.

How will the job affect the teen's schoolwork?

Accepting your child's promise of "Don't worry, I'll get it all done" is not the proper way to address this question. This is the time to sit down with paper and pen and write out a time-management plan.

Write down all the days of the week and all the hours in each day, and make a realistic plan for all activities.

How will the job affect the teen's sleep and eating habits?

Will your child have to get up earlier than usual? Go to bed later? (If he already has a hard time waking up in the morning, this should be a red flag!) Will there be time for regular meals, or will he have to go right from school to work without a break for a nutritious meal? How will you handle all of these details?

How will the job affect the teen's family relationships and leisure time?

Will the job replace quality time with family and friends? Will there be time for activities outside of school and work? Who will your child be working with? This is an important question because people he spends time with at work may well become his new circle of friends. What will be their influence on him?

Does your child understand the commitment?

A job is a mature responsibility with no room for calling in sick in favor of a friend's party or going to work tired from a late night at the movies. Beyond frivolous actions, keeping a work schedule may mean passing on fun activities to stay home and finish homework or chores. Working at an outside job should not take the place of having your child participate in chores at home; after all, he still is a productive member of the family. Is your child really ready for this new set of obligations?

What are the benefits of this specific job?

Once you've determined that having a job is the right idea for your child, take a fresh look at this specific opportunity. Is your child ready to jump because the job is offered? Take a look around and make sure that this is the right job. What will she be getting from the experience? What vocational skills and training will she gain? If the job is merely routine, repetitive la-bor, the glow may wear off quickly and the job could become boring. Is your child prepared for this? What is the goal for length of employment or possible advancement?

When you've decided to give your adolescent the green light on a job, show her that you support her — and let her know you believe she will succeed!

11

Raising a Moral Child

T HE SEARS FAMILY HOBBY is sailing. Riding the waves with kids provides many teachable moments. The importance of proper sail trim can be related to the importance of having rules for running your life. We can't change the wind or the waves, but we can decide our destination. We must trim the sails in order to get there, and if we run into a storm, we drop anchor and wait it out. Without these simple rules, the boat will drift aimlessly at the mercy of the wind and waves. We might be lucky and float safely in the right direction; more likely, we would end up on the rocks. Inner rules called morals keep our sails trimmed and our boat moving in the right direction in life. These rules also anchor us in rough times. If we follow these rules, we have a better chance of being happy. When we trim our sails just right, the boat moves in harmony with the wind and sea. When we trim our inner guidance system correctly, we'll feel in harmony with ourselves. We'll have a smoother sail through life when we make the right choices.

HOW CHILDREN LEARN TO MAKE MORAL CHOICES

Paula and her husband, Jeff, were discussing what makes children obey their parents. They had three children, kids who had the usual messy rooms and teased one another and squabbled. But generally they did what their parents and teachers expected of them. They were good kids.

Jeff insisted that it was because they knew what would happen if they didn't behave: they would be punished and would lose certain privileges. Knowing this, he felt, was what had kept him in line as a child and adolescent, and he expected his children to follow the same line of thinking. After all, why did he himself drive at the speed limit and stop at stop signs? So he wouldn't get a ticket, right?

Paula, however, had other ideas, based on her own upbringing. She had grown up in a home in which children were seldom, if ever, punished. It wasn't that her parents didn't care about her and her sisters, nor did they let their children do whatever they wanted. Paula and her sisters just never dreamed of misbehaving or defying their parents the way that many of their peers did. When they did behave in a way that their parents didn't like — say, they were unkind to one another or neglected responsibilities — one of their parents, usually their dad, would talk to them. By the time he was done talking about the offense, they wanted nothing so much as to live up to his high expectations for them. Paula thought that her own kids were honest and responsible for pretty much the same reasons.

This was hard for Jeff to understand, but he had to admit that all three of their children followed rules reliably, got their homework done (usually), and stayed away from the kind of trouble that had tempted him as a teen. They seldom forfeited privileges, and when they made mistakes in judgment, they were always sorry and worked hard to regain their parents' trust. He also had to admit that as his children got older, it would be more difficult to punish them effectively.

Paula reminded him that when they were adults, their children would have to do the right thing on their own. Yes, the legal system would punish certain kinds of wrongdoing, but responsible adults are accountable mainly to themselves and to their families. Paula also observed that Jeff obeyed traffic laws even when there was no police cruiser in sight. Everyone's safety depended on drivers following the rules of the road.

Doing what is right because it is right is the hallmark of a moral person. Kids are successful when they take responsibility for making their own moral choices. This isn't the conventional meaning of success: it doesn't involve wealth, status, or power. But along with empathy and compassion, the ability to make moral choices is a quality parents wish to instill in their children — for their kid's own good, and for the good of the world.

How do children learn right from wrong? And what makes them choose to do right? Children don't form strong moral values on their own. They learn their values from their parents and their peers, in schools, in churches, and on the playground, through discussions and on-the-spot life lessons. Morals are "caught" as well as taught, and a child who is moral shows it through deeds as well as by words.

Paula and Jeff in the story above were well on their way to raising children who would become responsible, moral adults. They had built strong connections with their children over the years, and their kids trusted them. They had also given their children a strong spiritual foundation. When these children did the right thing, they felt right inside. When they contemplated making a wrong choice, they felt uncomfortable. Just as Paula remembered from her own childhood, there were certain things that were just not done "in our family." Her children did their best to live up to their parents' expectations.

Morals and values are not learned separately from the other qualities children need to be successful adults. Empathy is an important part of making moral choices, since the ability to understand a situation from another's point of view is at the heart of why some choices are right and others are wrong. Self-esteem and a sense of responsibility are also related to moral behavior. And all of these things children learn first from their relationship with their parents.

This chapter helps you understand how your child thinks about right and wrong at different stages of development. It also gives you the tools you need to raise children who want to do the right thing simply because it's right.

MORAL KIDS ARE KIDS WHO CARE

Empathy and compassion lay the foundation of morality. The Golden Rule (Do unto others as you would have them do unto you) is based on empathy. Before your child can treat others as he wants to be treated, he has to be able to get behind the eyes of that other person and understand how his actions affect others. This calls for compassion, as well as the ability to think through an action and its consequences before doing it.

Raise a connected child.

Empathy depends on *sensitivity,* to others and to oneself. The connected child, because of the mutual trust between him and his caregivers, develops a sense of well-being, an inner sense of rightness. Because his caregivers are sensitive to his needs, he learns to be sensitive to his inner feelings, to heed his inner voice. He also learns to be sensitive to and trust what his caregivers tell him about himself and what he should do. Their actions and virtues become part of him, so that sensitivity and trust are not so much qualities that the child has or aspires to as they are simply what he is. Trust makes limits and boundaries — other building blocks of a moral person — more meaningful to the child.

Some kids will lie to their parents when they get into trouble, and others will tell the truth. Why one child lies and another doesn't is based not only on the developmental stage and temperament of the child but also on the connection between the parent and child. For the connected child, to lie would be a *breach of trust.* The child knows this and will not risk falling out of his parents' esteem. The mutual trust between parent and child is so strong that the child can admit wrongdoing. Sure, even the most connected child will spin some yarns, especially in his preschool years, but as his own sense of right and wrong grows, he will be bothered by doing wrong because he knows this is not what his parents want from him. Con-

fronted with a situation that demands an on-the-spot choice, children will usually do what's easiest. For the unconnected child, it's often easier to lie. Unconnected children do not depend on caregivers' trust and regard for their sense of well-being, nor are they interested in how their actions affect others. For the connected child, it's easier to tell the truth because the pain of violating the trusting relationship he has with his parents would be more unbearable than the pain of admitting wrongdoing. The trustful child is more likely to become a truthful child.

Kids who have not been sensitively cared for may not be able to feel remorse or take responsibility for the way their actions have an impact on others' lives. Connected kids who care are bothered by how their actions affect others. They shy away from wrongdoing because they are aware that these actions will bring feelings of remorse. They prefer the good feelings that they have when they act right. Even when they stray from the straight and narrow — which connected kids will do at times — they have an easier time getting back on track because they know what it is to feel good about themselves, and they prefer that feeling.

We have observed that attachment-parented kids — connected kids — are likely to think and act morally. They are not kids who spray-paint graffiti on playground walls, are deliberately mean to other kids, or try almost anything to annoy their parents during adolescence. The internal sense of rightness and well-being that develops as a baby grows up in arms, at breast, and with his needs cared for becomes an inner guidance system that enables him to do the right things for the right reasons. In other words, the attachment-parented child likes the track he is on and is more likely to stay there.

HOW CHILDREN DEVELOP MORALS AND VALUES

Like other qualities described in this book, the ability to follow a moral code develops as cognitive and emotional skills grow. Three-year-olds' ideas about why one thing is right and another is wrong are different from those of ten-year-olds. Adolescents' moral reasoning is more sophisticated than preteens' but is still not fully mature. What you expect of children and how you teach them about morals depend on what and how they think at a given stage.

An infant has no abstract sense of right and wrong, just as he has little sense of being a separate self. He knows only what makes him feel safe and secure and what frightens him. "Good" means comforted, fed, at peace. Self-awareness and trust are the virtues learned in infancy, and are important to being able to do the right thing later in childhood.

Do as I say.

Enter the toddler, whose moral values come directly from her parents. Because of the connection established during infancy, the child knows that whatever the parents say can be trusted. And as the toddler begins to explore his world, parents have lots to say. Dad says hitting is wrong, so it's wrong. Mom says don't touch the lamp cord, so that's out-of-bounds. The toddler is learning that there are yeses and no's in life. He doesn't yet internalize them or remember them very well. He has to check in with Mom and Dad constantly, and they must be hypervigilant to keep him out of trouble. They also remove temptation from his life by putting away the breakables that he shouldn't touch and plugging the electrical outlets he shouldn't explore.

Toddlers also learn that sometimes they have to wait. They can't have a cookie before dinner.

Mom and Dad won't buy every toy they see at the supermarket. When parents and toddler are connected, the child trusts that what the parents say is right. Toddlers learn to respect and trust authority as they practice obeying the parents they love. They also learn that there are limits in life — they cannot do or have everything they might want.

Another vital morality lesson learned in the early years is that others have needs, feelings, and rights, too. Infants and toddlers are egocentric: everything in their world revolves around them. Other people exist only in relation to them. But as preschoolers become more independent, they are ready to understand the feelings of others. Now comes what we call transfer time — parents help the child transfer the sensitivity he received from his caregivers to others. Your three-year-old pushes another child in the play group. You say, "Katie, how would you feel if Mary pushed you?" A younger sibling is sick and the five-year-old is encouraged to help take care of her: "Susie feels sick and she doesn't want to get up. Could you bring her a glass of water?" Because this is what Mom says to do, and because this is how Mom and Dad have always treated her, the child is able to care for another's hurts. "We don't hit, we hug," "The doll belongs to Mary," "Billy's crying, let's help him feel better." Imagine if your little sponge soaks up half a dozen such morality lessons every day for several years. These positive lessons will become his pattern for living with others.

Do as I do.

Between three and six years of age, children's ability to *internalize* instructions grows. When your child was two, you may have had to repeat guiding words such as: "Pet the cat, don't pull her tail" every time your child encountered the cat (who probably soon learned to stay away).

A three-year-old remembers your admonition from one petting session to the next. Between the ages of three and six, children also internalize their caregivers' values. What's right for you becomes right for her. This is why wise parents and preschool teachers start their morality lessons with "we": "We don't hit, we hug," "We sit on chairs, we don't stand on them," "We say please and thank you." Children want to belong, to be part of this "we," so they follow the norms of the family or the classroom. You may hear your six-year-old tell a friend, "In our family we do such-and-such." As these norms become part of a child's self, these inner rules begin to direct the child's behavior — with frequent reinforcement, reminders, and occasional redirection from caregivers. With inner controls in place, the child now does the right thing because it feels right — and because Mom and Dad will approve.

"When I do this, then . . ."

The moral code of young children also expands with their ability to understand consequences. They can make the logical connection between *when* and *then:* "When I ride my bike out in the street, then my bike gets put away for a week," "When I hit, I must sit." The connected child does not like consequences, since they tend to remind him that he has violated his inner sense of rightness. The roots of healthy *guilt* are forming, reinforced by the consequences of wrongdoing. This is yet another way in which a child learns that "I feel good when I do right and feel bad when I do wrong." This inner feeling of remorse and guilt is what distinguishes the moral, connected child from the child who feels no remorse or believes that "whatever I do is okay, as long as I don't get caught."

A child's conscience begins to grow in infancy and early childhood, but it doesn't govern the child's actions until the middle years, when children begin to think more consciously about right and wrong. Conscience is what links a child's inner feelings to his outward actions. There's even a physiological basis for conscience. Consider the premise of a lie-detector test: people experience physiological changes when they tell a lie. A child with a conscience has the ability to figure out whether an action is right or wrong, not because people in authority say so or out of fear of punishment but because the child knows it and feels it — in his mind and perhaps even in his body. Those inner feelings of rightness, nurtured during infancy and toddlerhood, guide the behavior of older children,

---

THE PINOCCHIO PRINCIPLE

Here's one way to explain to children the concept of a conscience. This is how I presented it to six-year-old Matthew.

You have two voices inside you, a "do right" voice and a "do wrong" voice. Sometimes the "do wrong" voice is easier to follow. What it is suggesting may seem like more fun. But when you listen to this "do wrong" voice and do what it says, you won't feel right inside. Instead, listen to that voice that tells you to do right. That's the one that will make you happy.

When he was about six years old, I could tell that Matthew was developing the beginnings of a guiding conscience. As I caught him starting to fabricate an untruth, his eyes would meet mine and he would back off. As our eyes engaged, he would start smiling (so would I), as if he were saying, "No, Dad, that's not really true." From the look Matthew gave me, I believe he felt that lying would breach our mutual trust, and our connection.

teens, and adults. Connected children internalize the values of the significant people in their lives as the conscience that will guide them through life.

Surround the growing child with people who make healthy choices.

You want these impressions to become such a part of your child that when she is exposed to unhealthy choices — and she will be — they will disturb her. The child who enters the age of conscience building without an internal reference file is at a disadvantage, like a gardener who waited too long to plant crops. You may find that values taught later in childhood may take root, but the roots are not as deep as if they had been planted in the right season.

The big eyes and impressionable mind of a growing child continually scan the environment, trying to figure out what's normal, what's real. The first five to seven years are very important for modeling moral impressions. In those early years what a child sees and hears, he automatically sees as "the norm" or "right." If he sees you hit someone, he perceives that it is right, since you are his parents. Children store the impressions of all their persons of significance as model behavior worth imitating. Being so impressionable early in life is why we continually emphasize the importance of the first few years as greatly influencing whether or not kids turn out well.

Look for teachable moments to point out to your child how people of good character are the truly important ones. Suggest these examples to get your child thinking about what it means to be important:

- "That was kind of the sales clerk to offer to carry our heavy box. Helpfulness is a sign of a good person."

- "It was nice of that young man to get up and give the pregnant woman his seat on the bus. It's important to do that, you know."
- "Did you see how that player from the other baseball team came over to congratulate the pitcher on his shutout? That's good sportsmanship."

Character counts.

When you praise others for their humanitarian deeds or their simple acts of kindness, you are letting your child know how you expect him to behave and what kind of qualities you value in a person.

Another reason it's important to give your child the message that character counts is that any person can be a person of good character. Some people become prominent because of the talents they are born with, the business or fortune they inherit, or just a lot of good luck. Yet your child should realize that becoming a celebrity or a powerful person in business is not what makes someone a valuable human being. It's character that is most important — and your child has it within her power to grow up to be someone of good character.

The age of moral reasoning.

Between the ages of seven and ten, children form more abstract ideas about what is right and wrong. They use moral reasoning to determine how to respond to difficult situations. The battle cry of children developing this ability are those famous words from middle childhood: "It's not fair!" Children's strong sense of fairness helps them understand the necessity of rules and leads them to want to participate in making the rules. Though they still look to parents for guidance about right and wrong, they also begin to understand how something can be right or wrong on its own merits, without input from authority figures. In fact, children between the ages of seven and ten may question whether parents and other persons of significance, such as teachers, coaches, and ministers, are right about an issue. As children begin to think about morality for themselves, authority figures no longer appear infallible.

As their ability to judge whether something is right or wrong matures, you get a second chance to teach values to your children. Kids who have had healthy models in the preschool years are usually more discerning at this stage. Yet even if your child hasn't had the best models in the early years, you now have an opportunity to actively teach your child to make moral decisions.

PRETEENS AND TEENS

As children move into adolescence, they look to peers for acceptance. This is also a time when they sort out which values they want to make their own. They may try on different value systems to see which ones seem to fit their lives and boost their self-image. Preteens and teens are quick to sniff out hypocrisy in their elders and may question ideas of right and wrong that don't make sense to them. They use more sophisticated moral reasoning as they get older and are able to see many sides to a question. Whereas children ages seven to ten tend to think in black-and-white, right-and-wrong terms, older children and teens understand that moral questions do not always have simple answers. They are able to think beyond their own interests to the good of society and can be very idealistic.

Preteens and teens look to parents for affirmation and for advice, but they no longer see parents as almighty authority figures. Rather than giving orders and expecting to be obeyed, parents of teens must be prepared to act as consultants. In order for you to be a trustworthy adviser who has a positive influence on his moral choices, you must work at staying connected to your teen. Explain your reasons behind the various decisions that affect him and the rest of the family. Listen to his opinions and his rants about unfair teachers and unfeeling

SCIENCE SAYS:

Children from open-discussion families are more morally mature.

Studies show that individuals who come from families that encourage open discussions about controversial subjects show more "morally mature" thinking. A California study of a thousand college students looked at the relationship between a student's level of moral reasoning and the previous parenting. Students who scored high on moral reasoning came from families that discussed subjects openly. Other studies have shown that highly permissive parents who do not expect obedience from their children and who praised them when they didn't deserve it produced "me-firsters," children whose only thoughts were to satisfy themselves. Studies also show that the other extreme — overcontrolling parents — produced conformist teenagers who couldn't think for themselves. Families who gave their children a voice in decisions produced teenagers who were able to reason morally. It seems that giving children opportunities to preach to themselves is the best way to teach lasting moral lessons.

friends, and as you help him interpret situations from others' viewpoints, be sure that you seek to understand his.

Discussing TV programs with kids is a great way to talk about moral choices. For instance, you notice your teen watching a TV program that fosters some lifestyles contrary to your family's values. Watch for a while with your teen, then talk about what's going on: "What made that character do that?" "What would you do in that situation?" "What do you think is the right thing to do?" You can also discuss current news stories and social issues with your teen. There's plenty of material for practicing moral reasoning in daily headlines about controversial public figures with questionable private lives and financial interests. Encourage your children to express their opinions and participate in lively, open-ended family debates. Respect your children's viewpoint, even if you don't agree.

MORAL NORMS

At all stages of moral development, children are searching for norms: "How am I supposed to act?" "What's expected of me?" "What do my parents and friends believe is right?" The connected child is able to sort out answers to these questions. She is firmly grounded in her parents' norms — "This is what we believe and how we act in our home." She knows the behavior that's expected of her and can see the consequences of misbehavior, since her parents have mapped this out clearly. Because she trusts her parents, she is not confused or worried about what is right and wrong. With these secure boundaries, she is able to ponder moral questions and arrive at valid answers. There is great freedom and comfort in knowing secure boundaries.

The unconnected child has a more difficult time grasping what's right, what's wrong, and what's normal. As he tries to figure out what's expected of him, his right choices may go unnoticed and unrewarded and his wrong choices may bring him lots of attention, albeit negative. The unconnected child may become an angry child, because the way he is treated violates his sense of fairness and trust. He has no one he wants to please and no boundaries, but he knows that he *should* have them. Many times when I've seen an unconnected ten-year-old in my office, I can't help but think, "This is one angry kid."

Alternative values.

Children who are unsure about moral norms, because they have not learned them at home, may have a difficult time staying on track when confronted with alternative values. Children from homes in which values and virtues are not discussed and taught are easily swayed by the values of their peer group or by whatever feels good. With no inner sense of well-being to guide them, they are like a boat without a rudder or anchor, adrift in a sea of moral uncertainty. They ride whatever current comes along, whatever makes them feel good for the moment. On the other hand, the connected child has an inner moral code that is part of his *self.* Behavior that goes against it upsets his sense of fairness and well-being. The morally connected child becomes the morally selective one. He adopts those values that contribute to his well-being and shuns those that don't.

It might seem that the morally unconnected child is freer, but actually he isn't. Because he is not morally grounded, he is easily influenced by people who take advantage of him and by cultural trends that have little to do with what will make him truly happy. The morally grounded

---

PARENT TIP:

Give your children a moral inheritance. It's the lifelong asset they are least likely to lose.

---

child, on the other hand, is really freer. Because he wastes less energy searching for what's right, wrong, and important in life, he is free to divert this energy to achieving his goals in life. He doesn't bounce around from track to track, because he knows where he is going and why.

Monitor influences on your child's moral norms.

As children begin to spend more time away from home, in school or other programs, you need to be mindful of what values they are being actively taught and what values they are learning from others' examples. Some connected kids feel confused once they enter school and begin talking with peers from homes with different values and different degrees of parental protectiveness. Many children who are securely attached to their home caregivers enter school armed with enough self-confidence that they are not disturbed by the different behavior of the kids at school. Others may wonder about why their peers do what they do, or why the teacher treats one child differently from another. The connected child enters school with a high standard of expectations and, with continued monitoring from his parents, will seek out peer influences that are compatible with these expectations.

What about exposing your children to different moral norms so that they learn to become more tolerant? On the surface this might seem logical, even politically correct, but there are problems with this approach. Some parents feel it's healthy for their children to learn about lots of different value systems while growing up so they will be more "open-minded" as adults, but throwing your child into the melting pot of diverse values at too young an age, before his own moral norms are well established, may produce a child who is so confused that he develops no deep value system, or one that is improperly based.

So should you instead protect your children from all outside influences and any ideas that are different from your family's values? There are risks involved in raising a child in a bubble-like atmosphere. Parents who are overprotective may end up with a child who cannot think for himself, who is thus vulnerable to all kinds of dangers and temptations. Or this child may become very judgmental and automatically condemn anyone with different beliefs.

Somewhere between these two extremes is the right path for your child. Somewhere in the middle is the parent who helps the child establish a firm value system and guides him as he encounters other value systems. This parent teaches and models tolerance, even while letting the child know what his own values are. The child eventually formulates a belief system that is similar to the parent's, with a sprinkling of alternative, yet compatible, values learned from peers and other persons of significance.

Minimize bad impressions.

Children become who they are based on the impressions they receive while growing up. While you cannot, and should not, raise a child in a bubble, parents should do the best they can to foster good influences on their children and minimize the bad ones.

Monitor the media.

Researchers who study the effects of media on the behavior of children have discovered that negative images leave more lasting impressions than positive ones. Children are more likely to remember and copy violent scenes than acts of kindness. A child's developing mind is like a giant video library where he can click on "instant replays" of all those scenes — positive or negative — that he has stored. If the child repeatedly witnesses graphic scenes of violence, sexual insensitivities, and abusive language in movies and on television, these images get a lot of shelf space in the library of the child's mind. Consider the ten-year-old who likes to watch police shows on TV. He tells his parents, "Don't worry, Mom and Dad, that stuff doesn't bother me." Doesn't bother him? It ought to. This child has become desensitized. Fast-forward the life of this child to late adolescence or young adulthood. He gets into an argument with a girlfriend, and abusive language pours from his mouth. Or he doesn't let up on his advances when a girl says no, since movies with male heroes have taught him that girls mean yes even when they say no. When presented with a situation similar to one he has seen on television, he replays by reflex what he learned as a norm from television. (For more about media influences, see Chapter 16.)

Connected children whose parents have sensitively and selectively monitored their media exposure will be bothered when they see violence portrayed. When their moral norms come from real life in the home, the blood and guts of a murder scene will upset these children, as will abusive language and insensitivity. Some internal "not right" sensor goes on, and the child doesn't feel right watching this. Being bothered by bad impressions is a good sign. We are supposed to be bothered by such junk.

Screen persons of significance.

Not only do you screen the screen from a child, but you need to be selective about the people

your child comes into contact with: friends, teachers, coaches, scoutmasters, childcare providers, and ministers. The more contact and the more trust involved in the relationship, the more you should keep an eye on it. Some children are more easily influenced than others. If you know your child well, you'll be able to sense when someone becomes a bad influence.

Know your child's friends.

Besides knowing how your own child is developing morally, it's important that you know where his peers stand, since friends leave lasting impressions on your child — good and bad. You'll run into kids who will do almost anything to get the attention of the other kids, trying to lure them into watching a restricted movie on TV, testing limits at every opportunity, and modeling just about every negative value you'd like to keep away from your child. Talk to your child about how the "bad apple's" behavior affects him: "What did you think about Stuart's behavior tonight?" Approach your child without coming across as being judgmental. You first want to find out what your child thinks. This is a clue to where your child stands morally. You can make points with your child by pointing out how the other child's behavior makes everyone uncomfortable and really isn't popular after all.

One of the reasons we emphasize the importance of forming your child's values in the preschool years is that doing so enables you to send your child off to school morally literate. As he comes under the influence of peers, he has a road map of inner convictions that has been built up over many years. Values don't stick if they are tacked onto the child at the last minute like a holiday decoration or changed like a piece of clothing according to the fashion of the day. Once children enter school, they are on the receiving end of tremendous peer pressure. If the child does not have an inner guidance system telling her which choice to make, she will more readily become a victim of peer pressure. Schoolchildren are searching for direction, and they also want to belong. Your job as a parent is to channel these drives so that they lead your child to good influences, not bad ones.

Although you can't pick your child's friends, you can set your child up to make friends with kids whose morals meet your standards. If you spot kids who are turning out well, create opportunities for your children to get to know them better. When a new family with great kids joined our church, we invited this family over to our home for lunch and an afternoon of play. We followed up with additional invitations that set the stage for our children to be together, and they became the best of friends. Friends who model your values for your children reinforce what you have taught them. This is crucial when children reach the stage at which they begin to question their parents' values. Value-full friends act as booster shots to the values you instilled in your children in the early years.

HELPING YOUR CHILD THINK AND ACT MORALLY

Children need to learn to *think through what they're about to do*. This is the key to moral behavior. Teach your children to think before they act. In the preschool years you condition children to act a certain way rather than teaching them to make moral judgments. From ages five to ten, you condition them to think morally. In addition to knowing that stealing is wrong, the older child can begin to think about how bad the owner of the bike would feel if it got stolen.

Give your child "think before you act" drills.

Children are impulsive, some more so than others. Teach your child to "count to ten if you are tempted to haul off and hit someone." Help him imagine the consequences of an action before he acts. Teach a child to imagine what the other person may feel: "Suppose someone stole your ball. How would you feel? How do you think Sean would feel if you took his ball?" The frequent verbal reminders ("count to five," "stop and think!" "wait a minute . . .") become part of him, his way of thinking, his moral reasoning. Ten or fifteen years later your child is at a party where alcohol is being served. He is the designated driver, the one who will not drink so that everyone else gets home safely. Two different kinds of reasoning enable him to stick to the plan: he has been conditioned that you don't drink and drive, and he is able to imagine the consequences of doing such a stupid thing. He is used to thinking before he acts, since he was taught to do so in childhood.

Model moral thinking.

Let your child hear you think through questions of right and wrong. One day as Matthew and I were leaving the supermarket, I noticed that the cashier had given me too much change. I shared this information with Matthew as I decided what to do next: "The cashier gave us too much money back. This extra money does not belong to us, so it would not be right to keep it." Matthew listened, thought for a minute, and nodded agreeably.

Taking advantage of such teachable moments gives parents a chance to combat the "but everybody does it" kind of thinking that justifies an action. You both show and tell your child that you expect him to do the right thing, regardless of whether anyone is watching, re-gardless of whether anyone would find out that he kept money that wasn't his. In this kind of situation you might say to your child, "A lot of people would just keep the extra change. What do *you* believe is the right thing to do? How do you think you would feel if you kept the money that doesn't belong to you?"

As your children get older, you can share more complex moral decision making with them. Talk about why you give money to sup-port certain causes, why you believe certain actions are wrong, and why other choices may be difficult but morally correct. When con-fronted with tough questions ("Should we put Grandma in a nursing home?" "Should we tell the neighbors that their teens had a loud and noisy party while they were away for the week-end?"), explain the reasons behind your deci-sion to your child. Kids, particularly teens, need to know that doing the right thing isn't always easy but is nevertheless important.

Take responsibility for your actions.

Being a moral model for your child does not mean that you have to pretend to be perfect. We all blow it once in a while. It's okay for kids to know this about their parents. In fact, you can get a lot of mileage out of your mistakes. Suppose your lose your temper, slam the door, and tell your spouse that he or she is worthless and uncaring. You leave a shocked child and angry mate in your wake. Sit down, take a deep breath, cool off, and after you apologize to your spouse, talk with your child. Apologize for your outburst and let him know that you were wrong to act that way. We all make mistakes. When parents do something wrong, they can show their children how to take responsibility for their actions and correct them. Teaching your children this lesson is more important

than having them believe that you are right all the time.

Be real.

Children hate hypocrisy. Children notice when you do not practice what you preach, and they won't take your morality lessons seriously if you don't back them up with your behavior. I re-member Matthew glancing over at the speed-ometer and noticing that I was driving ten miles over the speed limit. I could see that he was confused. I was always telling him to do the right thing, and here I was doing the wrong thing. I caught myself: "Whoops, Daddy is not obeying the law." I slowed down. It was tempt-ing to justify my driving by saying, "Well, we're in a hurry, " but doing so would have been morally wrong. I did not want Matthew to get the impression that one obeys the law only when it is convenient and expedient.

Avoid power-based morality.

"If I catch you stealing again, I'll belt you even harder," yelled a dad who was determined to teach his child right from wrong with the use of fear and force. This kind of morality lesson is more likely to produce an angry, rebellious child than one who follows an inner moral code. This child is more likely to expend his energy figur-ing out how to avoid getting caught rather than considering whether his actions are morally right or wrong. Also, the father's threats are sending the message that might makes right — that older, bigger people can enforce their val-ues by intimidating those who are less powerful. This won't produce children who do the right thing simply because it's right.

Help your child be a leader.

The family is a minimodel of society, in which children learn to respect authority and to become moral citizens. Children should respect authority figures but not accept others' values without question. You want your child to be a moral leader, not a follower. You want to raise a child who will take the lead in throwing out lawmakers who are not serving the best moral interests of the people, and who will work to elect better leaders. When children live with a strong guidance system at home, they are likely to make their parents' values a part of their selves. They then carry this guidance system with them into interactions with others. Instead of being swept along in the current of peer approval, they will set their own course, stay on it, and even swim upstream against the current if their peers are making unacceptable choices.

Train your child to be a leader.

Leadership qualities are tied to a child's temperament and personality, but parents also play a part in shaping children to become leaders rather than followers. Genuine leaders have strong convictions. They are not moral wimps. Unlike some of the modern-day politicians, whose policies and promises depend on the latest polls, connected kids follow their own deep convictions about what is right, what is wrong, and what is fair. Their sensitivity compels them to speak out against actions they believe are wrong.

Does this mean that kids who are firmly grounded in parental values have "zero tolerance" for ideas that differ from what they have learned at home? Connected kids have such firm convictions that they are deeply bothered by social injustice and the lack of values in society. Moral fervor can make some people intolerant. Yet one of the values parents can model for their children is tolerance and understanding of others' viewpoints. Children who are taught to think morally will consider others' points of view and will not stick mindlessly to their own convictions any more than they will blindly follow someone else's.

"But my child is too shy to be a leader," you may think. You can give her some help. Try these tips to set your child up to succeed.

- Encourage her to volunteer your home as a meeting place for school groups. Hosting a meeting gives a child a feeling of importance and sets the stage for showing leadership.
- Encourage your child to be part of school government.
- Often, having a parent volunteer to help with a project or event may be just the boost a child needs to get more involved herself.
- When your child feels passionately about a cause, encourage her to become involved and do what she can to make this a better world. Children and teens are very idealistic. Support them — don't be cynical or discouraging about their efforts.

Get involved in values education at school.

The answer to making schools safe and moral is not metal detectors and more security guards. Schools must teach empathy, compassion, and justice, along with social studies, math, and English. The U.S. Department of Education is now giving millions of dollars to school districts to develop programs to teach values.

It's understandable that parents would want to keep a cautious eye on the values schools teach, since schools have not always done well in this area. Educators have been told they may not impose their own values or religious beliefs on students, which has led to confusion about what values they *may* teach. Schools have tried the "values clarification" approach, which means that kids must figure out what their own values

KIDS WHO DIDN'T TURN OUT WELL
— WHAT THE GOVERNMENT DIDN'T DO

Read the headlines: ANOTHER SCHOOL SHOOTING! YOUTH ARRESTS FOR VIOLENT CRIMES ARE UP 50 PERCENT! Why these alarming headlines? Too many kids today are insensitive. Kids don't care. Criminologists have demonstrated that most criminals lack empathy. They aren't bothered by how their victims feel. They act before they think. Most likely, they were unconnected kids who became unconnected teens and uncaring adults.

The government's response has been to spend billions of dollars to put more police on the streets and build more prisons. But the government is funding the wrong end of the problem.

What would happen if the government were to use these billions of dollars for parent-education programs that would help parents learn about all the important ways in which they can prepare their child for success in life? What if disadvantaged mothers received generous financial subsidies to continue breastfeeding (like the successful program in Quebec, Canada, where mothers who qualify for the equivalent of our WIC program receive a financial incentive to breastfeed)? Imagine if every parent attended classes on babywearing, breastfeeding, child development, and discipline. What if the government made it financially possible for all mothers to stay home with their babies during the first two years?

Sure, there are many socioeconomic factors that contribute to high crime rates. Yet if we could curtail the flow of unconnected kids into the streets and replace them with kids who care, American cities would be safer and more sensitive places to live.

---

are without the guidance of moral norms. Values become a matter of what feels good.

However, schools are now beginning to teach the values that most cultures and religions hold in common: truthfulness, respect for authority, and compassion. Be sure you know what is being taught and how this is affecting your children. Ask them. If there are messages being sent that you don't agree with, or that you think could be taught differently, discuss them with your child, your child's teacher, or school administrators. It's important that parents be aware of not only the values that are actively taught in the classroom but the ones modeled by teachers, administrators, and other students. Be sure that the school is truly committed to these programs. If children see teachers acting contrary to the school's stated values, they'll conclude that values classes are phony — just words that sound nice, not words to live by. Schools that have incorporated character and values teaching into student life as well as the curriculum have seen a decrease in school violence and disciplinary problems.

Many children spend more time with their teachers and classmates than they do with their parents and therefore learn many of life's lessons from these persons of significance. One thing kids can better learn at school than at home is that while people look different, speak differently, and come from a wide variety of backgrounds, they hold certain basic values in common. Learning about common values from the perspective of different cultures helps children be more accepting of others and may help them overcome prejudices that might have been picked up at home.

SPIRITUAL VALUES

Many families' values and morals are grounded in religious or spiritual beliefs. What to tell your children about God, death, the soul, and angels is beyond the scope of this book. However, we do feel that successful children are spiritually aware and that parents must teach spiritual values to their children along with moral values and the other life skills described in this book.

Kids say: *Once I started believing in God like my parents do, I suddenly felt I had a purpose in life. (Jim, age fifteen)*

Many adults return to their own religious roots when they have children, or they seek out other spiritual traditions. Nurturing your own spiritual growth prepares you to answer questions your kids will ask. It also gives you the inner peace you need to live up to the demands of being a parent. How you practice your faith will determine how your children practice theirs. In this area, as in others, parents teach more by example than with words. A child who can trust his parents is more likely to trust God.

RAISING A SPIRITUAL CHILD

Over the years as we have studied families, we have noticed that adults and children who are spiritually grounded tend to be more successful. Remember that we have defined success not in terms of money, power, or status but rather as being connected to others, enjoying interdependent relationships, and feeling satisfied and happy. This kind of success depends upon a spiritual foundation. Whether your family's spiritual beliefs are based on the Bible, the Torah, the Koran, the teachings of Buddha, or another spiritual tradition, giving your children a sense of being connected to a being larger than themselves brings depth and richness to life and relationships. Many parents devote a great deal of effort to shaping their child's intellectual, emotional, or physical development, but they shy away from teaching spirituality. They are neglecting a critical tool for success.

In our families, spirituality means commitment to the ways of Christ and Christianity, yet for the purposes of this book, we use the term *spirituality* in a broader sense: having an inner life and belief in a supreme being greater than oneself and having these beliefs guide one's daily thoughts and actions.

While spirituality and morality are complementary, they are not synonymous. Morality is about right and wrong in human relationships and actions. Spirituality describes a deeper dimension of experience, one that looks for meaning and purpose in life and seeks relationships with that someone greater. Spirituality is not the same thing as religion, though many people find spiritual meaning in the teachings, rituals, and fellowship associated with organized religion.

Why spirituality is important to success.

Humans have a need to believe in someone greater than themselves. Comparing our own petty concerns and short span of life to the unfathomable size of the universe leaves us searching for direction, a meaning to life, and a purpose for living. Children tune in to these questions at an early age: "Where was I before I started growing in Mommy's tummy?" "Where is

Great-Grandma now? Where do people go when they die?" As they begin to think more clearly about these questions, they are not satisfied with explanations that tell them their life began by some quirk of nature and will end without meaning. Spirituality is especially needed in the high-tech world, where quick answers and instant gratification are available at the click of a mouse but ultimately prove unsatisfying.

Without support and encouragement for spiritual growth, children may grow up out of touch with their inner selves and unconnected to spiritual reality. Children who grow up without spirituality are at risk of feeling that their life is without meaning or purpose. Without the rudder of spiritual beliefs, they may drift in a sea of uncertainty, swept along by the crowd or the current popular-belief fad. Theologian and author Thomas Moore used the term *soul sickness* to describe the emptiness, meaningless-ness, disillusionment, and hunger for spiritual-ity experienced by today's youth. Because spirituality is something children can't see, mea-sure, or tune in to with a remote control, they need guidance if they are not to miss out on this important dimension of life. Children spend more time than we think soul-searching for deeper meaning to life: "How did I get here?" "Where am I going?" "What path do I take?" Spiritual guidance empowers children. It gives them a plan and a road map to help them answer these questions. It also gives them a sense of security, peace, and self-worth.

As a physician, I have frequently been im-pressed that spiritually grounded persons heal faster. I vividly remember one of my nine-year-old sick patients asking me, "Dr. Bill, would you pray for me?" That child was well on her way toward spiritual success.

TWELVE WAYS TO GUIDE YOUR CHILD'S SPIRITUAL DEVELOPMENT

We have noticed that children without a core of spiritual beliefs feel incomplete or alone, and are at greater risk of depression and feelings of low self-worth. For this reason, spiritually aware children tend to be more responsible and tend to make wiser choices. Spiritually grounded children believe that their lives have meaning.

1. Start early.

Your child's spiritual training actually begins with the way you parent. Spirituality requires children to trust in themselves and in relation-ships outside themselves, and trust is learned

---

SCIENCE ASKS:
Is the brain wired for God?

Neuroscientists, using new tools called SPECT cameras (the acronym stands for "single photon emission computed tomography"), can take pictures of radioactive tracing materials circulating through the brain to show which areas are used for different types of mental activity. Studies of people's brains during various spiritual exercises, such as deep meditation, show that specific areas of the brain are used for spiritual processing. This certainly suggests that brain biology supports the human need for spirituality. We would add that children's early experiences may influence the development of this wiring.

from responsive parents. Children's concept of God parallels their relationship with their parents. Children must learn how to trust their parents, whom they can see and feel, before they can trust someone they cannot see. Children who experience their parents as cold, uncaring, or unresponsive come to expect this lack of responsiveness in other relationships, including their relationship with the universe. Children who receive attachment parenting learn to trust their environment and their parents — and by extension, their spiritual longing. As the Hebrew psalmist observed in prayer, "You made me trust in you even at my mother's breast" (Psalm 22:9). Children who learn to trust right from the start will be able to trust their spiritual needs more easily. Attachment parenting also instills in the child the *capacity to connect,* and connectedness is at the heart of spirituality.

Why spirituality can't wait. Sometimes we hear modern parents say, "We want our children to be open to many religions rather than teaching them about only one. So we're going to wait and not teach them anything specific. We want to let them make up their own minds when they are older." For some parents, their hesitation may reflect their own rebellion against the rigid religious teaching of their youth. The truth is that putting off spiritual guidance does your children a disservice. As with moral or intellectual values, learning spiritual values follows a developmental process. Miss the windows of opportunity in the different stages of childhood and it's hard to catch up on spiritual values in adulthood. (See "internalizing" and "stages of moral growth," pp. 190.)

The idea that kids should be free to determine their own moral course without outside spiritual influence is not a new idea. Samuel Taylor Coleridge, the great English poet, was once talking with a man who told him that he did not believe in giving children any religious instruction. The gentleman's theory was that the child's mind should not be prejudiced in any direction. Children should be permitted to

CHILD'S RELATIONSHIP WITH PARENTS	CHILD'S SPIRITUAL VALUES
• Trust: Child knows that parents respond to her needs	• Trust in a responsive God
• Comfort: Parents comfort in distress	• Comfort in God, in nature, in others
• Connectedness: Child feels that he belongs	• Connection to others, to something bigger than self
• Love: Child feels that she is important and brings joy to others	• Love for self, for others, for God
• Desire to please: Parents are authorities	• Willingness to be responsible to self and others
• Forgiveness: My parents forgive me	• Acceptance of oneself and others

choose their religious opinions completely for themselves. Coleridge said nothing, but after a while he asked his visitor if he would like to see his garden. The man said yes, and Coleridge took him out into the garden, where only weeds were growing. The man looked at Coleridge in surprise and said, "Why, this is not a garden. There is nothing here but weeds." "Well, you see," answered Coleridge, "I did not wish to infringe upon the liberty of the garden in any way. I was just giving my garden a chance to express itself and to choose its own production."

2. Know thyselves.

Some parents' reluctance to teach their children spiritual values stems from their own uncertainty about what they themselves believe. As a teen in a spiritual-philosophy class in a Catholic school, I studied the principle *nemo dat quod non habit* (no one gives what he does not have). The feeling that they should offer spiritual guidance to their children often compels parents to examine their own spiritual values. This may begin with being part of the miracle of birth and taking on the responsibility of parenthood. As young adults become parents, they often shake off their spiritual complacency, reconnect with spiritual values learned in childhood, and search for new ways to express spirituality in their lives. Parents may begin to pay more attention to their own spiritual lives when their children enter school or begin to ask hard questions about God and death.

If you are still searching for answers yourself, be honest with your child about it. Don't try to fake conviction. What is more important is that you recognize that spirituality is important to you and that you let your child know that it is important to you. Even if you are uncertain of your own beliefs, give your child an honest

speech from your heart. You don't have to be a theologian to talk about spirituality with friends and family. Tell your child what you think and feel, then listen to what he thinks. You may be surprised to discover that your child's comments may point you toward the answers you've been looking for. Your child's exploration of the meaning of life and death will enrich your own.

3. Spiritual values are for everyday wear.

Teaching children about spirituality is not a once-a-week assignment. You can't delegate the job to a rabbi, a Sunday school teacher, or even to Grandma and Grandpa. Children need to see and talk about spiritual values in everyday life. To help your child "catch" the spirit, you need to emphasize spirituality as an important part of everyday living. Spirituality is not separate from everyday family life; it *is* family life. Marvel at the sky, the clouds, and the trees together, and talk with your child about how they came to be and who made them. Share how your beliefs help you through challenges and hard times, and show your child how to connect with his own spirituality in moments of need and sadness. Also share how these beliefs contribute to the joy and peace in your life. It's important that children learn that there is a spiritual dimension in daily living.

I often refer to sunsets as God's paintings.

4. Listen to your child.

You'll learn a great deal about where your children are spiritually from the questions they ask and the comments they make. Don't back away from tough issues. When children have questions about life after death, they expect a thoughtful answer. Even if you don't believe you have all the answers, at least discuss your ideas and your child's to the extent that your child perceives that this is a subject worth thinking about.

When preschool children go through that normal stage of magical thinking, they often experience saints, prophets, or angels as very real people in their lives. Sometimes a puzzling question ("How can God have eyes enough to see everybody?") can lead you into an interesting discussion with your child, especially if you are not too quick with pat answers. The questions and stories that are the product of a child's imaginative thinking are signs of spiritual inquiry and growth. The words and images they use to explain life's spiritual dimensions tell you about what they're thinking and feeling. Preschool children might imagine God as a superhero of some sort. Children may imagine heaven as a place full of candy and toys. It's important for parents, teachers, and religious leaders not to squelch this normal stage of magical thinking. Instead, reinforce what your child discovers through his imagination. Use these opportunities as teachable moments and relate your child's ideas to your family beliefs.

5. Watch for openers.

When your children ask about God or death or creation, seize the moment and talk with them according to their level of understanding. A discussion initiated by a child has greater potential for learning than when a parent introduces the subject. When watching the news or talking about world tragedies or inequities, interject comments about the spiritual aspects of such happenings. Most children have a spiritual hunger that needs to be fed and will welcome chances to talk with you about spiritual subjects.

6. Enjoy daily spiritual events.

In our families, mealtime and bedtime prayers and blessings have been an important means of transmitting our beliefs to our children. Our children listen to our prayers, as we ask God for both favors and forgiveness, along with the wisdom we need to meet the challenges of our lives. We also encourage our children to talk about what's going on in their lives, at school, at play, and at home, and ask for God's blessings on them. These rituals help children establish comfortable patterns that they can call upon throughout their lives to maintain their own spirituality.

Our children may hear many "Thank God" references throughout the day.

7. Make family rituals special.

Another way to focus on spiritual values in your family life is to plan and enjoy family rituals. Rituals signify a spiritual connection. Start them when your children are young and continue them into the teen years. Rituals don't have to be formal or complicated to make an impression.

Consider these suggestions:

- A family ritual might be something as simple as asking everyone to name something they are thankful for before digging into a holiday dinner.
- Celebrating the various holy days of your own religious tradition, or adopting those of others, helps children see what is sacred about your beliefs and how you make them central to your life.
- Take your children to weddings and funerals, civic ceremonies, and seasonal celebrations in

your community. Attending a friend's religious celebration helps your child respect other people's religious practices.

- Some Christian families celebrate their children's baptismal anniversaries as well as their birthdays. You might find other special days in your child's life to commemorate from year to year.

All of these activities show your child that people are connected in their joys and sorrows, and that our lives have meaning that we cannot always see.

8. Real men do it.

Polls have shown that mothers are more likely to be involved in praying with children than are fathers. This gives children, especially boys, the message that spirituality is primarily a woman's domain or that it is not important enough for both parents to become involved in. Just read the headlines and you'll see that today's boys are in need of spiritual values.

9. Join a spiritual community.

Parents as well as children thrive on the support available to them from communities of faith. Being part of a spiritual network, such as a church, synagogue, prayer group, or religious-education class will help you develop your own spiritual practices as you guide your child's development. Being part of a religious group also gives a child a feeling of belonging. The child feels that he and his family are not alone in their spiritual beliefs, since he knows other people who live and believe this way, too. Children benefit from getting to know a variety of people outside the family who are good role models. In a spiritual community, they also learn to care for others and enjoy the feeling of being cared for. Loneliness is very common in

children, especially teens. Being part of a group of people who share similar spiritual values is a healthy antidote to loneliness. It can help teens (and their parents) ride out the conflict-ridden orange-hair, nose-piercing stage and other strange adolescent behaviors and help kids eventually turn out well.

10. Read about it.

Encourage your child to enjoy books with a spiritual dimension. Picture books, traditional tales from many cultures, songs, and movies all convey spiritual messages to share with your children. (There's a lot of theology in the *Star Wars* movies.) Novels such as C. S. Lewis's series, *The Chronicles of Narnia*, contain lessons about love and sacrifice, along with plenty of thrills and adventure. The Old Testament is full of action stories. What could be more exciting than the children of Israel's escape from Egypt and the parting of the Red Sea?

11. Teach tolerance.

You want your children to respect the beliefs of others and be open to new ways of thinking about life and spirituality. One way to explain the many religions in the world is to say something like "People speak to God in different languages."

Exposing children to other beliefs won't dilute the message you're trying to get across. Instead, children learn that spirituality is important to lots of people and that "everybody believes, they just believe differently." It's also important to learn that everybody practices what they believe differently and that everyone's beliefs and practices should be respected. Some people light candles, some sing hymns, some lift their arms, some bow their heads, some fall on their knees. Spend your energy anchoring and grounding your child in your own family belief system rather than putting down the ideas of others.

12. Practice what you preach.

Children intuitively identify what's real, what's important, what matters. Children will learn more from how your beliefs translate into how you live than they will from what you say about what you believe. Guiding your children spiritually is a lot like instilling healthy nutritional habits. Show matters more than tell. Children learn by example. Children won't follow their parents' beliefs unless they see them in action.

Preteens and teens in particular can see through parents' shallow belief systems. As children grow older, parents must ease away from dictating how children should behave and get down to the basics of practicing what they preach. Children, teens especially, hold hypocrites in low esteem. Parents, however, have been known to drag children to weekly worship services or enroll them in religious elementary or high schools mainly because they think doing so will keep their kids on the straight and narrow. Children need to know that their parents' commitment to spirituality is real — not just a paranoid attempt to keep teens away from sex, drugs, and alcohol. Religion is not a pill to be swallowed just to get a person through a difficult season of his life, though some children learn this viewpoint from the adults around them. Developing mature spirituality is an ongoing process. For most of us, it's a journey rather than a final destination.

Forcing religion on unwilling and unready children without practicing it yourself causes teenagers to grow up resentful of parents' spiritual beliefs and unwilling to make spiritual commitments of their own. When children see parents acting contrary to their own spiritual values because of expediency or lack of commitment, they conclude that their parents' beliefs are not real. You are always onstage in front of your children. They want to see how you overcome challenges to your beliefs and to see you defend and nurture your spiritual values and put them into practice.

Throughout this book we have emphasized the importance of children learning to trust and building connections first with parents and then with others outside the family. Shared spirituality helps build trust and connectedness. It also gives children integrity and grounds their morality in lasting principles rather than in the intellectual fashion of the day. Guiding your children to spiritual maturity gives them a faithful heritage that can last an eternity.

If we fail to instruct our children in justice, religion, and liberty, we will be condemning them to a world without virtue, a life in the twilight of a civilization where the great truths have been forgotten.
                                    — President Ronald Reagan

12

Eleven Ways to Boost Your Child's Self-Confidence

WHAT CHILDREN BELIEVE about themselves is at the heart of what they become. A child whose self-belief is positive values the person he sees when he looks inside himself. He thinks of himself as a worthwhile person, and because he feels right about himself, he behaves in a worthwhile way.

There are lots of terms for positive beliefs about oneself: *self-esteem, self-respect, self-worth, pride, a "can-do" attitude.* We prefer the terms *self-confidence, self-worth,* or *self-belief,* which portray a deeper trust in oneself than the terms *self-image* or *self-esteem.* A child with healthy self-belief feels good inside. He carries a *sense of well-being* within himself and strives to maintain this feeling. When the child strays off the path — which all kids will do at times — some inner voice says, "This is not right." The child then works hard to right himself and regain that sense of well-being.

Self-belief defends children from people who belittle them or threaten their sense of well-being. Building up your child's self-belief is an effective way to protect her from bad relationships and from people who do not respect her. Kids with healthy self-confidence can stand up to peers who are tempting them with drugs or alcohol. They can say no to verbal abuse

from a teacher or coach. They are more likely to maintain their balance in a family or personal crisis. The child with healthy self-belief accepts and values his own emotions and can connect with others and their feelings. Self-confident children can sense what they themselves need, and they know how to ask for it.

A child with positive beliefs about himself does not necessarily sport a perpetually happy face. Yet he feels good about the person he is and enjoys the ability to handle life's ups and downs with an overall feeling of "rightness." He thinks of himself as valuable and worthwhile. Because children who feel right within themselves express this feeling in their behavior, they tend to be easier to get along with, make better decisions, and are more likely to resist peer pressure. Children with a healthy set of beliefs about themselves can appraise their strengths and weaknesses realistically, thereby empowering themselves to build upon their strengths and enabling them to work through problem areas.

A child who doesn't feel right often doesn't act right. A poor sense of self-worth leaves a child feeling that he can't get what he needs from the people around him and that he is of no value to anyone, even himself. This feeling leads to anger, distress, and behavioral problems. Because the child believes he is no good at anything, he doesn't trust himself. He whines and cries to get what he needs, or he yells and bullies. His parents and his peers don't like this behavior and react to it by scolding, avoiding him, getting angry, or punishing him, which only makes him angrier — or more passive. His behavior gets worse instead of better. Eventually, no one expects him to behave, so he doesn't.

Positive beliefs about oneself lead to high self-confidence, not in a narcissistic or arrogant sort of way but in a realistic way. A child's confidence is rooted in trust in his caregiving environment. When he can trust that his needs will be met, he feels worthy of having his needs met. Confidence means "trusting in," and when babies and children feel confident of their caregiving environment, they also feel confident about themselves.

Kids say: One thing I'm glad my parents never did is make me feel bad about being me. (Chris, age twenty-two)

Self-belief is contagious. Consider your friends and acquaintances. Why are some of your friends a delight to be around, while you dread being around others, who drag you down? How often do you try to avoid someone because "he's such a negative person!"

Try as many of these eleven self-belief boosters as you can.

1. BOOST MORE THAN BREAK A CHILD'S SELF-BELIEF

Sometimes it seems that a child's self-confidence is just one more thing for parents to worry about: Is my child healthy? Is he eating well? Does his winter jacket fit? And by the way,

how's his self-esteem doing? You don't need to measure your child's self-esteem daily, as you might take a temperature: "Billy's self-esteem is low today; his soccer team lost. I'd better find a way to give him a boost." Self-belief is more stable than the up-and-down fortunes of the soccer team or the A's, B's, and C's on a report card. Self-confidence does not rest on compliments, praise, good evaluations, sports victories, or congratulatory ice-cream cones — though these things may influence self-worth. A child's self-belief is based largely on the way he is treated by people who are important to him. When you as a parent are responsive to your child's needs, you are laying the foundation for her belief in her own worth and her ability to make things happen.

Throughout life your child will be exposed to people and events that contribute to his self-worth and to others who chip away at it. We call these *boosters* (positive influences) and *breakers* (negative influences). Your role as a parent is to be a builder, someone whose positive beliefs about your child help her think well of herself. You don't need a degree in psychology to raise a confident child. Much of parenting is easy and fun. Hold your baby a lot, hug your child often, respond sensitively to children's needs, treat your children the way *you* would like to be treated. All of these things help children believe that they are important people, worthy of love and respect. If you can put yourself in your child's place and hear with her ears the messages you send, you'll naturally concentrate on being a builder and recognize when the occasional "breaker" slips out of your mouth.

I believe that healthy self-esteem is developed very early by letting kids know that they are doing a good job, by letting them know that they are valued, and by helping them see their strengths — whatever level they happen to be. It's important to be clear about the end result and not fret about the little missteps along the way. To me, life is a journey, not a race, and I want my children to enjoy every step of the way.

2. BUILD BABY'S SELF-CONFIDENCE

The roots of self-belief are planted in infancy. What do you imagine an attachment-parented baby believes about herself? Her needs are appropriately and consistently met. She spends many hours a day being held in someone's arms, worn in a sling, nursed on need, and comforted when upset. Her environment gives her a calm, happy, secure feeling that becomes a part of her. Because of responsive caregiving, this infant grows up feeling that she is *worthy of attention.* Ever been in a situation in which you were on the receiving end of lots of special care? Didn't that make you feel as if you were someone special? That's how attachment-parented babies feel most of the time.

Babies learn about who they are from the way they are cared for. The prime builder of self-esteem in infancy is that key word *responsiveness.* Baby cries because of hunger or distress. Caregivers respond, and baby discovers that her actions can make things happen to help her feel better. As baby and caregivers repeat this cue-response pattern thousands of times during the first year, baby learns that her cues have meaning. As she forms the idea that she is a separate person, she builds in beliefs about her worth: "Someone listens to me, picks me up, feeds me . . . I'm valuable." She learns to recognize when she feels right, and when she feels wrong, she learns what to do about it.

When a baby's needs are not consistently met she learns to distrust her own cues and to distrust herself. She may feel confused and believe that her signals have little or no meaning, because she's never sure whether she will get a response. While in reality it's not her fault that no one is responding to her cues, this baby nevertheless concludes that she herself is powerless or worthless. In baby's egocentric view, what's wrong with her world is also wrong with her.

These early impressions take deep root in a baby's fast-growing brain. The connected infant enters childhood with a secure sense of well-being — one that is an inherent part of his self. This self-belief is difficult to dislodge; the child adjusts his behavior to maintain this sense of well-being. Sure, these children will falter at times, and some, because of circumstances or their own personality quirks, may face considerable challenges during childhood, but with positive self-belief established early in life, these children are very likely to wind up back on their feet. Children who lack this secure sense of self-worth have greater difficulty asking for what they need and want as they are growing up, and they do not feel in control of their lives and destinies.

Our number one theory with all of our kids was to give them the feeling of a secure, loving world in the first six months of their life, knowing that reality would come soon enough.

◆

Elizabeth notes: *As I watch my five-month-old son, Coleton, I am truly overcome by the fact that he is so very dependent upon others for survival. The simple fact that he can barely hold his head up, let alone move his body where he wants, makes me realize what an awesome responsibility we have to our babies. He's hungry; he cannot eat. He's wet; he cannot change himself. He's scared; he cannot move away from what frightens him. He desires to be held; he cannot express his wishes clearly. At no other time in* *my child's life will he be so dependent upon others to fill the most basic, yet most essential, of his needs.*

◆

By responding to our baby's needs, we begin to build positive self-esteem by communicating that his needs are important and that he matters to us. Babies are young for an incredibly short time — don't waste a moment.

3. MIRROR POSITIVE MESSAGES

Children continue to see themselves through their parents' eyes as they grow out of infancy and into childhood and beyond. A child's self-belief — for better or worse — depends on the messages he receives from his parents. During their first year, most infants receive mostly positive messages. They learn that they are loved, valued, and cared for, especially those who spend a lot of time in arms and at breast and have sensitive, responsive parents.

Children value the messages they receive from adults they trust. Attachment parenting at the beginning of life sets up the child to be very trusting, so the messages he receives from his parents as he grows have a great impact on him. They are meaningful because they come from people to whom he is deeply connected. The messages of love and attachment that the infant receives so frequently in the first year or two need to continue throughout childhood, although these messages take different forms as the child goes through different developmental stages. There is more to growing a confident child than just following the Baby B's of breastfeeding, babywearing, and bonding.

What messages do you reflect to your child? Are they predominantly positive or negative? Do you give her the idea that she's fun to be with, that you value her, that her opinions mat-

ter, that her behavior pleases you? There are many ways you can give your children these kinds of positive messages about themselves; while praise and compliments are certainly one way to help your child form positive beliefs about herself, your actions speak at least as loudly as your words.

We praise Thomas because we believe that positive labels can be of great assistance to the child in developing self-esteem and can actually be like self-fulfilling prophecies. I say, "Wow! Look at your room! You put every single toy away in its box. What a tidy boy you are!" He remembers the "tidy boy" idea and will be more likely to behave in this way again. Often he even praises himself. He says things like "clever Thomas!" when he does something clever.

4. PLAY WITH YOUR CHILD

Both children and adults learn a lot when they play together. When you take time to play with your child, you are saying, "You are worth my time. I like being with you." This is an important way to tell your child that the things she cares about are important to you. When you have fun together, your child's self-confidence grows.

Stepping out of your adult world and into your child's is not always an easy thing to do. As a busy person, I had a hard time learning to enjoy unstructured and seemingly unproductive play with my children. My mind would wander back to the "more important" things I had to do, and I would get restless. I felt I ought to be "doing something" (like writing a book about kids) instead of stacking blocks or rolling a ball with my own toddler. Yet as I began to realize how important these times were to my children, playing with them became more meaningful.

TURNING BREAKERS INTO BOOSTERS

Your child will not spend his or her entire childhood surrounded by positive messages that boost self-esteem. Your child will be the target of put-downs. Here's where you can turn a problem into an opportunity or teachable moment.

You hear your two children squabbling. "You're stupid," says big brother Aaron to Chris, and Chris crumbles. "That's a put-down," you say. Kids need us to identify a behavior without a lot of words. Aaron clearly needs an empathy lesson and a reminder of how much his younger brother loves and trusts him. But first you need to put Chris back together.

You might point out that even the best of friends and brothers sometimes say unkind things that they don't mean and that they're sorry about. You also remind Chris of all the smart things he does. You tell him that just being the younger brother doesn't make him stupid and that there were lots of things Aaron couldn't do very well when he was that age.

Next, take Aaron aside and help him imagine how he would feel if he were the target of "you're stupid." Do a little role-play (see p. 122). Put on Aaron's hat and play as if you're him and he's Chris: "Suppose you're Chris and I look you right in the face and say you're stupid. How would you feel? You're the older brother, and Chris loves and trusts you. He believes what you say. Suppose I say you're stupid, and because you love and trust me, you really think you are stupid. How does that make you feel?"

Play even became therapeutic for me. It forced me to leave behind my adult preoccupation and focus on the simple pleasures of playing with my child, who was, without realizing it, teaching me to relax. Here are some ways to enjoy playtime with your child.

Give your child focused attention.

If your body is with your child but your mind is elsewhere, your child will sense that you would rather be somewhere else. This is a lose-lose situation. Your child gets a negative message ("Daddy doesn't want to be with me") and concludes that she is not important. You lose the opportunity to relax and learn more about your child. Being able to slow down and enjoy the present moment is a valuable life skill, and learning it is one of the great benefits of hanging around with children. One of my cherished play memories is the fun I had in our "play cir-cle" with six-month-old Matthew. I sat him on the floor facing me with a few of our favorite toys and made a circle around him with my legs — a position that kept us focused on each other and provided support in case he started to topple over. This was the beginning of many hours of play between us. He had my undivided attention. He felt special, and so did I.

Make time.

A friend once asked me how I found time to coach our kids' sports teams, attend their performances, teach them the skills of skating and sailing, and have time to just hang around with them. I told him that because it's important to me, I make time. It's simply a matter of priorities. And very early on, your children perceive where they fit into your priorities. During playtime give your child the message "There's nothing I'd rather do right now than spend time with you."

While I was writing this book, our family got a new Ping-Pong table, and fifteen-year-old Matthew really got into the game. Frequently he would come find me while I was working and ask, "Dad, want to play a game of Ping-Pong?" Notice that he didn't say, "Let's play a game of Ping-Pong." He wanted me to *want* to play with him. When I realized this, I made a point of immediately acknowledging his request, no matter where I was in my book-writing schedule. "Sure, Matt, I'd love to," I would say as I put down my pen and tuned in to my child. A fifteen-year-old who wants his dad to play with him gets priority. The time you have with your children passes so fast, and it's like playing a tape you can't rewind. Enjoy these precious moments while they last.

Let your child direct the play.

Some adults, when they spend time with children, feel that it's their job to make playtime worthwhile. They decide what educational game to play, which story to read, or how to build the best block tower. The child goes along because she wants to please the grown-up, but whose self-worth is getting the boost here?

Activities initiated by the child hold her attention longer than ones suggested by an adult playmate. A child learns more from play when she gets to make decisions about what is going to happen. When you let the child choose the activity, you are saying, "I like to do the things you like to do." This is a self-belief-builder for kids. It makes them feel special and respected. Even if you're thinking you can't *possibly* play *another* game of free-wheeling checkers with your six-year-old, it's important to him. If you can smile brightly and say, "Okay, champ, go get the checkerboard!" you'll not only make him feel great, you'll teach him that it's okay to ask for what you want.

And if you *really* can't smile while playing another game of checkers, ask your child for another suggestion. Working with him to select an activity you both enjoy also sends a positive message. Children perceive when you are really into the game or just perfunctorily going through the motions more out of duty than desire. Go ahead and add your own personal twist to the time you spend playing with your child. It's easy to get bored the twentieth time you're asked to read *The Cat in the Hat*. Stop and talk about the story and add your own twist, such as: "What would you do if the Cat in the Hat came to our door?" Asking him what he thinks gives his self-belief a boost.

5. SHOW AND TELL YOUR CHILDREN THAT THEY'RE IMPORTANT

It may be obvious to you, but children often don't realize how important they are to us. Parents can get so busy with day-to-day living that they neglect to tell their children outright how much they love them and how important they are. So many times we think wonderful things about our children but neglect to voice these feelings when our children need to hear them.

- "There's nothing I'd rather do today than spend time with you."
- "I'm so proud that you're my daughter."
- "I'm glad you came along. It's so much fun being with you!"

Parents' actions also tell children that they are important to us. Every time you attend a child's choir performance, baseball game, or class party, you send a message that builds self-confidence. You are saying that the things that are important to her are also important to you.

BUILDING HEALTHY SELF-BELIEF IN CHILDREN OF COLOR

When we first moved into our neighborhood, my son, Andrew, and I went across the street to the playground. He began to play "tag" with the other two kids. The only way they would play with him was if he were perpetually "it." He had to do the chasing, even after he'd tagged one of them, or else they would just ignore him. Their mother sat watching, as if this were a perfectly natural way to play the game. After a while, I noticed Andrew getting frustrated and sad. It hurt me, of course, to see my son's feelings hurt this way. I called him over and told him, "You don't want to play with them, Andrew. They're not playing fair." As we walked home, I talked with Andrew about what had taken place, and admonished him never to allow anyone to take advantage of him in that manner.

This isn't just a story about kids who don't play fair. You see, my son is black, and the two other kids happened to be white. Were they playing this way because they were thoughtless or because they were prejudiced? It's unfortunate that race colors our perceptions of situations and of ourselves to such a large extent, but when it comes to the self-image of our children of color, it seems to me that it would be foolish, if not detrimental, to ignore this. Three strategies I use to ensure that my son has a healthy concept of who he is and what he can achieve in life are acknowledgment, affirmation, and positive exposure to diverse experiences.

It's important to acknowledge our history and culture, both within the context of the larger society and apart from it. Parents may have to supplement what their children learn in school about their history. I've used community activities, cultural events, art exhibits, visits to other cities, and explorations around our Philadelphia area, which has a lot of historic sites and a rich African-American heritage, to teach my son about his "roots." I also acknowledge African-American contributions to the larger culture by making sure that examples of the creative expressions of black artists, writers, performers, musicians, and inventors are evident in our home.

I've always paid attention to my son's personal interests and affirmed them. Early on, Andrew showed an affinity for science, particularly space and natural science, including animals. For years, we had memberships to our city's science museum, the Museum of Natural History, and to the zoo, and we still visit those places often. It wasn't long before my son began to see science as his area of expertise. He looked forward to choosing the more complicated topics for his science fair projects, probably, in part, because he knew he could count on my attention and support. In second grade, he got curious about computers, and I introduced him to educational software. Now, at 11, he uses the internet to do homework research, but he's mostly into computer games. I check out the games he plays, and I talk to him about the kind of thinking, graphic design, and technical skills it takes to create a computer game. (Somebody had to develop that stuff, and probably made good money doing it!) At the end of fifth grade, he proudly brought home a certificate for outstanding achievement in computer skills. He feels very confident now in his ability to utilize and trouble-shoot computers.

Having these and other areas of expertise affirms my son's identity as an intelligent boy with numerous possibilities for a secure future. I believe they provide a kind of safeguard against internalizing the negative images, destructive influences, and discrimination he's likely to encounter as a young black man growing up.

I want to make sure my son's upbringing includes an array of experiences that broaden and prepare him to live and work in a multicultural, global society. Again, I've taken advantage of the numerous and varied attractions of the area where we live to add diversity to our family outings. I underscore that as residents and taxpayers, all of the public venues of our city are as much ours to enjoy as anyone's, from the art museum to a Japanese garden, to a horse-jumping competition. We're only limited by our imaginations.

I think it's very important for us to talk to our children about their future. That's how they learn of our expectations of them, and the way they begin to visualize their options. I take every opportunity to introduce my son to people, particularly people of color, who are succeeding in their chosen work, such as the president of a company I work with, or a relative who ran for mayor and is in state politics. I took Andrew along with me when I interviewed a leading astronomer for a magazine article and, over the years, as we've taken our pets in for care, Andrew has had interesting chats with our veterinarian, a profession he says he would be interested in pursuing. I make sure that positive role models, African-Americans being productive and doing valuable work, are part of my son's world.

Valerie Harris, Publisher and Editor
Black Parenting Today *magazine*
www.blackparentingtoday.org

You don't have to wait for a big event in your child's life to send this kind of message. Equally important are mini–confidence boosters — showing interest in a block structure your child just built, listening to a teen's new music CD, asking about something that's going on in their lives. All of these seemingly insignificant moments add up to a billboard-size message that says: You are a valuable person.

We want our children to always feel loved and supported. One way to do this is to leave brief, cheerful notes for them in unexpected places, such as tucked in a hat. This always puts smiles on their faces.

6. RESPECT YOUR CHILD'S OPINIONS

When you ask your child's opinion about something or listen attentively when she offers it, she feels important. When your child has your complete attention and senses that you are truly interested in what he has to say, he feels valued. Conveying that you value your child's viewpoint not only builds self-worth but also opens up avenues of communication. You're giving your child a chance to practice expressing himself in tactful, respectful ways.

- "Which dress do you think looks best on Mommy?"
- "Which movie do you think the family will like best?"

- "What do you think we should get your brother for his birthday?"

When you consider your child's opinion carefully, ask her about her reasons, and let her know that her input has helped you make a better decision, you reward her for thinking carefully and let her know that you respect her judgment. She'll feel more confident about herself as a result.

Kids say: I think one thing that's really important for a good parent to do is to take time to listen to your kids. Don't always yell at them if you think what they did is inappropriate or disrespectful. See things from their point of view before you lose your temper and start cutting strings for what could have been an excellent relationship by thinking things are only right if you have your way. You could be putting up the very wall in the parent-child relationship that most parents are trying to break down. (Amy, age twenty-one)

7. STAMP OUT PUT-DOWNS

While you can't (and probably shouldn't) shield your children from all the self-confidence breakers they will encounter outside your home, you can make your home a safe zone where children are encouraged to believe positive things about themselves. Ban put-downs from your home, especially the kind that older children direct toward their younger sibs. Be equally vigilant about friends and neighborhood kids. And it goes without saying that parents should be especially careful to avoid directing put-downs at their children.

A put-down, even one that is meant to be fun, can make a child feel small inside. A bit of good-humored teasing is okay between brothers and sisters, but blatant put-downs ("You are so dumb" or "Everybody knows your handwriting is terrible") are out-of-bounds. Teach your children that you expect them to pull each other up, rather than put each other down. Siblings have great influence on each other's feelings of self-worth. When you hear crippling words such as "You're dumb!" or "You're weird!" label them as put-downs the instant you hear them. "That's a put-down."

A mother in our practice told her children how devastating put-downs are, especially to younger children. She explained how calling someone an unkind name makes that child feel angry and makes the child want to continue the very behavior that triggered the name-calling. She told her children, "Instead of yelling, 'You're stupid,' at your brother, look him square in the eye and say, 'That was a stupid thing to do, and I know you're smarter than that.' Then help him clean up the mess, or do whatever needs to be done." This is good advice for siblings and for parents. Remember to model this behavior yourself the next time you encounter spilled milk or mud tracked through the kitchen. You'll get a more positive reaction than you would if you just started yelling.

Squelching name-calling can also be an empathy lesson. "You imbecile!" yelled fourteen-year-old Jennifer at her annoying seven-year-old brother, Alex. Alex didn't know what an imbecile was, but by the tone of Jennifer's voice, he knew he didn't want to be one. Here's a situation the wise parent would turn into an empathy lesson and tell Jennifer, "Suppose you were seven and Alex was fourteen, and you were called the imbecile. How would you feel?" Appeal to the normal sensitivity of older children and they are likely to change their behavior without a long sermon. Doing so with Jennifer privately, once her anger has subsided, will have better results.

8. PROTECT YOUR CHILD'S SELF-CONFIDENCE

In the preschool years, the home environment naturally has the most influence on a child's self-esteem; ideally, home should remain the most important impact throughout childhood. But as children mature, they become involved with people and activities outside of the home, which also influence what children believe about themselves.

The deeper the roots of homegrown self-confidence, the better equipped kids are to enter school and interact with peers in a way that builds up their self-worth rather than pulling it down. In fact, we have noticed that connected children shine in social groups. Because of their sensitivity and ability to empathize, they get along well with most kids. Because connected children are more comfortable with themselves, they are able to feel comfortable with others. Their inner feeling of rightness and sense of well-being guides their choice of friends. Because of this internal guidance system, they are less influenced by peers with incompatible values. Connected children are often very discerning about friendships. Rather than forming numerous superficial relationships with lots of kids, they may have fewer, but more meaningful, relationships.

Screen your child's friends.

Keep a watchful eye on your child's friendships. Although children need to choose their own friends, parents should closely monitor the relationships. More often than not, connected children seek out compatible playmates on their own; they don't like to be with friends who threaten their feelings of self-worth. Examine how your child is feeling at the end of playtime with a particular friend. Is she happy and at peace, or ornery and upset? Do she and her friend share an equal, give-and-take relationship, or does one dominate the other? If you feel that a particular friend is a positive influence on your child, encourage the relationship; if not, discourage it.

One day my daughter Emma had over an older girl whom she greatly admires. The two of them were drawing. Her friend, who's quite artistically talented, drew a picture of a beach scene, and then Emma began one. Her friend said, "No, that's not how you draw the beach!" I was ready to step in and say that it was fine to do things differently, but before I could enter the room I heard Emma say, "That's okay, I like the way I'm doing it!" It really showed me how confident and comfortable she is with her own abilities and how she was not swayed by another's opinion.

Make your home kid-friendly.

Making your home inviting to your child's friends gives you the opportunity to observe your child in social situations. Sure, having groups of kids around may mean you have a bigger mess to clean up and a higher grocery bill, but the security of knowing your child's friends and how she gets along with them is worth the inconvenience. Being the home in your neighborhood where kids like to congregate gives you an advantage by putting you on the spot for disciplinary intervention, either in private time with your child or in group therapy if the whole pack is getting out of line.

As children ease into independence, they often take two steps forward and one step back. Expect your child to retreat periodically to the security of home and family after ventures into the social jungle. This is why it's so important for school-age children to maintain a strong attachment to parents and family. Even connected kids who are able to follow their own inner compass in new situations and relationships will need periodic doses of homegrown confidence.

Screen other influences.

A child's self-esteem depends not only on the messages he receives from parents and friends, but also on those that come from other trusted caregivers — *persons of significance* in a child's life, such as coaches, teachers, scoutmasters, ministers, and relatives. Once upon a time, persons of significance in a child's life came primarily from the extended family, but in today's mobile society a child is exposed to a wider variety of influences. Today's parents need to be especially vigilant about their children's role models. In fact, the more your child likes and trusts a particular person, the more vigilant you need to be about the messages that person sends your child. Ask yourself, "Is my child receiving good, appropriate messages from this person?" Sometimes you just have to rely on your gut feeling about that other person. If you are not

---

HELP CHILDREN LIKE THEIR OWN BODIES

Unfortunately and erroneously, our world places high value on a person's appearance. Today's hottest celebrities are usually young, physically beautiful, and very thin. Television commercials focus on ways that men and women alike can become more dazzling and attractive. These societal messages not only distort our children's impressions of what "real" people look like, they also create impossibly high standards against which our children measure themselves.

For the sake of our children's self-image and good health, we parents must counteract the messages in the media and focus our children on the reality that true human beauty has nothing whatsoever to do with a certain standard of packaging. Yet what a child sees in the mirror greatly influences her self-worth. Here are some ways parents can help children like what they see:

• *Model healthy dietary and exercise habits in your family.* A child who is well nourished and physically fit will be happier with her body. (See Chapter 6 on family fitness and nutrition.)
• *Tell your child you like his body and what he can do with it.* "I love to see you run!" "You dance so gracefully!" "You look terrific!"
• *Avoid comparisons,* such as "Your sister has nice, long legs," "Your brother is so strong."
• *Never tease a child about her body.* Don't allow kids to criticize other kids' bodies. Model this behavior yourself as well. Avoid descriptive words with negative connotations, such as "skinny," "shorty," "clumsy," "chunky," and "klutzy."
• *Realize that how your child looks now is not how he will look as an adolescent or adult.* Most kids go through a sloppy stage when they don't seem to care about their appearance or hygiene. This will pass, especially if you model, rather than preach, neatness. Many preteens, even kids whose parents are slim, go through a pudgy stage. When adolescent growth hormones kick in, the body stretches and that stored fat disappears. The pictures of the ten-year-old and the fourteen-year-old don't even look like the same child. If during this stage the child is not happy with her appearance, show her pictures of yourself at the same age, or just let her know that she'll soon stretch like her sister or her friend did.

comfortable with a particular teacher or coach being an influence in your child's life, arrange for a change. Your child spends six to eight hours at school every day — as much time as adults spend at their workplace. A teacher who belittles students or clashes with your child has a great deal of influence. We have always operated on the principle "when in doubt, take him out." (See "Screen Persons of Significance," p. 50.)

9. FRAME YOUR CHILD'S QUIRKS POSITIVELY

You can change how photos appear by changing the theme around them. Children with certain personality quirks or challenging temperaments are often tagged with unfair labels. The more the child hears this label, the more he may believe it and actually wear it. Your job is to quickly discount discouraging labels and replace them with encouraging ones. Framing is a powerful encourager, as you will notice in these examples:

Framing your child in a positive light not only squelches your child's critics but makes you look good in front of your child. If you as the person he trusts more than anyone in the whole wide world believes that he has these positive traits, he is likely to believe it himself. Besides, children expect their parents to look through external behavioral quirks and delve into the person inside.

Temperamentally difficult children, because they are both challenging and inconvenient, get tagged with unkind and unfair labels, such as "difficult," "exhausting," "draining," "uncooperative." With behavior shaping, nurturing, and positive framing, these early perceived liabilities in your child's temperament often turn out to be personality pluses. Many such children turn out well and exhibit strong leadership qualities, empathy, assertiveness, and very persistent personalities that make them determined to stand up for their own belief systems.

Quirky kids.

Framing is particularly important for children who have behavioral problems or rough edges to their personality that need smoothing. Focusing on the negative and always framing your child in a negative light is likely to make the child even more difficult and negative. While helping to fix what you perceive is "wrong" with the child, encourage what is right. Emphasize the pleasant parts of her personality more than commenting on the difficult areas. Temperamentally difficult children are set up for negative comments and actually are the ones who need the most encouragement.

Frame your own attitude positively. Let your children see how you keep your cool in the face of setbacks: "I'm sure happy I didn't get burned" as you spill your hot coffee. Attitudes

SOMEONE SAYS	YOU RESPOND
"He sure is stubborn."	"He does have a persistent personality."
"He seems so hyper."	"He sure is curious."
"She sure cries easily."	"She's very sensitive."
"She gets bothered easily."	"She's very compassionate."
"He sure is draining."	"He's very challenging and interesting."

are contagious. Joyful persons we interviewed attribute their positive attitude to the attitude modeling of their parents and other caregivers.

The most successful people are usually ones with the most positive attitude. When our children reach age seven or eight (the age at which lessons about life seem to finally sink in), I have an attitude talk with them that goes something like this: "You often can't control circumstances, but you can control your attitude toward them. Throughout life you'll encounter times when things just don't go your way — you strike out, you don't get invited to a party, or you get sick. Sometimes your reaction to what happens tears you up inside and is really worse than what actually happened. Keeping a positive attitude and filling your mind with positive thoughts ("I'm still a good player," "Wow, I could have been hurt a lot more!") can help you from getting stressed-out inside. As soon as you feel negative thoughts enter your mind, quickly tell yourself, 'Don't go there.' Instead, immediately click into positive thoughts." One of the most valuable success tools you can teach and model for your child is maintaining a positive attitude even in the face of adversity.

10. HELP CHILDREN DISCOVER THEIR SPECIAL SOMETHING

Success breeds success. Over the years, we have noticed a phenomenon we call the *carryover principle:* success in one area boosts a child's self-confidence, which then carries over into success at other endeavors. For example, one of our sons is a natural athlete but wasn't at all interested in academics when he was younger. Operating on the carryover principle, we encouraged his pursuit of athletics. As his overall self-confidence increased, so did his grades.

Once children excel at one thing, they learn what it feels like to overcome challenges and master a skill. They like this feeling and want to repeat it in other endeavors. People who are successful at one thing tend to be successful in many others.

Kids say: I think parents should always remind their children that they are important to them. They are beautiful in their own unique way. (Rachel, age sixteen)

Every child has a special something, a talent that, if encouraged and nurtured, blossoms into skills that bring a child much pleasure and also contribute to his self-esteem. Having a special area of expertise is especially valuable to children in large families, where children's individuality can sometimes easily be overlooked. If you child really wants to try something, find a way for her to do so. She's more likely to stick with and succeed at something she is passionate about.

THE WALL OF FAME

In our Sears's family gallery of accomplishments, our walls display Jim's sailing trophies, Bob's football photo, pictures of Pete playing soccer, Hayden's cheerleading trophies, Erin's horse-show ribbons, Matthew's Little League pictures, Stephen's baseball poses, and Lauren's soccer pictures. Every child is good at something. Discover it and encourage it. Frame it, display it, and make your kids famous — at home, anyway. Older children can see their years of achievement at a glance. This gives them a lift, especially during times when their self-worth needs a boost.

Every child is a VIP, yet children are important in different ways.

I encouraged my daughter to try everything until she found not only something she was good at but something she loved doing. This ended up being in the world of the performing arts — acting, singing, and dancing. I encouraged her by accompanying her to auditions, rehearsals, and performances. When she had trouble or failures, I listened to her vent and sympathized with her tears.

♦

Sports, music lessons — my daughter tried these things, but nothing really caught fire. Then she wanted very much to try figure skating. Must be the costumes, I thought, and we headed off to skating lessons. I figured this, too, would pass, but instead, she really worked hard at her skating and got to be quite good. Then she announced she wanted Irish dancing lessons (costumes again!), so I signed her up. She loves it and recently won a first-place trophy at a dance festival. At age sixteen, she is paid to help out with skating classes at the Y and with dance classes for younger kids. Now she says she really wants to study archaeology in college. If she really, really wants to do it, I figure she'll be a success.

If you have difficulty identifying your child's special something and motivating your child to develop it into a skill, try scouting or a similar program where everyone works hard and everyone's hard work is rewarded with badges. Scouting exposes your child to a lot of different kinds of activities, one of which may unlock your child's special something.

Sports as a special something.

Some of the happiest times in childhood come from participation in team sports. In addition to creating happy memories, involvement in sports tends to encourage healthy self-esteem.

Research shows that the longer kids stay in sports, the more likely they are to stay in school, get better grades, have higher self-esteem, and have fewer behavioral problems. Positive interaction with parents is one of the main reasons youngsters continue to participate in sports. (See *It's Just a Game! Youth, Sports and Self-Esteem: A Guide for Parents,* by Darrell Burnett, Ph.D., [Funagin Press, 1993].)

Participating in athletics benefits a child's self-confidence for a host of reasons. Playing on a team fulfills a child's need to belong to something bigger than herself; the identical uniforms, the team cheers, and the common goal help create a special kind of protectiveness among children. They join the team as disconnected individuals but unite and work together toward common goals. Involvement in sports also gives children an opportunity to learn and master skills, another path to boosting self-confidence.

Sports participation also presents some hazards to your child's self-esteem. I've had the privilege of fifteen years of coaching various kids' sports and have learned more about children from my coaching experience than from my psychology courses in medical school. Most children will play only as well as they're expected to. If a parent or coach keeps telling a child he is not good at a sport, he'll usually play accordingly. Most children trust most coaches. They are significant people in a child's life — for better or worse. Monitor the messages that come from coaches. While competition motivates some children, for others it makes life on a team difficult. Being a bench warmer or the kid who bats last can be tough on a child's self-worth. Here's what you can do to make your child's participation in sports a positive influence on self-esteem.

- **Match child and sport.** Part of knowing your child is knowing your child's capabilities. Figure out what sport he's good at and encourage him to try it. But let him choose what he wants to participate in.

- **Match child and position.** When I had children with marginal attention spans on my baseball team, I would try to position those kids as pitcher or catcher. They had to pay attention, or they'd get beaned with the ball. Interestingly, children who have attention problems often can go into a state of hyperfocus when playing a position that requires intense concentration, such as a goalie on a hockey or soccer team.

- **Match child and coach.** If you have a sensitive child whose self-confidence is easily undermined by harshness, yelling, and put-downs, avoid teams with drill-sergeant coaches.

- **Show and tell the coach.** Tell the coach about your child and what approaches you've learned best motivate your child. A wise coach will listen.

- **Remember that the sport is for the child, not the parent.** Your job as a team parent is to cheer for your child and the rest of the team, to support the coach, and to get your child to practices and games at the right time. Your child is not in sports to replay your own glory days as a high-school athlete or to make up for the Little League experience you missed out on as a child. It's easy for parents to become emotionally involved with a child's performance on the playing field, but doing so only puts additional pressure on the child to play well. If you are a jock dad and your child is more gifted as an artist than as an athlete, accept your child's uniqueness and encourage him along the path he should go, not along the path that you chose.

- **Be a model spectator.** Don't put down the coach for questionable strategy; don't deride the way another team plays; don't even bad-mouth the ump for bad calls. Children develop an attitude about a particular sport not only from the coaches on the field but from the parents in the stands. As one veteran coach colleague shared with me, "I love coaching the kids, it's the parents who are a problem."

- **Remember the reason your child is playing sports.** Kids play sports to learn skills, enjoy exercising their bodies, and have fun. Along the way they learn a few life lessons, like teamwork, how to handle winning and losing, and that hard work pays off. It's unlikely that you have brought another Tiger Woods or Michelle Kwan into the world. Just relax and enjoy the game.

Exciting the unmotivated child.

What about the child who you know has a certain talent but is just not motivated to work at developing that talent into a skill? If you recognize an ability in your child that she doesn't, encourage her. Be sure that you truly recognize the child's own talents and interests — not just an ability that you wish he had or, worse, that you wish *you* had.

Consider the dilemma of piano lessons. Is it wise to encourage your child to take piano lessons if she is reluctant? Madison's parents, sensing that she would enjoy music, encouraged her to play an instrument. Madison resisted. "I don't want to," she said. "I don't like to practice. I'd rather be playing outside." Eventually, Madison agreed to piano lessons but resisted practicing. Nevertheless, after a few months of lessons, her parents realized that she had a natural talent for the piano. Madison was still not excited about it. Should her parents allow her to drop the piano lessons, so as not to be pushy parents, or should they persist?

Madison's parents wisely persevered. They believed that skill development is important to a child's self-esteem, and they wanted her, for her own satisfaction, to develop her musical abilities. They encouraged her: "Madison, we love to hear you play." They really listened when she played and often asked for encores of favorite pieces. They rewarded her with a new dress for her piano recital. To get her into the habit of practicing, they made a rule: no piano, no TV. After six months of lessons, Madison mastered a few longer pieces and played them frequently. She liked how they pleased her audience, and most important, she liked how she felt when playing the piano. Now she enjoys playing the piano and practices willingly. She is self-motivated, and her parents can now back off.

Sometimes how you phrase a request makes all the difference and can ease your child into compliance. We had difficulty getting Matthew to practice piano, yet we wanted to encourage him to develop his natural musical talent. An encouraging word like "Matthew, how about some great music . . ." would often motivate him to sit down and play the piano. In this way, he played because he wanted to, or wanted to please us, rather than feeling compelled to.

Every child has a special talent for something. Developing this talent helps the child learn valuable skills — not just how to play the violin or how to pitch a baseball but how to work hard at getting better. Often you have to prime the pump with loads of encouragement and tangible rewards to get it going to the point that it runs itself. Those first steps up the learning curve on a musical instrument or in swim-

ming or gymnastics are hard, and children, who often begin an activity believing that they will be good at it immediately, can get discouraged. This is where wise parents let the child know that they expect him to stick with it. Once the child gets over the "my mother made me do this" stage, and begins enjoying the skill, he will be able to motivate himself better. He may even remember to thank you when he's grown up.

11. VALUE DOESN'T DEPEND UPON PERFORMANCE

While encouraging children and having high expectations can be a confidence booster, it's important that children perceive that their value as human beings is not tied to their performance or to fulfilling your expectations. Being expected to perform to gain love and acceptance is a tough assignment for a child, one that most children rebel against. Trying to live up to unrealistic parental expectations sets up a child for failure, and those feelings of failure will become part of his beliefs about himself, possibly for the rest of his life. Be sure that your words and actions let your child know that you love her because of who she is, not because of what she can do. Let her know that you expect her to do her best, no less and no more, and that you love her no matter what.

Children measure their own worth by how they perceive others value them. And in this measuring-and-testing society, in which children's scores and abilities are quantified from prekindergarten testing up to GPAs and SATs, there are plenty of opportunities for children to measure themselves against others. Your child may be batting a personal best of .400 this season on the softball team but still may feel inadequate if teammates are batting above .500. With all the opportunities for not measuring up, it's important that children be able to rely on their parents to love them for themselves, to celebrate their accomplishments, and to avoid measuring them against their peers.

What's important, anyway?

Children — and many adults, for that matter — tend to measure a person's importance by prominence or wealth. As children enter school and become more involved with peers, they become more aware of whose family has a bigger house or a fancier car, whose parents have higher-status jobs, or which children have more expensive toys. It's up to you to teach your children to value themselves and other people based on their character rather than by their titles or what they own. Character, after all, dictates true importance in the world as you want your child to see it.

Being different doesn't mean you're less important.

All human beings have limitations and imperfections, and these do not make us less worthy. No one is perfect, and no one should expect to be perfect. An art teacher once told an aspiring artist-friend who was having difficulty, "Leave in imperfections." Why? People are unique and interesting because of, not in spite of, their differences and flaws. As the song says, "Everything is beautiful in its own way." This is an especially important message for parents to give their children because children can be cruelly honest with one another and won't hesitate to point out differences. Parents should certainly not deny that these differences exist. In fact, explaining differences about disabilities helps demystify why some children must use a wheelchair and others have difficulty learning

to read or speak clearly. As you explain things to your child, you should also point out that as different as people may seem, we are all remarkably alike in many ways. Children with disabilities like to play with friends, watch television, listen to music, and have fun with their families.

If your child has a disability, set her up to

CHILDREN ARE RESILIENT

Don't fret about your past parenting. It's never too late to work on building your child's self-image. Children are resilient and able to bounce back from a difficult start. No parent gets everything right all the time; and in many families, financial circumstances, medical problems, or parents' personal struggles with self-worth keep them from being the parents they would like to be. Children, however, are able to pick out the prevailing messages in the family and form lasting impressions based on them. Lasting beliefs about oneself are not formed in a day, a month, or even in a year. As with every other facet of parenting, your child expects you to do the best you can, given the circumstances of the moment.

By the time our child was four years of age, I realized I had gotten into a more distant style of parenting, and my child and I weren't connected. I realized I needed to shorten the distance between myself and my child and gave her high doses of lots of focused attention. We spent lots of time just having fun with each other. In a way, this reconnecting process was like camping out with our child for a year, and it paid off.

succeed by helping her develop the skills and talents she does have. Be a facilitator. Set up the conditions that make it easier for her to do things for herself. Consider the child who is shy or has difficulty making friends, or has some physical limitation that causes her to be regarded as "different" by her peers. Throw a class party at your house. Invite your child's chosen friends on a special outing. Ask a friend or two to help with a special craft or cooking project on the weekend. Set up your child to shine, to have a special moment in the eyes of her peers. She'll get a confidence boost, and her peers will see a side of her they don't see at school.

13

Ten Ways to Encourage Your Child

JIM FASSEL, COACH of the 2001 Super Bowl finalist New York Giants, announced early in the Giants' football season, "We're going to the Super Bowl. I guarantee it!" Though far from being the favorites and despite a less-than-promising beginning to their season, they did indeed go to the Super Bowl. Why? What turned an average team into a great team? The coach believed in his players, so each player believed in himself. No one else thought they would make it as far as the Super Bowl, but their 41-0 victory over the Minnesota Vikings in the playoffs convinced NFL fans that they were winners. That's the power of encouragement and high expectations!

Encouragement means giving children the confidence they need to be all they can be. Think about what it means to *en*-courage. It means helping a child have the courage to try, to believe that "I can do it!" Encouragement is much more than praise, which just acknowledges something a child does ("Good job at cleaning your room!"). Encouragement helps a child keep working at something. It keeps her involved in the process of learning and trying. Children thrive on encouragement, messages that tell them they can be all they want to be and that help them recognize their progress and

potential. By encouraging children, you enable them to give themselves positive feedback, like *The Little Engine That Could.* The "I think I can" attitude stimulates children to believe in themselves and to keep trying until they accomplish their goals.

Kids say: My parents were confidence builders. They identified our strengths at an early age and affirmed and encouraged the development of those qualities. Frequently during family meals they would set aside a special time to affirm a particular family member. Those were very important times, not only for expressing love and appreciation but also for building confidence. (Marcy, age twenty)

Parents are usually their children's number one fans. They cheer at soccer games; applaud when their child gets a hit in baseball or softball; and attend band concerts, choir concerts, plays, spelling bees, gymnastics meets, and school awards nights. Supporting kids' academic, artistic, and athletic endeavors is important, but you can do more for your kids than just be there.

I tell my children they can be anything they want to be if they put their mind to it. It's a big world out there and they have an important place in it.

Kids who turn out well have parents who set high expectations for their children and encourage them in specific, genuine ways. Here's what we've learned about encouraging children to stretch themselves, learn, and grow.

1. BUILD A STRONG TRUST RELATIONSHIP

Encouragement begins with trust. "Consider the source" is good advice for evaluating both criticism and compliments. Words of encouragement are most valuable when they come from a trustworthy source. This is why we encourage you to use attachment parenting to build a strong, trusting relationship with your child. When your child trusts you, everything you do as a parent is more effective. Think for a moment how you feel when you're on the receiving end of praise or a compliment. Encouraging words mean more when they come from someone whose opinion you trust. If your children have learned that they can trust you to respect and care for their needs, they will also believe you when you say, "You can do this." When children trust that you believe in them, they are more likely to believe in themselves.

Kids say: I think parents should always make sure their children know when they're proud of them. (Bill, age fourteen)

2. STAMP OUT DISCOURAGING WORDS

"Where seldom is heard a discouraging word . . . ," goes the ballad "Home on the Range." Ponder for a moment what *dis*courage implies — taking away a child's courage, undermining confidence, lowering expectations. Discouraging words that tell a child he can't do something or isn't good enough become self-fulfilling prophecies. Your child perceives that you don't believe he can do it, so why should he believe he can? Common discouragers include the following:

Generalizing.

"You *always* mess up that play." "You *never* clean your room." Nobody's bad all the time, but statements like these tell a child that you are hypercritical. The child then perceives, "I'm basically incompetent." It would be better to offer an encouraging word when your child makes mistakes, such as, "Even great kids make foolish choices," or "You're too smart for me to allow you to make unwise choices." By limiting the discussion to the present problem and reminding your child that he's not usually like this, you empower him to do better next time.

ENCOURAGING WORDS

Let your attitude, and your home, be filled with words of genuine encouragement, such as:

- "You can do it!"
- "Great job!"
- "Yessss!"
- "Way to go!"
- "Yes, you can!"
- "Wow!"
- "Great idea!"
- "I knew you could!"
- "Awesome!"
- "You can handle that!"
- "Keep it up!"
- "You've just about got it!"
- "You're almost there!"
- "You've got it!"

Comparing.

"Why can't you make A's like your sister?" The child perceives, "I'm not as good as my sister. My parents don't love me as much." Putting down a child in this way will make him feel that he truly is not as good as his sister. A better approach would be to say, "Do you really believe that getting C's is the best you could do?" or "We expect you to do your best, so we'll look at the effort column more than the grade."

Replaying.

"That's the third time you . . ." A child perceives that "Dad is keeping score" or that "Mom must believe that I am bad most of the time." Again, you're taking the focus away from the present situation and leaving the child feeling worthless. Although you want to be aware of whether your child is developing a pattern of misbehavior inappropriate for his age, dredging up past offenses usually doesn't help prevent future misbehavior. Talk about the present offense with your child, and the causes for it. Figure out how you can help him maintain better control over this behavior.

3. WRITE ENCOURAGERS

Our children appreciate the little love notes that we sprinkle around to motivate and encourage them.

- A well-timed Post-it on the bathroom mirror that says, "You can do it!" encourages the child who later on that day will compete in cheerleader tryouts.

- Place a little Post-it on the top of a pile of completed homework that says, "Done!"

- An animated e-mail sent to your child's mailbox is a nice high-tech touch.

- Paste a little note on a pillow after your child has cleaned his room that says, "Nice work!"

- A happy-face picture in a child's lunch box encourages a great afternoon.

- As your child opens his book at school to a chapter he studied so hard the night before, he sees a little note with a happy face with a reassuring caption, "We're thinking about you," or "We're praying for you," as he begins his test.

4. PLAY THE ERASE GAME

Children need to receive constant messages from persons of significance about what's important and what's expected. Here's a way to give your children the message that it's important to encourage one another and that, in fact,

---

ENCOURAGING SIGNS

Encouraging your child doesn't always have to involve words. Use body language. Give your child the thumbs-up sign as she steps up to bat or prepares to compete in the gymnastics meet. Raise your eyebrows and open your mouth in a "wow!" expression when admiring your child's painting. Catch her eye and smile as the band concert is about to begin. Stop and listen while she practices violin. When your child is kind to another, reach over and warmly squeeze her hand. Sometimes your actions can say a lot more than words.

you expect it. When you hear one sibling insulting another, wave your hand in front of the speaker in a wipe-away gesture. Say, "Stop," or "Erase." Children immediately get the message that discouraging words are not acceptable and will not be tolerated. Don't waiver, joke, or give your child any ambivalent messages that these words are okay. Children look for opportunities to test whether you will remain firm about family principles. Teach them that you are. Most children will naturally use, shall we say, colorful language with their peer groups. But you can balance out this tendency by expecting them to use better language at home.

5. GIVE "WE" MESSAGES

We have gotten a lot of mileage out of the appropriate use of "we" in our family.

- "We practice piano."
- "We brush our teeth every night."
- "We go to church every Sunday."
- "We say thank you, I'm sorry, excuse me. . . ."
- "We don't stand on chairs."

"We" messages are much more meaningful to the child than "I" messages ("I want you to clean up your room") or "you" messages ("You should clean up your room"). "We" conveys an expectation, the family norm, sort of like the "everyone is doing it" belief that school-age children are often motivated by. It capitalizes on the natural desire for children to seek out what's important. "We" tells him so. It denotes that some behaviors are not optional — they're expected. Using "we" also eliminates the need for inappropriate praise and gives your child the message that he is doing exactly what you expect, and he should not expect to be praised for do-

ing so. You can acknowledge expected behavior, such as "Glad you finished brushing your teeth early so we'll have more time for stories," but you don't have to praise this expected behavior.

6. SHOW GREAT EXPECTATIONS

Children very often live up — or live down — to their parents' expectations. Praise a child for being kind and she will look for more opportunities to show kindness. Tell her she's not very good at softball and she'll probably start dropping easy fly balls. Children know what their parents expect from them, even when the expectations have gone unsaid. Parents' expectations become part of children's beliefs about

---

SCIENCE SAYS:

Students study up to their expectations.

In their book, *Pygmalion in the Classroom,* psychiatrists Robert Rosenthal and school principal Lenora Jacobson describe a study they did involving children from kindergarten through fifth grade. They told the children's teachers which students in their classrooms had "exceptional learning abilities." But the teachers did not know that the researchers had chosen these "exceptional" students at random. When the students were tested at the end of the school year, the students who the teachers had been led to believe had exceptional learning abilities had made much greater academic progress than their peers. In essence, the teachers had been programmed to expect more from certain students, and these students thus expected more of themselves and delivered.

themselves. Having high expectations for your children helps them believe that they are capable, talented, and likable.

We frequently use terms like "sharp eyes," "quick thinking," "extra helpful," and "very considerate," to praise our children. These are terms we feel identify the traits we want to help our children develop.

Aim high.

Parents' expectations are a very powerful motivator for children. Let your children know that you expect them to do their best. You're not wishing or hoping — you expect that they can and will do their best. As your child searches for norms to follow in life, make sure that he realizes that doing his best is not an option: it's the norm, the way it is.

Of course, it's important that your expectations about your child's talents and direction in life are realistic. You want your children to be all *they* can be, not just what you want them to be. We are frequently asked what we did to influence our three eldest sons to become doctors. Sometimes I'll answer these queries by joking, "It was entirely their choice — they could choose what medical school they wanted to go to." But really, our children were more influenced by what I did than by what I said. They observed that I felt good about helping other people feel better. They had opportunities to see me at work, since I always had a small office in our home for seeing sick children after hours. I also took them on hospital rounds and let them hear me giving telephone advice. They saw that I enjoyed what I did, and of course, children are fun-oriented. They saw the fun of medicine before they realized that they would have to do a lot of hard work before they started having fun. As they got older I also let them know that no matter what you do,

whether it's being a doctor or a concert pianist, there is a "grunt work" stage that takes perseverance to get through and that you often have to do work you don't want to do in order to get to where you want to be. And I did drop a few hints here and there: "You know, Bob, I think you'd be a great doctor. . . ."

"Be a good one."

An encouraging message we gave our children is that whatever you chose to do, do it well. Marv Levy, former coach of the four-time Super Bowl team Buffalo Bills, was expected to use his Harvard education to excel in the business or academic world. Instead, he pursued his dream of being a football coach. When he announced to

---

AN ENCOURAGING FISH STORY

Michelle Borba, in her book *Parents Do Make a Difference,* relates the following story:

A local fisherman told us about one of the residents several years ago who, tired of his pet fish, dumped them into the lake. The fish, Japanese carp, were no more than three inches in length at the time. The fisherman explained a fascinating principle about the breed: The carp's length is affected by the size of its container. He told us that carp contained in a small aquarium grow to about three to six inches in length. If you put the same fish in a larger tank, they'll grow to be six to ten inches long. If they're in a small pond, they can become almost a foot in length. Because the fish were thrown into the lake, they grew to be over two feet in length. . . . It seems the fish grew bigger because they had the opportunity to do so.

his father that he decided to be a coach, his surprised dad responded with an encouraging, "Be a good one."

7. PUSH RATHER THAN PRESSURE

"When am I pushing too hard?" concerned parents often ask. There is a fine line between encouraging and pushing. Encouragement motivates a child to *want* to accomplish a feat, based on his innate talents — with a little help from those he trusts. Encouragement becomes pushing when parents try to get a child to do something or develop some skill that he doesn't really want to, perhaps because he believes he lacks the talent. Pushing becomes pressuring when parents try to force a child where he doesn't really want to go, and it can backfire. Encouragement resonates with the child's own inner beliefs and desires. It's a positive force.

For wise parents, what the child wants to do and is capable of doing coincides with the parents' wishes for the child. But there are times when parents of kids who turned out well have insisted that children learn certain skills at certain ages, regardless of whether they want to or not. Take piano lessons, for example. How many of us remember our mothers "pushing us to practice" when we would rather have been out playing ball? Yet many of us wish that our parents had pushed us harder to learn a musical skill; as adults we now regret that we didn't develop the ability to play a musical instrument. As a mother of three children who turned out well told us:

Practicing piano twenty minutes a day is not going to kill any child. We simply let our children know that this is a normal expectation in our family, it's what we do, sort of like the routine of brushing your teeth. They never felt that practicing was an option. It was an expectation. Now, as adults, each of our children plays a musical instrument, just like their mother told them they would.

8. MODEL AN "I CAN" ATTITUDE

Whether you think you can or whether you think you can't, you're right.

— *Henry Ford*

Motivational speakers proclaim, "Success comes in cans, not cannots!" Your attitude about tackling new challenges is contagious. Let your children know when you take on a tough job that a "can do" attitude is what makes success possible. Many times when I have been talking to editors about book deadlines, our children have heard me say, "Yes, we can finish by then." They hear a ring of enthusiasm and confidence in my tone of voice that says, "I can take on this challenge." Then, over the next few weeks, they see me focusing on finishing the work. They learn that it takes time and effort, along with self-confidence, to complete challenging projects. This model has helped them attack challenging projects in school and elsewhere.

Kids say: They exuded an attitude of support that helped me believe that I could do anything, and should at least try everything. They did not overbook my schedule but exposed me to athletics, music, and the arts at an early age. (Marcy, age twenty)

"E" is for effort.

One of the most encouraging messages you can give your children is that you expect them to *do their personal best.* Encourage effort, not only results. It's easy to become preoccupied with all the ways we keep score in this society — grades,

---

PERSEVERING WORDS

"You can get it done."
"You can reach your goal."
"Don't quit."
"Keep trying, you'll finish it."
"Stick to it."
"Hang in there."
"Keep trying."
"Keep at it."
"Don't give up."

SUCCESSTIMONIES

The following are stories we have heard about people who succeeded by overcoming handicaps and discouraging setbacks. They persevered and believed that they could accomplish their goals.

- Michael Jordan was once cut from his high-school basketball team.
- Walt Disney was fired from a newspaper job because he didn't have any great ideas. He went bankrupt a few times and was advised to "Get rid of the mouse because there is no potential in it."
- Thomas Edison and Winston Churchill were considered failures in school.
- Albert Einstein didn't talk until age three or read until age nine. He didn't do well in high school and failed his college-entrance exams.
- Abraham Lincoln was demoted from the rank of captain to private.
- Beethoven was told by his music teacher that he would never succeed as a composer.

---

sports statistics, percentiles on standardized tests — and neglect to notice the effort the child made. Encourage effort; praise perseverance.

Perseverance is high on the list of traits of children who succeed. It's more important than talent or IQ. People who are less than gifted, physically or intellectually, nevertheless work their way to the top if they persevere. Working harder at something is a great equalizer in an achievement-oriented society. A less gifted person can achieve as much, and even more, success as one who is gifted but less disciplined.

A classic example of a successful person persevering to succeed is Winston Churchill, whom we discuss at length in *The A.D.D. Book.* By today's standards he would have been labeled A.D.D. and had repeated school failures. Yet he went on to become one of the world's great leaders. Why? Because of his perseverance, for which he is best known by his motto: Never give in. For Churchill, perseverance was the most important key to success.

Thomas Edison is another historical figure we portray in *The A.D.D. Book,* and surely had he lived today, he would have been tagged a "hyperactive kid." But through perseverance he went on to become a great inventor and truly

merits the label of a successful person, since the lives of many people are literally brighter because of Edison's inventions. As with Churchill, his perseverance was the key to his success, as evidenced by the familiar Edison quotation: "Genius is 1 percent inspiration and 99 percent perspiration."

Love them no matter what.

While encouraging children and having high expectations can be a confidence booster, it's important that children perceive that their value as human beings is not tied to their performance or to fulfillment of your expectations. Being expected to perform to gain love and acceptance is a tough assignment for a child, one that most children rebel against. Trying to live up to unrealistic parental expectations sets up a child for failure, and those feelings of failure will become part of his beliefs about himself, possibly for the rest of his life. Be sure that your words and your actions let your child know that you love her because of who she is and not because of what she can do. Let her know that you expect her to do her best, no less and no more, and that you will love her no matter what.

9. LEARN FROM MISTAKES

We all know that Babe Ruth once held the record for hitting the most home runs in a single season. But did you know that the same year he hit the most home runs, he also set a record for striking out? People who persevere, try hard to excel, and venture into many areas are likely to make more mistakes. You want your children to learn that it's okay to make mistakes. The real issue is what you learn from a mistake so that you don't keep making the same ones over and over.

Kids say: My parents did not always interfere but let me learn from my mistakes as long as it was not too harmful. (Madison, age seventeen)

Children need to learn that it's all right to mess up and that it's normal not to be perfect. But they should also be taught to take responsibility for their misjudgments. Actually, by watching our children, we learned that mistake-free living was not only impossible but also unhealthy. Our sixth child, Matthew, was very hard on himself when he didn't get something done perfectly, and we realized that he was picking up on his parents' tendency to become angry at our own mistakes. Perfectionism wasn't doing Matthew any good, and we reasoned that it probably wasn't good for Mom and Dad, either. So we began to lighten up on ourselves; consequently, Matthew learned to live with his mistakes as well. Now when someone in our family makes a mistake, we say, "What can we learn from this?"

All children make mistakes. Our job as parents is to turn mistakes into important opportunities to learn. Unfortunately, parents' first response when a child makes a mistake is an emotional one, one that sends the message that mistakes are terrible. Reactions such as "How can you be so clumsy!" or "What's the matter with you?" turn mistakes into signs of personal shortcomings. Better responses focus on the fact that the child is a capable person who, like all capable people, makes mistakes now and then. Try one of these the next time your child makes a mistake: "You almost got it right," "That's okay, try again," or "Oops, here's a sponge."

Model mistake-correcting.

One way to help your child learn to accept mistakes is to admit your own mistakes and then take responsibility for correcting them. Lighten up on yourself. When you spill a cup of juice, say, "Guess I win the family 'Messy Award' for the day."

Be sure your child perceives that you have an accepting attitude about mistakes. We have made a deal with our children, "If you tell us about the mistake you've made, no matter how big it seems, we promise not to get angry with you — provided that you tell us the lesson you've learned and how you are going about correcting your mistake."

Elizabeth says: When Vanessa was about three years old, she attempted to pour a glass of juice. The liquid missed the glass and spread over the floor. She looked up at me with horror in her eyes, but I just said, "Oh-oh, you better get a towel." She wiped up her mess and asked me to pour the juice. "You can do it," I reassured her. "Try again." She did, and again most of the juice missed the glass and landed on the floor. I helped her wipe up the second mess, and she then assumed I would pour the juice. Instead, I helped her by steadying her hand on the carton, and she successfully poured her glass full. The delight on her face said it all: "I did it!"

We have tried to teach our children to focus more on solutions than on problems, which, incidentally, is one of the keys for success in the corporate world. Learning to turn problems into opportunities helps a child bounce back from mistakes and earn a second chance. In fact, taking a problem and turning it into an opportunity is one of the hallmarks of some of the most successful corporate executives. Computer-age children are finding that mistakes are a normal way of life. When the computer makes an error, we don't even call it a "mistake," we call it a "glitch."

10. HELP YOUR CHILD GET AN A FOR ATTITUDE

Why are some people more enjoyable to be around than others? One explanation is attitude. That's what attracted me to my wife, Martha. Her positive attitude made her a nice person to be around. I liked being with her and wanted to be around her all the time. Attitudes are contagious, and Martha's attitude toward life and people improved my own.

A positive attitude can make the difference when getting a promotion or convincing your proposed mate to say, "I do." Attitudes affect our lives in concrete ways. Studies have shown that optimists generally live happier, healthier, longer, and more successful lives than pessimists. Parents shape their children's outlook on life. Here are some simple ways you can help your child become a positive person.

Put on a happy face.

Children use parents as mirrors. They look to parents for cues about their own feelings and reactions. If you reflect an upbeat attitude to your children, they perceive that being positive and hopeful is the norm. Even when you're feeling worried or stressed, try to greet your children with a smile and a positive attitude. A happy or just a calm conversation with your child can put your worries in perspective and brighten your outlook. A scowl from you can leave your child worried or frightened, even though your frown has nothing to do with his or her behavior.

Look at the bright side.

Show your children how to make the best of bad situations: "But, Mom, we lost the game!" "Yeah, that's tough, but your team is really improving. And you scored your first goal!"

"All this rain means we can't go to the park today. Let's go to the library instead. It's a nice place to be on a rainy day!"

Program the positive.

I often remind my children, "You can't always control circumstances, but you can control your reaction to them." This is true from moment to moment and over the long term as well. In fact, I believe (and science is beginning to confirm) that a child's growing brain is programmed with predominantly positive or negative attitudes, based on the child's experiences. The statements

"She's such a positive person!" or "He always seems so negative!" may have roots in the biology of the brain, as well as in psychology. When you see your child dwelling on a mistake or misfortune, help him find a way to get out of that rut. Acknowledge his sad or shameful feelings, but then help him find a new way of looking at things. If your child didn't make the basketball team or the season is just not going well, get him thinking about the soccer or the gymnastics season ahead. Or remind him that not having to attend basketball practice means he has more time to do other things he enjoys.

Dress up when you're down.

Help your child learn to figure out what she needs to do to turn negative emotional states into positive ones. Your own example will present teachable moments. When it's clear to your child that you're having a bad day (and children are very good at sensing a parent's mood), stop and flip the emotional switch from negative to positive. Say, "I'm not going to let myself feel this way. What can I do that would help me feel better?" Think of some options: "Let's get dressed up and go out and have some fun," "It's a beautiful evening — what if we sit outside and watch the moon?" "Cooking something yummy always makes me feel better — let's make cookies!"

Turn problems into opportunities.

Edison saw darkness as an opportunity to invent the lightbulb. Whenever your children are confronted with a problem, try to help them turn it into a positive, or at least a learning, experience. For example:

Social problem: Your eight-year-old comes to you sad that her best friend is mad at her.

Social opportunity: Help your child find a way to reconnect with her friend: "Remember how you and your friend are both good skaters? Let's ask her to go to the ice rink with us on Saturday."

Whenever our children have gotten themselves into a mess, we tell them, "Don't dwell on the problem; look for solutions."

Broadcast good feelings.

One day we had a guest in our home whose body language from head to toe said she was a very negative person. After the guest had left, we asked our children how being around that person had made them feel. They didn't feel good. We pointed out that her attitude had affected everyone around her. This communication phenomenon is known as *emotional broadcasting*.

TRY THE SANDWICH TECHNIQUE

There are times when you have to point out children's mistakes, but some children at some stages are very sensitive to criticism. Try sandwiching the bad news between layers of encouraging words: "Trevor, you're a smart boy. We know, and you know, that you can make good grades. And, you're not lazy. We don't expect this D in spelling to continue. We know you have the ability to do better. How do you feel about the D? . . . I'm sure you'll feel a lot better next semester when you pull up that grade." Sandwiching constructive criticism between compliments is a valuable communication tool to use with adults as well. It makes the listener more receptive to your criticism. In fact, the conversation may be perceived more as encouragement than as a put-down. And it achieves the results you want — that the child do his best and achieve the grades he's capable of.

We also pointed out that presenting a positive attitude can make everyone around you feel good, even in difficult situations.

One of our favorite stories to tell our children is about the little oyster who got a grain of sand under his shell. This little speck was irritating, yet as hard as he tried he couldn't get rid of the grain of sand. So, he said to himself: "Since I cannot remove it, I shall try to improve it."

As the years went on, that small grain of sand that had bothered him so much grew into a beautiful pearl.

During my fifteen years as a Little League baseball coach for the many Sears athletes, I have noticed that in our annual draft sessions, one of my fellow coaches seemed to pick the most successful player year after year. I asked him for the secret of his success. He said, "I draft attitude."

14

Kindness and Manners

H E'S SUCH A KIND KID!" "She's such a nice person to be around!" These are words parents like to hear about their child. Where do these qualities come from? Although pleasant personalities are rooted in the genes, kindness and politeness are learned in the home. Would you put your sixteen-year-old in a car and let him drive away without teaching him the rules of the road? Politeness, respect, and kindness are the rules of the road of life, and teaching them to our kids helps ensure a safe and enjoyable journey — for the children themselves as well as the people with whom they share that road. You want good manners to become a habit, a part of the child's self. Children who are kind and thoughtful and have good manners will be more readily accepted than ones who are lacking in these qualities.

One day as I was walking through a school, an eight-year-old girl accidentally backed into me and stepped on my foot. Within a millisecond she turned and said, "I'm sorry." She looked me in the eye, with a concerned expression on her face. What struck me about her polite response was that it happened so quickly; as if by reflex, she replayed a pattern of association that had been ingrained in her from early childhood and repeated hundreds of times. Polite-

ness was such a natural part of her response that she didn't have to think before she acted. That's a well-mannered child.

TEN WAYS TO TEACH KINDNESS AND MANNERS

My son is extremely polite, and people comment on this frequently. I think his good manners are a result of his innate desire to be a good person. I think that, on some level, he realizes that people respond to his good behavior, and so he continues it.

1. Teach manners early.

How early? Try infancy! From the moment your baby exits the womb, you begin teaching her how people treat people. As your six-month-old discovers all the things he can do with his hands, he grabs a handful of your hair and pulls — hard. You don't yell. Instead, you unfurl his strong little fists and tell him quietly to "be gentle." He learns to be gentle from your example, long before he understands the word itself.

From the beginning, I paid attention to how I communicated with my babies, be it a soft word or a gentle touch.

The root of good manners is respect for other people, and the root of respect is sensitivity. The hallmark of attachment parenting is sensitively responding to the needs of the child. Sensitivity is contagious, and with continued sensitive parenting, your child becomes an empathetic little person who cares about others' feelings. Even two-year-olds can learn to say "peas" and "tank oou." Though they don't yet understand the exact meaning of the words, toddlers soon conclude that "please" is how you ask for things and "thank you" is how you end an interaction. The more a child hears a word or phrase repeated, the greater the importance he attaches to it and the sooner he learns it. When you ask your toddler to give you something, open with "please" and close with "thank you." The child learns that these are important words because Mommy and Daddy use them a lot and have such nice expressions on their faces when they do. Toddlers parrot these terms and understand their usefulness long before they understand their meaning.

About three years of age, children begin to toddle away from a purely self-centered existence into one in which they become more concerned about those around them. They understand that when they take a toy from a baby, they cause the baby to cry. They begin to grasp the cause-and-effect relationship — that they are responsible for the baby's unhappiness. Children can also see that when they make funny faces and goofy noises, the baby laughs — that they are responsible for the baby's joy. They also discover that being kind to others brings them feelings of warmth and happiness, feelings that they like and that motivate them to be kind more often. Children also discover that saying "please" and "thank you" shows people that they appreciate them and that these words make others happy.

2. Model manners.

Between the ages of two and four is a prime time for modeling manners. During that time, what Mary hears, Mary says. Let your child hear "please," "thank you," "you're welcome," and "excuse me" frequently from you throughout the day. Use the same polite manners with your child as you would with another adult. Chil-

GIVING AND RECEIVING COMPLIMENTS

One of the many keys to social success is mastering the art of giving and receiving compliments. Sincere, thoughtful compliments make both the giver and the receiver feel good. Model this art for your child: "My, you look handsome tonight!" or "I like your new haircut!" Show your child that it's good to give yourself a pat on the back, too ("I completed my project at work right on time").

Children with low self-worth have difficulty giving and receiving compliments. They may feel unworthy to receive a compliment and can get so hung up on how someone else will take their compliment that they clam up. In this case, a little parental guidance is in order. Austin's elder brother just finished his school science project. You whisper to Austin, "Go tell David his science project looks great." If your child comes forth with an unexpected compliment to you, "Wow, Mom, you look great in that new dress!" be sure you receive this compliment well and acknowledge it: "Thanks, honey, what a nice thing to say." Your child's self-esteem gets a boost from seeing how happy you were because of what he said.

dren learn what they live, especially at this young age, so a child who has well-mannered parents is likely to become well-mannered himself. One time we were in a taxi and noticed how politely the taxi driver spoke. When we asked him where he learned to speak so politely, he responded: "My mom and dad were my teachers."

Go out of your way to set a good example for your child. Your neighbors' dog escapes from their yard. Do you complain: "There he goes again"? Or do you round up the dog and take him home? You're in line behind an elderly shopper who is struggling to get groceries out of his cart. Do you mumble a complaint about the holdup, or do you ask if he'd like some help? Do you rush ahead, or do you patiently allow a motorist to turn into traffic in front of you? Your children are watching!

3. Don't force-feed.

While it's okay to occasionally remind a child to say "please" when making a request, don't treat manners like a pet trick: "Now say the magic word, and I'll give you your treat." You run the risk of the child tiring of these polite words even before he understands them. Manners are a skill to be enjoyed, not forced. When you remind a child to "say please," do so politely, in a meaningful way: "You know, if you really want me to stop working at the computer and get up and help you find your teddy bear, I think it would be helpful for you to say please." You want your child to be sincere about being polite and understand why it's important to say please and thank you.

My son was playing basketball with a group of boys when a toddler walked across the court. My child gave the toddler the ball and let him throw it one time before moving him off the court. He was kind to think of what the toddler wanted.

4. Expect manners.

Parental expectations are one of the most powerful ways to motivate children. Children brought up in an environment where good manners are expected will use good manners. One day we noticed a family entering a hotel. The father looked at his two sons, ages five and seven, and said, "Now, chaps, do hold the door for the lady," which they did. When I commented on how well mannered his children were, he replied, "We expect it."

5. Teaching table manners.

Your child will eat almost 20,000 meals by the time he's eighteen — which makes the table a good place to teach all kinds of lessons, including how to participate in a conversation. Your family conversation at dinner will show your child how to behave when she is a guest in other homes. Teach your child to look at people when speaking to them, to speak clearly, and to answer questions in complete sentences, not mumbled grunts. Model for him the give-and-take of mealtime conversation. You get a chance to talk, but there are also times when you must listen and not interrupt. Children usually can't sit as long at a meal as adults can, so it's a good idea to teach them to ask, "May I please be excused?" when they are through eating and start getting restless. Children can then go play while the adults continue their conversation.

6. Write thank-you notes.

A handwritten thank-you note tells the recipient, "You are important enough for me to take the time to write this note." Be sure your child follows up gifts, kind acts, and special favors with a note of appreciation. You can instill this habit at an early age by asking children to draw thank-you pictures or by having them dictate their thank-you message, for you to write down.

While we believe that handwritten thank-you notes will never go out of style, our children will almost certainly confront new questions of etiquette as they communicate with others by e-mail or instant messaging over the Internet. These are brave new worlds for old parents like us, but twenty-first-century parents will certainly have to teach their children "netiquette" for getting along in cyberspace.

7. Teach telephone manners.

Most children love to answer the phone, so be sure you take the time to teach them how to talk clearly and what to say. It's heartwarming to have a call answered by a child who says, "Hello, this is Kyle. Yes, she's here. Just a minute, please," or "No, she's not here. May I take a message?"

8. Teach respect.

Since most people like to be called by name, children should be taught at an early age to look people in the eye and address them by name. This is a sign of respect, as well as a way to get someone's attention. (See related section, p. 158.)

But what name to use? Different families have different preferences. Some parents teach their children to address all adults outside the family as Mr. or Mrs. (or Ms. or Miss, depending on the circumstances). In other circles, kids are free to address their parents' friends by their first names. Some families always use "aunt" or "uncle" when naming those relatives. Some don't. Whatever is preferred in your family or social group, teach your child what is expected of her in different situations. When children don't know a person's name, they can still use polite openers, such as "sir," "ma'am," "pardon me," or "excuse me."

We've taught our children to call adults by "mr." or "mrs." unless they are specifically told otherwise. We tell them that this is a sign of respect.

If the person has a title, teach your child to use it: "doctor," "reverend," "professor." I remember once an airline-ticket agent addressed me as "mister," which I didn't mind at all, yet she quickly interjected: "Sorry, I mean 'doctor.' After all, you've earned it." That was quick-thinking manners.

Respectful listening is another social skill that's important for children to learn. Remind your child not to interrupt and to wait for an appropriate time to add comments. Teach children to look at and acknowledge people who are talking to them. Be a respectful listener yourself. When your child approaches to engage you in conversation, turn off the TV, turn away from your computer, make eye contact, and listen with interest.

9. Use PR (parental reminders).

During their preschool years, you teach your children good manners and polite speech by your example at home. Once a child enters school, he is exposed to other ways of behaving, some of which he will pick up on and you may not like. Children need frequent booster shots from their parents that "this is how *we* talk." Don't scold, just use PR — parental reminders said in such a way that the advice you're giving goes down smoothly. Emphasize the "we" in the PR: "This is how we talk and act in our home," "This is what we expect." Another powerful phrase is "in our family . . ." This reinforces the norms you have taught your children early in childhood and makes good manners an expected part of belonging to your family. Belonging is important to children, and you want that sense of be-

---

POLITE CORRECTIONS

Parents sometimes rebuke their kids' bad manners by correcting them harshly and impolitely: "Give that toy back to your brother, now!" "Where are your manners, young man?" Sometimes the "I mean business" approach is necessary to get your point across. But not always. Other times, try a softer and more polite approach, beginning with these phrases:

"It would be nice if you'd . . ."

"Next time it would be better if you'd . . ."

"What I'd like to hear you say is . . ."

"Do you think there's a better way to handle this?"

"Do you remember when we talked about? . . ."

"I noticed that you said . . ."

---

longing to the family to be more important than doing what it takes to belong to the peer group.

Another time to issue a parental reminder is prior to a significant social event. For example, if your child is about to welcome a houseful of guests for a birthday party, preview what's expected of him: "Remember to greet each person at the door and say, 'Thank you for coming,'" "When you open your presents, look at the person who gave you the gift and say something nice about it." Children want to be kind, but many are not aware of the right way to act or what to say. Help them build a repertoire of polite phrases that they can replay as they face different social situations. Teach your child a multipurpose expression to use when trying to gain another's attention, squeeze through another person's space, or after emitting bodily

noises. "Pardon me" or "Could you please repeat that?" are much easier on the ears than the more usual "What?" or the more abrasive "Huh!" Practice these phrases at home so that when your children are out of range of parental reminders, they will still remember what to say and do.

10. Explain the why of manners.

Good manners will come more naturally if you teach your child why they should be used. "Good manners are really just good human relations," says Letitia Baldridge in her book *More Than Manners! Raising Today's Kids to Have Kind Manners and Good Hearts* (New York: Rawson Associates, 1997). She refers to manners as acts of goodwill toward others. Help your children recognize their own good feelings when others are kind and polite to them. "When Hannah thanked you for helping her clean up the mess, how did you feel?" Children who are on the receiving end of kindness and politeness enjoy the feeling and are more motivated to do likewise to others.

Children may not fully understand the importance of shaking someone's hand and saying, "Congratulations," or "I'm sorry for your loss." It's up to you to help your children realize that these kinds of gestures help people stay connected and that a kind word or a hug may mean more than the child realizes.

When children understand why they should be kind and polite, their good manners become sincere expressions of their thoughtfulness and empathy, not just a parroting of polite phrases that please parents. Rudeness is disrespectful. A person who is sensitive to others will use good manners. Respect for other people is simply an extension of the sensitivity and empathy that are naturally a part of connected kids.

TEACHING THE ART OF APOLOGIZING

"I'm sorry!" "It's my fault!" "Excuse me!" Apologizing helps your child accept responsibility for herself and puts her on the road to making things right again. Apologies and forgiveness heal broken relationships. Knowing when and how to apologize will help your child succeed in life. Try the following tips:

Start apologizing early.

Teach toddlers to give a hug to "make it better" when they hurt someone. Model hugs for hurts at home so your little one will know just what to do. Verbally model a simple apology for a toddler and then help him say it with a hug.

Model apologizing.

When you blow it, admit it. "I'm sorry I yelled at you. You didn't deserve that outburst. I've had a hard day, but I shouldn't take it out on you." We've said these words, or similar ones, many times to our children. When parents apologize, children learn that we all make mistakes — it's normal and expected — and that taking responsibility for our mistakes and correcting them is also normal and expected. Children who grow up hearing sincere apologies from trusted authority figures and persons of significance will learn by example how to apologize themselves. Look caringly into the child's eyes, touch her shoulder, and speak sincerely from your heart. Your child will learn from you how to tell others that she is sorry.

Forgive and forget.

It's important for children to learn not only when and how to apologize but how to receive an apology. Forgiving completes the healing process. The offender feels better when the offended "drops the charges." Teach your child to say, "I forgive you," or "That's okay," in reply to an apology. A handshake, a hug, or a friendly touch on the shoulder reinforces the message that all is forgiven.

Model how to do so by saying you forgive your child when she apologizes for her mistakes. Hearing you forgive is important. Many children are not ready to say, "It's okay," after they feel they've been wronged. They need to learn that forgiveness is expected and speeds up the healing process and lets the relationship go on. Alexander Pope coined the famous saying, "To err is human, to forgive divine." We would add, "To forgive is just plain kind." Children need to learn not to hold grudges. Forgiveness clears the air.

One day, in anger, I called one of our children a "brat." I felt really bad that such a put-down came out of my mouth (even though she really was being difficult). I knew I had to apologize, so I hugged her and said I was sorry, but I still felt terrible. When she said in a childlike, sincere tone of voice, "It's okay, Dad," I felt so relieved — and I'm an adult. You can imagine how children feel when Mom or Dad tells them that they are forgiven.

Apologizing and forgiving are especially important between siblings. It's the parent's job to make sure the apology happens so that both children can start again with good feelings between them. A phrase we use in our family for handling sibling squabbles is to "make peace with each other."

THE REWARDS OF BEING KIND

Children should not learn to expect praise for every act of kindness. After all, you expect them to be kind and well mannered, and truly gracious do-gooders don't call a lot of attention to themselves. Yet it never hurts to give positive feedback or to tell a child that you are proud of her. You don't have to be cautious about using the phrase "I'm proud of you." And, of course, add, "You must be so proud of yourself!"

My five-year-old son is known for being kind. He often helps his classmates carry things or put their things away. He's even given his last cookie to a classmate who didn't have a dessert in his lunch. One day when we talked about his kind acts, he told me: "When I do stuff like that, my eyes get tears in them."

Dr. Chuck Wall, professor of management and human relations at Bakersfield College in California, was listening to yet another radio newscast describe yet "another random act of senseless violence." In his dismay over this constant onslaught of horrible news, he changed one word in this phrase and went to his class the next day with an assignment: Each student was to "commit one random act of senseless *kindness*." His actions started a grassroots awareness campaign that sparked the Act of Kindness Awareness Week, instituted by the U.S. House of Representatives. When we interviewed Dr. Wall for this book, he was excited to hear that we would cover the art of teaching kindness to children. He told us, "Though committing ourselves to the concept of an act of kindness is not the answer to all the ills of the world, we must begin somewhere." He went on: "An act that positively influences the lives of both the giver and receiver is a kindness. It doesn't have to cost money or be difficult to perform. It can be spontaneous or premeditated. It can be as simple as a smile or a 'thank you,' or as compli-

cated as starting a nonprofit organization to benefit those in need." According to Dr. Wall, "Kindness has four important parts: dignity, respect, compassion, and humility. If you have all these things in yourself, then you will be able to share them with others." Dr. Wall went on to suggest that people live by the phrase "Today I will commit one act of senseless kindness."

Every now and then you have the chance to witness a moment with your children that makes you realize you're doing something right. My four young children and I visited an animal hospital on a field trip with about six other families we did not know. There was an opportunity for the children to witness an operation on a horse through small viewing windows. One little girl, who was about three years old, was not tall enough to see through any of the windows and tugged on her brother, saying, "I can't see," but he ignored her. Then she went to her sister and repeated her cry, "I can't see, I can't see." The other mothers were chatting with one another and did not seem to notice. I was off to the side with a sleeping baby in my arms. As the young girl's cries went unheeded, she finally stepped back and said in a very sad voice, "I can't see," one more time. My daughter, Katie, who was six at the time, stepped away from her viewing window and said, "I'll lift you up so you can see." And she did. I was so amazed that being so young she could have compassion for a child who was not one of her own brothers or her sister. She held her there until the little one wanted down and ran off. Needless to say, I told her how proud I was and encouraged her to continue to think of others and how they feel. She is nineteen now and still a very kind and compassionate person who is always trying to think of how it feels to be in another's shoes.

15

Building Successful Sexuality

A HEALTHY ATTITUDE TOWARD SEX and toward oneself as a sexual person is part of what it takes to feel happy and successful in life. In this book we have defined *success* largely in terms of relationships, and for most people their most important relationship is the intimate one they have with their mate. In addition, how children feel about their own sexuality is part of their self-image. Positive feelings about being a boy or being a girl are part of the overall structure of positive self-belief.

How do parents of kids who turn out well teach their children about sex and sexuality? Schools, for better or worse, teach children about sex; families model *sexuality*, which means teaching children not only the "facts of life" but attitudes as well. The most important lessons are not the ones delivered in big talks about "the birds and the bees." Your child's sexual self-image depends more upon the example you set and the attitudes you model than it does on how well you explain the facts of life. Yes, talking with your child about sex and being sure that he or she has the facts straight is a good thing for parents to do, even if you have to overcome some uneasiness to stutter through these conversations. But facts children can get from a book or in a health class at school. What

to do with their sexuality, how to live as boys and girls, then as men and women, is a far more important success tool.

TEACHING SEXUALITY EARLY

Like so many other qualities, sexuality is first learned in infancy. Your child learns about his physical self from the messages you send through your *loving touch*. How you care for and caress his tiny body tells him that touching feels good and that being close to another body is comforting and soothing. When you rub his back, carry him in your arms or on your body in a baby sling, put him to breast, or gaze into his eyes, you are speaking love in a language that even a tiny baby can understand.

Sexuality is giving and receiving touch.

Your baby is learning that people show love by the way they touch each other and that it's good to touch and be touched by people who love you. Babies find human touch very calming. Studies of premature infants have shown that these babies breathe better, have steadier heart rates, and sleep more peacefully when placed skin-to-skin between their mothers' breasts.

When baby falls asleep after nursing with his cheek on mother's breast, or when he cuddles comfortably on Dad's chest, he is learning to enjoy physical closeness. Babies who are on the receiving end of the high-touch attachment parenting learn their earliest lesson in sexuality: to be comfortable touching and being touched.

Sexuality is being sensitive.

Another lesson about sexuality that babies learn already in infancy is sensitivity. Babies whose parents respond sensitively to their needs will grow up to be sensitive themselves. They will understand their own feelings better and be able to identify with the emotions of others. They will have higher-quality relationships as a result. They can be honest about their own needs and boundaries, and will be more likely to be respectful of others'. As discussed in Chapter 7, romantic love is often called "mutual empathy."

Sexuality is trusting.

Trust is another part of healthy sexuality that begins in infancy. The connected child learns trust from her parents and carries this trust into later relationships. Being able to trust someone is essential to intimacy, and using good judgment about where to place one's trust is important to happiness in life. When a baby or child constantly receives messages that his parents respond to whatever is bothering him, he will be more likely to trust his parents' advice about relationships and sexual behavior in the teenage years. Parents who trust their children and respond to their expressions of need raise kids who learn to trust themselves. They are less likely to be swept along by peer pressure or to settle for sex when what they are really seeking is love and closeness.

Sexuality begins with curiosity.

Children begin to explore their bodies already in infancy. Discovering everything the body can do is part of sexuality. This is the beginning of how children learn to feel comfortable as a "he" or "she." Children understand that bodies are made of legs and arms, tummies, toes, chins, ankles, and genitals. Between the ages of two and five, children discover all the ways in which men are different from women, fathers are different from mothers, and brothers are different from sisters. As infants, they learned that although Mommy is the one with the breasts and the milk, Daddy is also a source of comfort and definitely a source of fun. Babies pat breasts and rub beards.

Lots of learning about sexuality takes place in the years before children enter school. Kids begin to identify with the parent of the same sex and become curious about the bodies of others. What could be more fascinating than the differences between boys and girls? At this age children can sometimes be found in the bedroom or bathroom exploring one anothers' bodies. This activity is more about satisfying curiosity than about sexual arousal. How parents react, however, can have a lasting effect on children's acceptance of their own and others' sexuality.

So what do attached, connected, levelheaded parents do when they discover their child and a friend with their clothes off, "playing doctor"? Compose yourself and be careful not to say something that shames the children. Don't tell them that they're "dirty" or "bad" or "shameful" or that their behavior is shocking. Get behind the eyes of your child, who probably just wants to know what other kids' genitals look like. Treat the situation matter-of-factly, because this is actually a teachable moment, a chance to talk about differences between boys and girls and to introduce some ideas about privacy and private parts.

Sexuality needs privacy.

Explain to children that private parts are those parts that are covered by your swimsuit. You can tell your child that it's normal to be curious about others' bodies but that it's not right to look at or touch anyone else's private parts. Nor is it right for others to look at or touch his or her private parts. This is a key concept for children to learn at an early age, since understanding these boundaries is important not only to their relationship with peers but also to protecting them from sexual molestation. Here is where establishing a trusting relationship with your child beginning in infancy and continuing throughout childhood is crucial. The number of children who are sexually abused, often by people they know, is alarmingly high. Children who trust their parents will readily understand that it's not good to keep secrets from Mommy and Daddy — unless it's a good secret, for example, about a birthday surprise. Tell your child that they must tell you if someone touched their private parts. When children know from

---

PARENT TIP:
It's safe to tell!

Children are often afraid to tell their parents about sexual matters, such as someone's touching (or even molesting) them, because they fear their parents' reaction. We were proactive by reassuring our children that we would never get angry at them as long as they honestly confided problems to us, no matter how bad the situation seemed.

---

experience that they can talk with Mom and Dad about private parts in a comfortable, non-threatening way, they are better able to defend themselves against people who might hurt them.

Privacy boundaries within the family are a way of reinforcing what you teach your children about the privacy of their bodies. Different families have different boundaries, and much also depends on the age of the children. Teaching your child to knock on closed bedroom or bathroom doors is one way of helping him understand that one must ask permission before entering someone's private space. Allowing children control over their own bodies also strengthens their concept of personal boundaries. Ask, "Can I give you a hug?" before wrapping your arms around a child who might be otherwise engaged. Don't force children to kiss or hug friends or relatives. Don't tickle or roughhouse with a child who is asking you to stop.

Let your child know when you do and do not wish to be touched yourself. If you're sitting on the sofa in the evening, after a long day of work, child-chasing, meal preparation, and cleanup, and you really want to be left alone for a few minutes, teach your child to respect that need. Children of three and four can learn to do this, especially if you're prepared to hug them and play with them after you've had some peace and quiet.

Where do babies come from?

When do you give your child the big speech about babies growing in mommies' tummies, and (gulp!) how daddies help the baby start growing? Take your cues from your child. Answer questions as they come up. Wise parents don't impart this important information all at once, any more than they would expect their child to master ideas about time, gravity, or how the earth turns on its axis in a single sit-down session. Look for teachable moments: "Did you know that Colin's mom has a baby growing inside her? It's in a special place called the womb." Preschoolers are usually interested in short answers. Older children may have follow-up questions. If you want your child to trust you and come to you for information about sex and relationships as a teen, start the conversation in early childhood. Get behind your child's eyes and imagine what it is he needs or wants to know. Children of nine or ten, particularly girls, need to know about the body changes associated with puberty. Children who hear news stories about AIDS or homosexuality may need these issues explained to them in age-appropriate language. Open discussions about sexuality and sexual behavior are important at every age so that your child believes that sexuality discussions are not "bad" and that she can trust you to understand her feelings and give her the information she is seeking.

FOSTERING HEALTHY GENDER IDENTITY

Ideas about what it means to be masculine and feminine have changed a great deal in the past half century. Nevertheless, stereotypes about little girls and little boys persist, fed by the advertisers who want to capture the huge market and buying power of kids, preteens, and teenagers. In a world where parents and teachers tell children that girls can grow up to be lawyers and firefighters and that boys should learn to be sensitive and caring as well as strong and stoical, it's challenging for kids to figure out just what kind of a man or woman they will be.

In the 1960s and 1970s, social scientists and people in the women's movement argued that differences in the ways males and females behave were learned. The culture prescribed that boys were rough and tough and that girls were soft and sweet, and children adapted these behaviors based on messages they received from parents and teachers, media, and other influences in the environment. The problem with this is that girls often grew up believing they were less capable than boys in almost every area but nurturing children, caring for the sick, and doing housework. And boys were expected to be tough and never grieve or cry.

Attitudes have changed, and now girls play all kinds of sports in grade school and high school, they grow up to be business executives and physicians, and parents make a point of teaching their daughters to be assertive and independent. In theory, expectations for boys have also changed, allowing them to show their caring, feeling side and to place greater importance on family issues as they plan for careers. The reality is that women still come up against the glass ceiling in the business world, they're more likely to become pediatricians than surgeons, and companies that offer family leave to all employees find it's rare for men to take several months off to care for a new baby or an aging family member. Girls and young women still obsess about their looks and their bodies, encouraged by impossibly thin and beautiful models on television and in advertising. Boys, perhaps more than ever, define masculinity in terms of power, and many still repress their emotions, except for anger.

Research is beginning to reveal that there are differences between men and women in how the brain works. Biology may be at the root of some of our traditional expectations for boys and girls. Girls are often found to be more adept at tasks involving language and interpretation of social signals and feelings. Boys have an easier time with spatial thinking and math skills. They are usually more physical and more aggressive.

Clearly, both nature and nurture are at work as children learn what it means to be male and female. There are wide variations in behavior within genders. Boys can be as imaginative in playing house as girls can be. Girls may build elaborate structures from blocks or become very skilled at a sport. Parents need to encourage their child in his or her individual interests so that the child can develop into the best person possible. If this means your daughter takes ballet and your son plays baseball, fine. If you find that your daughter is the family athlete, encourage her. If your son prefers drawing and painting to hockey or basketball, give him the materials and classes he needs to excel. Above all, be sensitive to the entire range of emotions and ambitions that your child may express. Don't downplay a girl's desire to run for student body president or to choose a traditionally male occupation. Be open to your son's expressions of loss and frustration as well as anger and triumph.

Modeling a good marriage.

Parents are a prime source of information about gender roles for their children. Their own behavior toward each other and toward children of the same and the opposite gender sends important messages about what it means to be male and female. For example, it's important that children learn that both Mom and Dad are fair disciplinarians as well as loving caregivers. Kids need input from both parents on relationships, sports, careers, and academics. They also need to see that mother and father respect each other — that each has unique talents, some perhaps related to being a woman or a man, some that are theirs alone.

The relationship between mother and father shows children how adults care for one another. It's entirely appropriate for children to see hugging and kissing between Mom and Dad, as well as other gestures of affection. Equally important is that they see that mother and father treat each other with empathy and kindness. One day our eight-year-old, Erin, was being sassy to Martha. I took her aside and said, "Erin, I won't tolerate you talking to the woman I love like that." Ten years later Erin still remembers that lesson, and I scored points with my wife. It is not appropriate for a parent to put down his or her spouse in front of a child. This not only models poor attitudes about gender roles (women are "illogical" or men are "lazy"). It also shows kids that complaining, blaming, and verbally abusing others is okay. If you don't want your kids to treat people outside the family in a disrespectful way, be careful how you speak to your spouse.

Remember that you are raising someone's future spouse. Your marriage is a model of what your children's marriages will be. While nobody's marriage is perfect, you do want your children to learn key values from your relationship with your spouse — respectful ways of interacting, helpfulness, enjoying each other's company, and happiness and contentment with one's role as a spouse and parent.

My mother-in-law has often told me how she used to tell her son (now my husband), "I feel sorry for the woman who marries you." And she had good reason

---

A DAUGHTER'S TIP FOR FATHERS:

One day while I was preparing material for a talk to a group of new fathers, I asked our twenty-two-year-old daughter, Hayden, if she had any tips for me to give these men about raising daughters. She advised, "Tell them to act like the man they want their daughter to marry."

to say this. By doing everything for them, she taught my husband and his brother to be fairly helpless. I'm determined that when my sons choose who they will marry, my reaction will be "What a lucky girl!" because I have prepared them to be sensitive and helpful husbands.

TEEN SEXUALITY

When children reach puberty, questions of sexuality and sexual identity come to the forefront. Their bodies mature and they become capable of reproduction long before they are emotionally ready to become husbands, wives, and parents. Peer friendships become very important, and parents' influence seems to fade into the background.

As teens desire more independence, parents must let out the reins, but it's important to stay involved in your teen's life. Meet her friends, volunteer to be the driver when they need a ride, and welcome these kids into your home. Acknowledge that your teenager has sexual feelings and urges, and talk about them. Kids are exposed to sex and sexuality everywhere — on billboards selling cigarettes and beer, on television and at the movies, in the music they listen to, and in the lives of the celebrities they look up to. Help them see the difference between the values you have always taught them and those of the culture around them.

Most of all, help teenagers understand themselves. The trust and caring you have shown your child in the years leading up to puberty should make him more sensitive to his own feelings and reactions and to the feelings of others. If he is yearning for intimacy and connection, help him recognize that he can fill these needs with close friendships rather than with sexual activity. Help teens focus on long-term life goals — college, a good education, career, solid friendships, and eventually, marriage, sex, and children. Stay involved with your teen. (Teens really are fascinating people.) Don't just shake your head and give up.

Kids say: *One thing I'm glad my parents never did is let me have free rein when it came to high-school boyfriends. At the time, I thought they were so unfair, but in actuality they were just being good parents and not allowing the opportunity for hormones to rage unchecked. (Maria, age seventeen)*

Sexuality is an important part of life. Basically, you want to give your kids the message that it's great to be a man and it's great to be a woman. Neither gender is better or inferior, and sexuality leads to happy, fulfilling adult marriages. Approach this subject with the same caring and openness that you bring to teaching your child empathy or responsibility and you will give your child another opportunity for success.

16

How to Monitor Media and Technology Influences

IT IS LIKELY THAT THE AVERAGE CHILD spends more time each day in front of a screen than he does with his parents, so who's the more important influence? Whether screens (TV, movies, video games, etc.) contribute to or detract from a child's success depends on how appropriately parents and teachers monitor these electronic influences. Here are our concerns, along with practical ways for parents to monitor the media.

TAMING THE TV: WHY AND HOW

Would you let a stranger babysit your child? Would you allow your child to hang around with peers that promote values contrary to what you teach? That is what happens when you let this unmonitored tube into your home.

Consider these disturbing stats.

According to Nielsen data, the average American child watches twenty-one to twenty-three hours of television every week, or approximately three to three and a half hours per day. Another report shows that when computers, video games, and movies are added to TV viewing, the time children spend in front of a screen

may amount to forty hours a week, or as much as a full-time job. Reportedly, by the time children graduate from high school, they have spent 11,000 hours in classrooms, compared with 20,000 hours in front of screens of all kinds: television, videos, movies, video games, the World Wide Web.

Ponder this disturbing research.

In the January 2000 *Journal of the Archives of Pediatrics and Adolescent Medicine,* researchers at Stanford University report that cutting back on the time children watch television and play video games leads to a decrease in aggressive behavior. Third- and fourth-graders at one school were encouraged to reduce their usual TV and video watching while third- and fourth-graders at another school continued their normal viewing habits. Seven months later researchers compared the two groups and found that students who had limited their TV and video watching were less aggressive toward their peers on the playground.

In July of 2000 leaders from organizations such as the American Academy of Pediatrics, the American Psychological Association, the American Academy of Adolescent Psychology, and the American Medical Association met with public-health officials in Washington, D.C., to review thirty years of research on the effects of the media on children. They concluded that viewing violent entertainment can lead to an increase in aggressive attitudes, values, and behavior in children. Viewing violence in the media made children more likely to see violence as an effective way to settle conflicts. Children who are exposed to violent programming also have a greater tendency toward violent behavior. Another finding — and this is our greatest concern — is that violence in the media may cause children to become emotionally desensitized toward violence in real life. Researchers estimate that by the age of sixteen, children will have witnessed 200,000 violent acts, including 40,000 murders, on a screen. Because of the concern about the growing influence of technology on child development, the American Academy of Pediatrics recommends that doctors take a "media history" during school-age checkups.

These disturbing statistics are not a recipe for success. It has also been reported that academically successful children spend a great deal less time in front of a screen. Consider the following potentially harmful effects on the emotional and physical health of growing children:

Gives children a distorted perception of real life.

Remember, one way to help your child succeed in life is to give him a healthy perception of what the norm is and what's important. Screens do the opposite. Television highlights the abnormal. Children who watch a great deal of television have a distorted sense of reality. They may believe that the world is a meaner and scarier place than it really is. Children younger than eight do not have the mental ability to separate fantasy from reality, especially when

the made-up story on TV is made to look like real life.

Much of the programming on television, including news and "reality" shows, feeds the perception that the world is a violent and mean place. This viewpoint is not the road to happiness and contentment as an adult. For children to grow up emotionally healthy, they need to learn that life is, for the most part, peaceful and that being happy doesn't require constant stimulation and lots of material goods. This belief is in contrast to the values promoted by the fast-paced action dramas, which keep kids glued to the tube, and sitcoms that trivialize family relationships.

Fast cars, beer-drinking buffs, and sugar-coated fatty food eaten by thin, happy people all threaten to destroy kids' notions of what's good and "cool." Television also presents false models of how men and women are supposed to relate to one another. Fathers are portrayed as bumbling and wimpy, and mothers are portrayed as doing everything but nurturing children.

Promotes mental tune-out.

Watch a five-year-old "zoned out" on a TV program. The child's brain becomes a passive recipient of whatever is on the tube. At least most video and computer games are interactive. Eye doctors are also concerned about the effects on healthy visual development. A TV screen is only two-dimensional, so avid television viewers may not have sufficient opportunities to develop a three-dimensional depth perception. Eye doctors are concerned that excessive TV viewing may limit the development of proper eye mechanics. While watching TV, children tend to fix their eyes in one spot for long periods of time, which is counterproductive to learning to move their eyes from left to right for reading. Excessive TV watching, eye doctors fear, may interfere with the normal "wiring" of the visual attentive systems.

Not only visual development is a concern; hearing is, too. TV is more of a visual than an auditory medium. You don't have to listen well to follow most television programs. Speech pathologists are particularly concerned about the effect TV viewing has on how children learn language. One of the communication tools for success that we encourage throughout this book is active listening, which leads to imaginative listening. Children need practice paying attention to the speaker and then forming their own mental images about what they hear. When children are bombarded with TV images, their own ability to form imaginative pictures may become impaired.

Promotes obesity.

Studies indicate that adolescent obesity correlates directly with the amount of time spent watching TV. Television watching can contribute to obesity in three ways: Children's metabolic rate slows as they sit and watch TV, so they burn fewer calories. Second, they tend to munch mindlessly on junk food while watching TV, taking in unneeded calories. When tuned into the tube, children tune out their body's signals for appetite control. Kids can down a whole bag of chips without realizing it. Third, television advertising is full of unhealthy messages about eating.

The largest share of food advertising during children's programming is for products with low nutritional value, such as highly sugared and high-fat snack foods. This advertising pays off; that's why advertisers spend the money. Children exposed to this food advertising select more junk food.

Here's what we have done at our house to trim the TV-obesity connection. We put exercise equipment (a minitrampoline, an exercise bike, and jump ropes) in the TV room to encourage our children to work out while they watch. We don't allow snacking on anything but fresh fruits and vegetables during TV watching. Finally, we don't let TV advertising influence our choices at the supermarket. Instead, we use junk-food ads as an opportunity to talk to our kids about why these foods are not "grow foods."

Causes sleep deprivation.

Studies show that children who stay up late watching TV are likely to suffer sleep deprivation, which can result in poor school performance and inattentive behavior the next day. Violent programming can also contribute to sleep disturbances. In my pediatric practice, I frequently find that scary TV is a cause of children's nightmares.

Promotes short attention spans.

Attention problems are becoming epidemic among schoolchildren. Witness the long line in front of the school nurse's office as children with A.D.D. (Attention Deficit Disorder) line up for their "focus pill." Screens require only short attention spans, just the opposite of the concentration required for reading, studying, and listening in class. Studies of both childrens' and adults' brain-wave patterns while watching TV confirm that brain activity switches from beta (alert and attention-promoting brain waves) to alpha waves. Alpha waves are the kind of brain activity seen in someone who is bored or falling asleep. One of the most promising areas of research in helping children with attention deficit disorders is neurofeedback, a therapy that helps children focus their brain waves in just the opposite way that television does. Any connection between too much screen time and the epidemic of attention-disorder problems? We believe there may be.

Promotes unhealthy sexual attitudes.

Research shows that the average young TV viewer is exposed to more than 14,000 inappropriate sexual references a year. The characters, story lines, and even the costumes often promote sexual values that differ from what parents want their kids to learn.

Desensitizes youth.

As a father of eight and a pediatrician for thirty years, I am most concerned about how the electronic media can make youths insensitive. Remember, sensitivity and empathy are the keys to healthy relationships and success. Cartoons desensitize kids toward violence. So do video games. Toy ads are full of gender stereotypes. Sit-

coms geared for adults suggest that adults leap into bed together as a part of getting to know one another. One day I was strolling past a video arcade and decided to go in and watch. Two preteens were playing a video game about two snowboarders racing downhill. Seemingly harmless? The snowboarders began punching each other. What kind of sportsmanship is that? On to the next screen, where the characters were pulverizing one another. Then came the sword fights and various shoot-'em-ups. This is what preteens should do for fun? Try this test. Next time you notice your child watching something violent on TV or playing a violent video game, ask him, "Does that bother you?" If the answer is no, take it as a red flag. Squishings and shootings *should* bother children, unless, of course, they have become so desensitized that they don't even notice.

How this desensitization process occurs is well explained by the classic analogy of the frog in boiling water. If you put a frog in boiling water, he will immediately jump out to save his life, but when you put frogs in tepid water and gradually heat it up, they don't jump out. The change is so gradual that the frogs accommodate themselves to the new environment and don't try to escape. This is exactly what happens when children become desensitized to violence. They don't realize what's happening until it's too late.

TV AND PRESCHOOLERS

Little eyes and minds can't yet differentiate between fantasy and reality. Parents and other caregivers must be especially selective about media influences on preschoolers.

Be careful about cartoons.

Preschool children from two to five spend an average of 1.5 hours a day watching TV or videos. They often don't have a caregiver along-

---

BAD IMPRESSIONS

Throughout this book we have emphasized models as one of the primary influences on a child's success. An unfortunate fact of psychological life is that negative behaviors (e.g., anger and violence) are easier for a child to copy, and both research and experience have shown that children tend to remember bad examples more than good ones. Positive behaviors (e.g., humor and kindness) are more difficult to imitate because they require more creativity. Parents should not be lulled into a false sense of security because their child is seeing "only a few murders" on television or has gone to "only a few violent movies." Saturate your child's mind with examples of healthy behavior in the media, so that there is less room for negative ones.

side to talk with them about what's happening in the story when there's a shooting, squishing, or other violence. They're left to process this information on their own. Scary things happen in cartoons. Consider the death of the father, Mufasa, in *The Lion King*. Realistically, every cartoon should have a PG rating, meaning "parental guidance."

No TV for tots under two?

In 1999 the American Academy of Pediatrics issued a controversial statement that said no child under two should watch TV. That's because infants are often plopped in front of the "electronic babysitter" without a caregiver to supervise, interpret, or screen out unhealthy messages. The AAP was also concerned that TV watching is too passive and keeps toddlers from enjoying healthier activities necessary for their development. The great architect Frank Lloyd Wright attributes much of his building genius to his early start in playing with blocks. Preschoolers learn more from Play-Doh than from pushing buttons.

It's unhealthy "downtime."

Yes, children of all ages need some time to relax, but there are better ways than vegging out in front of a video. In fact, the quick-changing images on a television screen are likely to rev up kids' minds rather than relax them. While a nonviolent comedy can be relaxing for children and adults to view together, TV is generally too fast-moving for an infant. Best to stick to a caregiver's hugs and lullabies, and rocking chair.

HOW PARENTS CAN MONITOR THE TV

Does all this mean that you simply should not allow your children to watch TV, surf the Net, or play video games? No, but you must teach your children to watch TV wisely, and you must monitor what and how much they watch. Here are some ways to turn television into a harmless household member, and sometimes even a healthy influence.

Just say no!

There are times when you have to put your foot down. Even when kids claim that they know the difference between reality and fantasy on television, the line is less defined than they think. If they say, "Oh, Dad, that doesn't bother me," come back with "How do you know it doesn't?" or "It should bother you." Once, when I saw eight-year-old Matthew watching a cartoon that violated every value that we wanted him to learn, I said, "Matthew, that stuff pollutes your mind. Do you know what 'pollute' means?" He answered, "To put bad stuff into it." Matthew got the message. If the values that your child is viewing threaten what you're trying to teach, take a stand. Don't allow her to watch these programs. Tell your child, "Because I love you and care about what kind of a person you will grow up to be, I can't let you pollute your mind by watching this program." Children will understand this and respect you for it. This is another one of those times when it's helpful to begin sentences with "In our family . . ."

Watch wholesome entertainment.

Once upon a time there was wholesome family entertainment, but thanks to special effects, stunt doubles, and Hollywood's way of upping the ante in action movies, what used to be considered "wholesome" now bores desensitized children. Some programming that is marketed as relaxing escapism can actually excite children, creating turmoil rather than peace. If your child is already addicted to movies and videos overloaded with shoot-'em-up, fast-action special effects, you may need to reprogram your child. Try weekly family video nights when you rent some of the old classics, such as *Lady and the Tramp* and *Charlotte's Web* and watch them together. Better yet, try reading books aloud together as a family. Robert Louis Stevenson's *Kidnapped,* for example, and the Harry Potter books have plenty of action, but the reader or listener must create the pictures in his own head.

Sneak-preview the program.

If your child insists on renting a video or watching a TV program that you think may be unsuitable, let him know your family's policy — that any questionable program must be previewed by you. Usually you'll know within the first ten minutes whether this program meets with your approval. Check out these web sites for previews of movies, videos, and music: www.kids-in-mind.com and www.screenit.com.

Notice how the program affects you.

If you don't preview the entire movie or program, be sure to watch it with your child. If the program bothers you, assume that it does (or should) bother your child. Talk about what's going on and why it's objectionable. Use your own feelings as the barometer and select family programming accordingly. Ask yourself, "Would I want my child to imitate these characters?" If your answer is no, shut it off, or at least watch with your child and discuss what you see.

Screen neighborhood TV.

You have a great deal of control over what your children watch in your home, but it's more difficult to monitor what they see at a friend's house down the street. Unless you know that there are like-minded parents in that house, make a rule that your child cannot watch television until you have talked to the friend's parents. When you are not at home, your substitute caregiver should enforce family TV rules. Before you leave, tell her — with the children present — what television programs or videos may be viewed while you are gone.

Ban TVs from bedrooms.

Parents who allow children to have their own television sets in their bedrooms are setting up the kids for trouble. When the tube is out of sight, it's out of your control. If your child is spending the night at the home of a friend who has a TV in his room, talk to the friend's parents ahead of time about how much and what kind of programming your child is allowed to watch.

While I agree with the American Academy of Pediatrics' statement that TV is not generally appropriate for children younger than two, I do think that there are ways in which parents can watch TV together with tiny tots and have fun. Interact with your infant or toddler while watching programs geared to small children. Mimic the antics of the characters with your toddler. In this way, the TV is being used as a prop for parent-child entertainment, not as an electronic babysitter. During the first two years especially, babies and toddlers need direct interaction with caregivers to develop to their full potential. Being passively entertained by the tube can impair development. Still, half an hour a day of interactive family TV with the tot can provide fun for the whole family.

"The TV needs to go to sleep . . ."

But not with the child. Be careful about using television as an electronic sleep-inducer. Even the most wholesome cartoons and programs can contain images that cause nightmares. Yet there are times when tired parents welcome being able to sit down in front of a video and know that their child will be asleep before it's over. I can still remember rocking three-year-old Matthew off to sleep to *Lady and the Tramp*. Still, this isn't the best way to help children fall asleep. Tell kids that "the TV needs to go to sleep," and parent your child to sleep with a story instead.

Set ground rules early.

"How much TV is too much?" you may wonder. It's easier to prevent television addiction than it is to cure it, but kids have been known to go "cold turkey" on television and live to tell the tale. As a general guide:

- Birth to two years: 15 minutes a day
- Two to five years: half an hour a day
- Five years and up: an hour a day. Tape worthwhile programs on school nights and replay them on weekends or holidays.

Sometimes it's easier for parents to say "no TV" than to enforce time limits on television viewing. Remember that you control the electronic monster — you can always unplug it.

Try group therapy.

One of the most effective ways to distract your children from television watching is to give them lots of other things to do. Invite friends over frequently. Take kids to the park for an hour or more every day after school or during the summer. Encourage them to play outside, shoot baskets in the driveway, ride their bikes, make things, help you cook, look at books, play interactive games on the computer. Sign them up for sports teams and music lessons. Go places together as a family. Some children are better than others at entertaining themselves. If you have a child with couch-potato tendencies, you may have to invest some time and energy

in getting her away from the television, but it's an investment well worth making.

TV can be educational.

Of course, there is a positive side to television. Documentaries and other educational programs bring the world into your family room and expose your children to interesting sights and sounds that they might never see otherwise: giraffes running in the wild in Africa, aerial views of the Grand Canyon, live coverage of news and sports. Stimulating educational programs can open family discussions on all kinds of topics and inspire kids to learn more. Follow a political controversy or an election campaign with your children. Listen to their opinions and give them yours. Though you have to be careful about letting children watch the nightly news, since it is often filled with sensationalism and violence, other news programs can provide teachable moments. Following current events with your kids gives you a chance to find out about their moral values and their understanding of the world. It also gives you an opportunity to reinforce your values.

As with so many issues in child rearing, decisions about television watching require a balanced approach. Appropriate doses of educational TV can enlighten children about the world beyond their immediate community. Using television as an electronic babysitter while parents fix dinner or recover from a frazzling day is part of real life. Watching a movie can be wholesome family fun. But you can take control of what your child watches and how often. Stock a library of wholesome kids' videos that you have previewed with your child's personality and unique sensitivities in mind. Enjoy what's good on TV as a family, but be sure to enjoy lots of other activities together as well.

THERE'S A COMPUTER IN MY HOUSE . . . IN THE CLASSROOM . . . IN MY HAND!

Is technology taking over your home, as it has millions of others? Computer literacy is low on the list of success tools. This may surprise some, and some parents may not agree. Yet, as we have continually stressed, it's *relationships,* not technology, that determine success and happiness in life. Acquiring computer skills is relatively easy at any age. There are more important learning tasks for children to master: reading, thinking, acquiring compassion and empathy for others. When children grow up being more comfortable relating to machines than to people — parents, we have a problem!

The good news is that computers have greatly improved the efficiency of just about every enterprise. They bring encyclopedias of knowledge and interest into a child's room on a single CD-ROM. Computers streamline homework, facilitate writing and rewriting, and make term papers more presentable. E-mail has inexpensively connected people all over the world. Kids — and adults — find computers fun. Yet, buyer beware! Be sure the computer in your house becomes an asset to your child's success rather than a liability.

Concerns about Computers

Educators we have consulted fear that too much technology too soon may have detrimental effects on a child's developing the ability to learn. Here is a summary of their concerns and the consensus of their opinions.

May be inappropriate for optimal brain development.

Some educational experts believe that exposing a child to too much computer use too early is not developmentally appropriate, not only because it may hamper verbal and social skills but because it could interfere with the windows of normal neurological development. Children who are exposed to too much electronic learning too soon may develop more of a visual than auditory intelligence. Educators believe there are well-established windows of learning opportunities for the growing brain, yet no such window exists for computer learning.

Two schools of thought.

There seem to be two opposing viewpoints among educators. We'll call them technophiles and technophobes. Technophiles argue that early and extensive computer use in homes and schools prepares children for the "real world." Since the world is becoming dominated by technology, the earlier a child learns about it and gets with the program, the greater advantage she will have in the job market. Technophobes argue that the instant gratification and multimedia hype of technology prepare a child for an "unreal" world because he plays life on a screen rather than experiencing it with other kids. Technophobes encourage a developmentally appropriate introduction of computer skills into homes and schools. They fear that we are training a generation of emotionless technonerds who become competent relating to machines at the expense of competence relating to people. They believe children need to first go through stages in which they hop, dance, stack blocks, catch, sing, run, and play together, because for optimal brain development, children need to use all their senses.

Dr. Jane Healy, author of *Failure to Connect: How Computers Affect Our Children's Minds —*

*and What We Can Do About It,** sums up the technophobes' concerns: "Today's children are the subjects of a vast and optimistic experiment." Dr. Healy goes on to warn: "Encouraging children to 'learn' by flitting around in a colorful, multi-media world is a recipe for a disorganized and undisciplined mind. . . . Inundating youngsters with easy and amusing trivia is more likely to make them fools than wise men." The technophiles are more concerned with preparing children for the future. Technophobes want to put the brakes on the technobandwagon and let kids be kids. At least technophiles win on one count. Keyboards teach tots to type.

Edutainment versus education.

Professional educators are concerned about a growing trend they dub "edutainment," which describes software that mainly entertains kids under the guise of teaching them. Technophobes worry that children are so enamored with and overwhelmed by graphics and special effects that they may have trouble following a logical step-by-step thought pattern, which conscientious teachers who have to present the bare facts find it hard to compete with. They also worry that computers give children an unrealistic sense of instant gratification and access to information instead of having to work hard and think hard to solve a problem. Teachers fear that by being presented with material in living and constantly changing color, students will gradually perceive textbooks as unexciting and teachers as dull. In some ways teachers are being made to compete with software by being coerced to deliver material that "entertains" rather than teaches the child.

*We highly recommend this book for parents and educators who want to learn about the developmentally appropriate use of computers in homes and schools.

The real concern here is that this entertainment form of technolearning glosses over the fact that problem solving, in learning and in life, begins with simple hard work. Thus, early use of computers at home and in school is a good news/bad news scenario. The possible good news is that computers expose a child to information more quickly and, because of interesting visual and auditory special effects, the entertainment and graphics on computer screens hold a child's attention longer. The bad news is that children equate all learning with fun and are therefore less motivated to go through the hard work of learning.

Makes hyper kids more hyper.

Teachers worry that the growing number of hyper kids will become more hyper and that the growing number of violent kids, more violent. The fast-paced, point-and-click, constantly changing graphics make looking more fun than listening for the hyper child. For added effect, he can shoot, squish, or blow up his creation. The child who already has difficulty using his mind has no need to create imaginative scenes in his head, since his computer does it for him. Yet technocrats counter that computers may be a boon for children with learning disabilities and poor attention spans, since visual rather than auditory learning tends to help children with certain learning quirks. On the other hand, technophobes warn that children with hyperactivity and poor attention may be further harmed because the point-and-click feeds into their impulsivity and satisfies the instant gratification that marks many A.D.H.D. children. Educators warn that developmentally inappropriate use of computers and video games can feed into modern problems that plague many schoolchildren, such as A.D.H.D., autism, depression, and poor self-esteem, since these children seem to prefer machines to people.

Fosters watching rather than reading.

Educators debate whether children learn best from reading or viewing. In research studies, reading wins. Students compared for comprehension after reading from a screen showed poorer memory and less understanding than those reading the same information from a book. Educators fear that technotots will grow up finding reading relatively boring compared with the multimedia presentation of the screen. A related theory is the random point-and-click web surfing teaches children to think randomly, unlike the material that is presented in a serial and organized format of a book. However, technophiles argue that multimedia presentations of constantly changing sights and sounds engage the students' attention longer, and they frequently use the buzzword *interactive* as a selling point. Technophiles argue that show-and-tell (graphics plus text) has more learning value than telling or text only. Research has shown that children actually pay less attention (and, therefore, the brain is less active and making fewer connections) when they see a story depicted on video versus listening to it being told or reading it themselves in a book.

Studies have shown that schoolchildren using reading-software programs suffered a 50 percent drop in their creativity scores. But the study also found that no such decline occurred when the computers were integrated with regular curriculum and hands-on, creative activities.

The greatest concern expressed by educators is that too much technology too soon, and without human monitoring, may interfere with the normal timing of brain circuits for language development. Neuroscientists believe that there is a certain timing, or windows of opportunity, for various language pathways, such as a pathway for visual learning and a pathway for language learning. Neuroscientists are concerned that children who grow up connected to a computer rather than to people will develop pathways for visual learning at a time when the child should be developing pathways for language. Since computer graphics arouse the right brain (the side involved with sad feelings) more than the left (the side involved in happy feelings), neuroscientists fear that the technochild will grow up becoming more computer-competent and less emotionally and socially competent. Too much stimulation of the right brain too soon may predispose a child to depressive or anxiety disorders. Techno-educating is often dubbed artificial intelligence (AI), causing educators to worry that the overuse of technology may interfere with the natural development of human intelligence. They worry that schools may turn out good information gatherers rather than good thinkers.

Better late than early.

Why wait? The growing brain and personality of a growing child needs responsive human contact. From four to seven (the prime target age for computer marketing), children need to imagine, explore, learn, and practice language; to control their impulses and think before they act; and to learn how to feel for themselves and feel for others (empathy) and tune in and become comfortable with their own feelings. Screen time steals from the time that can be spent in this window of opportunity for emotional development. In the preteen years (nine to twelve) — another prime target for computer marketing — children begin to develop a higher level of moral reasoning. They're searching for values, wrestling with ethical concerns, and are developing a social conscience and competence. Spending time with violent, instantly gratifying computer games interferes with this development.

During these ages, children should be learning to relate to people rather than to machines. Also during these ages, children need to learn to be social rather than becoming isolated in the bedroom with a machine, which can contribute to antisocial attitudes. Wise parents and educators conclude that it's better to help children build their growing brains and humanize themselves before overexposure to computers and video games. As with so many things in real life, the question boils down to balance. First and foremost, humanize your child to social relationships and instill a love of learning. Then, as a bit of icing on the cake of life, help your children also become computer-literate. As Dr. Healy sums up: "Not too much, not too soon, not too inhuman."

Steals valuable time.

A final worry is that computer games and video games may steal valuable time that the child could be using to develop social and physical skills. These games are constructed to cause the child to be riveted (read: addicted) to this form of entertainment by providing instant rewards for continuing the game. The problem is that the child often has to blow up or kill something in order to "advance to the next level." At least these games are more interactive than TV.

WHAT PARENTS AND TEACHERS CAN DO

As discussed above, to build a well-educated and well-rounded person, it is important that children develop a love of learning, problem-solving skills, social skills, empathy and interpersonal relationships — and, by the way, computer skills. All are necessary to build a well-educated person, not just computer literacy. Consider the following points in helping your child become computer-literate, yet in a delved-out, mentally appropriate manner.

Don't feel pressured.

Don't feel pressured to teach your child computer literacy at the expense of social literacy. The whole technology industry is targeting tots and parents with the message that computer literacy is a ticket to success. But parents must always keep in mind that relationships, not machines, are the ticket to success. It's far more important to give your child valuable relationships with other human beings than to upgrade your computer every time the technology industry makes a faster, more efficient chip.

"Won't my child fall behind in school if we don't teach her how to use the computer at an early age?" Research has debunked the myth that children will be scholastically disadvantaged if they aren't computer-literate early. Kids who learn to use a computer at ten master these skills just as well as kids who began at five. There is no scientific evidence that links early computer training with later computer literacy. Yet, there is scientific evidence linking early verbal and social skills with later literacy in these areas. Although educators do believe that the computer is a valuable tool in the academic and business worlds, they also point out that using computers too much and too early can shorten attention span and dampen imagination. Learning at its best takes place in a social context, not in a one-on-one relationship with a machine. So don't feel pressured to make your toddler high-tech too early.

Also, don't pressure your school to get into a contest with other schools over who has the latest-newest-greatest computer lab. Schools, especially private ones, perceive that some parents may choose their school based on how high-tech it is, and they sacrifice other educational, athletic, and arts programs to stay in the high-tech scholastic race. Remember, it's primarily teachers that make a school great, not machines.

Be screen-smart.

As with limiting TV, balance is the key. Limit your growing child's time in front of screens of all types, lest they become addicted. If you allow a computer in your child's bedroom, monitor how he uses it. During screen time, use the computer interactively and take part in your child's computer explorations. Hold off on the baby software and hold your baby instead, and you're giving your child a smarter start.

Put mind before machine.

Picture two first-graders given the assignment to draw what they most like about their family. The computer wizard pulls clip art from the "mind" of the computer's hard disk and fabricates a technically perfect drawing. The other child starts with a blank piece of paper. He creates an image in his mind of what he wants to draw and uses his senses to translate what's in his mind to an image on the paper. While there is learning value to both approaches, the child who simply started with a bunch of crayons and a blank piece of paper is required to make more brain connections to create her art.

Why wait?

The question is not whether children should or should not become computer literate. The question is how much computer time and at what age. There is a growing body of educators who believe that it's better for children to learn the "old-fashioned way" first, with interpersonal contact — pupil-teacher interaction and student-to-student interaction — and wait until age seven to ten to tackle technology. The bottom line is some educational experts believe

that because computers foster visual rather than auditory learning, it may not be developmentally appropriate in schools before the age of seven. In this way, you teach children to relate to people before things and grow up to become masters rather than servants of technology.

VIDEO VIOLENCE IS COMING TO A SCREEN NEAR YOU

Warning: Video games may be hazardous to your child's emotional health.

Sounds like a warning on a cigarette pack, and justifiably so. Once upon a time TV was blamed for a variety of children's emotional disturbances, from obesity to aggression. Just as parents learned to tame the TV, along came another electronic influence that can undermine a child's success far more than television. Here's why.

Disturbing stats.

Video games are becoming the second-largest segment of the entertainment industry, second only to television. About half of all children have a video-game player or a computer on which to play the games in their own bedrooms. A study comparing parental rules for television viewing and playing video games showed that parents set rules for video games only half as much as they did for TV viewing, and the majority of parents did not restrict the type of game their children played. Eighty percent of the most popular video games feature aggressiveness or violence as the primary themes, and in 20 percent of these games the aggressiveness or violence is directed toward women. Surveys conclude that on a typical day, one in four American boys plays an extremely violent video game. And the sales of extremely violent games are climbing. By the time typical American children reach the age of eighteen, they have seen 200,000 acts of violence and 40,000 murders on some sort of screen.

Disturbing research.

Many studies have shown a definite correlation between the degree of violence in video-game viewing and the degree of aggressive behavior in the viewing children. In his book, *Stop Teaching Our Kids to Kill* (New York: Crown Publishers, 1999), Lieutenant Colonel David Grossman, a psychologist at Arkansas State University and past specialist as a "killologist," points out that willingness to kill another person is not a natural behavior, but one that has to be taught by repeated desensitization and exposure to violence. He goes on to reveal that part of teaching soldiers to kill demands a conditioned response so that shooting a gun becomes automatic. According to Colonel Grossman, the Marine Corps uses modified versions of grossly violent video games (like the ones that allegedly motivated the Columbine carnage) to teach recruits how to kill. They are used to develop the "will to kill" by repeatedly rehearsing the act until it feels natural. Obviously, this technology is much more dangerous in the hands of kids than among soldiers and police. Grossman refers to violent video games as "murder simulators."

Consider the following ways that unmonitored video-game playing can interfere with your child's success in life:

Conditions children to be violent.

Children are not born violent, they are made violent. They become conditioned to associate violence with fun, as part of "normal life." Are we bringing up a generation of soldiers, or are we bringing up children? The end result of unmonitored video violence is that we are training an army of kids. There is a psychological and physiological principle called "operant conditioning," a stimulus-response training whereby a person is conditioned to act, not think, in a stressful situation. This is how pilots train in flight simulators and the U.S. Army trains its soldiers. Could the video-game addict become conditioned to shoot or hit whenever provoked? Could these video games trigger what we call "instant replay," so that the player is conditioned to pull a trigger when seeing someone go after his girlfriend? We are concerned that this terrifying technology can fill a child's vulnerable and receptive brain with a whole library of scary instant replays so that by reflex, he replays one of these violent scenes when faced with a real-life problem.

INSTANT REPLAY

A child's developing mind is like a giant video library. He stores all he sees for later retrieval. If a child repeatedly witnesses graphic scenes of killing, hitting, yelling, or sexual dominance, this topic gets a lot of shelf space in his library. Years later, when presented with similar circumstances, like a conflict with a schoolmate or girlfriend, the teen or adult may instantly replay a similar scene from his video library, and shoot the person who stole his girlfriend. We wonder if the criminals who go berserk (translation: "temporarily insane") and commit hideous crimes are, by reflex, replaying what they were subconsciously already programmed to do.

Desensitizes children to violence.

Kids are becoming increasingly attracted to violence and numb to its consequences. They build up an immunity to violence and therefore need higher levels of violence as "booster shots." Since violence is actually unnatural for children, video games make it fun for them, which gradually conditions the child to believe that violence is natural. Colonel Grossman dubs this phenomenon as AVIDS — acquired violence immune deficiency syndrome. As violence goes on to desensitize children, they perceive violence as "cool." At a very young age, children learn to associate violence with pleasure and excitement, a dangerous association for a civilized society. As the desensitization process continues, parents should be aware of disturbing words, such as "It's just a game" or the most disconcerting "It doesn't bother me." It *should* bother them.

It's developmentally incorrect.

Children instinctively copy adult behavior, and violent imagery is much more easily stored in the memory than less violent behavior. Yet many preteen children have not yet learned to completely differentiate fantasy from reality. They view, interact with, and get involved with the video game but developmentally lack the moral judgments as to the rightness or wrongness of the action. They lack discernment. Violent screens put the wrong messages into children's vulnerable brains at the wrong time.

It's physiologically disturbing.

The "hype hormones" that are aroused by violent video games cause children to suffer serious consequences, such as nightmares, stomachaches, headaches, anorexia, and fatigue. Some studies have even related seizure activity to violent screen time. Violent video games have been found to stress the cardiovascular system, such as increasing blood pressure and rapid breathing characteristic of a physiological stress response. One study even reported an increase in the stress hormone adrenaline during video playing. A 1998 study showed that while playing video games, children experienced a high release of the brain neurotransmitter dopamine, which could be called the hype hormone.

It's more dangerous than TV.

During TV watching, children are just passive viewers of screen violence, yet with video games they can interact. With the push of a button or click of a mouse they can point and shoot, kill and squash — and they get more points for more killing. Video arcades are even worse. There is no parental monitoring and the joysticks are more like guns, enabling children to point and shoot. In some violent programs on TV, at least the bad consequences of violence are often pointed out and the bad guy often loses. With video games, on the contrary, the bad guy often wins, or at least gets to a "higher level." In fact, the violent characters are often more glamorized in video games than on television. With TV watching, many little brains just tune out, yet with video games teens often tune up. Instead of watching killings, the player can kill.

It's habit-forming.

More than 60 percent of children report that they play video games longer than they had intended. Once they get engrossed in a game, they get hooked on the hype and want to play longer. The games fit into the natural desire for children to get control over their lives, and video games give children a feeling of mastery that they may not have over other aspects of their lives. Playing violent video games is like a drug. Once the child reaches a certain level of violence and becomes bored — what is known physiologically as habituated — the child needs more of the "drug" to maintain the high level of excitement.

Interferes with self-esteem.

The most disturbing fact is that children who have the least amount of self-esteem and mastery over their life are the ones most attracted to video games. According to Dr. Jane Healy in her book *Endangered Minds,* boys who pursue violent video games are more likely to have low self-confidence in school and be less successful in personal relationships. Studies have also shown that for girls, increased time playing video or computer games is associated with lowered self-esteem. These games give children an out when they don't feel in with other groups.

It's poor role modeling.

Role-playing games (RPGs) allow children to play the role of violent characters. The roles of these characters become more attractive to the children, especially if they don't like their roles in the real world. Children learn that violent characters are cool, powerful, and, in some misguided way, successful. During video playing, children get instant gratification and can manipulate their roles. Yet in the real world they have to wait, and it's not always fun.

"It's a fearful world."

It's the nature of a growing child to view the world as a kind and safe place to live. Violent video games distort a child's perception of the real world as violent and fearful. Media researchers fear that children will grow up viewing the world as violent and dangerous — a viewpoint dubbed the *mean world syndrome.*

It's scary.

Many pediatricians rank screen violence as a public-health issue at the same level as smoking and cancer. In fact, the American Academy of Pediatrics advises doctors to take a "media history" during annual checkups of school-age children. Here is one graphic example. Scary technology now allows players to "morph" headshots of other people (such as other kids or teachers whom they might hate) onto the bodies of the characters in the video game in order to shoot their heads off.

Suggested parental guidance.

Just as you take preventive measures against your child getting involved in alcohol or drugs, take steps to monitor your child's exposure to video games, for which children don't even need an ID. Try these suggestions.

- *Just say no.* Develop a list of no-nos: no TV or video-game playing in the bedroom, no violent video games, and no unmonitored video arcades.

- *Offer less violent alternatives.* The more involved your child is in sports, arts, and social groups, the less he will need video games. Discover your child's special talent — that special something every child has — and nurture it. Give him opportunities to build his self-esteem away from the screen.

- *Monitor the screen.* Just as you would preview a TV program or movie, watch the video game with your child, and discuss the violent parts and why video violence is harmful to your child. As one mother in our practice said to her child: "I refuse to let you grow up to be a jerk." Her child got the point. Talk about how the game makes your child feel. Above all, don't let your children become desensitized to what they watch. If they say it doesn't bother them, simply say, "Well, it should."

- *Rent rather than buy video games.* This allows you to preview them before you've made a financial commitment. Preview the entire game, since in many games violence increases toward the end or once your child reaches higher levels. Walk and talk your child through the entire game.

- *Create a screen budget.* Allow your child a certain amount of screen time weekly, say an hour a day, and enforce it.

- *Evaluate the ratings — carefully.* Don't let your guard down because of the ratings. The Entertainment Software Rating Board (ESRB) rates video games according to EC (early childhood), E (everyone), T (teens), M (mature), and "adults only," which are not intended to be rented or sold to any person younger than eighteen years. Also, coin-operated video games now label videos. A green label suggests that the game is suitable for all ages. Yellow or red labels signal that the video may contain violence, sexual content,

or bad language. Although these ratings are a start, preview the E or ALL ratings anyway, since the level of violence the raters consider harmless may not be acceptable in your home. For more information about video-game ratings, consult: www.esrb.org; or order a discussion of the ratings by the American Academy of Pediatrics at www.aap.org/family/ratingsgame.htm

- *Encourage group games.* Encourage your children to play video games that involve more than one person, so that at least they learn some social interaction. And, of course, choose games that are less violent.

Allowing violent video games in your home could be considered a form of child abuse. In fact, it's visual abuse. The best medicine to prevent your child from becoming addicted to violent video games is to immunize him against such violence so that he remains "bothered" by violence. The best way to do so is to practice attachment parenting. Technology is taking over the home. Video games are here to stay, and parents can't always stop this technorace. The best we can do is provide speed bumps and restful pit stops to slow it down. There is a bright side to technology that parents should allow and a dark side to technology that we must stop.

Index